# Real Estate License Exams

FOR

# DUMMIES®
A Wiley Brand

## 2nd Edition

**by John A. Yoegel, PhD, DREI**
Certified New York real estate instructor

**Real Estate License Exams For Dummies,® 2nd Edition**

Published by John Wiley & Sons, Inc., 111 River Street, Hoboken , NJ 07030-5774, www.wiley.com

Copyright © 2013 by John Wiley & Sons, Inc., Hoboken, New Jersey

Published simultaneously in Canada

For general information on our other products and services, please contact our Customer Care Department within the U.S. at 877-762-2974, outside the U.S. at 317-572-3993, or fax 317-572-4002.

For technical support, please visit www.wiley.com/techsupport.

Wiley publishes in a variety of print and electronic formats and by print-on-demand. Some material included with standard print versions of this book may not be included in e-books or in print-on-demand. If this book refers to media such as a CD or DVD that is not included in the version you purchased, you may download this material at http://booksupport. wiley.com. For more information about Wiley products, visit www.wiley.com.

Library of Congress Control Number: 2013938099

ISBN 978-1-118-57283-2 (pbk); ISBN 978-1-118-57272-6 (ebk); ISBN 978-1-118-57279-5 (ebk); ISBN 978-1-118-57281-8 (ebk)

Manufactured in the United States of America

10 9 8 7 6 5 4

# Contents at a Glance

# Table of Contents

# Part III: It's All Mine: Owning and Transferring Real Estate .......... 77

## Chapter 6: Owning It: Estates and Interests .....................................79

## Chapter 7: Understanding Forms of Real Estate Ownership ...........89

## Chapter 8: Knowing the Limitations on Real Estate Ownership .......99

# Introduction

So you want to become a real estate agent? Welcome to the book that's going to help you become one. Being a real estate agent is an extremely attractive career for many people. If you like looking at houses and other kinds of property and enjoy meeting and working with people, this job may be for you. Add to that having a flexible work schedule, essentially running your own business, and being rewarded for working hard and smart, and you've pretty much described a career in real estate sales.

Somewhere along the line, however, you discovered that real estate sales is a licensed occupation. Don't worry, though; I wrote this book specifically to help you get that license. Ready for the full scoop? Read on, you soon-to-be real estate agent.

## About This Book

Every state requires real estate agents to have a license to practice their occupation. Every state, at a minimum, also requires that you take and pass a state examination to get that license. Most states require more than just an exam. After you've made up your mind to become a real estate salesperson or broker (brokers' licenses usually are obtained after you've spent time as a salesperson), you need to find out what the procedure is for getting your license in your particular state. Because most states have an educational requirement, I assume that you have to take a course before obtaining your real estate license. (For more on licensing procedures, see Chapter 1.)

So how does this book fit in with your education? I wrote it specifically with the idea of:

- ✔ Giving you material that is focused on the exam rather than general real estate practice.
- ✔ Providing you with an additional resource that contains explanations and examples of material that you may encounter in the classroom, in a textbook, or on the exam.
- ✔ Preparing folks in states that have no education requirements for their state exam.
- ✔ Providing practice exams with explanations of the answers to help you prepare for the exam.

As the title states, this book is designed to help you prepare for and pass the state exam. In it, I discuss a wide variety of topics, such as the basics of the job, different real estate laws, the details of owning and transferring property, and issues such as contracts, leasing, and environmental regulations. Think that's a lot? Well, I also cover everything you ever wanted to know about numbers stuff, from appraising property to calculating mortgages, taxes, and investments. And to pull it all together, each chapter contains review questions, and I provide four full-length practice exams (complete with answers and explanations) to help you get ready for the real thing.

If you're a regular *For Dummies* reader, you know that a *For Dummies* book takes a modular approach to giving you information. That means you can pretty much read a section or a chapter and get the information you need without necessarily reading the entire book. That's true of this book, too. Although you certainly don't have to read the entire book to get what you need from it, it's okay if you do. I also provide you with plenty of cross-references so you don't have to remember where related subjects are. And just like all Dummies books, feel free to skip sidebars; they offer good reading material, but their content isn't covered on the exam.

A few things I've written about in this book are common to most chapters. Understanding them can help you get the most out of what you read and study and will prepare you for the exam because you'll run into some of them there, too.

- ✔ I use the term "real estate agent" to mean anyone who holds some form of license to represent someone else for a fee in a real estate transaction. In most places, there are at least two levels of licensure: broker and salesperson. Some states have more than two. Unless I'm referring to a specific type of license, I use the term "real estate agent."

- ✔ The terms "real estate" and "property" are used interchangeably. Even though real estate has a technical definition that I give you in Chapter 6, conversational convention is to use those two terms to mean the same thing. The term "property" can be modified as personal property, which is also defined in Chapter 6. It can also mean "vacant land," but that is made clear as necessary.

- ✔ The term "land" usually means vacant land, or land without structures on it, but it may also be used as a reference to the land-only portion of a property that has a structure on it. For example, "He bought a piece of land on which to build a house." "Her house sits on very rocky land."

- ✔ The word "transaction" as I use it in this book involves any real estate deal. It can and often does mean a change of ownership, but it can also mean negotiating and signing a lease or some other real estate agreement.

- ✔ I use the words "convey" and "transfer" generally to mean a change in ownership. Real estate can be sold, given away, willed, and exchanged. All of these are conveyances or transfers of ownership.

- ✔ You may want to go to a party after you pass your real estate exam, but until then, I use the word "party" simply to mean a person or a company, as in, "There were two parties to the deal, a buyer and a seller."

- ✔ The terms "landlord" and "tenant" can often be substituted for the terms "buyer" and "seller" when discussing items such as a real estate agent's representation of someone. In other cases the references are a bit more specific, but you won't have any trouble figuring out what I'm talking about.

- ✔ When discussing the relationship of a real estate agent to the person he represents, I use the terms "principal" and "client" interchangeably. The agent represents the principal, also known as the client.

Before I go any further, I'd like to give you some general information about what this book is *not* about. Many real estate textbooks on the market are designed to teach you about real estate. Some of them are used as textbooks in prelicensing real estate courses. Without going into a long explanation about the different approaches that each of these books takes, I want you to be clear that this is *not* a real estate textbook.

You shouldn't base anything you do in your real estate practice on what you read in this book. That doesn't mean that this book does not contain accurate information about general real estate concepts. It does. But as I wrote this book, I had to leave out pieces of information or finer details simply because I don't believe you'll be tested on them. I think this book not only fulfills the purpose of preparing you to take the state exam, but it also provides a general overview of real estate issues. In all cases, whether in your real estate practice or sitting for the exam, you need to defer to information provided by your state licensing authority and any local prelicensing courses you may be required to take if it conflicts with the information in this book.

This book also does not provide legal advice. I am not an attorney. Real estate sales and related issues are full of topics that many people, including attorneys, believe are matters that require an attorney's advice or that are best left up to an attorney. I unequivocally advise you that in any issue involving a legal matter, first and foremost, consult an attorney.

One last thing I want to mention concerns the subject of construction — not of the sentences in this book but rather of houses and other buildings. A significant inconsistency exists between and among states regarding whether they require you to know anything about construction for a state-licensing exam. It's obviously a pretty detailed topic, and I do encourage you to learn something about construction techniques and materials as you start your real estate career. I even include some material about construction regulations in this book. (If you're curious, check out Chapter 8.) In the interest of space, however, because of this inconsistency we decided to leave out a detailed chapter on construction. You do, however, need to find out whether knowledge of construction techniques, systems, and materials is a requirement for your state exam and then study the appropriate material.

# Foolish Assumptions

I hope I'm not being too foolish, but the following are my assumptions about you, dear reader:

✔ You're going to take, are taking, or have taken a prelicensing course for the real estate license that you're seeking (salesperson or broker), or, if your state doesn't require a course, you've already checked to see what the state wants you to know for the exam.

✔ You're an aspiring real estate agent who needs a tactical guide to improving your score on the real estate license exam.

✔ You have a reasonably good command of the English language. Both state exam writers and I assume this. Don't get discouraged if English is your second language, though. You may want to read what I have to say about this topic in Chapter 2.

✔ You still have to work for a living because you haven't won the state lottery, and you know that real estate can be a great career.

# Icons Used in This Book

The following icons are designed to help you use this book quickly and easily. Be sure to keep an eye out for them.

This icon points out sample questions within chapter discussions.

Items marked with this icon may vary from one state to the next. I usually give some general information about the subject, but when you see this icon, you need to check out the specifics in your own state. Where do you look for those specifics? In general, if you're not required to take a course or use a textbook to take your state exam, all the material you need to read probably is available from your state licensing agency. (I give you information about how to find your state agency in Chapter 1.) In states where you have to take a course, make sure you look for and study those items that I mention as state-specific in your textbook or course handouts, or ask your instructor about them.

This icon points to information that's especially important to remember for exam purposes.

This icon presents information like a memory acronym or some other aid to understanding or remembering material.

When you see this icon, pay special attention. The information that follows may be somewhat difficult, confusing, or harmful.

# Beyond the Book

In addition to the informative, clever, and (if I may say so) well-written material you're reading right now, this product also comes with some access-anywhere goodies on the web. No matter how hard you study for the real estate licensing exam, you'll likely come across a few questions where you don't have a clue. Check out the free Cheat Sheet at www.dummies. com/cheatsheet/realestatelicenseexams for some helpful definitions of terms, explanation of ownership, and a reminder of the fiduciary responsibilities of an agent.

# Where to Go from Here

First things first: Contact your state real estate licensing authority and get the information you need for the kind of license you'll be applying for, such as a salesperson's license or a broker's license. (You can get information on how to find your licensing agency in Chapter 1.) If you're still not sure or you're a little confused about where you're headed, you may want to start your reading in Chapter 3, which explains the different jobs real estate agents do.

The information you want from your state includes a copy of the license law, an application, information on the content of the exam (if available), and any other information available about obtaining your real estate license. You may be able to get this information online. (If you're already a broker, you probably are familiar with most of this. If you're new to the field, you want the package of information your state sends out for people who want to become a licensed salesperson.)

When you get it, read the information carefully and take the next step. That may be enrolling in a course. In a few cases, it may mean studying the license law and the other information the state sends you. You have to do this anyway, but in states with no education requirement, studying this information and this book is your preparation for the state exam. In either case, check out the chapters in this book that correspond with the subjects required for the type of license you're getting (see the Table of Contents for help) and start studying. Before you actually take the exam, be sure to check out the information about the basics of the exam in Chapter 1 and my best studying and test-taking strategies in Chapter 2.

If I were your personal tutor as you embark on your real estate education, I'd instruct you to do the following:

- ✔ Go to class, pay attention, do the homework, and keep up with the reading.

- ✔ As you progress through your course, study the material in this book related to the material you're covering in class.

- ✔ After you've completed a section or chapter in this book, test yourself with the practice questions at the end of each chapter. Diagnose your need for more study accordingly.

- ✔ When you're ready to take the state exam, do the four practice exams in this book. Use them to diagnose your need for more study in specific areas. I've constructed the exams to make it easy to diagnose where you may need more study.

- ✔ Make sure you study your state real estate license law for state-specific information that you may need to know.

- ✔ Take the state test, pass it, get your license, and start earning your first million.

# Part I
# Putting Real Estate License Exams into Perspective

# In this part . . .

- This part kicks off with a look at the different real estate licenses and exams.

- I share some test-taking tip and tricks to help you pass your exam with as little stress as possible. Here you find advice for preparing to take the exam as well as hints to help you while you're in the middle of taking the exam.

- Just about everyone hates math questions. I give you some solid advice and tips for getting through the math sections of the real estate license exam.

- If you've ever wondered how the exams are scored, I offer a look at how the scores are determined and how you can achieve a high score.

# Chapter 1

# Sold! Taking a Glance at Real Estate License Exams

- - - - - - - - - - - - - - - - - - - - - - - - - - - - - - - - - - - - - - - - - - - - - - -

*In This Chapter*

▶ Uncovering the basics of license exams

▶ Recognizing registration rules

▶ Understanding what to take (and not to take) to the exam

▶ Finding out how exams are scored

▶ Figuring out what to do to retake the exam

- - - - - - - - - - - - - - - - - - - - - - - - - - - - - - - - - - - - - - - - - - - - - - -

A state exam is one of the steps you need to take on your journey to becoming a licensed real estate agent. You may think that it's the most intimidating step, but don't worry; that's where this book comes in. In this chapter, I provide you with information to make sure the exam process isn't a total surprise and show you a few specific details to check out in your state.

Because individual states issue real estate licenses, the ultimate authority on the state exam is your own home state. You'll probably get a copy of the state license law and the state-specific information you need about the exam from the instructor of the prelicensing course you may have to take. (See "Figuring out licensing procedures" later in this chapter for more details.) If you don't get the information from your instructor, or if you're in one of the few states that doesn't require a pre-licensing course, you can write to your state licensing agency or go online to find information. Different states have different agencies that handle real estate licensing, but using a search engine like Google can get you where you need to go. Just type in your state's name followed by the words "real estate license law," "real estate commission," "real estate board," or "real estate licensing agency," and see what websites are listed. If you don't have access to a computer, try calling information in your state capital and asking for the agency's phone number, using any of the names I listed.

## Checking Out Licensing and Exam Basics

Most states have at least two license levels for its real estate agents: salesperson and broker. (Briefly, a *real estate broker* is someone authorized by the state to perform certain activities such as sales on behalf of another person for a fee. A *salesperson* is someone licensed to do those activities but only under a broker's supervision. See Chapter 3 for more.) Some states may have other levels of licensing, such as a time-share agent, associate broker, or salesperson apprentice or trainee. In at least one case, a state is moving toward only one level of real estate licensing. In any case, a state agency administers real estate license exams in each state (different states may have different names for their licensing agencies). In the following sections, I give you the lowdown on licensing procedures, the differences between the licensing and exams for salespeople and brokers, and the format of the exams themselves.

## Figuring out licensing procedures

After you decide to pursue a career in real estate, the next thing you need to do is get as much information as you can about the procedure for obtaining your license. Every state has specific requirements regarding age, citizenship, criminal background, education, and so on. For specifics about all of these necessities, you need to consult your state's license law directly. Each state's real estate license law typically has provisions about how to become a real estate agent in that state. In addition, it often has specific requirements regarding procedures to follow in your actual real estate business. And by the way, state exams often contain a few questions about the requirements to get your license, such as how old you have to be or the citizenship requirements. You need to get a copy of your state's license law either from the state website or from your instructor.

Your state licensing system may treat real estate licensing educational requirements and testing in a wide range of ways. Very few states have no educational requirements whatsoever and require only that you pass the state exam. Other states require that you take (and pass) a minimum number of classroom (or online) hours of education before you sit for the exam. And still other states require you to take not only a minimum number of classroom hours, an apprenticeship, and more educational courses, but also a state exam after one or both classroom experiences. You likely have to take more coursework and pass another exam to become a broker, so expect to become a salesperson first, and get some experience before you can move up to the broker level.

Assume that where education is required — and it is in most if not all states — you have to pass a course exam in addition to the state exam. Your state may have only an attendance requirement, but be prepared for a course exam nonetheless. Where there is a course exam, it's usually similar to the state exam. This book helps you do well on both exams.

As for the state exam, some states allow you to walk in and take the state salesperson exam before you complete the required education. Not much point in doing so in my opinion, because the education always helps prepare you for the state exam. And the course exam is good practice for the state exam.

## Knowing the difference between salesperson and broker licensing and exams

In most cases, you're probably pursuing the first or basic real estate license level — in some states it's a salesperson's license; in others it's some form of salesperson trainee. How you move up the real estate ladder varies among the different states. The following illustrates two of the many possibilities.

In one case, you complete all of the necessary requirements, including taking and passing a state exam, to become a licensed real estate salesperson. And that's it. You can stay a salesperson for the rest of your career. To become a broker in this situation, you probably have to gain some experience, take additional coursework, and pass yet another state exam.

In the second case, you begin your real estate career by getting a license at whatever level your state provides as an apprentice or trainee, which can involve taking a course and/or a state exam. After a prescribed period of experience, you're required to move up to the level of a full-fledged, licensed salesperson, which can mean more coursework and another licensing exam. You can remain a salesperson for your entire career in this case, too. Moving up the next rung on the ladder to the broker's level usually involves additional coursework, an exam, and additional experience.

I need to add here that some states may have a way for you to skip part of the salesperson licensing procedure. Although it rarely occurs, doing so usually requires previous real estate experience. The experience may not exempt you from taking all of the required courses, but it may enable you to skip the salesperson exam. You can find out whether your state allows this exemption by checking the license law and speaking with your state licensing agency. The state has final say over what constitutes a qualifying equivalent but for example someone who has bought, sold, and leased a significant number of his own investment properties might have the necessary experience.

Your job as it relates to this book is to identify the particular exam you have to pass at this stage of your real estate career. If you're taking your first-ever exam, you're at the salesperson level or the salesperson trainee level. If you're already a licensed salesperson, you're shooting for the broker level. Then you need to find out the subject matter on the exam. In the vast majority of states, you're required to take coursework to get your license. Figuring out what you're tested on and using this book to help you is relatively easy. Just match up the material in the course with the various subjects in this book. If you're not required to take coursework to get your license, you can find out your particular exam's subject matter by checking with your state licensing agency and still use this book to provide information and further explanation of the required material.

I've written this book to cover as many of the subject areas as are typical on a variety of state exams. In general, fewer topics are covered on the salesperson's exam than on the broker's exam. Broker's exams cover more subjects because more topics have been added to the list of subjects you learned at the salesperson's level. For example, a state might test you on property management, which I cover in Chapter 3, on the broker's exam but not on the salesperson's exam. So if you're taking the salesperson's exam in that state, you don't need to worry about property management; however, if you're taking the broker's exam, it's time to brush up on your property management knowledge.

If you're using this book to prepare for a broker's exam, be aware that many brokers' exams presume that you learned and remembered everything you covered in your salesperson's course. Although the emphasis may be on broker subject matter, topics typically on a salesperson's exam are fair game on the broker's exam. So it's a good idea to review all the material from the salesperson's exam as well as the new broker's material you learned if you're taking the broker's exam.

The topics at the salesperson's level are usually covered at a more basic level than on the broker's exam. Definitions and terminology are most important on the salesperson's exam. The broker's exam doesn't cover just additional topics; it may require you to apply your knowledge to specific examples and questions.

Two other subjects that should be mentioned for special consideration and preparation are math and ethics. Where appropriate, math formulas and problems are covered in the individual chapters in this book. In addition, Chapter 18 covers a variety of typical real estate problems. The amount of math on the state exam varies by state. You need to know real estate math to be an effective real estate agent, but especially for you math-phobics you need to find out how much math is on your state exam.

Ethics is another subject that varies by state. You need to find out if your state has its own code of ethics for real estate agents or if it expects adherence to the code of ethics and standards of the National Association of Realtors. Most importantly for passing the exam, you need to find out how much emphasis there is on ethics questions on the state exam.

## Looking at the format and other exam details

At any point in time (for example, a week after this book comes out), a state may decide to change its exam content or structure; therefore, talking with any certainty about exam formats is pretty much impossible. Ultimately the format of the exam really shouldn't matter when compared with a mastery of the material you have to know. Different structures have different approaches to the same material. If you know the material, the structure won't matter.

Most (if not all) states currently use a multiple-choice question format. Most people feel more comfortable with this format, and students believe these exams are easier to pass because the choices already have been narrowed down for you. Because most states use this format, I've chosen to write all the practice questions in this book, including the four full-length practice exams, in a multiple-choice format. How's that for service?

Exams are either a single, undivided exam or broken into two parts: a general part that covers key concepts, such as forms of real estate ownership, fiduciary responsibilities, and fair housing law, and a state-specific part. In this book you see many state-specific icons directing you to information that may vary from state to state. This type of information may end up on the state-specific part of these exams. In addition, any questions about state license law are covered in the state-specific part of the exam. (For more about license law, see Chapter 3.)

You should check with your course instructor or the state licensing agency about the following exam details:

- ✔ Number of questions on the exam you're taking. The salesperson's and broker's exams may have a different number of questions.
- ✔ Whether the exam is a single exam or whether it's broken into general and state-specific parts. If the exam is divided into parts, find out how many questions are in each part. If the exam is given in two parts, must you pass both parts at the same time; if you don't pass one part but pass the other, can you retake the part you didn't pass.
- ✔ Whether the questions are multiple-choice or whether any other question format is used.
- ✔ The form of the exam (paper and pencil or computer).
- ✔ The time available to complete the exam.

There are a few other questions you should ask about exam procedures, such as what to bring to the exam. I give you this information in the following sections, as well as offer some hints about successful test-taking strategies in Chapter 2.

# Sign Me Up: Registering for the Exam

You've fulfilled all your state's requirements. You've taken a course, read the license laws, and so on. These procedures definitely vary by state. In general, though, you have to send an application to the state at some point so you can take the exam. You may have to send the state a completion certificate as evidence that you passed the required prelicensing coursework, and you probably have to submit a fee. Your state's exam regulations detail whether the fee needs to be paid with cash or by check, credit card, or another method. In the case of the salesperson's exam, some states require you to have your application form signed by a sponsoring broker. (You can find out more about the relationship between a salesperson to a broker in Chapter 3.) It's likely that have to register online to get a date to take the exam. After completing and sending the appropriate materials to the state licensing agency, you receive an entry permit in the mail or a printable one online allowing you to take the exam. You also receive information on where and when to arrive for the exam, as well as a list of anything else you might need to bring with you (see the next section). Read all of the information carefully and follow the instructions exactly. If you have any questions, contact the state licensing agency well before the exam.

Keep in mind that in some states may allow you to take the test by simply showing up at the exam site with identification and the fee in hand. This is usually referred to as a walk-in exam.

Whatever the procedure may be, find out what it is from your course instructor or the state licensing agency, and follow it carefully. It's silly and completely unnecessary to have your application returned because you forgot to sign it or sent in the wrong amount for the fee.

# Knowing What to Take to the Exam . . . and What to Leave at Home

The big day is almost here. You passed with flying colors whatever prelicensing course you had to take. You also filled out and sent in your application for the exam and got something back in the mail telling you where and when to show up. You reviewed everything in this book that applies to the test you're taking and you're ready to go. Now start packing.

In some places, the question of what to bring to the exam has produced an art unto itself. General security issues are in effect in many public buildings, and you also need to deal with security issues that are specifically pertinent to exam-taking. The key here is simple. Read all of the literature you can find from the state licensing agency or the testing company your state uses to find out about what you can and cannot bring to the exam. (Some states have contracted with private companies to administer exams; if this is the case in your state, you can get contact information about this from your state licensing agency.) If you have a specific question that isn't covered in the material, you can call or e-mail the state agency or testing company and get an answer to your question. In general, the items you need to bring are:

- ✔ **A calculator:** Pay attention to the requirements for a calculator. Calculators are usually required to be silent, battery-powered, and nonprogrammable. In general, anything that can carry text won't be permitted. Those of you who have a calculator feature built into your cell phones may not be permitted to use them. In some places, you have to sign a form indicating the kind of calculator you're using.

  One other point: If you're using a battery-powered calculator, change the batteries a few days before the exam, or bring two calculators. If changing the batteries in your calculator is really easy (you don't need a screwdriver or some other tool), you can also bring new batteries with you, just in case.

- ✔ **An entry permit:** Make sure that you bring the entry permit that you received in the mail after you sent in your application, because it and any other necessary paperwork may be the only documents that enable you to take the exam. Necessary paperwork varies from state to state, so it's pretty difficult to tell you exactly what you need to bring, but at a minimum you need that entry permit. In states that permit walk-ins at exams, you may need the application itself, plus the fee and probably one or two forms of identification.

- ✔ **No. 2 pencils:** You probably need some of those famous No. 2 pencils. Bring more than two with erasers. If you buy new ones, sharpen them before you go to the exam; don't depend on there being a pencil sharpener at the exam site. Sharpened No. 2 pencils are a little hard to carry. I always put them in a standard-size (No.10) envelope.

- ✔ **A pen:** Bringing along a pen with blue or black ink is a good idea in case you have to fill out some form that's better completed in ink than in pencil.

- ✔ **A photo ID:** An ID of some sort is pretty standard, so bring a photo ID with you. Not all photo IDs are created equal; for example, your state may not count your new photo ID library card. You may even be required to present two forms of ID. And if you're not a citizen, have the appropriate documentation with you showing your status.

- ✔ **A certificate from your prelicensing course:** Your state may require you to bring the certificate you received that shows that you passed your prelicensing course. In some cases, you may have already sent it in with your application and don't need to bring it. In either case, when you get the certificate saying that you passed the course, make sure you make a copy of the certificate and keep it in a safe place before you ever send it or give it to anyone. States have been known to lose documents. Some states require that the real estate school you went to send documentation directly from the school to the state certifying that you successfully completed the course. Check to see if your real estate school does that.

You probably won't be allowed to bring scrap paper, food, books, notes, and so on, to the exam. In a worst case, you may be turned away from the exam site if you have any of these items with you. In a situation almost as bad, you may be asked to leave the unauthorized item(s) in the hallway outside the exam room. If you need to bring food or water because of a medical condition, make sure you get permission first before the day of the exam. In addition, if you need to make accommodations for a handicap, like the use of a wheelchair, make sure those arrangements are made before the day of the exam.

# Scoring High: Figuring Out How Scores Are Determined

Information about scores is available from your state licensing agency or the testing agency (if any) used by your state. Here are a few points you may want to consider:

- ✔ Check out whether all the questions have equal weight. For example, a state may give an exam with 100 questions, all worth one point. But another state may give a two-part exam, with the first part having 80 general real estate questions worth one point each and the second part having 40 state-specific questions worth half of a point each. I've found in my teaching that this kind of information seems to provide comfort to the students because they feel like they know what's going on. To some extent, knowing which questions have more weight may guide your studying, but in any case, you have to answer enough questions correctly to pass.

- ✔ Scoring may vary from state to state; most places give you a percentage based on the number of correct answers given. Passing scores vary by state, as well. In addition, some states make you wait for the test results, sending them to you by mail, whereas some states may be able to give you the results on the same day you take the exam. Your state may just advise you if you passed or failed.

- ✔ What about getting the big prize — the actual license? In some cases, you can receive a temporary license on the day you pass the exam. In other cases, you get your license in the mail. And in other cases, you have to apply for the license after you get your test results.

Having more than one testing center, a state may vary its procedures from one place to another. One center might be equipped to give you your score and even a temporary license right away; another testing center in the same state may not be able to do that. If getting your license right away is important to you, especially if you have a hot deal ready to go as soon as you have your license, it may be worthwhile to travel a little further to get instant results.

# Take Two: Retaking the Exam

You need to know how many times you can retake the state license exam. Your state may allow unlimited retakes of the exam, or it may limit you to a certain number of retakes before requiring you to take the prelicensing course again. Whichever the case, if you do fail the exam and plan to retake it, don't wait too long. Try to retake it the next time it's offered. If you have to reapply to take the exam, do that right away. (But I know that you'll pass on the first try with the help of this book!)

The same applies if you have to take an exam to complete your real estate course. Find out how many times you can retake it and when and if you would have to retake the course itself.

The exam itself is actually pretty good practice for a second try. Remember the areas with which you had difficulty, and concentrate on those areas first as you study for retaking the exam. If you're lucky and live in a state where you receive some idea of the areas in which you were weak, use the information to study that specific material. You also can use the review questions and practice exams in this book to diagnose your weak areas. Checking out the studying and test-taking tips in Chapter 2 for even more help won't hurt, either. Above all, don't grow discouraged. Anyone can fail an exam, but only you can have the stick-to-itiveness to go back and try it again.

# Chapter 2

# Using Successful Study and Test-Taking Techniques

### In This Chapter

▶ Figuring out how to get ready for the exam

▶ Understanding tips on how to pass the exam with ease

*1* want to share something with you that I tell all my students on the first day of class. If you read through Chapter 3 and then the rest of the book, you learn that real estate sales and brokerage is much more than just driving people around and showing them houses. As you read this book, you also find out that you have to know much more information than you originally thought. At that point, your head may explode. Just remember, however, that what you're tackling is real estate sales and brokerage, not rocket science or brain surgery. It's doable by anyone with reasonable intelligence and a decent command of the language. You've already established that you're intelligent, because you've already taken the most important step as far as I'm concerned: You bought this book. So now, all things being equal, with the right preparation, you should do just fine on the state exam.

This chapter is all about preparing to take the state real estate exam and then taking and passing the exam. In the first part of the chapter, I talk about ways to prepare for the exam. In the second part, I give you some hints for doing your best on the exam.

# One Word to Get You Through: PREPARE

Every teacher with whom you've ever taken a class has told you that the way to successfully pass an examination is to prepare for it. Maybe that's all they said, leaving you hanging, or maybe they gave you a few hints. I try to do better than that by providing you with a detailed plan for getting ready to take the exam. The plan is based on steps characterized by the letters in the acronym PREPARE. Each of the letters represents a separate step in getting ready for the real estate exam. In some cases, each step is made up of several smaller steps.

I'm not in the habit of making guarantees, but what I can tell you is that if you follow these steps and put some reasonable time into mastering the material in this book, you give yourself an excellent chance at passing the state real estate license exam the first time you take it.

## Provide

You need to provide yourself with every opportunity to pass the exam. But, I bet you're asking, "How do I do that?" Follow these few simple steps for test success.

✔ **Get information about the state exam.** I discuss exam information in detail in Chapter 1, but it's important enough to repeat some of it here. No matter whether you're planning to take the salesperson or the broker exam, you need to find out what subjects, both general and state-specific, are on the test. (Take special note of the State-Specific icons throughout this book and the items in Chapter 23 to help you out.) You also want to find out about the exam's format, the number of questions on it, and the amount of time you have to complete the test. It may be obvious, but find out where and when the exam is given and how to get there. Remember to check out what you need to bring to the exam (and what you may not bring). Whenever you require special arrangements (for example, if you are handicapped or need to bring food into the exam because of a medical condition), find out about that, too.

So where can you get all of this info? Try contacting your prelicensing course instructor, your state licensing agency, or the testing company that's been hired to administer the exam.

✔ **Take enough time to study.** Regular study, instead of cramming at the last minute, consistently seems to be the best way to approach material like this. What's more, when you leave your studying to the last minute and some emergency develops (believe me, one usually does), you lose out on what little study time you have left. You don't have to be fanatical about keeping regular study times and hours. You may want to study half an hour or an hour every night and two or three hours on Saturday or Sunday. The point is, put in regular time during a longer time frame so you can grow more comfortable with the material, including this book, state-specific material, and the textbook for your prelicensing course.

✔ **A quiet place to study.** Although having a quiet place to study may seem obvious, it's worth its own note. Do what you have to, including going to the library if necessary, to crack the books in peace and quiet so you can concentrate and get the most out of your study time.

## Review

*Reviewing* means you've already read the material, and that's what I'm assuming here. After you identify specific subject areas on the state exam you plan to take (either the salesperson's exam or the broker's), you need to spend time studying those chapters in this book. Then it's time to review the information, and don't worry about what you need to review or how. I've got the scoop on vocabulary and terms, state license law, and state-specific items.

### Vocabulary and terms

Vocabulary is critical on all real estate exams, especially the salesperson's exam. So the words I've placed in italics throughout this book are the first items to review. Do what works best for you to focus on these terms. Highlight the term and its definition with a highlighter, if you like. And I don't mind if you write in this book! Wherever possible, I try to define a term in one sentence so that it's easier for you to focus on the definition.

# Breaking the language barrier

In recent years, real estate sales and brokerage have attracted large numbers of nonnative-born Americans: intelligent, sometimes highly educated people who often are quite accomplished in their own countries. Nevertheless, because these exams often concentrate heavily on understanding the terminology and the application of certain principles, language can become an issue for non-English speakers.

Depending on how serious the language issue is, you have these options for dealing with it:

✔ Though it's unlikely, find out whether your state offers the state license exam in another language. I don't know of any states in particular that do this, but you can always ask.

✔ If you need to, drop back for a while and take an English-as-a-second-language course. If the course allows you to use optional reading assignments, ask whether the teacher will allow you to use this book for a practice text.

✔ Offer your services as an interpreter in a real estate office to not only translate, but to learn many of the common terms and practices.

✔ Study the material in this book, paying particular attention to vocabulary and definitions, and take the exam. More important, if you choose this option, take it easy on yourself if you don't pass the exam the first time, don't get discouraged. Recognize that you're dealing with a language issue, and this has nothing to do with your intelligence. Keep studying, and take the exam again.

If you like copying information as a way of studying, you can make a list of terms and their definitions, or prepare a three-by-five file card for each term. Don't forget to put a little notation on the corner of each card to indicate what general subject the term relates to. Doing so helps you remember the material in context. Or you can carry the card idea one step further and prepare flash cards. Write a term on one side of the card and the definition on the other side. Then you can either have somebody quiz you or quiz yourself.

## State license law

All states have their own real estate license law material, which usually covers more than just how to get a real estate license. It often provides rules and regulations regarding certain business practices in the conduct of a real estate business. It will usually also cover enforcement of standards and disciplinary measures for real estate licensees. This material may be available in hard copy from the state licensing agency or downloadable from the state licensing agency's website (try an online search for your state's site), or it may be given to you if you're required to take a course before taking the exam. Read the material several times, noting those items like license requirements, fees, and business practices. For more on license law, check out Chapter 3.

## State-specific items

Throughout this book, when you see an icon like the one to the left, know that it refers to items that may be unique to your state. In addition to reviewing the general information in this book, make sure that you find out about and review information that you know is unique to your state. You get this information in whatever course you're required to take. For those of you in states that don't require a course, if the information is going to be on the exam, it's probably available in whatever booklet or other exam preparation material is provided by your state real estate licensing agency.

One way to get a good start is to check out Chapter 23. That's where I highlight ten state-specific issues to study and watch out for on the exam.

## Evaluate

As you prepare for the state exam, you continually need to evaluate how well you're mastering the material. The best way to evaluate your progress as you study is to answer the review questions at the end of each chapter.

As you read through the chapters in this book for the first time, you can answer the questions as a review of your reading. Don't write your answers in the book; use a separate piece of paper. Go over the answers and then reread the sections of each chapter that may be giving you trouble.

After reviewing all the material in the book, and particularly the vocabulary and terms, try sitting down with several sheets of paper and answering each chapter's review questions in order, as if each were a test. You can take whatever time you need, but keep a couple of nights or a weekend afternoon to finish. Just keep answering all the review-question tests one by one until you've completed all the chapter questions. Don't forget to score each test and make a list of your scores in the same order as the chapters. Then you can study the chapters in order of your lowest scores to your highest scores. Do the same with the required course textbook if it has chapter review questions.

Most people have limited amounts of time to devote to studying. Reviewing the real estate exam information in the way I describe in this section enables you to focus your time on the material with which you're having the most trouble. Just to be safe, review the chapters you do well on, but if you don't get a chance to, at least you know where to focus your limited time. After reviewing the material in areas where you're weakest, you can take the review-question exams again, if you like.

## Practice

After you review the material, evaluate your weak and strong points, and review the material again, it's time for a final run-through. Whenever you can schedule two hours or so, sit down with a piece of paper and the writing tool of your choice and take one of the 100-question practice exams toward the end of the book, such as the first one in Chapter 19. Score yourself, and go over the answers to the ones you get wrong (Chapter 20 has the answers). If something isn't clear, review that section of the book. And don't stop there. Do it again on another day with the second practice test in Chapter 21; the answers are in Chapter 22. Do this with all four practice exams. If you've done everything that I've asked you to do so far, in the order that I've suggested, I'd be surprised if you don't do well on the tests. But if your scores still are low, review the material again and then go back on another day and take the practice tests again. Keep doing this until you can pass them all.

You need to be able to find out the length (number of questions) of the state exam and the amount of time you're allowed to complete it. You can use that info to take a self-timed practice exam that simulates the conditions of the real thing.

## Arrive

Someone once said that 80 percent of success is showing up. To ensure that you arrive safely to take your state exam, in good humor, on time, and in the right place, you need to find out where and when the exam is scheduled and how long it takes to get there. With that information in hand, you need to get directions to the exam site (no winging it) and find out if you're likely to encounter any long waits to getting into the exam and if people routinely are turned away because of overcrowding at the test site. (You can get this information by calling your state licensing agency.) These factors may vary from one exam site to another, especially if your state offers the exam at more than one location. If your state administers the exam in several locations, pick one that's most convenient for you, which may mean a little further away but easier to get to or have better parking When I took my broker's exam, I chose to drive farther away to a suburban location instead of taking public transportation to the test site in the city. Do whatever makes you more comfortable and leaves plenty of time to be early. If you live far away from the exam site, consider arriving in the area the night before the exam and staying over.

## Relax

Relaxation part one: Relax the night before the exam. Don't study. Go see an early movie, rent a video, eat a light supper, read a non-real-estate book, and get to bed early. If you regularly meditate, jog, or take long walks, the evening before the exam is a good time for enjoying that kind of activity. Prepare everything you need for the next day, and have it ready to go.

Relaxation part two: Try to stay relaxed on the day of the exam. Eat a light, nourishing breakfast. Get to the test site in plenty of time, and follow the instructions to get a seat. If you can, close your eyes for a few seconds, take a few deep breaths, and remember that no one knows this stuff better than you do. Now sit down and feel yourself relax into the moment of actually taking the exam.

Relaxation part three: Stay relaxed during the test. You may get caught up in the moment, starting to rush and feel pressured. Every 15 or 20 questions, sit up straight, close your eyes, and take one or two deep breaths. Flex your shoulders and hands, then begin again.

## Enjoy

I know what you're thinking: "How can anyone ever enjoy taking a test?" You've studied. You've reviewed. You're relaxed. In short, you're prepared. In your mind you've already passed the exam and are making money working in real estate, maybe even having your own brokerage business in time. I hope you're getting the picture. Taking and passing the test certainly is a challenge, but it's one that with the right preparation (which you now have), you can easily meet. You're ready, and your real estate career awaits you.

# Trying Terrific Test-Taking Strategies

So the big day has arrived. You've made it to the test site in plenty of time. You're seated and have the exam in front of you. You've carefully followed all of the instructions about how to properly answer the questions. Now you're ready to go. In this section I give you some test-taking tips and hints to maximize your score. Nothing replaces hard work and preparation before the exam, and no strategy helps you pass if you haven't prepared well. But some of these hints should help you make the most of what you've learned as you answer the questions.

## It's all in the timing

The first thing you need to do is something you should have already done during your exam preparation — a little math equation. Divide the total number of questions by the total number of minutes you have to complete the exam. This information is available either from the state licensing authority or from your course instructor. Now figure out some benchmarks for yourself. For example, say your exam has 100 questions, and you get two hours to take the exam. That gives you a little more than a minute per question. At the one-hour mark, you need to have at least 50 questions completed. After the first half hour you need to have 25 questions finished. You may move faster in some sections and slower in others, but overall you need to maintain the right pace so you don't leave anything unfinished. Whatever the time frame for your exam, always be aware of how many questions you need to have completed at what point during the exam time. You never want to leave any questions unanswered.

Make sure that you finish the exam, because as an instructor, I can tell you that nothing is more heartbreaking than seeing someone fail an exam because he or she didn't finish. You see, I know that students usually know the answers to at least a few of those eight or ten questions they never got around to answering, and so they never get full credit for what they actually know.

So how can you avoid this dilemma? Go through the entire exam fairly quickly, question by question, answering only the ones you know right away. Read quickly, not carelessly. Make sure that you spend enough time with each question to understand what it's asking, and read through all the possible answers. If you get to a question you're not sure about, eliminating one or two wrong answers can save you time later on. If you're taking a test on a computer, carefully follow the instructions for skipping questions. After you've gone through all the questions once, go back and do all the questions that you skipped. If you're mathematically challenged, save the math questions for the end. Always remain conscious of the time so you're not spending too much time on any one question.

Quickly answering the questions you know gives you a couple of advantages. You're assured that you get to all the questions that you know how to answer correctly, including the ones at the end of the exam. When doing a quick pass over the test, you may find a question near the end that triggers a memory or gives you information that helps you go back and answer an earlier question. For test takers who have a phobia of math, a quick pass over the test enables you to skip the math questions without wasting a lot of time on them. And finally, you have an idea of how much time you have left to spend on the remaining unanswered questions, especially those darn math problems. (For tips on dealing with math questions, see "Number crunching: Tackling math questions" later in this chapter.)

Besides, you'll probably be pleasantly surprised at how many answers you know immediately. And that definitely is a great confidence booster.

The last thing you need to do is actually count all the marks you made on the answer sheet to find out whether that number matches the number of questions on the exam. (If you're taking the exam on a computer, you need to scan the questions and answers to make sure you've answered every one.) In addition, make sure you that you don't fill in two answers for one question. You want to confirm that the answers you choose are aligned correctly with the questions; if you entered something incorrectly, you may have to spend precious minutes fixing everything.

## *Reading everything carefully*

I shouldn't have to remind you about reading with care, but I'm going to. Read all the material about getting ready for the exam; read about what to bring to the exam; read the directions on the exam itself; and above all, read the exam. And I mean every word of every question and all the possible answers. Give yourself every chance to understand what each question is asking and what each answer is saying.

Remember that exam writers may give you a choice of (A) or (B) that looks really good, but choice (D) nevertheless is the best answer. You won't know that unless you read everything. Beware of the partially correct answer. An answer has to be completely correct to be the right answer, and only one of the choices is completely correct. On the flip side, you also need to remember that you may encounter questions in which all the answers seem wrong. Nevertheless, one of them *is* the correct choice. And that answer may very well be the best of a bad lot, so to speak. That's the one to pick.

## Avoiding too much analyzing

Don't think too much. I know that sounds bizarre, but trust me, it's good advice especially for students who have some background in one or more of the exam subject areas. I've seen students overthink or overanalyze a question to the point of getting themselves tied in knots, selecting the wrong answer, and wasting valuable time. This scenario seems particularly true for people with specific technical backgrounds. Maybe you have a background in environmental science, and in answering a question about environmental issues, you can probably come up with ten reasons why all the choices are wrong. Obviously one has to be correct. The level of knowledge provided in this book and in whatever real estate course you take is the level on which you're tested. So leave all that extra stuff you know at the door. If you've studied well for the exam, the answer that first comes to you is usually the best answer. When you start overanalyzing, you may be in trouble.

## Guessing

Even with all of your stellar preparation, some questions are just going to throw you for a loop, and yes, you have to guess. When it comes to guessing, find out whether any penalties are assessed for wrong answers. Of course, you lose points for each wrong answer, but through the years exams have been constructed so that a percentage is added onto your wrong answers as a penalty for guessing. I'm guessing that you won't run into this anywhere on a real estate exam, but you need to check it out just in case. Assuming you won't be penalized for guessing a wrong answer, when in doubt, guess. Don't leave anything blank. In fact, the last step you need to take on the exam answer sheet is counting up your answers to make sure that you haven't left anything blank. (For more about budgeting your test time, see "It's all in the timing," earlier in this chapter.)

The key to guessing is to increase your odds of guessing correctly. If you're given four choices to a question and have no clue as to the correct answer, you have a one-in-four chance of guessing correctly. However, if you can eliminate one or two of the answers as being wrong, you've increased your odds of getting the right answer to one in three or one in two. Most Las Vegas gamblers would take those odds anytime.

So how do you eliminate the wrong answers? For starters, if you're as well prepared as I know you'll be, the odds are in your favor. You most likely can pick out at least one wrong answer right away. After that, it may get a little tough. Try the following tips:

✔ Answers with words "always" and "never" often may be eliminated. But be careful: Some things are always true, but it may be a tipoff to eliminating one answer, such as always owing your full fiduciary responsibilities to your client. (Check out Chapter 4 for more.)

✔ Look for categories of answers. For instance, a question might ask about a landlord's interest in property. You've studied enough to reduce the possibilities to leased fee and leasehold so you've increased the odds of getting the correct answer (leased fee) to one in two. (You can check to see whether I'm right in Chapter 12.)

✔ A specific strategy may work for questions in which the last answer is "All of the above." If you're sure that two of the answers are correct, then choose "All of the above" because it's a good bet that the third answer is also correct.

I've seen a number of hints that help people guess at answers. The problem is that in every case, I can write a question that proves the hint wrong. The best way for you to answer exam questions correctly is to study, study, and study some more.

## Second-guessing

Never ever change an answer after you've written it down. It seems that if you're well prepared, your mind tends to recognize the correct answer in a multiple-choice question immediately. From my own experience with correcting exams, I can tell you that all too often, I see correct answers erased and changed to wrong ones. I don't see the opposite as often.

That said, here are two exceptions to the rule.

- ✔ If a later question helps you answer an earlier one. Say in question 42 you find information that helps you select a better answer to question 23. By all means, go back and change your answer.

- ✔ If you get a different answer when reviewing a problem in the math section of the exam. If you have time, go back and do all the math questions a second time. If any of your answers are different, consider changing them. (For more about math questions, see the next section.)

## Number crunching: Tackling math questions

Many test takers find math problems to be the most intimidating of all the questions they have to answer, but keep in mind that the math we're talking about is stuff you pretty much learned between seventh grade and your freshman year of high school. Memorizing a few formulas and conversion factors and doing lots of practice problems are tremendously helpful in giving you the confidence and knowledge to handle any math question.

For more details about real estate math, check out Chapter 18. Here are a few specific strategies that I give my students for dealing with math questions:

- ✔ **Don't waste a lot of time on the math.** If you're truly uncomfortable with math problems, save them until the end, and spend whatever time you have left working on them. Guess if you have to. (See the "Guessing" section earlier in this chapter for the scoop.)

- ✔ **Do the problem first, and get an answer before you look at the answers.** After thinking through the problem, you very well could have the answer correct.

- ✔ **Read the problem carefully to make sure you've done all the steps.** Exam writers frequently give you an answer that merely appears correct, but only because you didn't go far enough into the problem. For example, you may find an answer about area that is correct when written in square feet, but the problem calls for the answer in square yards. Or perhaps an answer needs to be in months, but one of the choices is the correct answer for a year. Don't forget to divide by 12!

- ✔ **Go back over the math problems, if you have time.** Fingers are big; calculator keys are small. You may write down a number from a calculator, then key it back in incorrectly. You may simply make a mistake. Do each math problem again and try to come up with the same answer twice. It's a good bet that's the right answer.

# Part II
# So You Want to Sell Real Estate: The Job and Basic Laws

## Top 5 Reasons for Working in Real Estate

- ✔ You get to work with people from all walks of life, from your neighbors to new arrivals from across the world.

- ✔ You can check out fabulous properties, from houses to condos to office suites.

- ✔ You enjoy a flexible work schedule that enables you to be home with family when you're needed.

- ✔ You learn about fair housing laws and get to make sure they're followed.

- ✔ You form long-term relationships with buyers, sellers, and other members of the community.

Learn why this is a great time to start your career in real estate in the article "Now's the Time to Become a Real Estate Agent" at www.dummies.com/extras/realestatelicenseexams.

# *In this part . . .*

✔ Agent, salesperson, broker, associate broker . . . I define these terms so you can decide which test (and career path) to take.

✔ I break down the different career opportunities, from brokerages and franchises to appraisers and inspectors.

✔ You examine the different types of agency relationships, including agents, principals, and customers, and you also look at agency law.

✔ Getting paid is always a valid consideration. I tell you how real estate professionals get that all-important paycheck at the end of a sale.

# Chapter 3

# The Job: It Isn't Just Driving People Around

Welcome to the wonderful world of real estate. I wish I had you here in my classroom so I could ask you, as I do of my students on the first day of class, why you want to get your real estate license. Sure, it's to make money, but what drew you to the field? Have you always been interested in houses? Do you want to become an investor or a property manager? Do the flexible hours and being your own boss appeal to you? Real estate is exciting, and it's constantly changing and growing. I'm going to give you some information in this chapter about careers in the real estate field. Some of the information is nothing more than background so that you have an understanding of what real estate agents actually do and where they do it. Although interesting, it's not likely to be on the exam.

The rest of the material in this chapter is fair game for state exam questions. Understanding the different responsibilities that brokers and salespeople have, how brokers and salespeople are paid, and the working relationship between brokers and salespeople is important material in some states for the broker's exam.

I also give you plenty of information about property management as a career within the real estate business. Depending on your state, you may get questions about this subject. A few job-related laws also are discussed. As a means of putting all this information into the right context, I also give you an overview of a typical real estate transaction.

## Who's Who in the Real Estate Business, and How Do They Get There?

You'd think that simply knowing what the main players do in a real estate business is pretty obvious, but I think that because of the terminology they share, the distinctions between the players gets a little muddled. So I'll try to clear up those distinctions for you and talk a little about laws governing real estate licensing in this section.

Here are quick descriptions of players in the real estate game.

- **Real estate agent:** This generic term pretty much refers to anyone who has a real estate license.

- **Real estate broker:** This person is the key player. Most states require you to have a broker's license to perform certain activities like sell houses for other people.

- **Real estate salesperson:** Salespeople are allowed to perform all the activities that the state requires a real estate license for. However, a salesperson cannot work independently; he must work under a licensed broker.

- **Associate broker:** This person has a broker's license but chooses to work under another broker rather than opening his own business.

Agency law covers the relationships of these folks to each other and to the public. For the full scoop, check out Chapter 4.

Regardless of whether you take the exam for a broker's or salesperson's license, your state's exam writers expect you to know the basics of who a broker is and what a broker does. So regardless of the exam, you should know the material that follows.

## The buck stops here: Brokers

A *real estate broker* is the person in the real estate business who's primarily responsible for various activities on behalf of the public. I admit that sounds pretty vague, so let me explain.

Every state has a state real estate license law, usually just called the state license law. The state license law governs these two primary factors in the real estate business:

- A general list of activities that can be performed only by someone holding a real estate license

- The requirements for obtaining a real estate license

The state license law may specifically address what real estate agents must do during the course of their activities, which includes things like presenting all offers to a seller as soon as possible.

A real estate broker is someone who is authorized by the state to perform a certain list of activities on behalf of someone else and collect a fee for doing so. A broker is often called a real estate agent, which is correct in the sense that the broker acts on behalf of someone else (a client).

The license law provides a list of activities that, if they're done for another person for a fee, can be performed only by someone having a broker's license. Although the specific activities may vary from one state to another, the list of activities requiring a broker's license generally includes negotiating any type of real estate transaction, including sales, leases, and exchanges. A licensed salesperson or associate broker may perform these activities but only under the supervision of a broker. (For more general info on state license law, see "Making it legal: Looking at license law," later in this chapter.)

You usually can do any of the previously mentioned activities on your own behalf without having a real estate broker's license. In other words, you can sell your own house by your-self without being licensed. The implication is that you also can help someone else like a family member sell a house themselves without a license as long as you don't collect a fee, but remember the gift of a fancy restaurant meal can be considered a fee. You definitely need a real estate license if you want to collect fees for your work.

## Movin' on up: Salespeople

A real estate salesperson is someone who either works as an employee for a real estate broker or more typically as an independent contractor paid by commission. (For more about the latter, see "My Own Way: Working as an Independent Contractor" later in this chapter.) Generally speaking a real estate salesperson is someone who can do all of the activities that a broker can do on behalf of a client, but must do so under the authority and supervision of a broker. Referring to a real estate salesperson as a real estate agent is somewhat accurate. The salesperson sometimes is viewed as a subagent of the broker but, in fact, has the same obligations as the broker with respect to a client. (See Chapter 4 for more about representa-tion in agency relationships.) In general you become a salesperson first, spend a number of years learning the business, and then become a broker. Of course, you can remain a salesper-son for your entire career. Though unusual at this time, in at least one state, *broker* is the only type of license available.

## In between: Associate brokers

Some states have an intermediate level of licensing that is called an associate broker. An *associate broker* has all the qualifications of a broker but doesn't want to operate his own real estate business. Associate brokers choose to work under the licenses of other brokers just like salespeople. Be sure to find out how your state refers to this level of licensing and what the qualifications are.

## Making it legal: Looking at license law

You need to go over your state's real estate licensing law in detail. Some questions about the law undoubtedly will be on your state exam. Although you need to become familiar with your state's law in its entirety, pay special attention to the following:

- ✔ Qualifications for real estate licensees-broker and salesperson and associate brokers
- ✔ Requirements for getting the various licenses
- ✔ License fees and other fees associated with licensing
- ✔ Continuing education requirements
- ✔ Special requirements after you get your license, such as requiring a broker to maintain a place of business
- ✔ Exemptions from licensing, such as for attorneys
- ✔ Activities that require a real estate license include
    - Standards of conduct and acceptable practice either with respect to the law and/or a code of ethics
    - Enforcement and disciplinary actions for license law and standards violations

## So what's a realtor?

Real estate brokers and salespeople often are referred to as realtors. Sometimes this reference is correct and sometimes it isn't. The word realtor specifically refers to someone who is a member of the National Association of Realtors (NAR). The NAR is a trade group that represents a large segment of the real estate industry. It forms a strong lobby and provides educational information such as conferences to its members. Generally speaking, you become a member of NAR by joining your local NAR-affiliated real estate board or association. You can contact the NAR through its website at www. realtor.com. A number of states have adopted or pointed to the NAR code of ethics as the code of ethics for real estate agents in that state, even if they're not members of NAR.

# What Does a Real Estate Broker/Salesperson Do?

Real estate brokers and salespeople do all of the things listed in your state's licensing law. (See the previous section for more.) Although the list of activities is fairly universal across the United States, it may vary in detail from one state to the next. For exam purposes, you need to know the specific activities that require a real estate license in your state.

## Perusing a list of common activities

Typical activities that require a real estate license are

- Listing a property for sale
- Finding buyers for property that is for sale
- Negotiating the sale or purchase of a property
- Negotiating a lease on behalf of a tenant or a landlord
- Representing someone in the exchange of properties
- Buying or selling options (the right to buy a piece of property at some time in the future) on real estate
- Collecting rents for more than one building owner

This list of activities is at best only a partial one. Your state law probably requires a license to perform most, if not all, of these activities; however, license requirements can include more or fewer activities, depending on the state.

## Checking out a typical real estate transaction

Because buying and selling houses is the primary business of real estate brokers and salespeople, I want to give you a brief and somewhat generic overview of a typical house sale involving real estate agents. (By "agents" here, I mean either a broker or a salesperson. Remember, however, that the broker is primarily responsible in a transaction, with the salesperson working for her.) I use the word "generic," because although many elements are common to all simple real estate transactions, transactions can include state and even regional differences in some specific elements.

### In the beginning, there was a house to sell

A couple decides to sell their house and enlist the services of a real estate agent. You're one of several brokers or salespeople the couple invites to their home to hear your listing presentation and explain what services you offer. In addition, you probably advise the couple on what price they are able to get for their house. After meeting with several agents, the couple chooses you, signing a listing agreement and agreeing to allow you to represent them as their agent in the transaction. (For more on listing agreements, see Chapter 4.)

As the couple's real estate agent, you begin marketing the property. In communities that have a multiple listing service (MLS), you enter their house information into a computer so that all other agents in the community can see what you've listed for sale. (See Chapter 4 for more about MLS.) In communities with no MLS, agents may spread the word around to other real estate agencies that they have a particular house for sale, and they may depend heavily on advertising. There may also be other formal or informal organizations or associations that permit sharing of listings so that a property gets the widest possible exposure to the market and to as many sellers as possible.

### Eureka, a buyer!

An agent across town who's been working to find a house for another couple sees your house on the MLS and gets in touch with you, asking for more details and making sure the house still is for sale. The cross-town agent then contacts his buyers, and they agree to take a look at the house. After seeing the house, they agree to make an offer.

The way a buyer's offer is presented varies in different communities. Sometimes the offer is made in person with the buyer's agent present. The offer usually is made in writing with a small check from the prospective buyer that's called a *binder* or *earnest money*.

 After a deal is agreed to, often after some negotiation, a contract of sale is prepared. Exactly who prepares the contract varies by state and region. In many places, however, the seller's real estate agent prepares the contract, sometimes filling in the blanks of a preprinted contract form, but in other places, only attorneys prepare the contract. After the contract is signed, the conditions within the contract are triggered. (For more about sales contracts, see Chapter 11.)

A typical real estate sales contract includes a provision for the buyer to obtain mortgage financing and may have provisions for the house to be inspected by a home inspector or engineer. The contract usually includes a provision that a *marketable title* must be conveyed. A *marketable title* means that a reasonable and proper search of the records has been conducted, showing that the title to the property has been documented from earlier owners to the current seller so that it can be conveyed (or transferred) without questions as to who the owner is. A records search that proves whether a title is marketable is called a title search. Title insurance also may be purchased (or even required) as part of the contract process to ensure that the title is legal. (For more on events before a closing, see Chapter 9.)

### All's well that closes well

When all of the contract provisions are satisfactorily fulfilled, the buyer and seller may proceed to closing, taking the real estate agent one step closer to getting paid. Pinpointing the actual moment when a real estate agent earns a commission is a somewhat complex issue (see the next section). In general, it occurs when a ready, willing, and able buyer brings an acceptable offer to the seller. Sometimes contract provisions, such as financing, must be satisfied before for a commission can be earned. By general agreement, the commission usually is paid at the closing. When more than one broker is involved, the broker representing the seller distributes the preapproved share of the commission to the buyer's representative. Each broker then splits a portion or percentage of the commission with the salesperson who worked the deal.

In many places, real estate agents run the show and are joined at the closing by the buyer, the seller, a representative of the bank, and sometimes an attorney. In other places, lawyers do the bulk of the work, and sometimes a representative of the title company may actually conduct the closing. In some states, the closing is done *in escrow,* which means that as all the paperwork is completed, it is sent to an escrow agent. When the escrow agent gets everything in order, he or she sends checks, deeds, and any other important documents to the appropriate parties. (For more on the closing process, see Chapter 9.)

After the closing, officially documenting the transaction by recording the deed in the local office of public records officially completes the transaction.

# How Does a Real Estate Broker/Salesperson Get Paid?

A real estate agent gets paid for performing a service, which is usually bringing a buyer and a seller together to complete a property sale. Some confusion may exist as to when a commission actually is earned. In most cases, the commission is earned when a *meeting of the minds* is reached between a buyer and a seller — in other words, when a ready, willing, and able buyer is presented to the seller and all the terms of the contract of sale have been met. What sometimes is confusing to buyers and sellers is that the commission most often is paid at the closing, long after their meeting of the minds, when ownership of or title to the property actually changes hands. The payment of the fee at the closing is done as a convenience to the seller, who often has no money readily available except after the house is sold.

Commissions frequently are shared among two brokers and two salespeople. Here's what I mean: Salesperson *A,* who works for Broker *A,* lists a house for a potential seller. Salesperson *B,* who works for Broker *B,* represents a buyer who buys the house from the seller who listed a house with Broker *A.* Before the sale is complete, Brokers *A* and *B* agree how they'll split the commission. After completing the sale, Broker *A* — the listing broker — receives a commission check from the seller and keeps his firm's part of the total amount and then gives the remaining portion of the total commission to Broker *B.* From their respective proceeds, Brokers *A* and *B* give prearranged portions of their commissions to their respective salespeople.

As you can see, a real estate salesperson doesn't get paid directly by a client. The broker receives the fee for any services rendered and then pays the salesperson. This arrangement often is written into state law. In a typical situation, a salesperson may receive a check for the commission at the closing, but the check needs to be made out to the broker. The broker then pays the salesperson from the proceeds of that sale. The split between the broker and salesperson is entirely negotiable, varies from one brokerage to another, and may depend on the experience of the salesperson and the volume of business that salesperson generates.

State law and federal law, specifically the Real Estate Settlement and Procedures Act which I discuss in Chapter 9, also cover prohibitions regarding nonlicensed persons receiving payment, finders' fees, commission, or kickbacks as part of a transaction — including any gifts, vacations, or other nonmonetary compensation received as part of a transaction. Suppose, for example, that in return for a percentage of the fee you earn, you arrange for a friend who runs a beauty salon to steer real estate buyers and sellers your way. Unless the beauty shop owner has a real estate license, you'd be violating any law that your state may have regarding kickbacks. (See why checking out your state laws is so important?)

In an arrangement where the buyer is represented by a buyer's agent, the buyer's agent sometimes may be paid by the buyer. I know it seems a little odd that I use the word "may," because, after all, you'd think the person being represented *should* pay the fee. A peculiarity in the law nevertheless enables a broker to agree to represent one person but be paid by another. For instance, the seller may pay the buyer's agent. I discuss more about payment in general in Chapter 4.

For more on myths regarding commission, check out "The price isn't right: Price fixing," later in this chapter. For the scoop on figuring a commission, see Chapter 18.

# Working Hard: Career Opportunities

Real estate agents (either a broker or a salesperson) can work in a number of places. In some cases real estate training can provide good background for jobs that may not require a real estate license. In this section, I give you a little background on each of these possible areas of employment. It's unlikely that you'll get any exam questions on this material, but you might want to know what some of the employment possibilities are.

## Considering independent brokerages and national franchises

The vast majority of real estate agents are employed as salespersons working for independent brokers. An independent broker may have more than one office and be affiliated with a multiple listing system, which enables brokers to share information about properties that are for sale. (For more on multiple listing systems, check out Chapter 4.) Many independent brokers have chosen to affiliate themselves with national franchises. These arrangements vary from a fair amount of control and standardization from the franchise's headquarters to an extremely independent operation in which the local broker pays a fee paid to maintain an affiliation with the national franchise. The benefits of franchise affiliations often are related to the nationwide exposure they provide through major advertising. Franchises frequently provide access to the training programs they require their salespeople to complete.

Of course, you definitely need a real estate license to work at a brokerage.

## Checking out corporations (in and out of the real estate world)

The sole purpose of some companies is to buy properties and then lease them out. These are real estate investment companies working for themselves. They may build on and then hold their properties or buy properties with existing structures. These companies may need people to locate properties to invest in (see Chapter 17), or they may need property managers (see "Taking care of business: The duties of a property manager," later in this chapter). As long as you're working for the company and managing properties it owns, you may not legally need a license to do the work; however, you need to find out whether any of your state's regulations require a license under those circumstances. On the other hand, if the company provides real estate property management services to other people or companies, a license is more likely to be required.

In addition, large corporations, particularly those with significant space or location needs, sometimes hire in-house real estate people. These jobs can involve leasing office or retail space for the company or buying land to locate company facilities. Depending on the company, you may find yourself leasing office space for a new company operation, buying a piece of property to locate a new gas station or fast-food restaurant, or negotiating with someone for an oil/gas lease. Although real estate training is good background for these jobs, a real estate license more than likely is unnecessary from a legal perspective. A company may, however, want you to have a license as part of your qualifications.

## Building business with builders

When you're working with a builder, your job may range from finding land for the builder to build on to selling the houses or other buildings the builder may construct. The main distinction that determines whether you need a license when working with a builder is whether you're working for that one builder as an employee, in which case you most likely do not need a license. You most likely need a license when working for one or more builders for a fee as an independent contractor (not as an employee).

When working with a builder you may find yourself working as an on-site salesperson. You may be spending plenty of time at the building site, showing people new homes or working with them as they select a design and special features or options for the new home the builder will build for them.

## Going into government

Local, county, and the federal government often hire people to perform real estate services. Typically, large governments employ people to maintain records, sell surplus property, buy property for various purposes, and obtain easements. As a government employee you are most likely exempt from needing a real estate license. People directly employed by one owner to handle their real estate transactions are generally exempt from license requirements, just as you would be if you sold your own house. In this case the employer is the government. In some states there is a specific exemption in the license law for government employees doing real estate work as part of their job.

Note that government jobs that deal with real estate are fairly specialized and not widely available.

## Appreciating appraising

Appraising is a field that's related to but distinct from a career in real estate brokerage. Although the knowledge you gain in coursework and experience as a broker or salesperson is useful in appraising, a separate license and education are required to become an appraiser. An appraiser's job is to estimate the value of a piece of real estate in a variety of circumstances.. The vast majority of appraisals are done for mortgage-loan purposes. Lenders hire appraisers to estimate the values of properties as a basis for the loans that the lenders extend to buyers.

You can get more information about the appraisal career field at www.appraisal foundation.org. For more on appraising property in general, see Chapter 14.

## Homing in on home inspections

Many buyers have the homes they're considering inspected by home inspectors before buying them. Although you don't need a real estate license to be a home inspector, some states provide for the licensing of home inspectors. You can get more information about this career field at the National Association of Home Inspectors website at www.nahi.org.

# Property Management: A Special Kind of Career Opportunity

Property management is a specialized job within the real estate field. Because most property managers have duties for which a real estate license is required, and they usually perform these activities for more than one client, real estate agents usually must have a real estate license to be a property manager. A license may not be required in some instances, though, such as when a property manager is an employee of a real estate investment company. If you're interested in this career field, you should check out your home state's requirements for property managers.

In this section I discuss the duties and responsibilities of a property manager and the basic details of a property management agreement. For more general information, check out *Property Management For Dummies* by Robert S. Griswold (John Wiley & Sons).

Some state license exams have questions about property management.

## Taking care of business: The duties of a property manager

The duties of a property manager generally are defined as maximizing income and maintaining or increasing the overall value of the property being managed. I tell you more specifically here about how a property manager is responsible for the financial and physical condition of the building and cover a manager's duties in actually renting out a property's units or floor space and handling insurance.

### Financial responsibilities

Some of a property manager's duties include the following responsibilities:

- **Creating an annual operating budget:** This task includes analyzing the building's income and expenses over time. The manager also examines ways to reduce building expenses. (For more about analyzing properties, see Chapter 17.)
- **Collecting rents:** A manager usually creates some system of collecting and accounting for rents.
- **Setting rents:** The manager examines the rents and vacancy rates for competing buildings in the area and either sets rental rates or recommends rates to the owner.
- **Paying bills:** A manager is typically responsible for paying bills for operating expenses and repairs and maintenance.
- **Preparing periodic financial reports:** These reports relate to the building's financial condition and its income and expenses.

### Physical responsibilities

The building manager also is responsible for properly maintaining the property's value, its physical condition, and the physical condition of its buildings. These duties include the following:

- ✔ **Physical analysis of the building:** The property manager analyzes the building with a view toward immediate and long-term repairs and improvements that might be made to enhance the desirability of the building and allow for higher rents.

- ✔ **Preparation of capital and repairs budgets:** Using the property analysis as a basis, the property manager creates a capital budget that includes larger improvements and repairs to the building. Capital budget items typically include the replacement of major fixtures, such as roofs, boilers, and air-conditioning units, while repair budget items deal more with making repairs and maintaining those same fixtures.

- ✔ **Maintenance:** Part of the manager's responsibilities is arranging for routine cleaning and maintenance of the building and grounds, including scheduling janitorial services, preventive maintenance, and needed repairs on equipment like the boiler. The manager typically hires outside people to do these jobs, has his own employees for this work, or uses a combination of the two.

### Rental responsibilities

A manager usually is responsible for renting the space in a building. I say "usually" because sometimes an owner takes care of this task directly or hires a real estate agent other than the manager to find tenants and negotiate leases. You can find out more about different types of leases and their provisions in Chapter 12.

Advertising for tenants is another rental responsibility. "For rent" signs on the building and print ads in appropriate media, such as newspapers for apartments and specialized publications for office or industrial space, can be useful. Billboard, direct mail, and Internet advertising also may be used. Radio and TV ads usually are less effective but may prove useful in some markets. One commonly held belief is that recommendations by satisfied tenants may be the most effective advertising for a building.

The manager is also responsible for providing necessary services to the tenants as agreed to in the lease, for trying to settle any disputes that may arise with tenants, and for engaging in eviction activities if necessary.

### Insurance responsibilities

Property managers sometimes analyze the insurance needs of a building they manage or call in insurance experts to do it. Unlike a single-family house, which usually has a single insurance policy that covers a number of things, large complex buildings may require different types of insurance policies to cover specific items. Proper insurance coverage is part of an overall risk management plan that a property manager needs to consider.

In general, managing risk, or in some way dealing with potential liability issues, can be handled by a system known as CART, or controlling, avoiding, retaining, and transferring risk. These four general risk management options are described in the list that follows:

- ✔ *Controlling risk* means anticipating it and preparing for it. Emergency lighting systems are an example of controlling risk.

- ✔ *Avoiding risk* means removing the source of danger. Storage of paint or other flammable materials can be removed from the building and moved to another location.

✔ *Retaining risk* means accepting the liability. This step sometimes is taken when the risk of something happening is small; or, in essence, when you agree to pay whatever liability costs arise from the building's funds when a particular event does occur. *Self-insurance* is another way of describing this situation. An alternative to retaining risk is purchasing insurance coverage with a very high deductible (the payment made by the owner before insurance kicks in).

✔ *Transferring risk* means buying the appropriate type and amount of insurance to cover the payment whenever an insured incident occurs.

The following are types of insurance that are available to cover different types of risks:

✔ **Boiler and machinery insurance:** Because of the substantial cost of heating units and air-conditioning systems in large buildings, a separate type of insurance is needed to cover the replacement and repair of this type of machinery.

✔ **Casualty insurance:** This type of insurance covers losses caused by theft, vandalism, and burglary.

✔ **Co-insurance:** This coverage essentially is for situations in which the owner takes on part of the risk by self-insuring for a portion of the risk. Incorporating a large deductible before the insurance policy starts to pay off is one example.

✔ **Errors and omissions insurance:** This type of insurance can cover property managers against any errors they make in the performance of their duties. This insurance doesn't cover losses caused by fraud or other dishonest or malfeasant activities.

✔ **Fire and hazard insurance:** Depending on what it covers, this type of policy sometimes is called an all-risk, all-peril policy. It basically covers loss of the property caused by fire, storms, and other types of damaging conditions. This type of policy usually does not cover flooding and earthquake damage.

✔ **Liability insurance:** This type of insurance covers losses caused by injuries that are the result of negligence on the part of the landlord. The classic case is the person who falls on an icy sidewalk that the landlord was supposed to have cleaned.

✔ **Rent loss insurance:** This insurance sometimes is called business interruption insurance or consequential loss insurance. It pays the owner of the building for the loss of rent from tenants if the building is destroyed by fire.

✔ **Surety bond:** Technically a surety bond provides payment whenever something is not done within an agreed-upon period of time. However, the coverage provided by surety bonds has come to mean making up for losses caused by dishonest acts of an employee. For example, this type of insurance covers a loss that is the result of rents being stolen by the rent collector.

## Can you manage?

If you're interested in the field of property management, you can get more information from the following:

✔ The Institute of Real Estate Management (www.irem.org) is connected to the National Association of Realtors. You can get information and training from this organization. They award the Certified Property Manager (CPM) designation.

✔ The Building Owners and Managers Association International (www.boma.org) is another source of information particularly with regard to the management of commercial buildings.

✔ Information and sometimes training and professional designations also can be obtained from the International Council of Shopping Centers (www.icsc.org), the Urban Land Institute (www.uli.org), the National Apartment Association (www.naahq.org), and the International Real Estate Institute (www.iami.org/irei).

# Saying yes: The property management agreement

The basis for the relationship between a property manager and a property owner is a contract called the property management agreement. Although every agreement is unique, particularly with respect to the details of duties, responsibilities, and payments, certain elements need to be specifically addressed in any property management agreement, including:

- ✔ **Who:** The parties to the agreement (both the property owner and the property manager) need to be clearly identified. In any partnership situation, both partners need to sign. The appropriate corporate officer needs to sign for a corporation.

- ✔ **Where:** The property to be managed needs to be clearly identified at least by its address and possibly by legal description. You can check out the specifics of legal description in Chapter 9. If any elements of the property are not to be managed by the property manager, they need to be identified. For example, if a building has a large empty piece of land next to it that is leased as a parking lot for use by an adjacent building, the owner may not want to have you manage that lot.

- ✔ **How long:** The term or length of the agreement needs to be stated. Owners tend to want a short time frame; managers want a longer one. A minimum of one year is the general recommendation, because that gives managers a chance to show their skills and recoup some of their initial expenses in setting up a management program for the building.

- ✔ **What — manager's duties:** The manager's duties need to be clearly defined and stated. All parties to the agreement need to know whether the manager will collect rents, pay bills, contract for maintenance, and so on. (For more, see "Taking care of business: The duties of a property manager," earlier in this chapter.)

- ✔ **What — manager's authority as an agent:** A property manager usually is considered a *general agent.* As a general agent, the manager usually has authority over a range of activities on behalf of the owner. The extent of this authority needs to be spelled out in the agreement. For example, the agreement needs to flesh out whether the manager has the final word in setting rent rates or must first check with the owner for final approval.

- ✔ **What information and when — reporting:** The principal form of communication between a property owner and a manager are the periodic reports prepared by the manager. The timing and content of these reports are negotiable and vary with the type and complexity of the building being managed. Monthly reports are typical and can contain a variety of income, expense, vacancy, expiring leases, and maintenance information.

- ✔ **Who pays what — allocation of expenses:** This part of the agreement states which costs, if any, are paid out of the manager's fees rather than from the income of the building. For example the manager may be responsible for the costs of advertising, especially if the manager receives an extra bonus for new leases.

- ✔ **How much — the fee:** The fee for any management agreement is completely negotiable, but it's usually based on one or more of the following:

  - Commission on new leases

  - Fixed fees

  - Percentage of the gross (before expenses are deducted) or net (after expenses are deducted) income from the building

  - A combination of any two or three of the first three

- ✔ **What the landlord wants:** A clear statement of the owner's objectives for owning the building can be made part of the management agreement or addressed in some other written format, such as a letter of understanding between owner and property manager. Regardless of how the owner's objectives are handled, the manager must have a clear idea whether the owner is seeking long- or short-term profits or other financial objectives from his investment. Furthermore, it's equally as important for the manager to adequately meet the owner's objectives without compromising her honesty or ethics.

# Managing a Real Estate Office: You're the Boss, Ms. or Mr. Broker

If you're taking the state examination for the salesperson's license, you probably can skip this section, but if you're taking the broker's exam, you need to read this section. Some states expect aspiring brokers to know something about the administrative duties and responsibilities of running a real estate brokerage, including supervising people who work for you, training those people, and setting office policies.

## Keeping an eye out: Supervision

State laws may vary, but in general, a broker is required to supervise the people who work for her. This extremely specific requirement makes the broker responsible for the actions of salespeople who work for her. This responsibility extends to violations of the state licensing laws, fair housing laws, and illegal or fraudulent activities. The extent of liability and punishment is, of course, determined by state licensing officials, and in the case of criminal or civil actions, by the courts.

The type of questions you're likely to get on this subject fall into these two categories:

- ✔ What your state law has to say about brokers' responsibilities with respect to supervising their salespeople.

- ✔ The expectation that you'll know most of the important points of the state licensing law with which you and your salespeople are expected to comply. (See "Making it legal: Looking at license law," earlier in this chapter.)

Although this material may be information you found out about when pursuing your salesperson's license, you still need to review the specific information that applies to your state's broker's exam.

## Teach me! Training

Brokers are expected to provide training to their salespeople. Most states require prospective salespeople to receive formal training through prelicensing courses before they can get a salesperson's license. Even though this training gives you the basic background and the minimum amount of knowledge that the state requires you to have to work as a real estate agent, it often does not cover the day-to-day real world activities of an agent. Brokers are expected to provide that day-to-day type of training. After you get your salesperson's license, you can stay a salesperson forever. In most states, however, if you want to become a broker, you're required to gain some hands-on experience.

## Setting office policy: Rules are rules

Formulating and periodically updating an office policies and procedures manual is a suggested means of at least partially fulfilling your training and supervision obligations as a broker. This manual is distributed to all employees along with training in the policies and procedures of the brokerage. Because most salespeople work as independent contractors (see the next section), the policy and procedures manual needs to rely on words like *suggested* and *recommended* rather than *must*. The subjects contained in an office policy manual can range from dealings with attorneys and other professionals to record keeping, using supplies, and attending sales meetings.

# My Own Way: Working as an Independent Contractor

Most real estate salespeople work as independent contractors for their brokers. This typical working relationship between a salesperson and a broker affects everything from taxes to daily work. In this section I'll explain this relationship and some of the issues you need to understand for exam purposes.

The best way to understand work status as an independent contractor is to contrast it with a regular employee. A real estate salesperson can work as an employee for a broker, but doing so is not the norm. Although he is the boss, the broker doesn't have the same detailed authority over an independent contractor as with a regular employee. The two main differences are

✔ Employees must work the hours the employer tells them to work. The employer also must take out taxes from the employees' pay and pay Social Security on behalf of the employees.

✔ Independent contractors are responsible for paying their own taxes and Social Security. They can deduct certain business expenses from their pretax pay that an employee can't deduct. Independent contractors can work their own hours and basically do the job in their own way. An employer cannot force an independent contractor to work certain hours or attend certain meetings, because that can jeopardize the independent contractor status of the salesperson.

# I Get It! Job-Related Laws to Understand

A few common misunderstandings about the real estate business are pretty serious issues because they deal with federal antitrust laws. State exam writers expect you to be able to answer questions about them.

Violations of the Sherman Antitrust Act can result in fines paid to the federal government of varying amounts and up to triple the damages paid to the injured party.

## The price isn't right: Price fixing

First of all no rule says that a real estate agent must be paid on a commission basis. Just to be sure you're clear on this, a *commission* generally is a percentage of the final sale price of the property that usually is paid upon completion of the sale. (See "How Does a Real Estate Broker/Salesperson Get Paid?" earlier in this chapter for more.) Pay by commission is a common practice across the United States, but has never been established as a requirement by any government or private agency.

No such thing as a standard commission exists. No state that I know of sets commission rates. No local real estate board or other association of real estate agents has the authority to set commission rates or create any standardized fees for services. In fact, any attempt among real estate agents to create a standardized fee schedule is and has been viewed as violating federal antitrust laws. The fact that many brokerages in a particular area charge the same commission is a matter of competition and individual business decision.

The Sherman Antitrust Act, which is a federal law that prohibits activities that are considered to be in restraint of trade, forbids any type of price fixing in any industry. In simple terms, what that means is that if I own an appliance store and you own an appliance store, we can't get together once a month and decide that we're both going to charge the same price for a washing machine.

In the real estate industry, antitrust laws essentially have been taken one step further as a result of a famous court decision in a case called *United States versus Foley.* The result of this case determined that even if no actual consultation occurred between individuals about price fixing, the mere discussion among competitors of prices for services is considered an invitation to fix prices and therefore violates antitrust law. As a result, the industry operates on the principle that discussing fees between brokers is illegal unless the brokers are cooperating on the same deal. Fees may be discussed in-house between brokers and salespeople and brokers, salespeople, and clients. In other cases, the courts determined that local boards of realtors can't dictate, recommend, or publish rate schedules.

## Bad break: Market allocation

The Sherman Antitrust Act also has a provision against market allocation that affects real estate professionals. *Market allocation* is an agreement among competitors to divide the market in some way.

Consider two brokers, for example, who own their own brokerages and meet and agree that one of them will handle all the listings west of Main Street and the other will handle all the listings east of Main Street. Add to the mix two other brokers who meet and agree that one will handle only houses worth more than $300,000 and the other will handle only houses under that price. All four brokers have violated the Sherman Antitrust Act's provision against market allocation.

## Feeling shunned: Group boycotts

Group boycotts — when competitors get together and agree not to do business with someone — violate the Sherman Antitrust Act.

Say *X* Brokerage and *Y* Brokerage don't like the way *Z* Brokerage does business. They meet and agree not to make any referrals to *Z* Brokerage. The *X* and *Y* brokerages have just violated the Sherman Antitrust Act prohibition against group boycotts. However, an individual broker can decide not to do business with another broker because he believes the other broker acts unethically. It's getting together as a group to boycott that's against the law.

## What's your condition? Tie-in arrangements

Any requirement to buy one product or service on condition that you buy another product or service is called a *tie-in arrangement* or *tying agreement* and is an antitrust violation.

Say I am a broker who owns a property that a builder wants to buy. As part of the sale, I require that the builder relist the property with me (list back) when he sells it. Because I required the builder to list the property with me as a condition of my selling it to him, I broke the law.

# Review Questions and Answers

For the most part questions in this section are aimed at people taking the broker's exam. In general, the exam may focus on broker responsibilities, license law issues, and the independent contractor status of salespeople. The antitrust questions may be on both the salesperson's and the broker's exams. You also need to check whether property management is a subject you're expected to know for the test at the license level you're going for in your state.

1. A salesperson paid an hourly wage and expected to be in the office from 8 a.m. until 2 p.m. to answer phones is probably a(n)

    (A) independent contractor.

    (B) employee.

    (C) contract agent.

    (D) associate broker.

    *Correct answer:* (B). A person required to work certain hours and paid an hourly wage is usually considered an employee. An independent contractor is allowed to work her own hours and is usually paid for her productivity by commission. An associate broker is not a status of employment but rather a licensing level. I made up the term "contract agent."

2. A division of a community along geographic lines for purposes of listing homes for sale by two salespeople working for the same broker is

    (A) market allocation in violation of antitrust laws.

    (B) legal.

    (C) a tie-in arrangement.

    (D) an in-house boycott that is illegal.

    *Correct answer:* (B). The allocation prohibition is between two brokers not within one brokerage, which makes the situation in the question completely legal.

3. Broker Bob will not give any referrals to Broker Jane because he believes she acts unethically. He tells no one about this. He

    (A) is violating the antitrust law regarding group boycotting.

    (B) is entitled to his opinion but needs to have checked with his local Board of Realtors first.

    (C) is violating no antitrust law.

    (D) needs to refer business to her because he has no proof of her behavior.

    *Correct answer:* (C). No group is involved here. As long as no fair housing or civil rights laws are being violated, an individual generally is permitted to do business with whomever he or she wants.

4. Who sets the commission rate in a real estate brokerage office?

    (A) The state real estate commission in each state

    (B) The local Board of Realtors

    (C) No mandatory rates are in effect, but rates need to follow the published rate schedule.

    (D) The broker who owns the business

    *Correct answer:* (D). Antitrust laws state that no group of brokers can get together to set rates or publish fee schedules, and states don't set them, either. Answer (D) is the common and legal practice in the industry.

5. Broker Helen allows her dentist to use her vacation condominium for a week for free to thank him for sending her a person who listed a house with her. Helen

    (A) did nothing wrong.

    (B) violated license law.

    (C) violated the antitrust prohibition about tie-in arrangements.

    (D) should have checked with the state real estate commission first.

    *Correct answer:* (B). State license laws generally prohibit the payment of fees or gifts to non-licensed individuals as part of a real estate transaction. So Helen did something wrong, it's not an antitrust violation, and there's nothing to check because it is a license law violation.

6. A property manager is employed by the XYZ Real Estate Investment Company to manage its properties. The manager

    (A) most likely does not need a real estate license.

    (B) most likely needs a real estate license.

    (C) does not need a real estate license if the owner of the company has one.

    (D) needs a license only to collect the rents.

    *Correct answer:* (A). Check your local state for the specific regulations, but generally an employee of a single company managing its own real estate need not have a license.

7. Property managers are usually considered

    (A) special agents.

    (B) general agents.

    (C) universal agents.

    (D) contractual agents.

    *Correct answer:* (B). A general agent handles a range of activities on behalf of a client. Special agents handle only one activity like selling a piece of property, and universal agents act on behalf of a client in all real estate matters (I cover these two categories in Chapter 4). I made up contractual agents.

8. What type of insurance secures against employee theft of rent collected?

    (A) Workers' compensation

    (B) Surety bond

    (C) Liability

    (D) Business interruption

    *Correct answer:* (B). Workers' compensation insures against employee injury. Liability insurance insures against injury to a member of the public injured on the property. Business interruption insurance (also called rent loss insurance) provides payments to the landlord when rents can't be collected due to some disaster like a fire. Surety bonds insure against an employee's dishonest acts (like the one in the question).

9. The amount of compensation received by a property manager is

    (A) set by the local real estate board.

    (B) set by the local property owner's association.

    (C) a matter of individual negotiation.

    (D) always based on a percentage of gross rents.

    *Correct answer:* (C). This is the same as setting commission rates. It's all negotiable.

10. Because of the independent contractor status of most real estate salespeople, a broker

    (A) should not bother with a policies and procedures manual.

    (B) is not responsible for his salesperson's actions.

    (C) is responsible for his salesperson's actions only with respect to fair housing law violations.

    (D) need not withhold Social Security taxes unless they are employees.

    *Correct answer:* (D). One of the distinguishing features of independent contractor status is that the broker doesn't have to withhold payroll taxes or Social Security payments. That doesn't relieve the broker of his responsibility for his salesperson's actions. All of the other answers are therefore wrong.

# Chapter 4

# Understanding Agency Law

● ● ● ● ● ● ● ● ● ● ● ● ● ● ● ● ● ● ● ● ● ● ● ● ● ● ● ● ● ● ● ● ● ● ● ● ● ● ● ● ● ● ● ● ● ● ● ●

## In This Chapter

▶ Choosing and establishing an agency relationship

▶ Looking at the duties of an agent to a principal and a customer

▶ Finding out who pays an agent and when

▶ Discovering how to end an agency relationship

● ● ● ● ● ● ● ● ● ● ● ● ● ● ● ● ● ● ● ● ● ● ● ● ● ● ● ● ● ● ● ● ● ● ● ● ● ● ● ● ● ● ● ● ● ● ● ●

*M*y guess is that the kind of agent you're most familiar with is the Hollywood agent. And that's as good a place as any to start talking about what the word *agent* means. Before and after the big parties and movie premieres, what does an agent do? An agent represents a client, and that means that agent always works for the client's best interest in any deal that the agent negotiates on behalf of the client. The agent tries to get the client the best role in the movie for the most money or may try to get the client a bigger dressing room at the studio.

Real estate agents are no different. They represent their clients and always work in their best interests. Except that the work isn't about better movie roles and bigger dressing rooms. It's probably about a better price for a house or a faster sale. Regardless of whether they're located in Hollywood or Topeka, or whether they're negotiating salaries or house sales, the relationship between agents and the people they represent comes with duties, responsibilities, and expectations.

In this chapter, I discuss the all-important agency relationship and its main players. I talk about how to establish such a relationship and define the elements of relationships between agents, principals (who are also called clients), and customers. I tell you about payday (who pays an agent and when), and I let you know how to end an agency relationship.

Every chapter in this book is important and fair game  for the questions on the real estate exam that you're going to take. That said, be sure to pay particular attention to the information in this chapter. People who buy and sell houses and other real estate continue to misunderstand the agency relationship. Although the situation has been getting better, various states are aggressive in making sure that their real estate agents understand the agency relationship, can act accordingly and appropriately, and can explain its nuances to the people who use their services. Specific types of agency relationships and laws governing agency vary a great deal from one state to the next, but the information I give you in this chapter is pretty much generic and therefore applicable in most (if not all) states. As such, you need to pay particularly close attention to the way your state deals with the entire subject of agency so that you know exactly what the agency rules are and how agency relationships are conducted. Through the years, the states have increased the number of hours they require in coursework on agency law, which, in turn, means that more emphasis is placed on this subject in the state's licensing exams. So be prepared for a bunch of questions about agency law on your state's exam.

# You're Hired: Becoming Someone's Real Estate Agent

In this section, you find information about some very important parts of agency law, who you represent, and how the agency relationship is established between you and that client.

## Picking sides: Representation in agency relationships

You'd think that defining or establishing just who you represent is an easy question to answer. In fact, you're probably amazed that I'm telling you right now that many real estate agents, buyers, and sellers either are confused about what constitutes an agency relationship from the beginning or seem to forget about it along the way. I explain why this confusion exists at the same time that I give you information that clarifies who you represent in a real estate transaction.

### Getting to know you: Agents, principals, and customers

Several people are involved in any given agency relationship, but first, I need to make sure that you understand who *you* are within that arrangement. An *agent* is someone who is authorized to represent the interests of another person. The three different types of agents, in the order of least to most authority, include

✔ **Special agents:** An agent who is hired by someone to represent that person in one transaction. A real estate agent who represents someone in the sale or purchase of a house is considered a special agent. In some states, this type of agent also is called a *specific agent.*

✔ **General agents:** An agent who represents someone in a range or group of activities. A property manager, who collects rent, pays bills, authorizes repairs, and negotiates leases, among other tasks, usually is considered a general agent (see Chapter 3 for more on property management). In some states the universal agent (see the next bullet point) is called a general agent, so make sure that you know the correct terminology for your state.

✔ **Universal agents:** An agent who acts on a client's behalf in all matters and situations. Someone who has a power of attorney to act on someone's behalf in all real estate matters is an example of a universal agent.

I talk about the relationship between brokers and salespersons in Chapter 3, but I want to say something more specific about brokers, salespeople, and the agency relationship. Licensed real estate salespersons work for and under the authority of a licensed broker. The agent in an agency relationship is the broker. The salesperson is considered an agent of the broker and a *sub agent* of the seller or buyer (depends on who the broker is representing), forming one of the more common types of subagencies. However, enlisting the help of other brokers in the sale of a property is equally as common an idea. This can be done through a local multiple listing service (see "Looking at listing agreements" later in this chapter) or with individual brokers. These other brokers, who often are called cooperating brokers, also may become sub agents of the seller. (It's not common to enlist the aid of other brokers when a broker is representing a buyer.) The point is you need to check out the specific responsibilities of sub agents and characteristics of sub agencies in your home state.

## But I never said that: Vicarious liability

There's a problem with the subagency relationship I described earlier. When using a cooperating broker or agent, the client can be held liable for the actions of the subagent. Let me give you an example. Say Client Jones wants to sell her house and hires Broker A to be her broker; that is, her agent. The client gives her broker permission to get the help of other agents to sell the house. Broker A puts the word out that this house is for sale, and Salesperson C who works for Broker B comes along and starts to show the house. In the course of showing the house Salesperson C makes a remark to a potential buyer that they might not be happy in the neighborhood because it's very ethnically uniform with many immigrants from one country. The buyer takes offense and considers this a violation of fair housing law. The buyer would be justified in filing a complaint against Salesperson C, Broker B, Broker A, and Seller

Jones, because even though the seller has never even met Salesperson C, he is working for her as a sub agent. The courts in these cases have often been reluctant to place blame on the unsuspecting seller/client. States have taken steps to eliminate this situation.

At least one state has created something called the Broker's Agent in an attempt to avoid the sub agent dilemma. In this arrangement when the client's broker enlists the help of other agents, the other agents become sub-agents to the broker but not to the client. In other cases individual multiple listing systems no longer consider cooperating brokers to be subagents of the seller but rather sub-agents of the listing broker. Although sub agencies with vicarious liability to the seller are gradually being eliminated, you should check to see if your state has dealt with the issue and how.

In addition to an agent, a few other key players in agency relationships are the following:

- **Principal:** A *principal* is the person you represent as an agent. This is the person you have the agency relationship with.
- **Client:** A *client* is another name for a principal.
- **Customer:** A *customer* is the other party to the transaction. In a typical real estate transaction, there's you (the agent or sub agent), the principal or client (such as a seller), and the customer (such as a buyer). The customer is considered and sometimes referred to, particularly in exam questions, as the third party.

### One or the other: Single agency with sellers or buyers

Most real estate agency relationships are *single agency relationships,* meaning you represent either the buyer or the seller. You know who these two people are, but which one is the principal (client) and which is the customer? The short answer is the principal (client) is the person with whom you have an agency agreement, that is, the person you've agreed to represent. The customer is the third party, that is, the person you do not represent. And this lineup is the same regardless of whether you represent a buyer or a seller. This is important but not necessarily easy information to understand, so let me illustrate. Broker A is hired by Seller A to represent her in selling her house. Buyer B hires Broker B to represent him as a buyer's agent (don't worry; I cover buyer's agency in a little while). In these two relationships Seller A is the principal or client of Broker A. Buyer B is the principal or client of Broker B. Now let's say Buyer B wants to negotiate to buy Seller A's property. Seller A now becomes the customer to Broker B, while Buyer B becomes the customer of Broker A. There are other possible relationships; however, this is where it begins, in the single agency relationship between agent and client with the customer being the third party.

Okay, although "warning" may be a strong word, this is the point in the explanation where many people begin to get confused. But you need to remember that the reason for the confusion is pretty much because of the way the real estate business has worked for 10,000 years. (All right, maybe not 10,000 years, but who knows, a real estate agent may have been trying to sell someone a nice cool tropical cave with an ocean view sometime back in the Stone Age.) The fact is that in most places, since real estate brokerage became an occupation, real estate agents represent the seller, yet spend most of their time with the buyer. If you've either bought or sold a house and used a real estate agent, you probably have a good idea of what I'm talking about. The real estate broker signs an agreement to act as an agent to sell someone's house, but the agent may not see the seller again except occasionally to bring people to the house to see it. Meanwhile, the agent spends every Saturday driving Mr. and Mrs. Buyer around looking at houses. Mr. and Mrs. Buyer are the customers. Nothing's wrong with this scenario; it's just that the agent, who's spending a lot of time with them, is so nice and helpful, and might even make a good match for their single cousin, actually represents the seller. But the Buyers begin thinking the agent represents them. And sometimes the agent begins to act like he does, too.

In an attempt to clarify things, particularly for buyers, something called buyer agency has been developed. *Buyer agency* is when the agent represents the buyer instead of the seller. In this case, the buyer is the principal or client and the seller is the customer. The existence and legality of buyer agency varies from state to state, so you need to check out how buyer agency works in your state and any specific buyer agency laws that your state enforces.

### A neat trick: Representing both sides in dual agency

*Dual agency* is a situation where both sides in a transaction, typically a buyer and a seller, are represented by the same real estate agent. Dual agency may actually be illegal in your state, but it's legal in enough states that I can give you some information that should get you through any test questions about the subject. You need to find out from your home state's specific laws whether dual agency is legal, and if so, under what circumstances.

Here's an example: Suppose you agree to represent Mr. and Mrs. Buyer as their buyer's agent to find a house. After working with them for several months with no success, you get a call from Mr. and Mrs. Seller, who want you to represent them as their agent to sell their house. Just to be clear, you now have agency agreements with both Mr. and Mrs. Seller and Mr. and Mrs. Buyer. At this point there's no dual agency or problem. However, you now show Mr. And Mrs. Seller's house to Mr. And Mrs. Buyer, and the Buyers agree to make an offer. You are representing both sides in this transaction. That's dual agency. If your state allows it, the usual way to make this legal is to inform the Buyers and the Sellers of your dual agency status and get their consent to continue representing both parties. This is called obtaining informed consent. This is sometimes referred to as *limited agency* because each client doesn't receive the full range of your fiduciary duties. For example, neither party can receive your undivided loyalty. I discuss specific fiduciary duties later on in the chapter in "Keeping the Faith: The Relationship Between an Agent and a Principal."

### The man (or woman) in the middle: Transactional brokerage

In some states, the idea that a broker is really a kind of middleman in a transaction between two parties is being given serious consideration. Some states have passed laws creating what is called *transactional brokerage,* providing for a situation in which a broker represents neither buyer nor seller but yet can complete a transaction and be paid for it. In such an arrangement, the broker brings the buyer and the seller together, negotiates the deal, and handles some or all of the paperwork. The major difference is that the transactional broker would not represent either side in the transaction. You need to check with your state's real estate law to find out whether this type of arrangement exists, and if it does, how your state has named the new arrangement, what brokers are called in this situation (because they may no longer be considered agents), and what the basic duties and responsibilities are, because they aren't fiduciaries. As you look for these laws in your state be aware that some states refer to this arrangement as non-agency and to the broker as a facilitator or intermediary as well as a transactional broker. (See "Keeping the Faith: The Relationship Between an Agent and a Principal," later in this chapter, for more on fiduciary responsibilities.)

### *Letting everyone know: Agency disclosure requirements*

A famous study some years ago indicated that a majority of buyers thought they were being represented by the real estate agent who was driving them around town looking at houses. In almost all the cases, the real estate agent was representing the seller, but because the agent was spending so much time with and being so helpful to the buyer, the buyer thought he was their agent and not the seller's. As states began recognizing the confusion that exists regarding who represents whom in a real estate transaction, they've enacted laws requiring real estate agents to tell prospective clients and customers who they represent. These laws, where they exist, are referred to as *agency disclosure laws.* Agency disclosure clears up any confusion for buyers and sellers as to who, if anybody, is representing them. It also gives them an opportunity to get an agent to work for them if they're not being represented. Disclosure typically is given in writing to both buyers and sellers. You need to find out what disclosure requirements, if any, exist in your state. (For more about the responsibility of disclosure, check out "You'd better tell: Disclosure" later in this chapter.)

## Establishing the agency relationship (and doing it in writing)

Representing a party to a real estate transaction as an agent and (hopefully) getting paid for it are based on the agency relationship that you established with that party. The information in this section about how you can establish agency relationships is pretty universal, so it applies in most (if not all) states. Nevertheless, you need to check whether your state's licensing law recognizes or prohibits any of the following ways of establishing an agency relationship and whether your state perhaps recognizes other ways that I haven't covered.

An agency relationship can be established either by means of an agreement between the parties, an agent and a principal (client), or by means of the actions of the two individuals. The first of the bullet points that follow is the former, and all the rest are the latter. You should remember that although I give examples of agents selling houses to illustrate the following types of agencies, if the statute of frauds in your state requires that all real estate agency agreements be in writing, then it's unlikely that you can collect a commission by any of the non-written agencies. (For more on the statute of frauds, see Chapter 11.)

- ✔ **Express agency:** *Express agency* is where the agency relationship is created through an agreement in which the agent and the principal state their intentions to enter into an agency relationship, that the agent will represent the principal. The parties state or express their intentions in words, either orally or in writing. Whether an oral agreement establishing an agency relationship is binding varies from state to state, so check it out. It may also be possible for an oral agreement to establish an agency relationship but not be enforceable by you, the agent, to collect a fee. The typical written agreement is a listing agreement or a buyer's agency agreement, both of which I discuss in the next two sections. The written agreement is the most appropriate and legally safe way to create an agency relationship.

✔ **Implied agency:** *Implied agency* establishes an agency relationship through the actions of the two parties. Although nothing formal has been said or written down, the agent and the principal *act* as if they have an agency relationship. Creating an implied agency may not have been what the two parties intended, but an agency relationship can be created anyway. If you find these circumstances hard to imagine, check out what happened to Ms. Seller.

Ms. Seller is selling her home by herself and puts up a for-sale sign on the lawn. You drive by, see the sign, and stop in. You identify yourself as a real estate agent and ask some questions about the house. Ms. Seller tells you she doesn't want to list the house for sale with any brokerage. She does tell you to feel free to bring any possible buyers around who might want to see the house. The next day you bring Mr. and Mrs. Buyer, who really like the house and want to make an offer. You tell Ms. Seller and begin negotiating a deal. If the matter comes down to commissions and lawsuits, only a court can finally decide, but you and Ms. Seller probably have established an implied agency relationship because of both your actions.

✔ **Agency by estoppel:** An *agency by estoppel* is created when a principal doesn't stop an agent from going beyond the agent's normal duties, which thus gives the impression that an agency relationship has been established. Say you're the owner of a building and you tell your agent to show an apartment to a possible tenant. The agent goes ahead and negotiates a lease even though you didn't give the agent any direct authority to do so. The tenant assumes the agent has the authority and an agency by estoppel has been created.

✔ **Agency by ratification:** An *agency by ratification* is created by accepting circumstances that created the agency after the fact. Suppose a real estate agent, without authorization and without ever speaking to the seller, negotiates a deal for a house that's for sale by the seller. One day the agent arrives with a completed contract simply awaiting the seller's signature and acceptance of the deal. An agency by ratification probably has been created when the seller ratified what the agent had been doing by accepting the deal. I say "probably," because the agent wants a fee for his services and may have to sue the seller to collect. When that's the case, the courts determine whether an agency relationship existed from the beginning of the negotiations — based on the fact that the seller accepted or ratified the agent's behavior by accepting the deal.

✔ **Agency coupled with an interest:** An *agency coupled with an interest* is a situation in which an agent has some kind of interest in the property that's being sold. For example, suppose a part-time broker is also an architect. The broker/architect agrees to design some houses for a builder who's giving the broker/architect the listings for the sale of the finished houses. In essence the broker/architect made an investment in the project, so the builder can't cancel the agency agreement. If this sounds like a tie-in arrangement and an antitrust violation (see Chapter 3), remember that the broker/architect isn't making one activity conditional on the other. A tie-in arrangement would've been created if the broker had said that if the builder wanted him to sell the finished houses, the builder also had to hire him (as in pay him) to design the houses. In an agency coupled with an interest, it's as if the broker/architect was investing in the project.

Most agency relationships are established in writing with different agreements for buyer and seller agency relationships (see "One or the other: Single agency with sellers or buyers," earlier in this chapter). Listing agreements involve sellers, and buyer agency agreements involve buyers. (How did you guess?) Within the two categories are different kinds of agreements. Many details within various types of agreements are similar with respect to the duties to be performed. The differences usually deal with circumstances under which an agent will or won't get paid. The issue of payment of the broker's fee, which is covered in more detail in "Making Money (No, Not at the Copy Machine)" later in this chapter, usually is related to who is the procuring cause of the buyer or seller. The *procuring cause* means the person who found the buyer or seller and made the transaction happen. Often it's referred to as the person who brought about a meeting of the minds between a buyer and a seller. It also may be defined as the broker who brought a ready, willing, and able buyer to the deal in terms acceptable to the seller.

# FSBO — What in the world does that mean?

Don't you hate when teachers use acronyms or initials without explaining them? Well, when I took my prelicensing courses I had a teacher who used FSBO a few times and never explained what it meant. He pronounced it "phizzbo," and I thought maybe it was some kind of antacid for those tough days selling real estate. The sad part is that I was too embarrassed to ask what it meant. I never forgot that, and now when I teach my classes, I try never to use letters or abbreviations without first explaining them, and I encourage all my students to feel free to ask questions about anything they don't understand, no matter how dumb they think a question sounds. You can rest assured that if you don't understand something, other people in the class probably are having the same problem. So ask those questions. Remember it's your money and it's your chance to learn. Oh! I almost forgot. FSBO means For Sale By Owner. Maybe that's why the teacher didn't want to explain it. For Sale By Owner means NCFB — No Commission For Broker . . . and that really will give you heartburn.

## Looking at listing agreements

A *listing agreement* establishes an agency relationship between an agent and a property seller. The agent agrees to represent the seller in marketing the property. Here are the names and descriptions of the four types of listing agreements in the order that they are more commonly used:

- ✔ *Exclusive right to sell listing:* In this type of listing agreement, a broker is given the exclusive right to market a property on behalf of the seller. The broker is paid regardless of who sells the property, an especially important point because it distinguishes this type of listing agreement from the others. I'll clarify: The owner always retains the right to sell his or her own real estate, even so, while the listing agreement is in effect, if the owner sells the property without any help from the broker, the owner still has to pay the agreed-upon fee to the broker.

- ✔ *Exclusive agency listing:* In this type of listing agreement, a broker is hired to act as an exclusive agent, representing the owner in the marketing of the property. The broker, of course, earns a fee if the property sells. However, if the owner of the property sells the property without any help from the broker, the property owner won't have to pay the broker a fee.

- ✔ *Open listing:* Notice anything missing from the name of this type of listing? The word "exclusive" is taken out because the property owner has the right to use as many brokers as are needed to sell the property. No broker has the exclusive right to represent the owner. This type of listing sometimes is called a *nonexclusive* or *general listing.* The owner who sells an open-listed property without any help from a broker is under no obligation to pay a fee to any broker. If a broker does bring a successful buyer to the property, the owner must pay the broker a pre-agreed to commission.

- ✔ *Net listing:* A *net listing* is a listing for which a broker is hired to sell the property for a certain amount of money called the *net amount* or *net price.* The broker keeps any amount in excess of the net price. So if you take a net listing on a house for which the owner wants to net $200,000 from the sale, and you sell it for $225,000, you get to keep $25,000 as your fee. *Note:* Net listings are illegal in some states and discouraged in others. Some states allow it only if the maximum commission to be earned by the agent is made clear to the seller in writing in the original listing agreement. Check out your state law about this kind of listing. Questions about net listings tend to be favorites among test writers, especially if it's illegal in your state.

In addition to these four types of listings, you may encounter something called an option listing. An *option listing* is not as much a listing as it is a clause in any listing agreement that gives the broker the right to buy the property. Check out your local state law to find out whether option listings are allowed and what conditions or requirements may be imposed when using an option listing. You can see the danger of a conflict of interest here so states that do permit them tend to regulate them.

More people have probably heard about multiple listings than have heard about the listing agreements we just talked about. Don't get confused. A *multiple listing service* or *multiple listing system* (MLS) isn't really a type of listing as much as it is a marketing service that permits brokers to share listings with other brokers. A broker gets a listing to sell a house and then puts it on the local MLS. Tens, if not hundreds, of other brokers look at that listing, and one of them may have a buyer for the property. In an MLS arrangement, the broker who has the agreement with the principal is the one who earns a commission on the sale, although he often may split that commission with other brokers who helped bring about the sale.

Because multiple listing systems have more to do with marketing than anything else, rarely are there any questions about them on state exams. I mention the multiple listing systems briefly here just in case it happens to be used as an incorrect choice on a question or possibly as a correct choice for a question that has to do with which choice is not a type of listing agreement.

### Examining buyer agency agreements

Traditional real estate brokerage continues to primarily represent sellers; however, as buyers became aware that they didn't have representation in real estate transactions, buyer agency agreements were developed to enable the buyer to become the principal and thus have all the advantages of being represented by a real estate agent. The several types of buyer agency agreements differ primarily in the circumstances under which the broker is paid. Here are typical agreements:

- *Exclusive buyer agency agreement:* This agreement makes the broker the exclusive agent for the buyer, and no matter who finds the property that the buyer is seeking, a fee is owed to the broker, if and when the buyer buys the property. Even if the buyer buys property directly from an owner with no broker involved, the buyer still has to pay the exclusive agent a fee. This type of agreement is also called an *exclusive right to represent.*

- *Exclusive agency buyer agency agreement:* This agreement makes the broker the exclusive agent of the buyer, but it requires the broker to be paid only if the broker finds the property that the buyer ultimately purchases. If the buyer finds property and buys it without help from the broker, the buyer owes no fee to the broker.

- *Open buyer agency agreement:* This agreement enables the buyer to enter into agreements with any number of brokers and is therefore not an exclusive type of buyer agency agreement. The buyer pays only the broker who finds the property that the buyer buys. The buyer owes the broker nothing, if the buyer finds and purchases a property without help from the broker.

The buyer or the seller may pay the fee in a buyer's agency agreement. Fiduciary responsibility (see the next section) doesn't follow the money. A buyer's agent who owes complete fiduciary responsibility to the buyer can be paid from a portion of the commission paid by a seller to the seller's agent. This is no different from when a fee is split in a co-brokering arrangement in which both brokers represent the seller. See "Making Money (No, Not at the Copy Machine)," later in this chapter, for more.

# Keeping the Faith: The Relationship Between an Agent and a Principal

The elements of an agent's responsibility to the principal are summed up in one word — fiduciary. *Fiduciary* means faithful servant, and an agent is the fiduciary of the principal. (In real estate transactions, the principal is also known as the client and can be either the seller or the buyer — see "Getting to know you: Agents, principals, and customers," earlier in this chapter.) The agent faithfully represents the interests of the principal above all other interests including the agent's own.

The specific fiduciary responsibilities of an agent have been handed down by practice and common law — what people have done and how the courts have interpreted those actions. Some states examined the fiduciary duties of real estate agents and incorporate them with their respective real estate license laws. Don't forget that the agent owes a fiduciary obligation to the principal or client. I discuss other duties and obligations that are due the customer in "Meeting Obligations: The Relationship Between an Agent and a Customer" later in this chapter.

Although I discuss fiduciary responsibilities so that you have a good general understanding of the subject for exam purposes, you nevertheless need to check out your local state's interpretation of fiduciary duties so you're more in line with specific questions you may encounter on the state exam. Because fiduciary responsibilities are the basis of the agency relationship, exam writers want to make sure that you understand your obligations as an agent. Be prepared to answer several questions on this topic on the state exam.

## Who has the money? Accounting

As a real estate agent, you handle money and sometimes large sums of it. Most often you'll handle the money that goes with the buyer's offer to purchase a property that is variously called the *binder* or *earnest money.* These funds are credited to the buyer and become part of the down payment. Eventually they belong to the seller but may be held by the broker for a considerable amount of time. The check may be written to the broker. Other funds from the buyer or the seller also may be entrusted to the broker.

The duty of accounting for all the funds that are given to you for safe keeping (yes, that don't belong to you) is part of your fiduciary responsibilities. Most states require that funds that belong to clients and customers be kept in a bank account that's separate from the broker's business account to avoid *commingling* or combining of client and customer funds with the broker's business or personal funds. Commingling is illegal even if you don't actually spend the money on yourself and can account for every penny. *Conversion,* or the act of using client or customer funds for the agent's personal or business expenses, also is illegal.

## Better be careful: Care

Care is a broad and general word that best can be described as agents using their best efforts and skills on behalf of their clients' respective interests. Activities such as helping a seller client determine a fair asking price for a property and then making every reasonable effort to market the property are expectations of the client under the care provision of fiduciary duties. Advising a buyer to hire a home inspector and providing the buyer with information about pricing of other properties are normal parts of the care provision when the buyer is the client.

## Shhhhh! It's a secret: Confidentiality

The agent is expected to keep all information that can harm the client's interest in the strictest confidence in addition to any personal information the client wants to be kept confidential, even if, in the agent's opinion, the information won't harm the client were it known. A seller client's desperate need to sell a property because of a financial situation needs to be kept confidential. A buyer client's equally desperate need to find a house before the school year starts needs to be kept confidential, and so does the buyer client's ability to pay more for a property than he or she is offering. Any client information that can be used to benefit the interest of the customer over the client must be kept confidential.

In some places, the duty of confidentiality is considered to be part of the fiduciary duty of *loyalty*. (See "A friend to the end: Loyalty," later in this chapter, for more information.)

## You'd better tell: Disclosure

The fiduciary duty of disclosure requires you, as an agent, to reveal any facts you're aware of that benefit your client. Disclosure applies to information that may benefit the client even if the client hasn't asked about it. As the agent, perhaps you know that the town is undergoing a tax reassessment that drastically may change the taxes on all the houses in town and your buyer client wants to buy a home for the first time and doesn't have a clue what a reassessment is. (You, of course, can at least answer state exam questions about reassessment because you read Chapter 16 in this book, right?) As a buyer's agent, you're required to tell your client about the proposed reassessment, even though they didn't know enough to ask about it.

Disclosure also applies to information that can hurt your customer's interest and that your customer has asked you to keep confidential. Perhaps your buyer customer reveals to you some recent financial difficulty that may make getting a mortgage difficult. Regardless of whether your buyer customer asks you to keep the information secret, you need to tell your seller client about the possibility that the buyer may have difficulty getting a mortgage to buy the house. (See "Meeting Obligations: The Relationship Between an Agent and a Customer," later in this chapter, for more on an agent's responsibilities to a customer.)

Disclosure is interpreted broadly. For example, the agent's duty to promptly give all offers to the seller client is considered part of disclosure. An agent who decides to buy his principal's property is something that must be disclosed. An agent buying a house that he has listed for sale is called *self-dealing*. Other people involved in the transaction, like a family member of the listing agent who is interested in buying the property, is information that has to be disclosed. If the information can help your client in any way or might harm him if he doesn't know it, it must be disclosed.

Keep in mind that the disclosure that is part of an agent's fiduciary responsibility isn't the same as a seller's obligation to disclose latent and material defects. In many states, a seller (whether or not she uses a real estate agent's services) must tell the buyer any bad news about the property that isn't readily visible by a normal inspection (rather than a special professionally done home inspection) and/or would have a material impact on the buyer's decision to buy the property. You should also remember that this type of disclosure isn't governed by the fiduciary duty of confidentially (see the previous section) or obedience (later in this chapter). See "Discovering defects," later in this chapter, for more.

One reason why states adopt agency disclosure rules, where agents must tell all those involved exactly who they represent and what that means, is the fiduciary requirement of disclosure to the principal. Too often, buyer customers begin to get so comfortable with the real estate agent that they reveal information that can hurt them in a negotiation and which the agent must reveal to his seller client. The customer either forgets that the agent represents the seller or never fully understands exactly what that means in terms of fiduciary duties. (For more, see "Letting everyone know: Agency disclosure requirements" earlier in this chapter.)

## A friend to the end: Loyalty

*Loyalty* means always putting your client's interests above everyone else's, including your own. You may want to read that last phrase again — including your own. You must never profit by doing something against your client's interest.

Say, for example, that you represent a buyer who wants to offer $200,000 for a house. You know the seller will take $180,000, and you're being paid a percentage of the total commission paid to the seller's broker based on the final sale price of the house. That means the higher the price of the house, the more money you make as the agent, right? I'm going to be blunt: Even though disclosing the seller's acceptable price is against your interest and you'll make less money, you nevertheless have to advise your buyer client to make the lower offer. If you don't, you're violating the fiduciary duty of loyalty and profiting at the expense of your client.

## Yes ma'am: Obedience

Obedience, as a fiduciary duty, requires you as an agent to follow the instructions of your principal. Obedience is sometimes referred to as *faithful performance*. The only limitation on adhering to the duty of obedience is if the client's instructions are illegal or unethical. If your seller client gives you instructions that violate some provision of fair housing laws regarding marketing the property, your fiduciary duty of obedience doesn't require you to break the law and obey the client's order. I cover fair housing laws in Chapter 5.

The obedience requirement also doesn't extend to keeping things confidential regarding problems with the property itself. If your seller client instructs you not to tell potential buyers about a leaky roof, you wouldn't obey the client, because buyers have a right to have that kind of information.

# Meeting Obligations: The Relationship Between an Agent and a Customer

Clients or principals clearly benefit from representation by an agent. Customers, who sometimes are thought of as the third party to a transaction, have rights, too. Remember that the customer can be either the buyer or the seller, depending on who the agent is representing as a principal. The agent is obligated to see that the customer gets whatever the customer is entitled to. Although not quite the same thing as a client-agent customer relationship, a seller working alone may also have obligations to the buyer. The agent's obligation to the customer is outlined in most places as providing

- ✔ **Honest and fair dealing.** Agents must be honest and fair with their customers, including properly accounting for the funds left in their possession (see "Who has the money? Accounting," earlier in this chapter).

- ✔ **Reasonable care.** Agents use their skills and expertise to help their customers, provided that doing so doesn't compromise their clients' interests.

- ✔ **Disclosure of material facts.** Check out the sections that follow for more about the specifics of disclosure of information to the customer.

Beyond the agent being trustworthy in handling the customer's funds, the customer mostly is entitled to information. I talk about several kinds of information that the agent is obligated to provide regardless of whether the customer is the buyer or the seller. The types of information principals and agents are obligated to reveal vary from one state to the next and frequently are interpreted by the courts. I only briefly mention the various things that you may have to reveal, so be sure to find out what your state expects an agent and a client to reveal to the customer. Just to be clear in case you didn't catch this, the seller acting alone, without representation, may have disclosure obligations to the buyer as governed by your state even though no real estate agent is involved. Expect there to be a question or two on the state test about this. Remember that disclosure of these facts applies to the customer, whether it's the buyer or the seller. In most cases real estate agents deal with seller clients and buyer customers, so most of my examples approach the issue from that perspective.

## *Discovering defects*

*Latent defects* are problems with the property that the buyer customers or buyer agents wouldn't find out about through a normal inspection. Some states interpret latent defects to mean structural items and safety items. Structural items are things like problems with the foundation. On the other hand, the things that need to be revealed usually are called *material defects.* The word material, in this case, means important. A latent defect, such as a crack in the plaster in a closet, wouldn't necessarily be a material defect because it's not very important and probably wouldn't affect the decision of the average buyer to buy the house.

Disclosure of environmental risks, particularly the ones that pose health hazards, may also be information that you have to disclose. A leaking underground oil tank or the presence of a nearby nuclear power plant has to be disclosed to the buyer customer.

The seller may also have an obligation to reveal material or latent defects. In some states real estate agent liability has been reduced by the adoption of specific forms that must be used as seller disclosure statements in which the seller is responsible for telling potential buyers about the condition of the property. Check this out in your state. These forms may more or less be mandatory or may carry financial obligations with them, as in money paid to the buyer if they're not completed by the seller. The agent often advises the seller of these obligations or tells them to check with their attorney. Get the details on what disclosure forms your state may have.

## Looking at stigmatized properties

*Stigmatized properties* are properties where events that make the property less desirable to some people have taken place. The event doesn't have to be documented as fact (actually happened) for the property to become stigmatized, but an agent may still have an obligation to tell a customer about it. A known murder or suicide can stigmatize a property, because some people don't want to live in a house where something like that occurred. Reports of a house being haunted by ghosts can also stigmatize a property, even though no hard evidence proves the haunting. Stigmatized property is an extremely state-specific item of disclosure because of varying interpretations by different states and different court decisions regarding the requirement for disclosure. Be sure to check this out because you as an agent may have disclosure obligations and therefore may be tested on this on the exam.

## Respecting Megan's Law

The interpretation of Megan's Law, a federally enacted law that requires registration of sex offenders with the police and possible notification of neighbors regarding the location of a sexual offender, varies by state. Interpretations regarding the responsibility of real estate agents with respect to providing this information to prospective buyers also differ. Some states may require disclosure of the sex offender's whereabouts to prospective buyers. Some may require disclosure only in response to a direct question or providing a response that includes information about the sexual offender registry. Check out your local state's requirements to be sure. And remember you may have different obligations depending on whether you've got a buyer or seller client or customer.

## Finding out about fraud and negligent misrepresentation

"This is the prettiest house on the street." When you, the seller's agent, say that to a prospective buyer, they realize you're giving them your opinion. They can also quite easily check it out for themselves. What you've just done is puff the property. *Puffing* is exaggerating the virtues or benefits of a property. It isn't illegal, and it's done all the time.

On the other hand, if you say property values are going to go up 10 percent a year for the next few years, you seem to be stating a fact, but the buyer has no way to check it out, because no one can predict the future. As the agent, you're perceived to be the expert and customers have every reason to believe you. However, if you're wrong, you could be in trouble. Worse yet is an outright false statement that you know is wrong: "No, sir, there are no plans to extend the six lane road past your house." In court, which is where you may end up, your actions in either of these examples can be interpreted as *fraud* or an intentional misrepresentation done in order to sell the property.

Negligent misrepresentation is a little trickier than puffing and fraud. If you don't know something, you can't be expected to disclose it. Sounds right but it isn't. *Negligent misrepresentation* is when you don't disclose something, because you don't know it, *but you should have known it.* As a real estate agent, the public expects a certain expertise, knowledge, and level of care to be evident in your work regardless of whether you're dealing with a customer or client. The location of the new highway that will bring truck traffic down the residential street of the house you're trying to sell has been all over the local papers. Because you don't read the local paper, you neglect to mention this information to your buyer from out of town. By not telling your customer, however, you may have committed an act of negligent misrepresentation because the buyer expects you to know about such things.

# Making Money (No, Not at the Copy Machine)

A discussion about how real estate agents are paid usually follows a discussion about agency relationships, because agents get paid if and when they fulfill their agency duties and complete the work of the agreement they've signed; helping someone sell or buy a propertyv. Like any job, agents get paid when they accomplish what they were hired to do. The problem with the real estate business is how you define the phrase "accomplish what they were hired to do." And, because several people are involved in a typical real estate transaction, including a buyer and seller and possibly two brokers, who pays what to whom, why, and when isn't as straightforward as when you get your paycheck every week at the office. In this section I give you information about some of the issues that exam writers like to deal with regarding how agents earn their pay and how that relates to agency law. (For more information about agents' payment, see "Looking at listing agreements" and "Examining buyer agency agreements" earlier in this chapter.)

I also give you some generally applicable information about fee arrangement in this section. But remember all of it is subject to your specific state's laws and regulations and to interpretations that your state courts may have made.

## Pay up! Deciding who needs to pay an agent

In a normal business arrangement, the person who hires you pays you. But who said real estate is normal? In this section, I take a look at some possible fee arrangements.

In many, if not most, real estate transactions you're hired by sellers to be their agent. You owe them your fiduciary responsibilities and they pay you. So far, so good.

But what about when you're hired by the buyer as a buyer's agent? You owe your fiduciary responsibilities to the buyer. Yet, in many buyer agency arrangements, you'll still be paid by the seller. Feel free to read that sentence again; it's correct. You owe your loyalty and all your other fiduciary duties to the buyer but will be paid by the seller, because of a simple rule that you need to remember.

Generally speaking fiduciary responsibility does not follow the source of the fee. This means that you can represent Person *A* and be paid by Person *B* even if your job is to represent Person *A* against Person *B*.

Looking at an example of a seller paying a buyer's agent may help you understand. Broker *A* is hired by Seller *A* as a seller's agent. Broker *A* will be paid a fee, usually in the form of a percentage commission based on the sale price of the house. To sell the house quickly and at the best price, Broker *A* puts the word out among other brokers in town that he has a house for sale, which is what usually is called a listing. Broker *A* may do this informally by phoning a few other brokers in the area or through a multiple listing service, which is a more formal arrangement for sharing listings (see "Looking at listing agreements," earlier in this chapter), and he offers to split the commission with any broker who brings someone to him who buys the house. Most likely he eventually executes a written agreement for sharing the commission with the other broker. Broker *B* is acting as a buyer's agent for Buyer *B* and brings Buyer *B* to Seller *A*'s house. Buyer *B* likes the house and buys it. Broker *B* will be paid a share of the commission that Broker *A* offered. Remember, Broker *A* gets paid by the seller, and throughout the transaction, Broker *B* represented the buyer.

The seller doesn't always pay the buyer's agent's fee. The buyer can and sometimes does pay his broker's fee himself, an arrangement that is particularly true in the case of a buyer signing an *exclusive buyer agency agreement* in which the buyer must pay a fee no matter how he finds a property. So even if the buyer ends up buying a house directly from an owner with no broker involved, he still must pay his agent a fee.

Finally, where a buyer's agent and a seller's agent are involved in a transaction, it's always possible for the buyer and the seller each to pay their own agents. Just remember, your fiduciary responsibilities go to your principal, which is the person who hires you, even if you receive your fee from someone else.

## Ready to go: Knowing when an agent should be paid

A question in the real world, and on state exams, is this: When, during the process. do real estate agents earn their fees? The answer is when the broker produces a *ready, willing, and able buyer*. A ready, willing, and able buyer is someone who agrees with the seller to all the terms of the deal and is prepared to do whatever it takes to buy the property. For example, if the buyer doesn't have the full price in cash, he gets a mortgage. The broker in this case is considered the *procuring cause,* a fancy term for the person who brought the deal together.

An interesting factor that you notice about this answer is that it talks about the transaction from the seller agent's point of view, because most agents still represent sellers. Although buyer's agency is growing, buyer agents' fees still are paid primarily by the seller (as you found out in the previous section). So don't grow confused or worried about a question that deals with when the agent's fee is earned. The ready, willing, and able buyer answer should be fine.

Another factor to notice about the definition of when a fee is earned is that it says nothing about actually transferring ownership of the real estate from one person to another. A fee is earned when the minds of the seller and buyer meet in an agreement — a *meeting of the minds* — which simply is another way of saying that the buyer and the seller have agreed to the terms and are prepared to complete the transaction. A fee may well be owed to the broker, even if property ownership doesn't change hands.

If a seller agent produces a ready, willing, and able buyer who's ready to buy the property at the seller's price and has the money to do so, and for some reason, the seller changes his mind and refuses to sell the property, the broker still is entitled to a fee. Generally, when-ever the broker is the procuring cause of the transaction, and the seller client does some-thing to cause the sale not to happen, the broker is entitled to compensation.

# Parting Is Such Sweet Sorrow: Ending an Agency Relationship

A real estate agency relationship can end in a number of different ways. Depending on the reason for the termination, the particular circumstances, and what is negotiated, the broker may or may not be entitled to compensation. You also need to remember that the fiduciary duty of confidentiality survives the ending of an agency relationship. A broker may not reveal information received from a client even after that client stops being the broker's client. Here are some of the ways an agency relationship can be ended:

✔ **Completion of the terms of an agreement:** This method of ending a relationship sometimes gets forgotten. The relationship ends when you do what you agreed to do. Obviously, the agent receives payment in this situation.

✔ **Expiration of the time period of the agency agreement:** Agency relationships tend to be written for limited time periods, with six months being typical. If the agreement expires and no sale has been accomplished, the agency relationship ends with no payment to the broker.

✔ **Destruction of the property:** If the property is destroyed by a natural or other disaster, such as a fire, a flood, a tornado, and so on, the property that was for sale no longer exists in its original form, so the agreement ends. No commission is paid. And yes, the owner can relist the now-destroyed house and semi-vacant land for sale.

✔ **Taking of the property through an eminent domain proceeding (condemnation):** See Chapter 8 for more about eminent domain. Because the property doesn't belong to the seller anymore through no fault of his own, no commission is owed.

✔ **Bankruptcy:** A bankruptcy filing by either of the parties (principal or agent) can end an agency relationship. It is unlikely that a commission is owed.

✔ **Agreement by both parties:** Both parties agree to end the agency relationship before the terms of the agreement are met. In other words, no transfer of property takes place. An ending like this might result in some payment to the seller's broker for things like advertising costs.

✔ **Death or declaration of incompetence:** When either party dies or is declared incompetent, the agency relationship is ended and no commission is due, but a broker may seek to collect some costs like advertising from the estate.

✔ **Renunciation or revocation:** *Renunciation* and *revocation* indicate the desire of one party but not the other to end the agency relationship. Permission to end the relationship this way varies from state to state, so be sure to check it out. The technical terms for this method of ending a relationship are *renunciation by the agent* and *revocation by the principal.* Depending on the particular circumstances, one of the parties may be able to collect money from the other.

The information in this section on ending agency relationships is pretty general. But you definitely need to check out whether any of these methods are permitted in your own state or if other ways of ending an agency relationship are acceptable.

# Review Questions and Answers

Who you represent and your obligations are the essence of your work as an agent. And state test writers want to make sure you understand all of this. Expect a fair number of questions on this material on both the broker's and salesperson's exams. The salesperson's exam likely will ask more definition-type questions, and the broker's exam will expect more understanding and the ability to apply the law to short case studies. One other thing: You may want to re-read this chapter after you've completed the rest of the book. Agency is often taught near the beginning of a prelicense course and as you can see it appears early in this book. You need to know something about agency as you go through the rest of the material; however, it's been my experience as an instructor that students often have more questions about agency toward the end of the course than they did at the beginning because they have more context in which to understand agency obligations. And I often find the best of students can be confused about agency law even as they complete their prelicensing course. So be patient with yourselves, and ask lots of questions in class. Instructors don't know what you don't understand unless you ask.

1. A real estate broker generally acts as what type of agent?

    (A) Universal agent

    (B) General agent

    (C) Special agent

    (D) Ratified agent

*Correct answer:* (C). Remember the fact that as a real estate agent, you usually handle one special transaction rather than all (universal) or some (general) transactions for a client.

2. To whom does an agent always owe her fiduciary responsibility?

    (A) Buyer

    (B) Seller

    (C) Customer

    (D) Principal

*Correct answer:* (D). The principal is always the one with whom you have an agency relationship and therefore is the person to whom you owe your fiduciary responsibility. Either the buyer or seller, in given situations, can be the principal. So neither buyer nor seller can be answered as "always" being the object of fiduciary responsibility. In terms of customer and client, it's the client who's the principal, not the customer.

3. A real estate broker takes a listing to sell someone's house. What is the relationship between the broker and the seller?

    (A) Agent-principal

    (B) Client-customer

    (C) Agent-customer

    (D) Principal-principal

*Correct answer:* (A). Sorry folks, no fancy explanation here. The listing agreement is the usual way that an agency relationship is established between a broker and a seller. An agency relationship is between an agent and a principal. Remember that the principal is also called the client.

4. A broker will earn a commission on the sale of a property whether or not she was the procuring cause of the transaction under what type of listing agreement?

   (A) Open listing

   (B) Multiple listing

   (C) Exclusive agency listing

   (D) Exclusive right to sell listing

   *Correct answer:* (D). Multiple listing is not really a type of listing. In an open listing and the exclusive agency listing, the broker gets paid only if she finds a buyer and makes the sale happen.

5. An agent representing both a client and a customer would be practicing

   (A) single agency.

   (B) dual agency.

   (C) exclusive agency.

   (D) open agency.

   *Correct answer:* (B). Dual agency is the best answer. It can't be single agency, because even though the situation may have started out that way, something that shifted the customer to a client status occurred. Exclusive agency is too vague, although exclusive agency listings exist. It isn't open agency, because although open listings are a possibility, no such thing as an open agency exists.

6. What kind of relationship exists between an agent and a principal?

   (A) Exclusive

   (B) Special

   (C) Compensatory

   (D) Fiduciary

   *Correct answer:* (D). You'll have to remember this one. An exclusive relationship may or may not exist, depending on the type of listing agreement that is signed. Most agents in a single transaction are special agents, but you can also be a general or universal agent. No relationship called compensatory exists, although the word can confuse you, because you expect to be paid for being an agent. The question needs to be read in the broadest way possible. Any and all agents and principals have a fiduciary relationship.

7. What part of fiduciary duties requires the agent to use her skills and abilities in her client's best interest?

   (A) Obedience

   (B) Care

   (C) Disclosure

   (D) Confidentiality

   *Correct answer:* (B). All of the other choices are part of fiduciary duties. Obedience is following your client's orders. Disclosure is telling your client everything he needs to know for his benefit. Confidentiality is keeping your client's information secret. Reread "Keeping the Faith: The Relationship Between an Agent and a Principal" until you can distinguish among and between examples of each duty.

8. Accounting requires

(A) a monthly expense statement provided to the client.

(B) the conversion of funds to pay expenses.

(C) commingling of funds.

(D) no commingling of funds.

*Correct answer:* (D). You may not see a lot of questions like this one, but I wanted to give you one anyway. It isn't a very good question in my opinion because the statement "Accounting requires" is too vague. Don't forget that you're taking a state real estate exam. Sometimes an assumption is made in the wording of a question such that you know that you're dealing with a question in a real estate context. So an accountant may think a client needs to get a monthly statement of expense, but a real estate agent wouldn't think that unless he were a property manager and had specifically agreed to provide the statement to his client. Those circumstances are, however, too narrow for the monthly statement answer to be correct. Conversion is when a client's money is used for broker's expenses, and commingling is when the broker mixes a client's money and his own business or personal money in the same account. Both are illegal.

9. Your seller client needs to sell his property quickly to take a job in another city. What do you do with this information?

(A) You tell buyers this so the house sells quickly.

(B) You keep this information confidential.

(C) You tell the buyers only if they ask.

(D) You reveal this information only to a buyer's agent.

*Correct answer:* (B). Confidential it is. The confidentiality of this type of information is absolute. If the seller authorizes you to reveal the information to generate interest in the property, then you can reveal it only after explaining to the seller that he may end up with a lower price because of it. This information is personal to the seller's circumstances. Remember that if the information is about the property (like a leaky roof), it may have to be revealed to the buyer.

10. Which of the following types of information does not have to be disclosed to the seller client?

(A) The buyer's financial condition

(B) An offer that the agent feels is unacceptably low

(C) The fact that the buyer owns a part interest in a sailboat with the agent

(D) The occupation of the buyer

*Correct answer:* (D). You may have found accepting this answer tough. The buyer's financial ability to go through with the deal is important information. All offers need to be transmitted to the seller promptly. A partnership in a sailboat may not be a close relationship, but it nevertheless is a relationship that needs to be disclosed to the seller. The buyer's job is an important piece of information only if it affects his financial ability to complete the transaction.

# Chapter 5

# Knowing the Fair Housing Laws for Selling Real Estate

As a real estate agent, whether broker or salesperson, you're expected to know and abide by fair housing regulations. Real estate agents are key players in promoting fair housing and preventing discrimination in housing. State exam writers expect you to know about fair housing laws at the federal level, because those laws apply to all parts of the country. Many states, counties, and cities have enacted additional fair housing laws that supplement federal law. State examiners expect you to know about these local laws. As you study for the state licensing exam, you need to be sure to find out about fair housing laws that apply only to your state or local municipality.

In this chapter, I talk about laws the federal government has adopted to prevent discrimination in the sale and rental of land, houses, and apartments. These federal fair housing laws are a series of separate laws that were enacted at different times. I also talk about groups that are protected by these laws (called protected classes) and the specific discriminatory actions that are forbidden. And to top it all off, I also give you information about how the law is enforced as well as a few exceptions to the law.

## Practicing Fair Housing: The Basics

The basic concept and goal of fair housing laws at the federal, state, and local levels is to prevent discrimination in housing and permit people to have an equal opportunity to live where they want to live. A student of mine once said that the only form of discrimination that's legal is monetary. An ad campaign promoting fair housing a while ago stated something to the effect that the only color you can discriminate against is green, as in the color of money.

In this section, I discuss specific federal laws that deal with housing discrimination, including some dates that you definitely want to remember. I also explain an interesting case that shows that a law is a law no matter how old it is. In addition, I talk about state and local laws, and the all-important fair housing poster.

As a broker who hires people, you also need to be aware of and abide by nondiscrimination laws with respect to hiring practices. Generally speaking, equal employment laws aren't taught in real estate courses and are rarely tested. However, if you're a candidate for the broker's license, you need to find out whether your state's exam requires you to know anything about equal opportunity employment laws where hiring practices are concerned.

# Understanding federal fair housing laws

Real estate agents primarily deal with and apply federal fair housing laws throughout the United States. In this section, I give you information on several federal laws, and I can pretty much guarantee that you'll see a few questions about these laws on the exam.

I discuss another set of laws related to fair housing in Chapter 15. That chapter is about financing real estate, and the laws I discuss there deal with providing equal opportunity and disclosure in the all-important mortgage loan process.

### The 1866 Civil Rights Act

In 1866, right after the end of the Civil War, the United States Congress passed the Civil Rights Act of 1866. This law essentially prohibits discrimination in the purchase, sale, lease or conveyance of real property (real estate and personal property) on the basis of race or color. The language of the act is clear insofar as it basically says that without any exception whatsoever, all citizens shall have the same rights regarding property regardless of race. The other unique thing about this act is that enforcement is accomplished by taking the case directly to federal court.

Although the act itself is important, an almost equally important 1968 court case that involved the act resulted in a landmark decision in fair housing law that you should remember. The case, *Jones versus Alfred H. Mayer Company*, essentially affirmed the fact that the 1866 act prohibited any discrimination on the basis of race by private individuals and the government *with no exceptions*. This case was filed shortly after the enactment of the Fair Housing Act of 1968 (see the next section).

The lack of any exceptions to the 1866 Act is important, because more recent fair housing laws actually include exceptions. Because it was enacted first and still remains on the books, the 1866 act is deemed valid even today, having been affirmed in the *Jones versus Mayer* case as superseding later laws with respect to exceptions regarding discrimination on the basis of race. Because of that, no exceptions exist with respect to racial discrimination in housing. For more, see "Bending the Rules: Understanding Exceptions to the Law," later in this chapter.

### The 1968 Fair Housing Act

The Fair Housing Act of 1968 is more technically known as Title VIII (read "Title Eight") of the Civil Rights Act of 1968. This act, the first in the 20th century, prohibited certain actions that were viewed as discriminatory with respect to housing and specifically defined groups, called protected classes, to which it applied. Unlike the 1866 Civil Rights Act (see the previous section), it included specific exceptions.

Together with the 1866 Civil Rights Act, the Housing and Community Development Act of 1974, and the Fair Housing Amendments Act of 1988, which added even more protected classes to the list, the 1968 act forms the basis of fair housing standards as they apply to real estate agents throughout the United States. The 1968 act is enforced by the Department of Housing and Urban Development (HUD).

These laws are best understood when they're broken down into what you can't do (prohibited acts), who you can't do it to (protected classes), and exceptions to the law. Presenting them this way enables me to cover this material within the context of what I discuss in the rest of this chapter. Check out "Don't Do It: Avoiding Discriminatory Actions," "Feeling Safe: Identifying Who's Protected," and "Bending the Rules: Understanding Exceptions to the Law" for more details.

The current protected classes under the federal law can be remembered with the acronym FRESH CORN, which stands for:

**F**amilial

**R**ace

**E**qual

**S**ex

**H**andicap

**C**olor

**O**pportunity

**R**ace

**N**ational origin

## Researching state and local laws

State and local governments like counties and cities have gradually adopted their own fair housing laws. These local laws need to be viewed and obeyed in addition to and not instead of federal law. The general rule regarding situations in which federal and local laws cover the same issues is that the more restrictive or stricter law applies. Local provisions usually don't add prohibited activities; federal law is pretty comprehensive with respect to prohibited discriminatory practices. Local provisions that are sometimes added include additional protected classes, or groups that require relief under the fair housing laws. For example, some cities and several states have added sexual orientation as a protected class to their fair housing laws. In addition, exceptions that the federal law permits sometimes are removed at the local level. (For more, see "Bending the Rules: Understanding Exceptions to the Law," later in this chapter.)

Megan's Law is a federally enacted law that promotes registration of convicted sex offenders after they're released from prison and take up residence in a neighborhood. Megan's Law has raised issues of the civil rights and rights to privacy of offenders in local jurisdictions. So you need to check with your state to determine your obligations as an agent to provide information to prospective buyers regarding the presence of sex offenders in the neighborhood. (For more, see Chapter 4.)

For exam purposes and, of course, for purposes of your future real estate practice, you need to research and find out as much as you can about any local, state, or municipal laws that supplement federal fair housing laws. Pay careful attention to any additional prohibited acts, additional protected classes, and exceptions to the exceptions.

### Displaying the fair housing poster

The Department of Housing and Urban Development (HUD), which is responsible for the Federal Fair Housing Act, has created a fair housing poster that must be prominently displayed in all real estate offices. Failure to display the sign can be considered noncompliance with fair housing law and will be used as evidence of discrimination whenever a complaint is brought against the real estate office. HUD also requires that its fair housing logo or other such appropriate wording be used in all real estate advertising.

## Don't Do It: Avoiding Discriminatory Actions

The basic provisions of the Federal Fair Housing Act of 1968 define certain actions that are considered discriminatory and prohibit them. I don't personally know the legislative background that went into writing this law, but it appears that Congress was trying to be specific enough to deal with people who may try to split hairs in attempts to circumvent a law that might simply have stated: "Do not discriminate." Specific activities, therefore, are listed in the act. I discuss and provide examples of each activity that's included. Remember these actions are considered discriminatory with respect to housing and are not permitted. For exam purposes, make sure you understand and remember prohibited activities and can identify them if they're presented in questions featuring short case studies. For more about groups that are protected, see "Feeling Safe: Identifying Who's Protected," later in this chapter.

### No way: Refusing to sell or rent

This prohibited action is easy to pinpoint. Declarations like, "I won't rent you an apartment or sell you my house because you are (fill in the blank with a protected class: any race, color, religion, sex, ethnic background, familial status, or handicap)." Of course, a specific reason doesn't have to be mentioned for this kind of refusal to be considered discrimination.

### On one condition . . . or a few: Changing terms for rental, sale, or services

A landlord or owner is prohibited from changing the terms or conditions of a rental or sale of a property for different tenants or buyers as a way to discriminate. Here's an example I use in my classes: You own an apartment building and have extensively researched damages commonly done by various types of individuals and developed a detailed schedule of security payments based on race, family status (with children, or not), and marital status. Is this activity legal or not? Emphatically, not! Even though you supposedly have objective data and probably claim that you're not using this activity to discriminate but rather only to protect yourself, it nevertheless is viewed as discrimination.

### You need not apply: Discriminatory advertising

Discriminatory advertising is prohibited. Although discriminatory advertising is easy to understand, it may be a little confusing to apply. The obvious and outright discriminatory advertisement is, for example, "Apartment for rent, Latinos not welcome." You'd probably never be able to place such an ad in any reputable newspaper anyway, and even if you could, you'd be breaking the law. Suppose, however, that you place an ad in a suburban newspaper for a new housing subdivision that includes a picture of several White families sitting around the backyard barbecue. Such an ad also is considered discriminatory, because the ad can be viewed as welcoming only White people to the development. The reverse also would likely be considered discriminatory. For example, an ad showing only Latinos in the backyard might be viewed as an attempt to steer that ethnic group to that neighborhood. You can read about steering later in this chapter.

HUD issued guidelines that must be followed in real estate advertising. These guidelines cover primary areas of possible discrimination:

- Advertising that uses certain words, phrases, pictures, or other visual representations that are discriminatory.

- Using certain types of media as a means of discrimination. For example, advertising in media only available to or likely to be seen by targeted groups (protected classes) or in reverse not seen by those groups such as a local newspaper that is read by a White ethnic group.

HUD provides fairly specific information about what language is and is not acceptable in real estate advertising. For exam purposes and for real-world applications, remember that the use of certain words or phrases is prohibited even when your intent is not to discriminate. The categories of the prohibited language with some examples include:

- **Code words, catchwords, or catchphrases:** These prohibited words may be a little more subtle or regional in nature. Obvious phrases like "integrated neighborhood" cannot be used. Words like "exclusive," although more subtle, may convey a racially exclusive or ethnically exclusive message and therefore are to be avoided.

- **Color:** No use of words describing color as it relates to race or ethnicity is permitted. For example, "White" or "Black."

- **Familial status:** The term "familial status" generally refers to the presence or absence of children in the family. Although marital status is not a protected federal class, HUD guidelines prohibit advertising that states or implies "married couple only" or other similar language.

- **Handicap:** "Property not suitable for a handicapped person" or any language that suggests an exclusion like that is forbidden. Inclusive words like "Apartment is handicapped accessible" are acceptable.

- **National origin:** The use of words that describe national origin like Italian, Mexican, and so on are prohibited.

- **Race:** No use of racially descriptive words, such as Asian or Caucasian, for example, is permitted.

- **Religion:** Words describing religions, like Catholic, Christian, non-Christian, and so on, is prohibited.

- **Sex or gender:** This category tends to be a problem more with rental housing than housing that's for sale. Any gender-preference words are prohibited. An exception is made for people who want to share an apartment or house with a roommate of the same sex. So you can advertise for a female roommate to share an apartment, but you can't advertise for only a male tenant for a rental apartment in an apartment house you own.

In addition any photos, drawings, or symbols that may imply preference with respect to any of the above categories are prohibited — for example, showing a picture of a church next to the house you're advertising for sale. Describing the location by using potentially biased references, such as "near the Catholic church," is prohibited. A reference to a known discriminatory facility must also be avoided. So you won't advertise a house for sale "near the XYZ Country Club" when the country club is known to discriminate in its membership policies.

Prohibited language, photos, symbols and so on are considered discriminatory at their face value, or as they appear, meaning that good intentions don't count. Furthermore, discriminatory language can't be used to describe a tenant or buyer preference, the neighborhood, or the dwelling itself. So "Good Christian building" is just as bad and just as prohibited as "Apartment for rent: Only Christians need apply."

Avoid using welcoming and inclusive terms, such as advertising that states specific groups are welcome. The use of the HUD fair housing logo and words to the effect that fair housing guidelines apply are the proper ways to say that all groups are welcome to buy or rent.

One other factor that HUD addresses in its guidelines is the use of terms that have lost their original religious or exclusionary meaning. For example, an ad placed during December that reads "Give yourself a Christmas present with a new house" would not be prohibited.

## All lies: Telling someone that property isn't available (when it really is)

If a house has been sold or an apartment already rented, so be it. But tell someone that an apartment is already rented when it isn't or that a house isn't available for sale when it is, and that's considered discrimination and therefore is prohibited. This form of discrimination may seem obvious and almost not worthy of its own rule. And although the background of this prohibition has faded into obscurity, I believe it had something to do with property owners saying that a dwelling unit was unavailable and then defending their action by indicating what they meant was that the unit was unavailable to a particular person.

## Scaring people into selling: Blockbusting

*Blockbusting* generally is defined as encouraging people to sell their homes because of the entry or potential entry into the community or neighborhood of a particular group of people. The group usually tends to be different in some aspect, such as race, color, or country of origin. The fear that blockbusting generates is the possible loss of property value, and the idea behind it is to induce panic selling and generate listings of houses to sell or bargains for developers. The prohibition of blockbusting is particularly aimed at members of the real estate industry, because agents benefit from panic selling by getting new listings, but investors who use blockbusting techniques for profit may also be guilty of discrimination.

## Telling people where to live: Steering

*Steering* is guiding, encouraging, or inducing people in some way to move to or stay away from a certain area or neighborhood, and it's illegal. Overt steering is easy to understand and avoid. Subtle forms of steering in the name of being helpful, like saying, "This is a good neighborhood," or "You wouldn't be happy here," also should be avoided. Participating in what I call self-steering is equally prohibited. What I mean, for example, is that a couple that asks to be shown houses "only in White neighborhoods" can't be accommodated. You must tell them that you can show them houses that meet their needs and financial situation in various neighborhoods, and then do so. And by the way, although avoiding discrimination is easy when someone says "White neighborhood" or something like that, it's sometimes a little more difficult to acknowledge the problem when someone asks for a neighborhood where a particular language is heavily spoken, because the family just came to this country. Specifically accommodating a request like this is still considered steering, and it's illegal. Again, you can show the family a variety of houses that meet their financial and space needs and then let them decide. In some states offering opinions about the quality of the local schools is also considered steering and should be avoided. Though probably not on the exam, real estate agents should provide the same information about a house to every prospective buyer. Providing different information to different buyers, especially when protected classes are involved, could be viewed as discrimination. You can read about protected classes in the section "Feeling Safe: Who's Protected" a little later on.

## No money for you: Changing loan conditions

Once upon a time it was a common practice to not lend money to unmarried women regardless of their income or employment status. It was also common to not count a married woman's income in the mortgage loan calculation because she'd likely quit work to have children. Nowadays, any such actions, including discrimination on the basis of the other protected classes such as race or ethnic background, are forbidden. You can read about laws prohibiting discrimination in mortgage lending in Chapter 15.

## Put away that crayon: Redlining

*Redlining* is discrimination in the lending of mortgage money based on location. This happens when a lending institution determines that for various reasons it will no longer make loans in a particular area. It figuratively or literally draws a red line around a particular neighborhood on a map and refuses to make loans on properties in that neighborhood regardless of the personal income qualifications of the borrower.

In 1977, as a result of past redlining activities, the federal government passed the Community Reinvestment Act, which requires certain financial institutions such as banks to develop and implement programs for reinvesting in their neighborhoods through mortgage, home improvement, and other types of loans. These financial institutions come under periodic review to determine whether they're in compliance with the act.

## You can't join: Denying membership in real estate organizations

One of the more blatant forms of exclusionary discrimination is denial of membership in a multiple listing association to certain racial or ethnic groups. Because these associations share property listings of houses that are for sale, such a denial has a direct effect on keeping communities segregated. (For more on multiple listings, see Chapter 4.)

A more subtle form of this type of illegal activity is a club, group, or association that meets periodically to share property listings where a multiple listing system doesn't exist. Denial of membership in such a group is a prohibited action. The prohibition extends to any brokers' organization and includes professional real estate organizations.

# Feeling Safe: Identifying Who's Protected

Federal fair housing laws protect essentially everyone. The government, however, has created *protected classes* — groups against which you can't discriminate. They're not so much groups of people as they are characteristics that can be used for the purposes of discrimination . . . and of course, should not be. In the sections that follow, I review federal, state, and local protected classes.

## Knowing the federal protected classes

Since the adoption of the 1968 Federal Fair Housing Act, the history of federal fair housing legislation has been one of extending nondiscrimination protection to more and more groups. The following is a summary of the legislative actions, when they were added, and the classes they protect. You can expect questions on the state exam about the protected classes and when they were added, and you may see questions that are like case studies.

- **1866 Civil Rights Act:** Protects against racial discrimination
- **1968 Federal Fair Housing Act:** Protects race, color, religion, and national origin.
- **1974 Housing and Community Development Act:** Protects against sex (gender) bias.
- **1988 Fair Housing Amendments Act:** Protects the handicapped and familial status (presence of children). Take note that *handicaps* include persons with AIDS as well as alcoholics (but not drug addiction) in addition to conditions like visual, hearing, and physical handicaps and mental disability. (For more about laws related to the disabled, see "Extra Coverage: Protecting the Disabled from Discrimination," later in this chapter.)

## Recognizing state and local protected classes

Finding out whether the state or local governments (counties, towns, villages, or cities) within your state have added protected classes to fair housing laws is one of the most important steps you can take in preparing for the exam. Two of the more common classes these days are marital status and sexual orientation. In addition, mental disabilities may be more specially defined and protected in your state.

In addition, local exceptions to the exceptions may have been adopted, meaning that although federal law may permit an exception, local law may not. Questions based on state or local fair housing laws are fair game in state real estate exams. And remember that if a local fair housing law and a federal fair housing law are different, the stricter applies.

# Bending the Rules: Understanding Exceptions to the Law

The 1968 Federal Fair Housing Act was written with certain exceptions, or cases in which people, in a sense, can discriminate in housing issues. In addition to remembering the exceptions themselves for test purposes, you need to remember these two important factors with respect to these exceptions:

✔ Even if an exception is legal for an individual (such as the owner of a single-family home selling her house), a real estate agent is not permitted to participate in the exception. Real estate agents are held to a higher standard in fair housing matters.

✔ Discriminatory advertising may not be used; again, even when the exception itself is legal. The owner of a single-family home can't use discriminatory advertising in selling her house, even though she could discriminate in the ultimate sale itself.

Don't forget that regardless of exemptions permitted by the 1968 Federal Fair Housing Act, the 1866 Civil Rights Act permits no exceptions with respect to race. The exceptions in the 1988 Law are as follows.

✔ **Age:** An exemption is provided to housing protections afforded to age and familial (children) classes that's intended for older people. Housing may be restricted to people 62 years of age or older or 55 years of age or older in cases where at least one occupant per unit is 55 and at least 80 percent of the units are occupied by people ages 55 or older. In these cases children may be excluded.

✔ **Owner-occupied housing:** Multifamily housing of two to four units, where one of the units is owner-occupied, is exempt from fair housing laws.

✔ **Private clubs:** An organization that restricts its membership may provide restricted housing to its members, as long as it doesn't offer housing to the general public.

✔ **Public-law occupancy standards:** Local maximum occupancy standards aren't superseded in their application by the Fair Housing Act. For example, if a local law provides a maximum occupancy of two people per bedroom and you rent out a studio apartment in a building you own, you can't be forced to rent the apartment to a couple with a child.

✔ **Religious organizations:** Housing sponsored by a religious organization may be restricted to members of that particular religious organization, provided the religion doesn't discriminate in its membership policies.

✔ **Single-family housing:** The sale or rental of a single-family house is exempted from the rules of the Fair Housing Act if the owner doesn't own more than three units at one time, and neither a broker nor discriminatory advertising is used. If such a property is sold, no more than one house can be sold during every two-year period.

## It may have happened to you . . . or your grandfather

I'd like to share a true story with which I end my fair housing classes. Many years ago, my father was a plumber. His shop and many of his customers were located in a typical ethnic neighborhood of first- and second-generation immigrants. In this case, the immigrants were German. My father, born in the United States, was of German descent.

One day a customer called on him to provide an estimate on some bathroom repairs. The bathroom was old and located in an old three-family house. My father encouraged the owner to remodel and upgrade the entire bathroom with a new tub, toilet, sink, vanity, and tile work. Somewhat conspiratorially, the customer said that he didn't want to spend the money because the neighborhood was changing. When I was young, the word "changing," in that context, usually meant some "lower class of people," as perceived by the residents, was moving into the neighborhood. My father, knowing the neighborhood quite well, didn't know what the man meant and responded with a questioning look. The building owner answered the questioning look by saying, "Italians just bought the house down the block." But that's not the punch line. The Italians who bought the house down the block were my aunt and uncle, specifically my Italian American mother's sister. And that, as a famous radio commentator used to say, is the rest of the story. I include this story in class to remind my students that discrimination can happen to anyone for any reason and in fact may have happened to one of their parents or grandparents in the past.

# Extra Coverage: Protecting the Disabled from Discrimination

The disabled are protected as a class with respect to fair housing law. Landlords must permit tenants to make reasonable changes to an apartment to accommodate their handicap. Tenants are responsible for returning the apartment to its original condition.

However, another law relating to the protection of the disabled normally is covered on the test. Congress passed the American with Disabilities Act (ADA) in 1992 to ensure not only protection from discrimination but also to provide access to public spaces. This law, which affects public and commercial buildings, requires buildings to be accessible to handicapped persons. It also requires new multifamily housing of four or more units built after March 13, 1991 to be handicapped accessible. The rules vary slightly for buildings with and without elevators. Employers, including real estate brokers, must be aware of the necessity of their places of employment being accessible to handicapped employees and the handicapped public at large. Real estate agents also need to be aware of ADA regulations with respect to commercial or other public buildings with which they may be involved.

# Staying Strong: Enforcing the Law

Complaints regarding violations of the Fair Housing Act must be made to HUD within a year of the event. HUD conducts an investigation and may attempt to remedy the situation by getting the property owner who violates the law to stop the action and take steps to prevent it from happening again. Those with complaints may also file a suit in federal court within two years of the violation.

If HUD finds a property owner guilty following an administrative hearing, it may impose fines of up to $10,000 for the first offense, up to $25,000 for the second offense if it happens within five years of the first, and up to $50,000 for a third offense, if it happens within seven years of the first event.

In addition, anyone who brings a HUD complaint can sue in federal civil court, where generally no limits are placed on monetary damages that can be awarded.

Remember that a violation of the 1866 Civil Rights Act prohibiting racial discrimination may be brought directly to federal court.

# Review Questions and Answers

Questions on the state exam normally involve knowing which laws are which, what groups are protected, and what the exceptions are. At the salesperson's level you can expect the questions to be straightforward. At the brokers level the questions may require a bit more interpretation of the law. Remember to check your state law regarding state and local fair housing rules and additional protected classes.

1. Inducing people to panic sell by telling them that a "lower-class immigrant group" is moving into the neighborhood is called

    (A) steering.

    (B) redlining.

    (C) canvassing.

    (D) blockbusting.

    *Correct answer:* (D). Blockbusting is inducing people to panic sell in order for the real estate agent or a developer to make a profit. Redlining is discrimination in the lending of mortgage money based on location. Steering is directing people to or away from certain neighborhoods as a means of discrimination. Canvassing is sending out letters or knocking on doors to see if you can offer your real estate services to people. It is a fairly normal way of doing business.

2. "Sorry, we don't make any loans on houses in that neighborhood" is an example of

    (A) blockbusting.

    (B) steering.

    (C) redlining.

    (D) an acceptable business decision.

    *Correct answer:* (C). Redlining is a practice where banks and other lending institutions refuse to make loans in certain neighborhoods regardless of the qualifications of the borrower. Blockbusting is inducing people to panic sell to make a profit (for example, by getting listings to sell property). Steering is directing people to or away from certain neighborhoods as a means of discrimination. These actions are all illegal.

3. Which of the following would be unacceptable under the federal fair housing law?

    (A) The resident owner of a three-family house refusing to rent to an Asian man.

    (B) A senior residence for people over 62.

    (C) A private club of graduates of an exclusive prep school.

    (D) Baptist Church sponsored housing available only to Baptists.

    *Correct answer:* (A). Answers (B), (C), and (D) all fall under the exceptions to the law. There are no exceptions with respect to race. For more on exceptions, see "Bending the Rules: Understanding Exceptions to the Law," earlier in this chapter.

4. Mike the seller refuses to sell his house to a Black couple.

    (A) He is breaking the law under the 1968 Federal Fair Housing Act.

    (B) He is breaking the law under the 1866 Civil Rights Act.

    (C) He is breaking no law as long as he doesn't use a real estate agent or discriminatory advertising.

    (D) He is breaking no law as long as he owns fewer than three houses and this is the only one he sells in two years.

    *Correct answer:* (B). (B) is correct because race was eliminated as an allowable exception by a court case that upheld the 1866 law. (A) is wrong because the 1968 law provides an exception to the owner of a single-family house. (C) and (D) are wrong because there is no exception with respect to race, so Mike is indeed breaking a law.

5. The fine for a third violation of the federal Fair Housing Act can be as high as

   (A) $10,000.

   (B) $25,000.

   (C) $50,000.

   (D) unlimited.

   *Correct answer:* (C). $10,000 is the maximum fine for a first offense, and $25,000 is the maximum fine for a second offense. There are no unlimited fines.

6. A deed restriction says that a property cannot be sold to a person of Native American ancestry. Which of the following is true?

   (A) The deed restriction supersedes fair housing law.

   (B) The fair housing laws do not apply to Native Americans because technically they are part of the Indian Nation.

   (C) Fair housing law takes precedence over the deed restriction.

   (D) This type of restriction was automatically removed by a treaty in 1888.

   *Correct answer:* (C). A deed restriction must be legal to be valid (see Chapter 8 for more on deed restrictions). These restrictions, many involving race and some referencing ethnicity common in some areas, are illegal and therefore invalid because of the 1866 act or the 1968 Act. I made up (B) and (D).

7. Which of the following advertisements for a house for sale would probably be acceptable?

   (A) Quiet Christian neighborhood

   (B) Fill your Easter basket with a new house

   (C) Husband's dream workshop

   (D) Two blocks from the local Episcopal Church

   *Correct answer:* (B). In HUD's determination, holidays like Easter and Christmas have lost their uniquely religious context and are therefore acceptable to use in advertisements. "Quiet Christian neighborhood" targets a particular religious group. "Husband's dream workshop" can be viewed as being sexually discriminatory because wives can also enjoy a dream workshop. "Two blocks from the local Episcopal church" is incorrect because references to landmarks referring to a specific religion are deemed unacceptable by HUD.

8. Under federal fair housing laws, which of the following is legal?

   (A) Refusing to rent an apartment to a man because he's gay

   (B) Refusing to sell a house to someone because he's Buddhist

   (C) Showing a White couple houses only in White neighborhoods because they asked you to

   (D) Charging different security deposits based on the number of children in a family

   *Correct answer:* (A). Sexual orientation is not a protected class in the federal law. It may be in your state, but that's not what this question says. Always make sure to read questions carefully, and be sure to check your state and local fair housing law to see if sexual orientation or other classes in addition to the federal ones are protected.

9. The Civil Rights Act of 1866 is enforced by

    (A) HUD.

    (B) federal courts.

    (C) state courts.

    (D) the Federal Equal Opportunity Commission.

    *Correct answer:* (B). The other answers are wrong because lawsuits under this law must be brought in federal court.

10. Which of the following is legal?

    (A) A broker offering discounts to members of a certain ethnic group as a way of encouraging them to integrate an area

    (B) Refusing to make a mortgage loan to a Black family with poor credit history

    (C) A broker advertising property exclusively in Spanish-language newspapers

    (D) A broker providing information on the demographics of a neighborhood including statistics on race and ethnic background

    *Correct answer:* (B). Money is the only legal basis for discrimination. All the other answers are wrong because they are discriminatory on some other basis that is prohibited by law.

# Part III

# It's All Mine: Owning and Transferring Real Estate

## Various Divisions of the NW Quarter Section
### 2,640 feet = 1/2 mile

| | | |
|---|---|---|
| N 1/2 of NW 1/4 of NW 1/4 **20 acres** | NW 1/4 of NE 1/4 of NW 1/4 **10 acres** | NE 1/4 of NE 1/4 of NW 1/4 **10 acres** |
| S 1/2 of NW 1/4 of NW 1/4 **20 acres** | SW 1/4 of NE 1/4 of NW 1/4 **10 acres** | SE 1/4 of NE 1/4 of NW 1/4 **10 acres** |
| W 1/2 of SW 1/4 of NW 1/4 **20 acres** | E 1/2 of SW 1/4 of NW 1/4 **20 acres** | SE 1/4 of NW 1/4 **40 acres** |

2,640 feet = 1/2 mile

1/4 section = 160 acres

**web extras** Learn about laws limiting what can built on private property in the article "What Do You Mean I Can't Build That" at www.dummies.com/extras/realestatelicenseexams.

# In this part . . .

- ✔ I give you an overview of liens — their priorities, types, distinguishing traits, creations, and removal.

- ✔ I give you information about land-use regulations, from making master plans to understanding zoning ordinances to construction regulations. Then you can check out eminent domain and what the government can and can't do.

- ✔ Deeds are an important part of the job of the realtor. Here you can find out what's required to have a valid deed and learn about the various types.

- ✔ You examine the title closing process, and I share what you need before, during, and after to make closing on a property a success for you, the buyer, and the seller.

- ✔ I explain that there are several different ways a property can be involuntarily lost, from the forces of nature to the government, even due to death. As a real estate sales person in today's market, this is important information.

# Chapter 6

# Owning It: Estates and Interests

. . . . . . . . . . . . . . . . . . . . . . . . . . . . . . . . . . . . . . . . . . . . . . . . . . . . . . . . . . . . . . . . . .

*In This Chapter*

▶ Discovering different ownership terms

▶ Finding out about all types of estates

▶ Understanding the rights that go with owning real estate

. . . . . . . . . . . . . . . . . . . . . . . . . . . . . . . . . . . . . . . . . . . . . . . . . . . . . . . . . . . . . . . . . .

$O$wning real estate is different from owning almost anything else. For one thing, you can't move it anywhere. For another, you can do so many things with it. Real estate is literally the foundation on which people live their lives. It's exclusively yours and, subject to certain legal limitations, you can pretty much do what you want with it, on it, under it, and over it. When you drive across your neighbor's property to get to your land, it's because your neighbor has given you the right to do so. Real estate is a unique commodity, and owning it has its own unique laws and practices.

This chapter discusses the unique aspects of owning real estate and introduces you to the concepts that are specific to real estate ownership and the various rights that come with owning property. I talk about the specific terms that are used to describe real estate ownership and about a concept called the bundle of rights, which is about the rights you get when you own real estate. I also discuss some additional rights that go with owning real estate, specifically air and water rights.

Although the concepts in this chapter are pretty much universal to all states, I nevertheless point out a few things that are specific to individual states. You need to find out about the concepts that apply specifically to your home state.

# What Do You Own? Understanding Ownership Terms

You buy a car; you own a car. You buy a table; you own a table. Most of what is so different about owning a piece of real estate is about terminology that has evolved over time to precisely explain what people are talking about when describing real estate ownership. Remember, although I define the terms as they're properly used for exam purposes, you also need to be aware that in the real world, some of these terms are used interchangeably.

## Looking at land

*Land* generally is thought of as the unimproved surface of the earth. It's the dirt, so to speak, with nothing built on it. Because of the complicated nature of ownership rights, when people say they own a piece of land, in reality, they also own the area under the surface down to the center of the earth and the air above the ground surface into outer space or infinity. (For details, see the "It's My Right: Different Ownership Rights" section later in the chapter.) Although practical matters make using all that space difficult at best, stop dreaming about immense skyscrapers; the fact is when you own a piece of land, the right to build that skyscraper is exactly what you own. Land ownership includes all the natural elements or features on the land like trees and rocks. Even if the rocks are gold. The related term *site* usually refers to land that has been improved in some way and is ready to be developed. In common usage, however, someone may refer to "the site of the new subdivision" but mean the unimproved land where the subdivision is supposed to go.

## Recognizing real estate

The term *real estate* means the land and all natural and artificial improvements permanently attached to it. The term real estate refers to the physical thing that is owned as opposed to the rights of owning the land and its improvements (see the next section). The word *improvement* means something that is built on and permanently attached to the land. A house is an improvement, and so are detached garages, landscaping, walks, and driveways.

## Defining real property

The term *real property* means land, natural and artificial improvements, and all the rights, benefits, and interests that go with owning a piece of land and the improvements. These rights include all surface, subsurface, and air rights that are automatically included with ownership of the land. (For the scoop, see "It's My Right: Different Ownership Rights" later in this chapter.)

## Checking out personal property

You're probably wondering why, if this book is about real estate, you need to learn about personal property. The answer: You need to know about personal property so you can tell the difference between it and real estate, and the difference almost always is covered on the test. *Personal property,* sometimes called *personalty,* is anything that is portable, movable, and not permanently attached to the real estate. *Personal property* sometimes is defined as anything of value that isn't real estate. Anything ranging from furniture to a car is considered personal property.

Personal property that becomes real estate is called a *fixture*. From a real estate perspective, the principal difference between personal property and a fixture is that personal property goes with the owner when a piece of real estate is sold, and a fixture stays with the property. Say you have lumber delivered to the house to build a deck. At the time of the delivery, the lumber is personal property that goes with you if you sell the house. However, if you build a deck with the lumber and attach it to the back of your house, the lumber now is considered a fixture that, of course, stays with the house when you sell it.

Ornamental trees and bushes are considered fixtures that remain with the real estate when it's sold. In cases where the seller wishes to take certain plants with her, like Grandma's prize rosebushes, she would have to dig them up before listing the property for sale or specify in the contract that they are to be removed. Agricultural crops, however, are considered personal property. A farmer who leases some farm land has the right to his crops even when his lease ends before the end of the growing season. Crops grown on property just before it's sold generally are considered to be the personal property of the seller. A small technicality here is that although the farmer is entitled to crops he's planted, he would not be entitled to the apples on his apple trees after he sells the property.

When a question arises about whether a piece of personal property is a fixture, these four so-called legal tests commonly are used to make the determination:

- ✔ **Adaptation of an item to the real estate:** This factor occurs when an item of personal property is customized to fit in the house. A custom bar in a finished playroom is a good example.

- ✔ **Existence of an agreement:** An agreement made in advance between two parties — a landlord and tenant, for example — can define what is considered personal property and what is considered a fixture.

- ✔ **Method of attachment:** Sometimes this legal test is called the method of annexation and deals with how an item of personal property is attached to the building. A bookcase with a single screw to hold it against the wall, for example, would likely be considered personal property. A bookcase that has molding and a base built around it to attach it to the wall would be considered a fixture, because it is more firmly and permanently attached.

- ✔ **Relationship of the parties:** The best example of this test is a commercial tenant in a rental building who attaches fixtures to the structure, perhaps jewelry cases in a jewelry store. The tenant normally not only is able to take them when he leaves but probably is required to remove them. Such fixtures are known as *trade fixtures*. If the tenant left the fixtures and the landlord wanted to claim them, they would be considered permanent fixtures at that point.

# Estates (Even Without the Castles)

Simply stated, the term *estate,* or *estate in land,* describes the extent and type of interest or rights that someone has in a piece of land. It essentially means the same thing as the bundle of rights theory (see the next section).

You need to bear in mind that neither the term "estate" nor the term "interest" necessarily means ownership. For example, the right to use a property granted by an easement is an interest in land. (I talk about easements in Chapter 8.) A lease also is an interest in land that also happens to be an estate in land, because it designates possession of the land, unlike an easement, which designates only the right to use the land. (I talk about leases in Chapter 12.)

In the sections that follow, I talk about a general concept called the bundle of rights. I also discuss different types of estates in land and how they fall into two main categories: freehold and leasehold. As you check out this material, concentrate most on terminology and on being able to remember the significant characteristics of each type of estate.

## Pick and choose: The bundle of rights

A concept that long has been associated with real estate ownership is the *bundle of rights,* which sometimes is called the bundle of rights theory. By picturing a bundle of sticks or logs, each of which represents a specific right associated with real estate ownership, you begin to get an idea of what I'm talking about. One key element of the bundle of rights theory is that you can remove one of the rights (one of the sticks) and separate it from the rest of the bundle.

One obvious right of ownership of property, for example, is the right to actually possess or occupy it. However, if I own an office building, I can give that right of possession or occupancy to a tenant through a lease. I may still own the building, but I've separated a part of my right to occupy the building from my bundle of ownership rights. Doing so severely limits my right to occupy that part of the building that I leased to a tenant, even though I still own the building.

The bundle of rights includes the rights to use and occupy, mine, farm, develop the property, the rights to will, give, and restrict others from using the property, and the right not to do any of these things with the property.

# Figuring out freehold estates

The essential characteristics of a *freehold estate* are that it must include ownership of real estate and that it lasts for an indefinite or indeterminate period of time that can be forever or for the lifetime of the person with the interest in the real estate. Fee estates and life estates are the two main types of freehold estates.

### Fee estates

Several fee estates exist. Each of the ones you need to be aware of for exam purposes is described in the list that follows. The term "fee estate" is really a general umbrella term for unlimited ownership rights subject to different limitations (if any).

- ✔ **Fee simple:** Also called *fee simple absolute* or *indefeasible fee,* this fee estate is the most complete form of ownership without limitations on rights of ownership, except for public and private restrictions on what can be done with the property. For example, zoning ordinances and deed restrictions are limitations on fee simple ownership. (See Chapter 8 for more.)

- ✔ **Fee simple qualified estate:** Also called a *fee simple defeasible estate,* this fee simple estate has some limitations on it. The three types of qualified fee estates are

  - **Fee simple condition precedent:** In this case, ownership, commonly referred to as title, won't pass from one person to another until a particular condition is met. An example is someone who donates property to the county for use as a park with the stipulation that nature trails must be built before the title passes to the county.

  - **Fee simple condition subsequent:** This form of estate is a situation in which the grantor — that is, the original owner — can reclaim property if some condition isn't met after title has passed to the next owner. A grantor who donates property to the county for a park where nature trails are to be built, for example, may reclaim the property because the county built a park headquarters building on the land rather than the nature trails that the donor had required under the original agreement. The right to reclaim the property is known as the *right of reentry.* The grantor would have to take specific action to reclaim the property.

  - **Fee simple determinable:** In this situation, title remains with the new owner as long as any conditions of ownership are being met. Say a property donated for a county park with nature trails stopped being used for that purpose. When that happens, ownership of the property automatically reverts back (is returned) to the original owner without the original owner having to take any action.

### Life estates

A *life estate* grants possession and limited ownership of a property to a person for the duration of the recipient's life or the life of another person. The main difference between a fee estate and a life estate is that a fee estate has no time limit and a life estate does. The two types of life estates are

- ✔ **Ordinary life estate:** An ordinary life estate is a life estate in which the length of time of the estate interest is the lifetime of the person receiving the life estate. One situation where this form of estate comes in handy is when a husband wants to provide a place for his second wife to live until she dies but doesn't want to shortchange the children from his first marriage. In that case, the husband/father creates an ordinary life estate granting ownership rights to his second wife for the remainder of her life with the children named as *remaindermen* (even if they are women) who are entitled to the remainder interest in the stepmom's place after she dies.

✔ **Life estate pur autre vie:** The French words "pur autre vie" mean "for another life." As opposed to an ordinary life estate, the length of the life estate in this case is for the lifetime of a third party rather than the person actually receiving the life estate. The example I use in class is a chronically ill nephew for whom you want to provide care. You own a second house that is empty at the moment. You give your nephew's mother (that could be your sister or sister in law) a life estate pur autre vie to live in the house for as long as your nephew is alive. Upon his death the house reverts, that is, automatically comes back to you. You have a *reversionary interest* in the property. If you happen to die before your nephew does, the house would revert to your heirs upon your nephew's death. Here's another scenario: You're helping your sister take care of your nephew while you're alive but want to make provisions for his care after you die. You can create a life estate pur autre vie through your will. In that case, the house reverts to your estate or designated heirs upon your nephew's death.

Some states have what are called *legal life estates,* which are life estates in one form or another that are created by state law. You need to check out whether your state has adopted any of these rights and find out details of how they work. General descriptions of four common examples of these legal life estates are

✔ **Community property,** which is a right of a spouse, entitling him or her to one half interest in real property that was acquired during a marriage.

✔ **Curtesy,** which is the right of a husband to a portion of real property that is owned by his wife — after she dies and even if she leaves it to someone else in her will.

✔ **Dower,** which is the right of a wife to a portion of real property that is owned by her husband — after he dies and even if he leaves it to someone else in his will.

✔ **Homestead,** which grants the family home a certain level of protection from creditors during the owner's lifetime.

## Surveying leasehold estates

*Leasehold estates* are considered interests in real estate because they give some rights to the tenant, such as a right to exclusive possession and use of all or some portion of the property, while the owner retains some rights, such as ownership, the right to collect rents, and the right to sell the property. Leases and the various leasehold-estate interests are covered in detail in Chapter 12. As estates, however, you need to remember two terms and whose interest they represent:

✔ The *leasehold interest or estate* is the tenant's interest in the real property. Remember, the tenant holds the rights assigned by the lease.

✔ The *leased fee interest or estate* is the owner's or landlord's interest in the real property. Remember, the landlord holds the fee or title to the property.

# It's My Right: Different Ownership Rights

A variety of rights come with real estate ownership. In this section I talk about the most important of these rights — water rights, air rights, surface rights, subsurface rights, and mineral rights. Whereas by no means the only rights contained in the bundle of rights (see the section earlier in this chapter), the rights I discuss here have particular features that are important to remember for exam purposes. Be prepared for a few definition-type questions and a case study or two that may require you to apply some of what you remember.

## Going for a swim: Water rights

Land that's adjacent to a body of water normally carries with it certain rights relative to that body of water. A real estate agent is expected to know something about what these water rights involve. Although water rights may vary according to local law in specific situations — and a buyer should always consult an attorney to be sure of what their water rights are — several common rights of use exist. These common rights are explained in the sections that follow.

### Littoral rights

*Littoral rights* are the rights commonly granted to owners of property that border a bay, a large lake, the ocean, or a sea. Owners of property abutting such bodies of water have an unrestricted right to use the water and ownership of the land up to the average or mean high water mark. The government owns the land below that point. Littoral rights are *appurtenant to the land,* which means they go with the land when you sell it, so don't think that you can still go swimming after you sell the land.

### Riparian rights

*Riparian rights* are the rights of property owners who own land abutting rivers and streams. The rights vary a little depending on whether the river or stream is considered navigable, or capable of supporting commercial water traffic.

When a river or steam is considered navigable, owners of property abutting the river own the land up to the edge of the water or the average or mean high water mark. The state owns the body of the water and the property under the water. On the other hand, when the river or stream isn't navigable, the rights of owners with property abutting the river or stream extend to the centerline of the river or stream.

In either case, owners of property that abuts a river or stream have a right to use the water, but they don't have any right to contaminate the water or interrupt or change the flow of the water.

### Watering rights

In agricultural areas, rights to water may be controlled by special agreement between property owners. In addition, where water is scarce, the *doctrine of prior appropriation* may apply. The doctrine of prior appropriation is state-specific and may be used in states where water resources are limited. Although implementation of the doctrine can vary from state to state, it basically places the right to control water resources in the hands of the state rather than individual property owners. Water rights, or the rights to use water, then are granted by the state to individual property owners. You may want to check whether your state operates under this doctrine and find out about some of the details of how it is implemented.

## Don't forget to look up and down: Other rights

Some of the rights associated with owning real estate have to do with what's going on over your head and under your feet. Ownership of land includes the ownership of the land down to the center of the earth and up to infinity. Although practical and legal limitations may inhibit your ability to actually use these rights, you nevertheless still have them.

### Up there: Air rights

A property owner has an unlimited right of ownership of the airspace above her land up to infinity; however, these rights may not interfere with aircraft traffic. Air rights frequently are thought of in terms of selling or transferring them to someone else. Picture a 3-story building in a downtown urban area on property zoned such that its owner can build a

20-story building on it. Although the owner doesn't want to build those additional 17 stories, someone else does. Assuming the construction, engineering, and legal aspects can be worked out, the owner of the property can sell the air rights of the property to someone else while retaining ownership of the land and the three-story building. The new owner of the air rights could then build up to 17 more stories of building space on top of the existing 3-story building.

### Down there: Surface rights

The most obvious rights that you get when you own a piece of property are the *surface rights,* which are the rights to do whatever is legally permitted on the surface of the property. Surface rights generally include construction of structures and physical improvements of all kinds as well as things like planting crops.

*Development rights,* or the right to build on a piece of property, are rights that can be sold separate from the land. Conversely, a county can buy development rights from a farmer to preserve the property affected by those rights for environmental purposes. The farmer/property owner is able to stay and keep on farming, but he can never develop the land with houses or other structures. The farmer can even sell the property, but the right to develop the land stays with the county. The new property owner must be content being a farmer.

Surface rights also include the right to give your neighbor a driveway easement across the surface of your property. I discuss easements in Chapter 8.

### Way down there: Subsurface and mineral rights

Because you own the property down to the center of the earth, you have the right to use the property beneath the surface or to permit others to use it. An example of subsurface rights is selling the city an underground or subsurface easement to install a sewer line across your property. Subsurface rights often are associated with mineral rights.

*Mineral rights* are the right to take minerals out of the ground. Today these rights are associated with oil and gas leases, which are agreements that landowners make with companies to take those specific resources or products out of the ground. These leases include the right to build structures necessary to extract oil and gas from the ground. In some places where valuable minerals were found many years ago, owners sold the property but retained the mineral rights. In areas where these transactions have occurred, seeing a deed that transfers ownership of the property excluding the mineral rights is not uncommon.

# Review Questions and Answers

Most material in this chapter is pretty standard regarding property ownership and rights associated with owning property. Although a few state-specific issues may be addressed on the exam, make sure you know the vocabulary well and can tell the differences among the terms; definitions are the most commonly questioned items on the exam.

1. Land, improvements, and all the rights of ownership is a good definition of

   (A) land ownership.

   (B) real estate.

   (C) real property.

   (D) property.

   *Correct answer:* (C). The statement in the question is the definition of real property. Land ownership and property are too vague relative to real property. The definition of real estate includes only land and structures, not rights.

2. Which of the following is not a fixture?

    (A) A fence

    (B) A dishwasher

    (C) A painting hanging on the wall

    (D) A dining room chandelier

    *Correct answer:* (C). You may think that fixtures can be only inside the house, but that isn't the case, so a fence is a fixture. The only other answer that may throw you a little is the chandelier, because many people take chandeliers with them when they move. When they do take a chandelier with them, they do so by prior agreement. The dishwasher is usually attached to the plumbing and electrical system in the kitchen and stays if no agreement exists to remove and replace it. Of course, if the dishwasher is your spouse, he or she will be going with you when you sell the house. The painting is correct because it is portable and not permanently attached to the structure, and unless an agreement exists to leave it, most people consider it to be personal property.

3. When a man wants to donate property to a conservation group, he agrees that the organization can take title to the property as soon as an education center is built on the property. What kind of estate is he creating?

    (A) Fee simple absolute

    (B) Fee simple condition precedent

    (C) Fee simple condition subsequent

    (D) Fee simple determinable

    *Correct answer:* (B). The word *precedent* means "before," so the education center has to be built before property ownership passes to the conservation organization. Fee simple absolute is the most complete form of ownership and has no conditions. The word *subsequent* in fee simple condition subsequent means "after"; the conservation group in this case has to build the education center after it receives ownership of the property. Fee simple determinable would have been correct if the language in the question had talked about an ongoing condition, such as "so long as the property is used for an education center."

4. Sally owns a house that she will allow her sister Fran to live in for the rest of Fran's life. Upon Fran's death the house goes to Sally's children. Which of the following best describes the interest Fran has in the property?

    (A) Ordinary life estate

    (B) Life estate pur autre vie

    (C) Fee simple condition subsequent

    (D) Leasehold estate

    *Correct answer:* (A). An ordinary life estate is an interest conveyed to a person that exists for as long as that person (the one who receives the interest) is alive. Life estate pur autre vie is a life estate that exists for the life of a third party — someone other than the person receiving the life estate. Fee simple condition subsequent is an actual transfer of ownership with a condition. Leasehold estate is the interest a tenant has in a rental situation. Don't be confused by the fact that the property goes to Sally's children upon Fran's death.

5. Joe rents office space from Fred. What type of interest does Joe have?

    (A) Leasehold interest

    (B) Leased fee interest

    (C) Fee simple defeasible

    (D) Fee simple absolute

    *Correct answer:* (A). Remember the tenant holds the lease. The landlord has the leased fee interest. Fee simple defeasible and fee simple interest are ownership interests in the property. Theoretically the landlord could have one of these interests, but because the question asks about the tenant's interest, only leasehold interest is correct.

6. You own property on a river that has regular commercial boat traffic. What rights do you most likely have with respect to the water?

    (A) You own to the centerline of the river.

    (B) You have no rights to the water.

    (C) You have rights to use the water and own to the edge of the river.

    (D) You can use the water and own the land under the water to the midpoint of the river, but the state owns the water.

    *Correct answer:* (C). Riparian rights, which is what you have on navigable rivers and streams, gives you rights only to the water's edge and use of the water. If the river weren't navigable, you would own to the centerline (A). (B) is incorrect because properties bordering water generally have some type of rights with respect to the water. (D) is a combination of statements that taken as a whole is incorrect.

7. What are the water rights called for oceanfront property owners?

    (A) Riparian rights

    (B) Littoral rights

    (C) Defeasible rights

    (D) Qualified rights

    *Correct answer:* (B). Littoral rights are those rights granted to owners whose land borders oceans, bays, and large lakes. Riparian rights are those rights granted to property owners of land next to rivers and streams. Defeasible rights have to do with a defeasible estate, which is an interest with certain conditions attached to it. A qualified estate is similar to qualified rights.

8. The right of the state to control water rights in some states is called

    (A) the bundle of rights theory.

    (B) littoral rights.

    (C) riparian rights.

    (D) the doctrine of prior appropriation.

    *Correct answer:* (D). The doctrine of prior appropriation exists in states where water rights are an issue and have to do with controlling the use of water. Littoral and riparian rights are rights automatically granted to land owners whose property abuts bodies of water. The bundle of rights theory is the overall theory of the rights property owners have.

9. The theory that best describes the rights that you get with a piece of real estate is

   (A) the doctrine of complete rights.

   (B) the bundle of rights.

   (C) the development rights theory.

   (D) fee simple absolute.

   *Correct answer:* (B). Fee simple absolute may have confused you here, but it isn't really a theory. Instead, it describes the highest form of ownership and may apply only in some cases. There is no such thing as the doctrine of complete rights or as the development rights theory. The bundle of rights theory is the best answer.

10. Receiving back the property you gave in a life estate when that life estate ends is best described as

    (A) conveyance.

    (B) transfer.

    (C) reversion.

    (D) remaindering.

    *Correct answer:* (C). Reversion is the correct term when a property interest automatically returns to you, that is comes back, which is the way the question is worded. A remainder interest conveys the rights to a third party, such as your children if the life estate ends after you die. Conveyance and transfer are generally associated with straight changes in ownership from one party to another.

# Chapter 7

# Understanding Forms of Real Estate Ownership

*In This Chapter*

▶ Finding out about owning real estate alone and with others

▶ Checking out special ownership of cooperatives, condominiums, and more

*R*eal estate ownership comes in many forms. You can own real estate by yourself. You can own it with your spouse. You can own it with partners. You can be part of a corporation that owns real estate. You also may own real estate in the form of a condominium or cooperative. In each of these situations, ownership issues and forms are slightly different. The form of ownership of a property usually is handled by attorneys. In some states, especially those where attorneys are less involved in real estate transactions, you may, as an agent, have to deal more directly with these issues. And speaking of states there may be slight differences from state to state with respect to some of these forms of ownership. Pay attention in class and note anything that might be unique to your state.

Regardless of how actively you're involved in form-of-ownership issues in a real estate transaction, state examiners expect you to know something about the various types of ownership. In this chapter, I give you some basic terminology and key features of the various forms of real estate ownership, such as owning property by yourself, with others, with a spouse, in a trust, and in a business. I also cover special types of ownership, such as cooperatives and condominiums.

Even in states where real estate agents do most of the work associated with buying and selling property, agents always need to be aware of the things with which they're not familiar. When ownership matters get the least bit complicated with regard to form, they need to and can refer clients and customers to attorneys skilled in real estate matters.

## *Real Estate Ownership: A Solo or Group Activity*

That real estate can be owned by one person, two or more people, a married couple, or some type of business is obvious, because as real estate law evolved, it had to deal with these various forms of ownership with different terminology and sometimes different conditions.

In this section, pay particular attention to the terminology and key differences among the various forms of ownership. Exam questions on this subject are likely to focus on recognizing these differences.

You see the word "tenancy" throughout this section. *Tenancy* means having an interest in a piece of real estate. Most of us associate the word with being a tenant, which essentially is what it means; however, it also means having an ownership interest in a property. On a state exam you see the word used in both of its meanings. By the way, the word tenancy comes from a Latin word that means "to hold."

## One is the loneliest number: Owning real estate by yourself

Owning real estate by yourself is called *sole ownership* or *tenancy in severalty*. I know, the law has done it again. Right about now you're asking, "How can you use the word 'severalty' when you mean only one person?" The answer's actually pretty logical if you remember one thing. The word "severalty" doesn't come from "several" but rather from *"sever,"* meaning to cut off. Sole ownership cuts off all other interests in the property. In other words, no one has an ownership interest in the property except the one owner.

## Join the crowd: Owning real estate with other people

Two or more people who aren't married can own property together in a form of ownership known as *concurrent ownership* or *co-ownership*. I describe two forms of co-ownership: tenancy in common and joint tenancy. Although these two similar forms of ownership are available to married couples, they may serve specific purposes of ownership for people who are not married but want to own property together.

### Tenancy in common

*Tenancy in common* is a form of ownership in which two or more people own property together. The fact that two or more people are buying property together as tenants in common is stated in the deed. If the form of ownership isn't otherwise specifically stated in the deed, in some states tenancy in common automatically is assumed when two or more people buy property together. (For general information about deeds, check out Chapter 9.) Probably the most common form of ownership where tenancy in common takes place is condominium ownership. See the section "More individuality: Condominium ownership," later in this chapter.

The principal features of tenancy in common are:

- ✔ **Undivided ownership:** The land itself is not physically divided into or split between multiple owners, but rather percentages or shares of interest are granted in the property as a whole.

- ✔ **Equal or unequal shares:** The percentage of ownership interest of each party need not be equal, so one person can have a 50 percent share, and two others can each have a 25 percent share in the same property, and so on.

- ✔ **Sale without permission:** Any owner can sell his or her share without having to receive permission to do so from the other owners. The new owner is a tenant in common with the previous owners.

- ✔ **No right of survivorship:** If one owner dies, she leaves her share to her heirs. The other owners don't have any right to her share of the property.

Tenancy in common might be the way two married sisters buy a vacation home to share. If one dies, her husband or children would inherit her part of the property. If one sister has more money invested than the other, there would be no problem because one would own, say, 60 percent of the property whereas the other owned 40 percent.

### Joint tenancy

*Joint tenancy* is a form of ownership with special features for two or more people. Joint tenancy is said to be created with these four unities:

- **Unity of interest:** Unity of interest means that each owner has the same interest in the property. If there are four owners, each has a 25 percent share in the whole property. If there are two owners, each has a 50 percent share. Some states now permit unequal shares in a joint tenancy. You should check out what the law is in your state.

- **Unity of possession:** Like tenancy in common (see the previous section), each owner's interest is in an undivided property. Although interest in the property may be divided, the land and building, if any, may not be divided. In other words, no physical division of the property exists. Each owner essentially owns a share in the property as a whole.

- **Unity of time:** Joint owners all take title (or ownership) to the property at the same time. A later owner cannot be added to the joint tenancy as a joint tenant unless new documents are executed, effectively creating a new joint tenancy. If one of the joint tenants sells her interest without this happening, that new owner becomes a tenant in common. A joint tenant also may sell his individual interest without the permission of the other joint tenants.

- **Unity of title:** Unity of title means that all the joint tenants names are on the deed together.

Any brother and sister who want to own a home together could buy a property as joint tenants. If one dies, the other automatically takes title (ownership) of the whole property.

Perhaps the most important difference between joint tenancy and tenancy in common is the right of survivorship that you have as a joint tenant and that you don't have as a tenant in common. The *right of survivorship* in a joint tenancy means that if one of the joint tenants dies, the other tenant(s) automatically take title to the deceased tenant's interest in the property. For example, if four joint tenants each own a 25 percent share of a piece of property, and one joint tenant dies, the three remaining tenants each has a 33⅓ percent share. That's why joint tenancy is a form of ownership that married couples sometimes use when they buy property. When one spouse dies, the other spouse automatically gets full title to the property.

You may want to check whether your state still recognizes the right of survivorship in a joint tenancy. Some states are doing away with that aspect of this type of co-ownership unless it is specifically stated.

## Getting hitched: Owning real estate when you're married

The law over time has developed special forms of real estate ownership for married couples. I describe the two common forms: tenancy by the entirety, and community property.

### Tenancy by the entirety

Tenancy by the entirety is a form of co-ownership specifically geared toward protecting the interests of married couples by providing a right of survivorship. A form of joint tenancy (see the previous section for the full scoop), the theory behind *tenancy by the entirety* is that a couple is treated as if it was one person owning property insofar as each spouse has an undivided and equal interest in the property. Upon the death of one spouse, the deceased spouse's interest automatically goes to the surviving spouse without having to go through the process of probating a will or other inheritance issues.

Another unique feature of tenancy by the entirety is that neither spouse can sell his or her share without doing so together. The entire property must be sold by the combined actions of both parties signing the deed. In the event of a divorce, a tenancy by the entirety is changed to a tenancy in common. (See "Tenancy in common," earlier in this chapter, for details.)

### Community property

Some states operate under community property laws. Under these laws, all property that a couple acquires during their marriage is considered jointly owned and equally owned by both spouses, regardless of whose actual income was used to purchase the property. Property acquired by one or the other spouse before the marriage is called *separate property* and is not subject to community property requirements. Property inherited during the marriage by one or the other spouse is also considered separate property. The essential elements of community property law are:

- Community property may be sold or mortgaged only by joint action of both spouses.
- Separate property may be sold or mortgaged by the person owning it (or bringing it to the marriage).
- No right of survivorship exists. Upon the death of one spouse, the surviving spouse retains title to his or her half of the property. The deceased spouse's half interest can be willed to anyone else.

You need to check how real estate ownership of married couples is treated in your state. Laws may vary from one state to another, particularly with respect to the specific implementation of laws protecting the rights of married couples in real estate ownership and whether community property is a recognized concept. Some states, for example, may use joint tenancy with a right of survivorship for married couples.

### State specific

As states begin to deal with the issue of same sex marriage and civil unions of one type or another, the laws regarding co-ownership of real estate will evolve. State exams are unlikely to contain questions this specific. Later on when you are practicing real estate you should research how your state laws work in this area.

## Who do you trust? Ownership in trust

Real estate can be held by a third party for the benefit of someone else. The main players are the *trustor* (the person who owns the property and conveys it to the trustee); the *trustee* (the person who receives the property and administers it on behalf of the beneficiary); and the *beneficiary* (the person who receives the benefits of the property, like rent on an apartment house, as a result of the administration of the property by the trustee).

Say, for example, you leave your apartment buildings to your brother in trust for your favorite nephew. You are the trustor, because you created the trust. Your brother is the trustee, and he administers the buildings according to the terms of the trust, which in this case would likely be that the income from the buildings goes to your nephew because he is the beneficiary.

Ownership in trust requires a special type of deed called (you guessed it!) a *trust deed* or a *deed in trust*. For more, see Chapter 9.

# *All business: Ownership by a business*

Ownership of real estate by business organizations is not so much about the forms of ownership as it is about the organizational structures of the businesses. You're not likely to be involved very often with this type of transaction in your everyday real estate practices, unless you work a great deal with commercial real estate and developers. State exam writers, however, expect you to know something about different business organizations and how they can own property.

You may hear the word "syndicate" in connection with business projects. A *syndicate* isn't a form of ownership. It's a term that generally describes two or more people or companies joining together to work on a project or form an ongoing relationship to own and manage buildings or other real estate.

Businesses (and syndicates) often purchase properties as investments. For more about investment properties and forms of investment ownership, see Chapter 17.

## *Corporations*

A *corporation,* for legal purposes, is treated the same as an individual owner when it comes to real estate ownership. Generally speaking, unless a corporation is involved in co-ownership arrangements with other corporations, it owns property in sole ownership or tenancy in severalty. I discuss tenancy in severalty in "One is the loneliest number: Owning real estate by yourself," earlier in this chapter. A few key features of real estate ownership by a corporation follow:

✔ People own shares in a corporation, but no direct ownership exists for individual shareholders in property owned by the corporation.

✔ Shareholders have neither authority over nor responsibility for management of corporation property.

✔ Shareholder liability generally is limited to the value of the shareholder's shares. For instance, if a shareholder owns $1,000 worth of stock in a real estate investment corporation, and the company loses a lawsuit for millions of dollars, regardless of whether the corporation has the money, the shareholder can lose only his $1,000 investment and no more than that. It should be noted that this protection is subject to court rulings in the event of a lawsuit.

✔ Profits that the corporation receives from the property are taxed before they're distributed to shareholders, who then pay taxes again on amounts they receive. The so-called S Corporation is a form of corporation with modified tax liabilities and is permitted by the government under strict rules.

## *Partnerships*

A partnership is two or more people or companies combining to do business. A partnership may be short-term for one project like buying, renovating, and selling a building, or long-term for ongoing investment and management of real estate holdings. Many states have adopted the *Uniform Partnership Act* and the *Uniform Limited Partnership Act,* which allow real estate to be owned in general or limited partnerships.

Partnerships are either general or limited. In a *general partnership,* all the partners share in the management and operational decisions over the business of the partnership. They also share in the liability for any actions the partnership takes without limit. The respective partners pay taxes according to their respective interests and liabilities, so that double taxation is avoided. On the other hand, in a *limited partnership,* one general partner usually manages the operations of the business, and a number of other limited partners have no management responsibilities. The liabilities of the limited partners are determined by and limited to the amounts of their respective investments in the company.

### Limited liability corporations

The limited liability corporation (LLC), or limited liability company, as it's sometimes called, is a hybrid organizational structure that has elements of a partnership and a corporation. Similar to a corporation, the liability of the individual members within the corporation is limited. Meanwhile, they pay taxes as if they're part of a general partnership (see the previous section). Management by members of the LLC also may be along the more direct lines allowed in a general partnership.

### Joint ventures

A *joint venture* is the joining together of two or more people or companies to do a single project like buy a house, renovate it, and sell it for a profit. A joint venture is somewhat like a syndicate in that it can own property in any of several forms, like tenancy in common, joint tenancy, or a corporation, among others (see the sections on these forms earlier in this chapter). However, ownership probably will include an ending date, because joint ventures aren't designed to be ongoing business relationships. A joint venture, like a syndicate, is really a name for two or more people or companies who want to cooperate in a real estate investment. The difference between a joint venture and a syndicate is that a joint venture brings people together for one real estate investment or project, whereas a syndicate usually does multiple real estate investments or projects at the same time or a series of individual projects over a period of time.

# Special Types of Ownership: Cooperatives, Condominiums, and More

Cooperatives and condominiums are popular forms of ownership for a variety of reasons, but primarily because they

- ✔ Usually are built to a higher density (more units per acre or in high-rise buildings), and they're often somewhat less expensive than a single-family house in the same area.

- ✔ Provide some of the advantages of homeownership, such as building up equity by paying off a mortgage, and tax advantages like being able to deduct real estate taxes and mortgage interest. (I cover mortgages in Chapter 15 and taxes in Chapter 16.)

- ✔ Provide the advantage of no outside maintenance, because the dwellings usually are maintained by a homeowners association in the case of condominiums or a board in the case of a cooperative.

These forms of ownership are unique because they involve ownership by more than one person, but the owners aren't known to each other nor are they in a business venture together.

I cover cooperatives and condominiums, plus planned unit developments and time shares, in the following sections.

## Share and share alike: Cooperative ownership

Strictly speaking, you don't own real estate when you're part of a cooperative. You own shares in a corporation that owns the real estate. As a shareholder, you receive a *proprietary lease* that enables you to occupy your apartment. For all intents and purposes, your ownership interest in a cooperative is treated like real estate, including the ability to finance your purchase just like a mortgage, except that your shares (and not the property itself) are pledged as collateral for the loan. In other words, if you can't pay off the loan, the bank can claim your cooperative shares in payment. (For more about mortgages, see Chapter 15.) Some of these expenses are deductible from annual personal income taxes, such as the cooperative owner's share of the property taxes.

A board of directors of the corporation makes rules and policies for the building, collects monthly fees from shareholders and maintains the building, and pays the taxes and any other expenses that may exist, like emergency repairs and a mortgage on the building itself. This mortgage on the building is generally referred to as the underlying mortgage and can sometimes make the monthly common charges a little more expensive than in a condominium because the share owners are responsible for payments on the underlying mortgage.

Two issues that frequently are considered disadvantages of cooperative ownership are

- **Shared liability.** Whenever shareholders default on their common charges (the payments all shareholders make to maintain the building and pay taxes), the other (paying) shareholders are liable. This issue can become serious whenever too many shareholders default on their payments and the other shareholders have to pay the share of the money that wasn't paid by the defaulting shareholders.

- **Cooperative board approval of newcomers.** This issue may be viewed as a negative or a positive, depending on your point of view. Requiring board approval of new cooperative buyers whenever someone sells shares in a cooperative is the fairly common practice. The requirement allows new owners to be screened for financial ability to pay their loans and common charges, but it also may hold up the sale of a unit while a prospective buyer undergoes the board approval process.

Cooperative boards in many places may not be required to reveal the reasons they turn down a specific buyer. Insufficient financial ability is generally the best reason to turn a buyer down, but other reasons — including illegal ones such as fair housing violations — may exist despite the fact that cooperative boards are subject to these laws.

## More individuality: Condominium ownership

Condominium ownership is a form of group ownership that involves actually getting a deed to your individual ownership interest. In general, the deed describes the airspace you own (in other words, the unit), which you own as a tenant in severalty, and your share as a tenant in common of the land under and around your unit. (See the "Tenancy in common" section earlier in this chapter for details.) A homeowners association usually collects set monthly fees, which pay for maintenance of the condominium building and complex.

Individual condo owners are responsible for paying their own property taxes, so defaulting on your tax obligations can result in a foreclosure on the unit but not on the entire complex. (For more about foreclosures, see Chapter 15.) *Condominiums* often are associated with complexes in the suburbs and are thought of as low-rise one- and two-story attached housing units. Condominiums, however, may also be found in high-rise buildings in urban areas.

You need to find out what the term "townhouse" means in your home state. Originally a term used to describe two- or three-story attached housing in urban areas, townhouses now are usually located in planned unit developments. Typically a townhouse owner owns the unit and the land under it and may even have ownership of small lawn or patio space. Because many early condos were built in a two-story townhouse style, in some areas common usage occasionally mixes the terms, calling condominiums townhouses regardless of the style.

## Mix it up: Planned unit developments

The planned unit development (PUD) is a somewhat hybrid form of ownership. In theory, a PUD is a large development often having mixed uses, such as different types of residential and commercial uses, and built by a single developer. In practice, a PUD may have only residential uses. Like a condominium, PUDs often are overseen by a homeowners association, and common charges paid by the homeowners go for outside maintenance. How a PUD often differs from a condominium is that the owner of a PUD unit also owns land beneath it.

In a condominium, you own the unit individually but the land under and around it as a tenant in common with others. (See the section on tenancy in common earlier in this chapter.) You generally don't own land individually in a condominium. You usually do in a PUD. You also usually own so-called common areas like recreation facilities, walking paths, and the internal roads as a tenant in common with others, just like a condominium. You should find out how the term PUD is used in your home state with respect to developments and property ownership.

## Check your watch: Time shares

In a *time share,* a person has either a fractional ownership in a property or the right to use a property for a limited period of time each year or both.

Ownership in a time share may actually convey a fee simple ownership interest in the property. In other words, you have unlimited rights to the extent of your ownership interest, even if that ownership interest is the last two weeks in August every year. (For more about fee simple ownership, see Chapter 6.) A time share owner may only have a use interest, which is permission to use the unit on a periodic basis, such as the first week in June each year. A person with a time share use interest (in other words, the right to use a dwelling for a defined amount of time) leaves ownership of the property in the hands of a corporation or an individual.

# Review Questions and Answers

Exam questions on the subjects in this chapter are about terminology and knowing the differences of different kinds of ownership and their main characteristics. Concentrate on key words and characteristics, and you'll do fine.

1. Ownership by one person is called

   (A) tenancy by the entirety.

   (B) tenancy in severalty.

   (C) tenancy in common.

   (D) joint tenancy.

   *Correct answer:* (B). All the other answers involve two or more people owning a single property.

2. Joint tenancy requires unity of interest, unity of possession, unity of time, and unity of

   (A) ownership.

   (B) deed.

   (C) finance.

   (D) title.

   *Correct answer:* (D). See the "Joint tenancy" section and remember the descriptions of the four unities. (I made up the other answers.)

3. The type of ownership available only to married couples that has the right of survivorship is

   (A) joint tenancy.

   (B) tenancy by the entirety.

   (C) tenancy in common.

   (D) community property.

   *Correct answer:* (B). Joint tenancy and tenancy in common aren't specific to married couples, and community property has no right of survivorship, leaving tenancy by the entirety as the correct answer.

4. In his will, Roger has his apartment house put in a trust to be managed by Alice on behalf of his son Jim. Which of the following is correct in this case?

   (A) Roger is the trustor, and Alice is the trustee.

   (B) Roger is the trustor, and Jim is the trustee.

   (C) Alice is the trustor, and Jim is the beneficiary.

   (D) Roger is the trustee, and Jim is the trustor.

   *Correct answer:* (A). The person giving the property or creating the trust is the trustor. The person managing the trust is the trustee. The person receiving the benefits of the trust is the beneficiary. Roger is the trustor; Alice is the trustee; Jim is the beneficiary.

5. In which of the following forms of co-ownership are all owners required to sign a deed of sale?

   (A) Tenancy in common

   (B) Joint tenancy

   (C) Tenancy by the entirety

   (D) Tenancy by survivorship

   *Correct answer:* (C). Tenants in common can always individually sell their interests in the property. Joint tenants, even though they receive their interest from the same deed, can break the joint tenancy by selling their individual interests; they're allowed to do this without the permission of the other joint tenants. Tenancy by the entirety is for married couples only and requires both parties to sign the deed of sale. I made up Answer D.

6. In what form of ownership does the owner get shares in a corporation rather than a deed?

   (A) Condominium

   (B) Planned unit development

   (C) Townhouse

   (D) Cooperative

   *Correct answer:* (D). Condominiums, planned unit developments, and townhouses are all real estate ownership interests; no shares are involved since the owner gets a deed. A cooperative is ownership of shares in a corporation. Though not one of the choices, remember that a proprietary lease permits a cooperative shareholder to occupy her unit.

7. Liability is limited to the investment in what type of business ownership of real estate?

(A) General partnership

(B) Syndicate

(C) Joint venture

(D) Limited partnership

*Correct answer:* (D). In a general partnership, all partners are liable for their actions without limit. Remember that syndicates and joint ventures aren't really forms of ownership but rather general descriptions of two or more people or companies cooperating to do one or more projects. The limited partnership is the only one of the four answers that limits the liability of the limited partners to their investments.

8. In what form of co-ownership does a deceased owner's share go to her heirs?

(A) Tenancy in common

(B) Joint tenancy

(C) Tenancy by the entirety

(D) Tenancy in absolute

*Correct answer:* (A). In tenancy in common, you can leave your real estate interest to your heirs. In joint tenancy, the property may not be willed to anyone outside the joint tenancy. When one of the joint tenants dies, her share goes to the remaining joint tenants. Remember that this is called the right of survivorship and may vary in some states. In tenancy by the entirety, which is a form of ownership for married couples only, the share of the deceased spouse automatically goes to the surviving spouse. It may not be willed to anyone else. I made up tenancy in absolute.

9. You're married and own property with your spouse. When you die, she will keep her half of the property, and you will be able to leave your half to your sister. You probably live in what kind of state?

(A) Community property state

(B) Joint tenancy state

(C) Tenancy by the entirety state

(D) Tenancy in common state

*Correct answer:* (A). Community property is the only form of ownership specifically for married couples that permits what is described in the question to occur. Joint tenancy isn't specific to married couples. Tenancy by the entirety is a form of ownership for married people in which the deceased partner's share in the property automatically goes to the surviving spouse. And although you may be able to create a scenario in which you own property as a tenant in common with your wife that allows you to leave half to your sister, this is one of those questions where the word "probably" should lead you to the better answer, which is community property state. It demonstrates the importance of carefully reading every word in a question.

10. A corporation owns property in what form?

(A) Tenancy in severalty

(B) Tenancy in common

(C) Joint tenancy

(D) Tenancy by the entirety

*Correct answer:* (A). Remember, a corporation is considered an individual person for legal purposes. The other answers involve multiple owners, and because a corporation is considered a single individual, tenancy in severalty is the only answer that works.

# Chapter 8

# Knowing the Limitations on Real Estate Ownership

*In This Chapter*

▶ Finding out about different private limitations

▶ Understanding government regulations that limit property use

▶ Checking out land-use regulations

**R**eal estate ownership conveys many automatic rights, such as the right to sell it or build on it. But those rights usually aren't unlimited. Your right to use a piece of real estate that you own often is limited by or subject to the physical, financial, or legal rights of others, including other people or the government. Sometimes the limitations simply prevent you from doing something specific with your property, such as building a commercial building in a residential area because of government restrictions on land use. A private, as opposed to a government, limitation may give the right to another person, usually the person who sold you the property, to determine the style of house you can build.

This chapter provides information about private and government limitations that are likely to be on the real estate license exam. I specifically discuss topics such as voluntary and involuntary liens, regulations concerning new construction, and much more.

## Carrying a Not-So-Heavy Encumbrance: Private Limitations on Property Use

An *encumbrance* is a right or interest in a piece of real estate that belongs to someone other than the property owner. Because someone else holds an interest in your property, that right is a limit or restriction on your use of the property. Encumbrances generally are considered private limitations; however, the government can make a claim on your property for unpaid taxes, which also is considered an encumbrance.

Encumbrances come in two flavors (no, not chocolate and vanilla):

   ✔ **Financial claims against the real estate:** These claims are called liens.

   ✔ **Limitations on the use of the property:** Included are easements, encroachments, and restrictions.

You can sample them in the sections that follow.

# Looking at liens

Real estate *liens* are financial claims against someone's property. Depending on its purpose, a lien exists with certain characteristics. How and why you permit someone to place a lien on your property has to do with the type of lien to which you're subjected. I talk about all that in the following sections.

### Abracadabra: Creating and removing liens

When you borrow or owe money, your real estate frequently becomes the security, called *collateral,* for that loan or debt. Collateral is an item of value you pledge in return for securing a loan. Okay so far? Even though you're actually borrowing the money, the lien attaches itself to the property like a leech. Thus the real beauty of a lien — not to you, of course, but to the person to whom you owe the money is that it stays with the property, regardless of who owns it, until the debt is paid. Although you may think that attachment is unfair, it helps guarantee payment of the debt.

When a lien is attached to real estate, it can limit ownership in a couple of ways. It can

✔ Mean the property can be sold against your will to pay off the debt, such as for non-payment of the mortgage or taxes.

✔ Show up when you sell your property. Because the new owner doesn't want to pay your debts, you have to pay what you owe to clear the debt and remove the lien before the property sale can be finalized. If you don't have the money to pay the debt when you sell the property, the debt then is paid from what you get from the sale. Removing a lien really is just that simple unless you can prove the lien was a mistake.

### Who gets paid first? Priority of liens

One characteristic of liens, the one that exam writers like to ask about, is called the *priority of liens.* A more appropriate term is *priority of payments* because it refers to who gets paid first when property is sold against the owner's wishes to satisfy a number of different debts. It also is referred to as the position of the person being paid, such as the "mortgage is in first position after taxes."

The first person paid from a court-ordered sale of a piece of real estate is the government. Real estate taxes take first position in the payment of liens. If several liens are attached to the property and one is for unpaid real estate taxes, the real estate taxes are paid first, including any special assessments, or special taxes above and beyond the general real estate tax. Payment of general and special assessment taxes takes priority over all other liens, regardless of when the liens were attached. (For more on tax liens, see "One size doesn't fit all: Types of liens," later in the chapter, and Chapter 16.) Sometimes, because of too many liens, a property may not be able to be transferred or sold, primarily because not enough money can be gained from the proceeds to pay off the debt. Once in a while, some of the lien holders will take less money just so the property can sell. Quite often it is the second mortgage holder in a foreclosure sale who has to settle for less.

Other than real estate tax liens, all other liens usually are paid off in the order that they were recorded in the appropriate local office of public records — the county clerk's office or some other office of public records. The particular state where you reside may have some variations on this general rule, but in most cases, the first-recorded, first-paid rule applies. If the real estate is sold to pay off one or more liens and money is left over after all liens are satisfied, the property owner receives the remaining money.

### It's all in the name: Liens' distinguishing traits

All liens have two specific traits: They're either voluntary or involuntary, and they're specific or general. Here's what I mean:

✔ **Voluntary or involuntary:** You either agree to have a lien put on your property or it's put there against your will.

- A *voluntary lien* is where the property owner willingly takes some action that enables the placement of a lien against the property. A mortgage is the most common example of a voluntary lien.

- An *involuntary lien* is placed on the property against the owner's will. If the property owner owes money to someone, such as the tax collector, and the owner doesn't pay, a lien is placed on the property. Because this type of lien was placed on the property without the owner's agreement, it is considered an involuntary lien.

✔ **Specific or general:** One other characteristic of a lien is identifying how many separate pieces of real estate it can be attached to.

- A *specific lien* attaches to only one property.

- A *general lien* attaches to a number of properties.

For example, if you own three properties and have a specific lien on one of them, no one can force you to sell either of the other two properties to pay off the lien. On the other hand, if someone places a general lien on the three properties you own, the lien applies to all the real estate that you own. In other words, all three properties are encumbered by that general lien.

Some general liens also can be placed against your personal property. For instance, income tax liens are general and can show up when you try to sell your yacht.

### One size doesn't fit all: Types of liens

You may wonder what types of liens can be put on real estate. In this section, I point out what actions prompt someone to place a lien on a piece of real estate and some of their characteristics. Pay particular attention to whether the liens are general or specific, and voluntary or involuntary. For some reason, state test writers love asking at least a few questions about these four types of liens:

✔ **Tax lien:** A *tax lien* is placed on real estate for unpaid real estate taxes. Remember the government organization or agency placing the lien is paid first, if the property is sold. Different levels of government from cities, towns, and counties can place tax liens on property. School districts and water and sewer agencies also can place tax liens on property. Tax liens are involuntary and specific.

✔ **Mortgage lien:** A *mortgage lien* is a voluntary, specific lien. In fact, it's the most common type of voluntary real estate lien. When you borrow money to buy or refinance a piece of real estate, you give the lender a lien against the property. Some states call this a *deed of trust lien*. Mortgage lenders are careful about wanting to be paid the money they loaned you. They usually make sure that no other liens take priority over their lien and that they have what is called a *first mortgage lien*. Any other liens are called *junior liens*. If the mortgage lien is in first position, the only other lien that can take precedence over it for payment is a tax lien.

✔ **Mechanic's lien:** A *mechanic's lien* is a lien placed on your property for nonpayment for work you had done on the property. For example, you didn't pay the plumber, so he puts a mechanic's lien on your property. A mechanic's lien is involuntary and specific.

Your state may allow brokers to place liens on real estate for unpaid commissions. This practice varies by state and may vary by whether the commission was earned from a sale of property or a lease negotiation. You may also be able to put a lien on the property for an unpaid commission, if the listing contract or the purchase agreement contains a clause that enables you to do so. So check it out.

Instead of a lien, your state may permit brokers to place a lis pendens on the property. A *lis pendens* isn't a lien but instead is a notice of a potential future lien. It's recorded in the public records to give notice to future buyers of the real estate.

Some states permit brokers to place disputed commission funds in an escrow account while the disagreement is resolved. This is not a lien.

✔ **Judgment lien:** *Judgment liens,* sometimes just called *judgments* or *money judgments,* usually are created as a result of a court action. Say someone sues you for a personal-injury claim, for example, and the court finds in favor of the person who sued you. If you can't pay immediately, the court may place a judgment lien against your property.

Judgment liens are involuntary and general. They're certainly involuntary, because you didn't voluntarily put up your real estate as security the way you do for a mortgage. A judgment lien is general because it affects all your real estate; however, it usually applies only to property located in the county where the judgment is issued. Nevertheless, a judgment lien can be filed in counties other than where you own property. In addition to real estate, judgment liens also can be attached to personal property, such as your car, boat, or antique furniture. Judgment liens, however, may vary from state to state, so you may want to check out specific laws in your state.

When property is sold for nonpayment of mortgage debt, tax liens are paid first from the proceeds, usually followed by mortgage liens, and then by other liens (mechanic's and judgment liens, for example) in the order in which they are placed on the property being sold.

## *Easing into easements*

An *easement* is the right of another person or entity to use someone else's property for his or her benefit. The other person or entity can be an adjacent property owner or another party such as a utility company. The easement can include the right to use the space beneath the ground, on the ground, or up in the air above the property.

The person or property receiving the benefit is called the *dominant tenement* or *dominant estate.* The property on which the easement was granted is called the *servient tenement* or *servient estate.* Don't worry so much about the words *estate* and *tenement;* the important words to remember are *dominant* and *servient.*

A way to remember: Think about the words serve and dominate. The property being used or serving the demands of the easement is servient. The property that benefits from the easement or dominates over the other is dominant.

You're probably thinking, "Why would you, as a property owner, actually let someone else use your property for his or her benefit? Or, for that matter, why would someone else let you use his property for your benefit? But, the fact of the matter is that many times two people voluntarily create easements. On the other hand, easements also can be created in a couple of not-so-voluntary ways.

Categories of easements are pretty simple and often are part of the exam. You'll see information about gross and appurtenant easements, which involve the person who benefits from the easement. I also give you some information about how an easement can be created against your will.

### *Running with it: Appurtenant easements*

Easements are defined by who benefits from them. An *appurtenant easement* benefits a neighboring property. By the way, don't get confused if your home state reverses these words and calls it an *easement appurtenant.* It's the same thing.

For example, your property can be landlocked, which means that it has no direct access to a public road. So to access your property from a public road, you must cross someone else's property. If that other property owner gives you a permanent right to drive or walk across his property so that you have access to yours, he's given you an easement appurtenant. Although as the property owner, you negotiated the easement for your use and benefit, the easement will continue after you and your neighbor sell your properties to other owners. So it is your property that actually benefits from the easement. Under the statute of frauds law, which exists in some fashion in every state, easements must be in writing to be valid.

Because an easement appurtenant attaches itself to a piece of property, it's said to *run with the land,* which means that whenever the property (dominant estate) that benefits from the ease-ment is sold, the new owner has the same rights to use the easement that the old owner had. Just in case I've lost you here, let's put that in terms of the example in the previous paragraph where you were given an easement to cross someone else's property. When you sell your property, the buyer obtains the same right that you had to cross the neighboring property.

Several appurtenant easements covered on the test include:

✔ A surface easement such as to build a driveway to get from a public road to your house

✔ An underground easement, for example to bring a water line from the city street main across your property to your neighbor

✔ An overhead or aerial easement to run an electric line to your house by crossing your neighbor's property

### So gross! Easements in gross

Another type of easement is called an *easement in gross*. This type of easement benefits another person rather than a piece of property.

Say, for instance, that the gas company has a gas main running parallel to the street in front of your house and wants to connect it to another line in the street behind your backyard neighbor's house. The gas company needs an easement in gross from you and your back-yard neighbor to install the connecting line across your respective properties.

Typical easements in gross that you may see on the exam are utility easements. For exam-ple, the city wants to connect two sewer lines by crossing your property with an under-ground pipe or the electric company wants to connect a line between two poles.

### In need: Easements by necessity

A court order creates an *easement by necessity* to permit someone to gain access to a prop-erty. For example, say Property Owner *A* sells Buyer *B* a back portion of land but neglects to give Buyer *B* an easement for access. If *A* then refuses to give *B* the easement, *B* can go to court and get it by court order — an easement appurtenant.

Easement by necessity doesn't necessarily mean that you can buy a piece of property with-out any access and expect the court to order a neighboring property owner to give you an easement under all circumstances. Usually a seller's refusal to provide an easement is the circumstance under which the court gives you the easement.

### The doctor didn't give you this: Easements by prescription

An *easement by prescription* is an easement that is created by the actions of one person against the interests of another person.

An example may help explain this type of easement: Every night when your neighbor Joe comes home, he drives his car across a corner of your property. The reason doesn't matter; he simply does it. You see him do it but never stop him, and he does it for a long time. Eventually you get tired of him driving across your property and tell him to stop, but he says, "No way, I've got an easement by prescription." Joe takes the matter to court, and the court agrees with him. Joe now has a permanent easement by prescription across your property. An easement by prescription is related to adverse possession, which is discussed in the "I thought I owned it: Encroachments and adverse possession" section later in this chapter. The principal difference is that a prescriptive easement gives you the right to use the property. Adverse possession gives you ownership of the property. Like adverse possession, easement by prescription is not automatic; it requires a court order as a result of a lawsuit.

When looking at Joe's case for the details of how an easement by prescription is created, the fact that Joe's actions had persisted for a long period of time came into play. So how long is long enough? That length of time varies according to which state you're in. Ten years usually is the minimum time, but it can be longer.

You saw Joe cross your property. His use was open and what lawyers call *notorious,* meaning it wasn't hidden. In a sense, by not telling Joe to stop sooner, you gave him silent permission to use your property.

Joe crossed your property every night, so his use was continuous during the period prescribed by state law without interruption. This scenario brings up another issue. Suppose that in your state, the period of time required for a prescriptive easement to be created is ten years, Joe sells his property after five years, and the new owner picks up right where Joe left off, continuing to use your property in plain view for another five years. Do you think he'll be able to claim a prescriptive easement? Much to your annoyance, the answer is yes, because of something called tacking.

*Tacking* is a factor that allows for the addition of the times during which several different owners continuously engage in the same use. So if five different successive owners use your property for the prescribed period of time — for example, your state's ten-year requirement — the latest owner's request for an easement can be granted by the court.

### Share and share alike: Party walls

In areas of the country where houses or other buildings are built side by side with no space in between, the outside wall that's shared by the two buildings is called a *party wall.* Each building owner owns half of the wall and has an easement for the other half. Fences on property lines and shared driveways work the same way. Agreements that deal with maintenance issues usually are in place for shared items like these. These party-wall easements are created at the time the buildings are built and sold. They're appurtenant easements because they benefit the adjacent property owner.

### It was fun while it lasted: Ending easements

Now that you've let Joe and others walk all over you, so to speak, just how do you go about getting out of an easement? Easements can be terminated in several ways, including:

- **An agreement or release:** The person who possesses the easement (dominant tenement) agrees to give it up or release the person across whose property the easement exists (servient tenement) from the obligation.

- **By merger:** *Merger* is a fancy word for the joining of the two properties involved. For instance, *A* has an easement to cross *B*'s property. *B* buys *A*'s property. The easement disappears.

- **By abandonment:** Use it or lose it. Say you had a driveway easement to some country property that you visit regularly, and for one reason or another, you stop going to the property. Eventually the easement may be considered abandoned and you can lose it.

- **The need no longer exists:** The need for the easement may no longer exist. Perhaps, for example, a new road is being constructed that allows direct access to the property.

Terminating an easement is not automatic. Usually some form of court action is needed to terminate an easement, unless the two parties agree, in which case some form of legal document agreeing to the termination of the easement needs to be executed and recorded.

## Providing help for the horses

Deed restrictions can be placed on a property for any number of reasons. A farm owner once subdivided his farm into lots that he sold off to individuals to build houses. Interested in horses, the farmer wanted to promote horsemanship in the area, so before selling any of the properties, he put a set of restrictive covenants on all the lots. First, because the old farm featured horse trails, the farmer restricted the new lot owners from blocking any of the existing trails. Even though driveways on the various lots were quite long, the farmer restricted them from being paved because pavement is bad for horse feet. (Okay! I know they're hooves.) And finally, because the zoning permitted smaller lots than the original size of each lot, he restricted any further subdivision of the lots so as to attract people who'd want larger lots for their horses.

## *It won't let you drive, but it's still a license*

A *license* is a temporary right to do something on someone else's property. A license usually is permission that's given for one-time specific use. Depending on the state law, the agreement can be either written or oral because it conveys no interest in the property but only short-term permission to use it.

Say, for example, your neighbor is building a house and construction vehicles need to have access to his property; however, until he installs his own driveway, the easiest way for them to get to his property is across your driveway. You give your neighbor a license to use your driveway for that purpose, but you retain the right to cancel the license at any time. This arrangement does not give your neighbor any permanent rights to your property.

## *No, you can't paint your house purple: Deed restrictions*

A *deed restriction* is a limitation on the use of your property that appears in the deed to your property and is put there by another person. In fact, it's specifically called a *private land-use restriction,* distinguishing it from the public land-use restrictions that I talk about later in this chapter. A deed restriction is considered a private agreement, because no one forces you to buy the particular property governed by it and if you do buy it, you voluntarily agree to abide by the restrictions. Deed restrictions also are referred to as *covenants, conditions, and restriction* (CCRs), or sometimes *restrictive covenants.*

You're probably already asking yourself how someone can agree to a deed restriction and why? I'll answer those questions next and give you some other important information about how deed restrictions work. (For more on deeds in general, head to Chapter 9.)

### *What is it I can't do?*

A deed restriction limits what you can do with your property. For instance, a deed restriction may limit you to building a house in only a certain architectural style or not allow you to build a house of less than a certain size.

Deed restrictions can limit almost anything you may want to do with your property. The only limit on the restriction is that it can't be something illegal. For example, a restriction that says you can't sell the property to a member of a particular ethnic or religious group is illegal and therefore invalid because it violates fair housing laws.

Deed restrictions bind not only the first person who buys the property after the restriction is put into effect but also all future owners, unless the restriction has a time limit.

Sometimes a deed restriction and public law cover the same issue but have different degrees of limitation. In that case, the more restrictive or limiting of the two applies. Local zoning, which is discussed in the "You're in the zone: Understanding zoning ordinances" section later in this chapter, may require a minimum of one acre for each house you want to build. But say that the actual size of the property you're buying is three acres, and the developer of the subdivision has put a deed restriction in place that says individual properties may not be sub-divided again. Even though the government, through the zoning ordinance, says you ought to be able to get three separate pieces of property out of your three-acre parcel, the deed restriction won't permit it. The deed restriction wins, because it's more limiting. Although not always the case, deed restrictions are often more limiting than local laws because they may be designed to do what local laws normally do not; for example, restrict the color you can paint your house.

### Who says 1 can't do it?

Anyone can put a deed restriction on his property that binds all future owners. Typically, though, deed restrictions are placed on a group of individual properties that have been created as a result of a subdivision. The restrictions are placed in the deed by the person creating the subdivision as each property is sold. Subdivisions are discussed in the "Many from one: Subdivisions" section later in this chapter.

The term *restrictive covenants* is used to mean a set of restrictions that applies to an entire *subdivision,* which is a large piece of real estate that's been divided into smaller properties to be built on and sold individually. Restrictive covenants cover all the properties in the subdivision.

Every property owner has the right to seek enforcement of a deed restriction through the courts. So if you paint your house purple, when a restrictive covenant prohibits using that color, any of your neighbors can seek an *injunction* to force you to paint your house another unrestricted color. However, if your neighbors ignore your new paint job for a certain length of time, they may lose the right to take you to court. The law of the state in which the property is located governs the time frame after which you can lose the right to seek enforcement of a deed restriction. The loss of a right that results from not using it is called *laches.*

## 1 thought 1 owned it: Encroachments and adverse possession

The ultimate limitation on the use of your real estate is losing the use of it or, in some cases, actually losing ownership of it. Loss of use or ownership doesn't happen automatically. It requires a court's decision.

### Crossing into the neutral zone: Encroachment

An *encroachment* is the unauthorized or illegal use of someone's property by another person. On one hand, an encroachment sometimes happens by mistake, as in the case of someone building a garden shed a few feet over the property boundary line onto your property. On the other, it can also be intentional. Someone, for example, may build a house on your country property. Yes, that really happens.

As is usually the case with unauthorized use and claims against someone's property, ownership or use is lost only as a result of court action. In a case involving a disagreement over a boundary line, court action may be necessary to resolve the dispute. Tell that to those feuders, especially when one of them claims they have the automatic right to that tomato garden because they've been using it for ten years.

### Staking a claim: Adverse possession

*Adverse possession* is someone actually claiming ownership of your real estate because of how they're using it. Say your neighbor puts up a fence ten feet onto your property. It was a mistake. He knows it, and you know it, but neither of you does anything about it. Not a big deal you say. He'll just have more lawn to mow and you less. No problem, right? Maybe it is, or maybe it isn't. If the fence stays and your neighbor uses your ten feet of property as though it's his own for the required period of time set by the state, he can go to court and claim ownership of the property by adverse possession. And he may even win. (For more details about adverse possession and other ways of losing ownership of property, check out Chapter 10.)

One point to note about adverse possession if you're thinking of building a pool on the county property behind your house. Government land is usually protected from an individual claiming ownership or use because of adverse use of the government owned land.

# Land-Use Regulation: A Major Public Limitation

A state's power to limit the use of your property is based on something called *police power.* You may think of police power in the usual way — traffic tickets — and you'd be partially right. The police power that every state possesses is a general power to pass laws for the health, safety, and welfare of the citizens of that state.

Although each state government may keep some of the power to regulate land use for itself, most of it is passed down to local governments like towns, cities, and counties. As a result the police power is passed down by the state through *enabling laws* or *enabling legislation* that it adopts.

Police power is pretty broad, and most of it has nothing to do with real estate. In this section, I talk about the part of police power that limits the use of real estate.

## To the drawing board: Making master plans

Most municipalities (villages, towns, and cities) create what are called *master plans* or *comprehensive plans.* These are written documents, usually including many maps, that are compilations of studies of current physical layouts of the municipalities, projections of how their governments want their municipalities to look in the future, and descriptions of what needs to be done to accomplish those projections. A municipality conducts a number of studies in completing its master plan. A partial list of these studies includes

- **Capital facilities:** The municipality takes inventory and analyzes its publicly owned buildings and parks.
- **Demographics:** Population characteristics of the municipality, such as age and level of education, are studied. These studies rely heavily on census data gathered by the federal government, which divides the entire country into *census tracts* from which it gathers population statistics as part of the federal census every ten years.
- **Housing:** The municipality examines its current and future housing inventory and needs. This study includes public and privately owned housing.
- **Infrastructure:** *Infrastructure* refers to roads, sewers, water lines, and other physical facilities that are important to the growth of a municipality. This study looks at current facilities and the need for new construction and improvements of these support facilities.
- **Land use:** Areas of land within the municipality are examined, usually on a map, with respect to their primary use, such as housing, shopping, offices, industrial, and agricultural.

Based on these studies, and usually with citizen input, the municipality sets goals for its future and develops plans to achieve those goals. One of the primary ways by which a municipality implements its master plan is through the adoption of a zoning ordinance.

## You're in the zone: Understanding zoning ordinances

A *zoning ordinance,* which in some municipalities is called the *zoning code,* is a set of rules that control what property in the municipality can be used for and regulates where on the land any buildings will be located, the maximum height of the building, and the amount of land it can cover. The zoning code essentially tells you what you can build, where you can build it, and how much you can build, all by designating zoning districts and establishing specific regulations for each district. A zoning district is an area that's designated for a certain type of use — housing, shopping, and so on. Typically a zoning ordinance divides a community into different districts for residential use, commercial use, agricultural use, and industrial use. Several districts may be designated in each of these categories. For example, one residential district may permit high-rise apartment buildings while another may allow only single-family houses.

### But I really want to build a skyscraper: Variances in zoning

Most zoning ordinances recognize unusual circumstances that require a certain degree of flexibility in applying zoning regulations. A one-property variation from the requirements of the zoning ordinance is called a *variance.* Variances can be granted whenever an owner can prove that a practical difficulty or hardship will result in an attempt to build on the land or show that existing zoning will deprive him or her of all economic use of the land.

For example, a zoning ordinance requires that a building must be set back 50 feet from the front property boundary line, but because of a rock outcropping that extends deep into the land from the back of the lot, the 50-foot setback would be impractical. A variance may be granted, permitting the building to be built ten feet from the front boundary line rather than the required 50 feet. This type of variance is called an *area variance.* A *use variance,* on the other hand, permits a different use of the land. One example of a use variance is a house with two apartments in an area that's zoned for single-family houses.

A state-specific item for you to look into is what board or agency grants variances in your state. Names like board of zoning appeals, planning and zoning board, or zoning hearing board are common, but be sure to check it out. Remember that a board in one locale may be a commission in another. You can probably get this information from your local building or planning department.

### On one condition: Special-permit use

Another type of variation from the requirements of the zoning ordinance for an individual piece of property, in some places, is called a *special-permit use;* in other places, it's called a *conditional-use permit* and in some places it may be called a *special-use variance.*

In any event, these variations are for uses listed in the zoning ordinance that are different enough from the permitted use within a zoning district that they require special review by municipal agencies. A nursery school in a residential neighborhood is an example of a use that may be appropriate in a residential zoning district but is different enough to make an additional review a good idea. The municipality may want to require the nursery school to observe specific hours of operation or install special safety features before issuing the special-use permit. These permits generally are issued to a property owner and either run for the length of ownership or for a specified period of time with the ability to renew them.

### I was here first: Nonconforming uses

A *nonconforming use* refers to an established structure on or use of a piece of real estate that wouldn't otherwise be permitted under current zoning. Nonconforming uses generally are buildings or uses that existed either when no zoning ordinance was in effect at all or when an old zoning ordinance was in effect that allowed such buildings and uses.

Perhaps your grandfather built a factory at the edge of town at a time many years ago when the area had no zoning ordinance. The factory continues to operate, but in the meantime, the town grew, and a zoning ordinance was adopted that zoned the area around the factory for single-family houses.

Although the specific regulations dealing with nonconforming uses vary from one place to another, the factory probably would be allowed to continue to operate. Typical regulations require the removal of the factory if it's ever destroyed or closed for an extended period of time. The site of the factory probably wouldn't be allowed to expand or change into another nonconforming use.

### Parking the car . . . and your family, too: Accessory buildings and uses

Zoning ordinances sometimes allow accessory buildings and accessory uses on a piece of property.

- *Accessory buildings* are buildings separate from the main building on a property that support or are related to the main building. A detached garage and a pool house are examples.

- *Accessory uses* are uses that are related to but a little different from the principal use of the property. A separate apartment for a family member in a district zoned for single-family houses is an example of an accessory use. Accessory uses can be in the principal structure or in an accessory building.

# Many from one: Subdivisions

A *subdivision* is one piece of land that has been divided into two or more (sometimes many more) pieces of land. These individual pieces of property often are called *lots* or *parcels*. The purpose of subdividing is to allow for the sale of the smaller individual pieces of land. Most subdivisions are created for building homes, but commercial or industrial properties also may be subdivided.

Most levels of government that have control over land use adopt subdivision regulations or land-development ordinances. These regulations are different from the zoning ordinance or master plan but may be adopted or periodically revised along with those two documents. You may want to find out in your state who adopts and enforces subdivision regulations. I give you some important information about particular aspects of subdivisions that may be on an exam.

### Knowing the main players and plans in subdivisions

Subdivisions are created by *subdividers.* (And you thought this would be hard.) Subdividers generally never get their hands dirty. Most of their work deals with lawyers, engineers, surveyors and sometimes developers. After a subdivision is approved, subdividers can sell the entire subdivision to a developer or builder. A subdivider can also sell individual lots with the promise to eventually put in roads, sewers, and water lines.

A *developer* actually, well, develops the subdivision, making physical improvements to it by putting in roads, utility lines, and other infrastructure elements. A developer sometimes builds houses for sale or sells individual lots to builders or people who want to build a house. A developer sometimes buys an approved subdivision from a subdivider or can act as the subdivider, too.

As you see there can be some overlap in these definitions, but it's good to understand that different people can be involved in the subdivision process, taking it from raw land to finished houses.

The specific legal requirements of a subdivision vary from place to place, but a typical subdivision proposal is based on a plat map. That's not a misspelling. A *plat map* shows how the entire property is to be subdivided, or broken down into the individual lots, by showing the precise boundaries of each lot. The area that's being subdivided often is broken down into blocks and lots, or sections and lots. For example, an entire subdivision may be divided into five blocks, with each block being divided into ten lots. The total subdivision would be 50 lots.

Something that you need to check out in your state is whether it has a specific law dealing with subdivisions, what the requirements of the law are, and especially at what lot count the law takes effect. Some states, for example, may require that an offering plan with details about the subdivision be filed with the state government before any lots are sold. This requirement may be in effect only for subdivisions of more than a certain number of lots. This type of state requirement is in effect regardless of whether the local government has approved the subdivision.

### Following the rules: Subdivisions and zoning laws

A subdivision must adhere to local zoning laws. Zoning is explained in the "You're in the zone: Understanding zoning ordinances" section earlier in this chapter. Here's an example of how zoning relates to subdivisions: You have a 50-acre piece of property that you want to subdivide. The local zoning code says that the minimum lot size for each new house is one acre. Knowing that 10 percent of the land typically is used for roads — in this case five acres — you're able to design the lots to take the most advantage of the land and can divide the remaining property into 45 lots. That's exactly what you'd do in a straightforward simple subdivision.

To allow for more flexible design of subdivisions, some municipalities have adopted density-zoning and cluster-zoning ordinances.

- A *density-zoning* ordinance permits the same overall density within the subdivision, which means the same total number of lots on the same overall size property as allowed by the zoning ordinance. The sizes of the individual lots, however, may be smaller or larger than the minimum required size. In the example I gave you, you still can get only 45 lots out of the whole 50-acre subdivision, but each lot can be bigger or smaller than one acre. As long as the average lot size is one acre the density zoning ordinance permits flexibility of design, lot layout, and road layout. It may also save money by reducing road length and utility (water and sewer line) costs.

- *Cluster zoning* goes one step further than density zoning. It clusters or groups lots together in a relatively small area to preserve a certain portion of the property as open space. You may, for example, be able to cluster or group the lots in your subdivision into a total of only ten acres. That leaves 35 acres without any buildings. Once again, you won't be allowed to create more than 45 lots, but in addition to preserving open space, cluster zoning also makes for shorter roads and water and sewer lines, which, in turn, results in savings to the developer. In some places, cluster zoning also is known as *conservation zoning*.

### Crossing state lines for real estate purposes

In this section, the subject of interstate land sales becomes part of the discussion; however, strictly speaking, it isn't a regulation about how land is developed but rather how it is marketed when subdivisions and land sales are discussed. And yet, it's important enough that state test writers want you to know something about it.

Land in one state has been offered for sale to people in another state probably for as long as people and land have been together in this country. Unfortunately buying land sight unseen is risky. Although many perfectly honest dealers do business in what are called interstate land sales, unfortunately many people have been victims of fraud in these types of deals.

The *Interstate Land Sales Full Disclosure Act* was enacted in 1968 to minimize fraud and dishonest dealings in the interstate land sales market. The act is administered by the Department of Housing and Urban Development (HUD).

The requirements of the act apply to interstate sales of vacant, or undeveloped, lots in subdivisions of 25 lots or more. The act doesn't apply if the lots are 20 acres or larger. However, the act requires developers to file information with HUD describing details of the project, including but not limited to utilities, recreation facilities, location of nearby communities, and soil conditions.

# Building a house out of paper: Regulations for construction

You thought it took bricks and wood and nails and cement to build a house, right? It does, of course, but it also takes lots of paper. Building construction, residential (houses and apartments) and non-residential (pretty much everything else) alike, is regulated in most parts of the country. The regulations are in place to provide for safe and, in recent years, more energy-efficient construction.

A *building code* is a regulation that provides minimum standards relating to construction, electrical, plumbing, and safety materials and practices and energy-efficient items such as insulation. Building codes are adopted and administered at the local (village, town, city, and county) level.

In some states, the state government adopts a building code and then requires each local government to use that code or one that is stricter. You need to find out whether your state has a statewide code and how it applies to the local municipalities. In states that have an arrangement where the local government can adopt a stricter building code, this issue is a favorite question on the real estate exam.

The building code also provides details that govern the construction process, and that's where all the paper comes in.

## Getting that house built

Although the process may vary from one place to another, you'd typically follow these steps to build a house:

1. **Draft plans.**

   Plans are detailed drawings of the building that usually are prepared and completed by the licensed architect or professional engineer that you hire. They usually include *specifications or specs* that provide written details of certain features.

2. **File an application.**

   You submit the plans along with an application to the proper government agency, typically the building commissioner or inspector or code enforcement department.

3. **Review the plans.**

   The building department officials review your plans to make sure they comply with all the ordinances and regulations of the municipality.

4. **Issue a building permit.**

   The building department then issues you a building permit, and you now can officially begin construction.

5. **Conduct inspections.**

An official from the building department inspects your project at various points during construction. Some typical items that are inspected include the foundation, framing, insulation, and electrical and plumbing work.

6. **Undergo final inspection.**

A building official inspects the project when construction is complete.

7. **Issue a certificate of occupancy.**

When the building department is satisfied that you've completed the project in accordance with your plans and all the appropriate codes and regulations, it issues you a *certificate of occupancy,* often referred to as the *C of O,* which is important proof that you've properly completed the project. When construction involves internal modification of the house rather than all new construction a *certificate of completion or compliance* may be issued in some municipalities.

8. **Throw a party.**

Although not an official part of the process, I can tell you that after having gone through it a couple of times in my life, you definitely deserve a party.

### *Now a few words on construction regulations from your state*

Most states have regulations concerning development. Some states have more than others. In preparing for the exam, you're going to have to hunt around a bit in your home state to find out about your state's development regulations. Finding what state agencies play a part in controlling development, what the major laws are, and what issues both deal with, probably is enough; however, if you have to take a prelicensing course, pay special attention to the state agencies and laws they deal with. If you don't have to take a course, in addition to reading this book, just study the material the state gives you to prepare for the exam.

Possible development issues that your state may deal with include the following.

- ✔ **State roads:** Find out who controls whether you get permission to put in a new driveway off of a state road. Usually it will be your state department of transportation or highways.

- ✔ **Fire and electrical concerns:** Your state may have a special agency or department that deals with regulations for electrical and fire safety issues.

- ✔ **Environmental issues:** Some states have adopted regulations that require consideration of environmental issues in the development of land. Although adopted by the state, they may be administered at the local municipal level.

- ✔ **Historic preservation:** Preserving area history is another factor where states have adopted regulations but delegated authority to administer them or adopt more stringent ones to the local municipality.

# *The Government Has Its Say: Other Public Limitations on Property Use*

Government plays a major role in how land is used. I actually need to say *governments* because public limitations on land use exist at all levels of government: village, town, and city (usually referred to as municipalities), and county, state, and federal. Government regulations on land use can and do limit what you can do with your property.

However, other government limitations on real estate have to do with what you expect the government to do for you in terms of services and buildings. You expect the government to build roads, bridges, parks, schools, and many other infrastructure facilities. The government needs money and land to accomplish these things, so it places limitations on land use that include its rights to obtain the land and money that it needs to do these things.

Most local governments depend on property taxes to pay for their services like schools and road maintenance. Because land doesn't go anywhere, it is always there, is hard to hide, and unlike salaries, its value is fairly predictable from year to year. It provides a good, stable source of income for local governments.

In this section, I talk about general concepts of public limitations on how you can use your real estate. With the exception of federal rules and regulations, all other specific limitations and how they are applied and enforced vary by state and even by municipality. Fortunately, most of the exam questions asked about this topic are about the general stuff. I point out some of the things that you need to check on for your particular state that may be on the exam.

## *The city wants to build a library: Eminent domain*

*Eminent domain* is the right the government can exercise to obtain ownership of your real estate against your will. Before you get too upset, I need to clarify that the government always has the right, like any corporation or individual, to negotiate with you to buy your property. Conversely, you are free to turn down the government's offer the way you would in any sale of your real estate. In most cases the government prefers negotiating when it needs land for something as opposed to exercising its right of eminent domain.

The government uses its right of eminent domain when it must have your land, and you refuse to sell it voluntarily. It does this through a *suit of condemnation.* This process sometimes is called *taking.*

Because the government has the right to take ownership of your property through eminent domain, it also has the right to take less than full ownership or less than the entire property. So the government can take the front ten feet of your land to widen a highway but leave you the rest of the property, or it can take the right to install a sewer line under your backyard without actually obtaining the land itself. This type of limited right is called an easement, which I talk about in "Easing into easements" earlier in this chapter, and can be either an easement in gross or an easement appurtenant.

The government must meet these three requirements to be able to obtain a property through eminent domain:

- ✔ The ultimate use for the land must be for a legitimate public purpose. *Public purpose* may be to build a road or a park or install a sewer line, among other things.

- ✔ A fair price must be paid to the owner. The price usually is determined by an appraisal and sometimes is challenged by the property owner obtaining his own appraisal.

- ✔ The government must follow all required legal procedures, or in other words, exercise *due process.* The specific requirements of due process vary from state to state but may include certain mandatory notices to property owners, minimum time frames for owners to be notified, and environmental reviews before the eminent domain action can be taken.

People always can fight eminent domain proceedings in court either because they believe that the use is not a legitimate public purpose or because they believe due process was not followed. In addition, they can argue about the value of their property. In a related type of argument with the government, they also can pursue inverse condemnation. *Inverse condemnation* is where a landowner sues the government because of a loss in value that is the result of a government action. Building a sewage treatment plant can reduce the value of nearby properties, for example. Neighboring property owners may sue the government for payment of their property value losses or to force the government to buy their properties outright.

## You didn't know the government was part of your family: Escheat

*Escheat,* which literally means transfer, is the process by which the state obtains property from people who die without heirs and without a will. The legal term for dying without a will is *intestate.* This state right prevents property from being without an owner.

In case you're wondering, obtaining property by escheat isn't a significant way for the state to get the property it needs for various public works, and it has very little to do with your future real estate careers. The term, however, almost always is included in a list of government limitations on real estate use, and more important, often appears on state real estate exams.

## Pay or lose: Taxation

Taxation of real estate is such an important subject that it has its own chapter: Chapter 16.

Why it's mentioned here is because in most discussions of government limitations on the use of real estate, taxation is included. After all, it's the way most local governments (towns, villages, cities, and counties) raise money to provide public services and buildings, and if you don't pay your taxes, you lose your property through a process called *foreclosure,* the most limiting kind of restriction someone can put on your property.

# Review Questions and Answers

Questions on the subjects in this chapter tend to be focused on general knowledge and definitions. State examiners don't expect you to become zoning experts, for instance, but they do want to know that you know the difference between a use variance and an area variance.

1. Which of the following is false?

    (A) Liens are encumbrances.

    (B) All encumbrances are liens.

    (C) Easements are encumbrances.

    (D) Deed restrictions are a type of encumbrance.

    *Correct answer:* (B). Among the several different types of encumbrances are easements and deed restrictions. Liens also are one type. So all liens are encumbrances, but not all encumbrances are liens. Remember — this question is asking you to select the answer that is not true.

2. Which statement is true about real estate tax liens?

    (A) They take priority over all other liens.

    (B) They are paid according to when they were recorded.

    (C) They take priority over all liens except the mortgage.

    (D) They are the only types of liens that do not attach to the property.

    *Correct answer:* (A). Real estate tax liens come first when property is sold for payment, regardless of when they are filed. There's no logic to this answer except that the government makes the rules, so you'll just have to remember that.

3. A judgment lien is

    (A) voluntary and specific.

    (B) voluntary and general.

    (C) involuntary and specific.

    (D) involuntary and general.

    *Correct answer:* (D). It's involuntary, because you didn't want it, and it's general, because it covers all your real estate and can include your personal property. You agree to a voluntary lien. Specific liens only apply to one property.

4. Ann buys property that is landlocked. Betty agrees to let Ann drive across her property to get to the main road. Ann has

    (A) an easement in gross.

    (B) an easement by the entirety.

    (C) an easement by necessity.

    (D) an easement appurtenant.

    *Correct answer:* (D). An easement appurtenant benefits a neighboring property — in this case, Ann's property. An easement in gross benefits an individual. No such thing as an easement by the entirety even exists. An easement by necessity may be granted by the court whenever someone refuses to give an easement. In this case, Betty agreed to give Ann the easement.

    Something else you need to notice in the question is the use of the term "landlocked." Test writers expect that you to know that it means a property has no direct access to a road.

5. The loss of the right to enforce a deed restriction because of a failure to enforce that right within a specified time frame is called

    (A) statute of limitations.

    (B) laches.

    (C) restrictive covenant.

    (D) statute of frauds.

    *Correct answer:* (B). Statute of limitations usually applies to criminal prosecution and civil suits. Restrictive covenants are the basis for filing for an injunction. Statute of frauds is something I cover in Chapter 11.

6. The right of the government to take your real estate against your will is known as

    (A) escheat.

    (B) negotiation.

    (C) eminent domain.

    (D) zoning.

    *Correct answer:* (C). Eminent domain is the right of the government to take your property even if you don't want it to. Escheat is the government getting your property after you're dead. Negotiation is with your cooperation so it isn't against your will. Zoning limits the use of your property but does not give ownership to the government. The use of the word "take" in the question is typical when referring to eminent domain.

7. A detached garage on a house lot is an example of

   (A) an accessory use.

   (B) an accessory building.

   (C) a variance.

   (D) a special permit use.

   *Correct answer:* (B). Remember an accessory use supports the primary use on the property. The key is that the question asks about a building.

8. The plan showing the individual lots in a subdivision is called

   (A) the master plan.

   (B) the plat map.

   (C) the zoning plan.

   (D) the lot-and-block plan.

   *Correct answer:* (B). The possible confusing answer here is the lot-and-block plan, because you may remember that many subdivisions are divided into blocks and lots. But that isn't what the subdivision plan is called.

9. The term used to describe roads, sewers, water lines and other municipal service facilities is

   (A) utilities.

   (B) demographics.

   (C) accessory uses.

   (D) infrastructure.

   *Correct answer:* (D). Go back and look at your definitions. And remember that test writers expect you to understand words like municipal, which means governmental unit (usually local), and facilities, which can be almost anything that's physical but isn't movable.

10. What document do you check to determine the amount of insulation needed in a new house?

    (A) Zoning ordinance

    (B) Deed restriction

    (C) Building code

    (D) Subdivision regulations

    *Correct answer:* (C). Zoning ordinances tell you what you can build and where you can build it, but the building code tells you how it can be built. I imagine an energy-conscious person can put an insulation restriction in a deed but doing so is so unlikely that (B) wouldn't be the correct choice here. Subdivision regulations normally don't deal with building specifications.

# Chapter 9

# Transferring Ownership: Deeds and Title Closing

. . . . . . . . . . . . . . . . . . . . . . . . . . . . . . . . . . . . . . . . . . .

. . . . . . . . . . . . . . . . . . . . . . . . . . . . . . . . . . . . . . . . . . .

**Y**our job as a real estate agent all comes together when ownership of a piece of real estate goes from one person to another. You'll probably get paid only if ownership of the property is *transferred* as a result of a sale or an exchange. By the way, another term that means the same as transferred in real estate language is *conveyed*, and I use the two words interchangeably. From the real estate agent's perspective, after a deal has been reached, a few more steps still need to be taken by either or both the agent and attorneys to change ownership of the property from one person to another.

This chapter gives you important information about how ownership of property is transferred from one person to another. I talk about the documents that are needed, such as the deed, and how property is described so that no mistakes can be made about who owns what. And I discuss a process called title closing, where ownership of the property actually goes from one person to another.

*Title* in real estate terms means ownership. So rather than use the word ownership, most people in real estate work say things like "The title was conveyed on Tuesday" to indicate when ownership was transferred. Unlike with automobiles, the title is not a document. And as already mentioned, the words *convey* and *transfer* apply to ownership of a property moving from one person to another, regardless of circumstances. Whether you're talking about a gift, sale, or exchange, title is conveyed or transferred.

# Doing the Deed: Delving into Deed Basics

The *deed* is an extremely important piece of paper, a document that transfers title to a property from one person to another. It's important not only because it transfers title, but also because until you convey title to someone else, it serves as proof of your current ownership. It also serves as a permanent record of your ownership.

In this section, I give you information about what specific factors and terms must be included in a deed to make it valid, and I talk about some other language in the deed that can affect how you use the property and spell out some information about different types of deeds for you. This section also includes some information about how real estate is described so that no one can question who owns what.

## Making it right: Requirements for a valid deed

The requirements for a valid deed have been passed down through history by common practice and law so that no one can have any misunderstandings about

- ✔ What is happening when the title to a property is conveyed.
- ✔ Who owns the property now.
- ✔ To whom the property is being conveyed.
- ✔ What (exactly) is being conveyed in terms of the property boundaries.
- ✔ What rights are being transferred.

Because of the importance of establishing and proving property ownership, all states have adopted legislation called the statute of frauds. The *statute of frauds* requires that all real estate transfers of title be in writing. Depending on your state, and sometimes even where you happen to be within your state, attorneys are required to prepare deeds, the exact form of which may vary somewhat; however, the essential requirements for a deed, and therefore the conveyance, to be valid *are the same.* The requirements that follow are listed in the general order in which they appear in most deeds.

- ✔ **Grantor:** The *grantor* is the current owner of the property who is conveying the title to someone else. The grantor must be legally competent and of legal age. In most places, the minimum legal age of competence is 18, but you may want to check what it is in your state, though it's unlikely to be a specific test question. Remember the grantor can be selling the property, exchanging it, or giving it away. The grantor could be a corporation or multiple parties if it's a co-ownership situation.

- ✔ **Grantee:** The *grantee* is the person receiving title to the property. An important factor in naming the grantee in a deed is that the grantee be named in such a way as to avoid any confusion about who he or she is. So, if the grantee is John Smith III, then he better be named that way in the deed, especially if John Smith I and John Smith II are still around. Addresses for both grantor and grantee are also sometimes required. Grantees can also be corporations or multiple parties.

- ✔ **Consideration clause:** The deed must contain words that indicate that the grantor is receiving something of value in exchange for the property. Generally, money is being received, and the *consideration clause* needs to state the amount. In some places, the phrase "ten dollars and other valuable consideration" or something similar is used for the consideration. No, the buyer did not get a super bargain as some people might think. The reference to ten dollars is used to hide the actual amount paid for the property if someone wants to keep that information confidential. I show you how you may be able to find out what amount was actually paid in "Recording the right documents" later in this chapter. When the property is a gift, the words "for love and affection," or similar phrasing, are used.

- ✔ **Granting clause:** A *granting clause* states that the grantor is conveying ownership of the property to the grantee. In fact, the *granting clause* also is known as the *words of conveyance.* (In Chapter 6, I tell you what it is you really own when you own a piece of real estate.) The granting clause includes words that describe exactly what rights the grantee is receiving in the deed and whether the grantee is taking title to the property with another person.

- ✔ **Habendum clause:** The *habendum clause,* which contains the words "to have and to hold," further defines the rights being granted to the grantee. (For those of you who've already tied the knot, the habendum clause may sound a little like you're getting married again.) The words in the habendum clause must agree with the words in the granting clause.

The inclusion of a habendum clause may vary from state to state because it has to match the granting clause anyway.

✔ **Legal description:** I provide detailed information about different ways a property can be described in "Painting the right picture: Property descriptions in deeds" later in this chapter. For now, though, just think of the legal description in this section as wording that's designed to leave no doubt about the exact boundaries of the property being conveyed.

✔ **Exceptions and reservations:** In Chapter 8, I give you information about the limitations that can affect how the property is used through such things as deed restrictions and easements. This part of the deed is where those restrictions or limitations are described.

✔ **Grantor's signature:** The grantor must sign the deed for it to be valid. Usually, if more than one person owns a property, all the owners must sign. In some states a husband or wife who own property by themselves may have to have the spouse also sign the deed even though the spouse does not have title to the property. An attorney-in-fact can be permitted to sign the deed in most states. An *attorney-in-fact* is someone who is appointed by a power of attorney, which is a legal document signed by someone giving another person authority to act on his or her behalf, in this case to sign the deed. An attorney-in-fact doesn't necessarily have to be a lawyer. In some states, a third party must sign the deed stating that the grantor actually is the person who signed the deed.

If the grantor is a corporation, other rules may apply. A resolution by the corporate board of directors or the majority of the shareholders usually is necessary to convey property owned by a corporation. One or more duly authorized corporate officers must sign the deed. (See Chapter 7 for more about ownership by a business.)

✔ **Acknowledgment:** An *acknowledgment* is a way of proving that the person who signs a deed signed it voluntarily and is, in fact, who he says he is (or who she says she is). An acknowledgment normally is witnessed and attested to by a notary public, before whom you produce evidence of your identity and indicate that you're signing the deed of your own free will.

An acknowledgment technically is not required for a deed to be valid; however, in most states, a deed without an acknowledgment cannot be recorded in the official public records. You can find out more about recording a deed in "Recording the right documents" later in this chapter, but remember it is usually not necessary to record a deed for the transfer of title to be valid. It's an awfully good idea but not mandatory.

✔ **Delivery and acceptance:** The conveyance of title to a piece of real estate has not officially taken place until the grantor delivers the deed and the grantee accepts it. The term *passing title* refers to the acts of giving and receiving the deed. The date of the transfer of ownership is the date the deed was delivered and accepted. An exception to this timing in some places occurs when closing in escrow, which is discussed later in the section on "Closing in escrow." In that case, title passes when the deed is delivered to the escrow agent.

## *The deeds of the many: Examining various kinds of deeds*

I'm sure you hope that only one kind of deed exists, but alas, I'm sorry, real estate grasshopper, you must deal with several different kinds, at least for the exam. Different deeds serve different purposes, and although all convey ownership, they differ in the kinds of warranties or guarantees they provide for the grantee. Although not required for a deed to be valid, many deeds provide for different warranties made by the grantor to the new owner. The various types of deeds also may differ because of who the grantor of the property is and why the property is being conveyed. Ultimately, these factors are mostly the stuff lawyers revel in, but most states want their real estate agents to have at least a basic knowledge of the different types of deeds.

You should check out the most common types of deeds used in your state and find out whether they have names that are different than the ones I listed. You can get this information in your prelicense course, the textbook you use, and any handouts the instructor gives you. As you read this section for the exam, keep in mind that you usually can tell one type of deed from another by the different warranties provided and the different purposes for which the deeds are used. And state test writers expect you to know only the basic information. You may have plenty of questions that you need to ask your lawyer, but don't worry about them for the exam. I list the different types of deeds in the sections that follow.

Title insurance usually is purchased regardless of the kind of deed that's conveyed. Even when the grantee receives a general warranty deed with all the guarantees back to the first owner, title insurance assures the new owner that if a title problem ever comes up, the grantee will be protected and compensated. In addition, title insurance usually is required by the bank or lender, whenever you borrow money through a mortgage loan to buy the property. (For more, see "Proving marketable title" later in this chapter.)

### General warranty deed

*General warranty deeds,* which sometimes are called the full covenant and warranty deeds, provide the greatest protection and warranties by the grantor to the grantee. The warranties, which are usually called covenants, are listed here in the order in which they usually appear in the deed.

- **Covenant of seisin:** Would you believe that some people can't even agree on the spelling of this? So watch for seisin, too. *Seisin* is the guarantee that the grantor is the owner of the property and has the right to transfer ownership.

- **Covenant of quiet enjoyment:** No, this warranty doesn't mean that the grantor promises that your neighbor won't play the radio after 11 p.m. *Quiet enjoyment* means that the grantor guarantees that no one else can come along and claim ownership of the property. It also means that if a later party's title claim is found to be better than the owner's title, the grantor is liable and must compensate the grantee for any losses.

- **Covenant against encumbrances:** The grantor guarantees that the title to the property has no encumbrances like an easement or lien. Easements are rights that enable someone else to use some of the property, and liens are financial claims against the property. You can find out more about encumbrances in Chapter 8. The only exceptions to this warranty are encumbrances that are specifically stated in the deed.

- **Covenant of further assurance:** In this covenant, the grantor promises to obtain and provide documents necessary to clear up any problem that comes up with the title.

- **Covenant of warranty forever:** This assurance sometimes is referred to simply as warranty forever. The grantor guarantees to pay all costs to clear up any title problems at any time in the future.

A particular feature of a general warranty deed is that warranties cover any title problems that may have occurred during the ownerships of all past owners. The reason a general warranty deed provides the greatest title protection to the grantee is because this deed provides the most complete set of warranties and the grantor is responsible for all previous owners' actions with respect to title problems.

### Special warranty deed

*Special warranty deeds* contain only two warranties. The first is that the grantor has title to the property. The second is a guarantee that nothing was done to affect the title during the grantor's ownership, and if a problem did exist, the grantor will correct it. The differences then between a specific warranty deed and a general warranty deed are the number of warranties and the fact that the grantor takes responsibility for things that happened only during his ownership. In some states, the special warranty deed is known as a *bargain and sale deed with covenants against grantor's acts.*

Because of the limited warranties, people acting as third parties — that is, they don't actually own the property they are conveying — sometimes use special warranty deeds. The executor of an estate, for example, uses a special warranty deed to convey property belonging to an estate or trust.

### Grant deed

Grant deeds are used in a few states and provide limited warranties. The grantor guarantees that the property hasn't been conveyed to anyone else, that no encumbrances limit the use of the property except the ones specifically listed in the deed, and that if the grantor later obtains any other title to the property, it will be conveyed to the grantee. These guarantees are limited to the period of time the grantor owned the property. The grant deed is used in only a few states, but if yours is one, you need to remember this information.

### Bargain and sale deed

The distinguishing feature of this type of deed is that it has no warranties. That the grantor has full title to the property is implied. Essentially it gives no protection to the grantee. This type of deed sometimes is used in foreclosure and tax sales. You can read about foreclosure in Chapter 15. Warranties can be put into the deed to make it similar to the special warranty deed, and in that case, it's referred to as a bargain and sale deed with covenant against grantors acts.

### Quitclaim deed

The *quitclaim deed* provides no warranties to the grantee and gives no implication of how much or how good the grantor's title to the property is. It conveys to the grantee only that much ownership interest that the grantor may have. Quitclaim deeds often are used to clear up a cloud on the title. A *cloud on the title* is something that makes the title less than complete, like someone appearing to occupy the property without the owner's permission or indicates that some other ownership interest may exist, like two properties abutting a private road with both claiming ownership of the road. Quitclaim deeds sometimes are used for uncomplicated transfers of property ownership within a family.

### Trust and reconveyance deeds

A *trust deed,* which sometimes is called a *deed of trust* or *deed in trust,* is used to convey ownership by a *trustor* to a *trustee* for the benefit of a *beneficiary* as security for a debt. Here's an example: Party *A,* the trustor, borrows money from Party *B,* the lender, and then signs a trust deed conveying ownership of the property for which he borrowed money to Party *C,* the trustee, a third party. The lender is the beneficiary. If Party *A* pays all the borrowed money back to the lender, Party *C* then reconveys the property back to Party *A.* If Party *A* fails to repay the debt, Party *C* sells the property and gives the money to the lender to pay off the debt.

On a related note, a *reconveyance deed* is used to reconvey title to property from a trustee back to a trustor after a debt for which the property is security has been paid off.

### Trustee's deed

A *trustee's* deed is given by a trustee when ownership of property held by a trust is conveyed. Say, for example, that a young child owns property held in trust until he reaches legal age. The trustee of the trust can use a trustee's deed to convey that property to someone if the trust decides to sell the property.

### Court-ordered deeds

Deeds often are issued as a result of legal proceedings. An *executor's deed* in the case of a deceased person's estate and a *sheriff's deed* in the case of a sale of property seized by a local unit of government town or the bank are two examples of such court-ordered deeds. State law establishes these deeds, and state law governs their form. You probably won't find many questions on your state exam about this topic, but you need to check it out just in case.

# Painting the right picture: Property descriptions in deeds

Describing the boundary lines of a piece of land as accurately as possible in a deed is extremely important. Why this is so important is simple. When you get to the end of your land, you find yourself about to step onto someone else's land. Contrast that with owning a car. I know what my car looks like, and I know where I park it. No doubts exist about where the car begins and ends. Not so with real estate. (By the way, throughout this section I use the terms land, property, and real estate interchangeably.) Property descriptions of the kind we're talking about and the kind typically used in deeds are descriptions of the boundaries of the land but don't include any descriptions of the buildings on the land.

All property owners would want to know exactly what they own but it is especially important because many government land use regulations that govern what you can do with your property involve the size, shape, and boundary lines of the land. Read more about this in Chapter 8. Accurately describing your property is equally as important when transferring title from one person to another. The grantor needs to know exactly what he or she is selling, giving away, or exchanging, and the grantee needs to know exactly what he or she is getting. This property description usually is referred to as the *legal description of the property*. Legal descriptions are prepared in one of three standard ways that I describe in this section. A few math questions that relate to a property's description may be included on the exam. I also discuss the measurement of elevations for property descriptions and clue you in on two ways that you *can't* describe a property.

As you're going to see, three systems of preparing a legal description can be used anywhere in the United States. Some parts of the country rely more heavily on one system than others. Exam writers like to ask about all three systems regardless of what state you're in, but they probably emphasize the system used in your state. So study all three systems and especially your local system of legal description. No one is trying to turn you in to a *land surveyor*, the professional who surveys the property, locating the property boundaries on the ground and prepares these legal descriptions. Exam questions tend to be recognition type questions, the kind that require you to be able to tell the difference between the characteristics and key definitions of each system of legal description. But the questions can get a little more detailed. I go over this in the following sections.

## Meeting your boundaries: The metes and bounds system

The *metes and bounds system* of legal description uses specific locations, distances, and compass directions to describe the boundaries of a piece of property. Starting at what is known as the place or point of beginning, the description follows a line or curve in a specific direction for a precise distance to another point. At that point the direction changes and the boundary line is then laid out again in a specific direction for a precise distance.

A simple metes and bounds description might then read:

*From a place or point of beginning 100 feet North to a point then East 100 feet to a point then South 100 feet to a point then West 100 to the place or point of beginning.*

For fun, try drawing this description with pencil and paper. Remember that when laying out a property like this, as you face the paper, north is up, south is down, east is to the right, and west is to the left. What you end up drawing is a square. In reality, metes and bounds descriptions usually are not so simple. The directions often are broken down into degrees, minutes, and seconds, which all are precise points on a compass. The distances sometimes are measured down to inches.

Turning points especially in older descriptions of the boundary lines often refer to natural features like a rock or a stream. Sometimes the boundary of someone else's property is used as a reference. But property owners change, rocks move, and streams dry up. Over time natural and ownership references have been replaced by artificial markers placed permanently in the ground or simply by points known to the surveyor. Sometimes marking only the place or point of beginning is sufficient rather than marking every turning point. The term *monument* describes any point in the surveyed boundary that is noted on the survey. Monuments, which usually are turning points, can be man-made or natural.

The metes-and-bounds description is clearly stated in the deed. On a large property, with a boundary that features many twists and turns, a metes-and-bounds description can be lengthy. The description also can be used to draw a map referred to as a survey map or simply survey. A *survey* is the actual determination of a property's boundaries on the ground. A *survey map* or *sketch* is a representation or drawing of the property's boundaries, sometimes showing structures that are situated on the property.

The metes and bounds system of describing property boundaries is the oldest property description system in the United States. It remains the primary way of describing property boundaries in the eastern part of the country, particularly in the states that formed the original 13 colonies.

### *You're so square . . . more or less: The rectangular survey system*

The *rectangular survey system,* often referred to as the *government survey system,* is based on a system of lines that form rectangles and squares throughout the United States. The first sets of lines respectively are called *principal meridians,* which run north and south, and *baselines,* which run east and west. The principal meridians and baselines are based respectively on lines of longitude and latitude. Just in case you were out the same day I was in high school, longitude and latitude are imaginary lines that divide the earth through the north and south poles (longitude) and run parallel with the equator (latitude). Principal meridians, baselines, and where they intersect (cross each other) are used as the basis for formulating property descriptions in this system. They are the starting points for describing a property's boundaries. The following is a list of helpful terms:

- **Quadrangles:** The basic squares of land of the rectangular survey system, *quadrangles* (also *government checks,* or just *checks*) are 24 miles square (that means each side is 24 miles long) and are delineated by a principal meridian and a baseline. Quadrangles have an area of 576 square miles, more or less, and are divided into 16 townships.

- **Townships:** The divisions of a quadrangle, *townships,* are six miles square (six miles on each side) and are delineated by township lines. Townships have an area of 36 square miles, more or less, and are each further divided into 36 sections.

- **Sections:** The divisions of a township, *sections,* are one mile square and have an area of one square mile, or 640 acres. Sections can be divided in several ways, but basically for purposes of the United States Geological Survey (USGS), they are divided in quarter sections.

- **Quarter sections:** The divisions of a section, *quarter sections* are formed by dividing a section into fourths that are delineated by their direction from the center of the section (northwest — NW, northeast — NE, southeast — SE, and southwest — SW). Quarter sections have an area of 160 acres.

- **Half sections:** *Half section* is a description of any two abutting quarter sections within a section, usually accompanied by a directional notation indicating the half of the section in which the two quarter sections are located. Half sections have an area of 320 acres. So there can be the north, south, east, or west half section.

Because of the curvature of the earth, the lines in the government survey system are only theoretically straight. Imagine trying to draw straight lines on a rubber ball. Although the lines start out the same distance apart, they get closer together as you get near one or the other end of the ball. *Correction lines* and *guide meridians* were established to correct this problem in the government survey system. Correction lines occur at every *fourth township line* or every 24 miles north and south of the baseline. The guide meridians occur every 24 miles east and west of the principal meridian. An area bounded on two sides by guide meridians and on the other two sides by correction lines is called a *government check, check,* or *quadrangle,* which is 24 miles square, meaning each of its boundaries is 24 miles long. A government check represents an area that measures 576 square miles. Remember that although these correction lines and guide meridians are the way the government deals with the issue of the earth's curvature, it isn't the way the government survey system describes land. In reality, because of this earth curvature issue, many sections and townships vary from their exact area measurements. A system of *fractional sections* and *government lots* are parts of standard practice to account for these discrepancies.

So how does the system describe land? Using principal meridians and baselines as points of reference, land areas are divided by two kinds of lines, township lines and range lines. *Township lines,* which run east and west, parallel to baselines, are horizontal parallel lines that form township tiers. Think about two lines running from left to right across this page about an inch apart. The *range lines* run north and south parallel to the principal meridians. These range lines form ranges. Think about two more lines running up and down the page on top of the first two lines, also about an inch apart. You got it. Tic tac toe. Where the two range lines and two township lines intersect, they form a township. Now the way it really works is for the this page to be filled with the lines going up and down and right to left so you have many townships. The township is the basic unit of measurement in the rectangular survey system. The area created by the intersection of a township line and a range line is a township The townships are consecutively numbered by their location within the intersection of multiple range lines and township lines. The boundary of each township is six miles long so a township contains 36 square miles and is described as being 6 miles square. These townships are not the same as political subdivisions.

Each *township* is further divided into 36 sections of one square mile each, or 640 acres, by horizontal and vertical section lines. Sections also are numbered consecutively. Section one within any township is always located at the upper right or northeast corner of the township. The numbering then moves from right to left across that first upper tier. The numbering continues directly beneath the sixth section, except that it progresses from left to right on the second tier. The numbering changes directions in the third tier from right to left — see Figure 9-1. In other words, after section number 6, it drops down to 7 on the next tier then goes left to right to number 12. Then the numbering drops down to 13 and goes right to left again and so forth.

Each section of 640 acres can be divided into halves and quarters called, get this, half sections and quarter sections. These divisions mean just that, for instance a quarter section always contains 160 acres, or a fourth of the total 640 acres in a section. See Figure 9-2. Specific directional references are needed in the actual description to locate a particular piece of property but for finding out how large a particular piece of property is, only the fractions matter.

|  | 6 | 5 | 4 | 3 | 2 | 1 |
|---|---|---|---|---|---|---|
| **Figure 9-1:** | 7 | 8 | 9 | 10 | 11 | 12 |
| Townships are divided | 18 | 17 | 16 | 15 | 14 | 13 |
| into 36 sections | 19 | 20 | 21 | 22 | 23 | 24 |
| numbered consecu- | 30 | 29 | 28 | 27 | 26 | 25 |
| tively. | 31 | 32 | 33 | 34 | 35 | 36 |

**Various Divisions of a Section**
5,280 feet = 1 mile

| | |
|---|---|
| NW 1/4<br>**160 acres** | NW 1/4<br>of NE 1/4<br>**40 acres**    NE 1/4<br>of NE 1/4<br>**40 acres**<br><br>SW 1/4<br>of NE 1/4<br>**40 acres**    SE 1/4<br>of NE 1/4<br>**40 acres** |

N 1/2 of SW 1/4
**80 acres**

S 1/2 of SW 1/4
**80 acres**

W 1/2 of SE 1/4
**80 acres**

E 1/2 of SE 1/4
**80 acres**

5,280 feet = 1 mile

1 section = 640 acres

**Figure 9-2:** Sections can be divided in a variety of ways, including quarters and smaller sections.

Each half or quarter section can be further subdivided into halves and quarters. So you can refer to the south (S) ½ of the northwest (NW) ¼ of a section in a township, for example (see Figure 9-3 for a variety of divisions in a quarter section). Figuring out the size of that piece of property, which sometimes is called a parcel, is simple, if you keep in mind that you're always dealing with a section of 640 acres. Putting the above description into words is half of a quarter section. Doing the math, it's ½ × ¼ × 640 = 80 acres.

# School days

When a township was laid out into sections, the town fathers and mothers wanted to make sure land would be available for public purposes, in particular, schools. You know how mothers and fathers are when it comes to their kid's education. Well, anyway, Section 16, a little north and west of the township's center (refer to Figure 9-1) was designated for school use. Parents thought its central location made getting to school a little easier for students. If any income was derived from the land in Section 16, such as lumber sales or rents, those fees went to support the school. Section 16 of the townships, therefore, became known as the school section.

**Various Divisions of the NW Quarter Section**
2,640 feet = 1/2 mile

| | | |
|---|---|---|
| N 1/2 of NW 1/4 of NW 1/4 **20 acres** | NW 1/4 of NE 1/4 of NW 1/4 **10 acres** | NE 1/4 of NE 1/4 of NW 1/4 **10 acres** |
| S 1/2 of NW 1/4 of NW 1/4 **20 acres** | SW 1/4 of NE 1/4 of NW 1/4 **10 acres** | SE 1/4 of NE 1/4 of NW 1/4 **10 acres** |
| W 1/2 of SW 1/4 of NW 1/4 **20 acres** | E 1/2 of SW 1/4 of NW 1/4 **20 acres** | SE 1/4 of NW 1/4 **40 acres** |

2,640 feet = 1/2 mile

1/4 section = 160 acres

**Figure 9-3:** A quarter section can be split into smaller parts.

A full rectangular survey system property description might read:

> The SW ¼ of the NE ¼ of the NW ¼ of Section 6, Township 4 South, Range 5 East of the Third Principal Meridian. (This description refers to a 10-acre parcel of land.)

The description probably would include the state and county in which the property is located and use abbreviations so in the example Township 4 South would be T4S. Whenever properties have irregular boundaries, the land may be further described using one of the two other systems described in this section.

You're likely to see at least a few questions on calculating the area of a part of section, and you'll also see questions about terminology and some of the measurements that the rectangular survey system uses. You may even see a question or two about the numbering system used for sections. I've included samples of these types of questions in the review questions at the end of the chapter as well as in the practice exams at the end of the book. Because the rectangular or government survey system was instituted when the United States was a brand new country, it was used to describe most of the land west of the original 13 colonies, so most of you are likely to see some questions about this system.

### Block party: The lot and block system

The last of the methods for preparing legal property descriptions is known by various names, including the *lot and block system, the recorded plat system, the recorded map system, the lot block tract system, the recorded survey system,* and *the filed map system.* You can find out the name commonly used in your area when you take your prelicensing course. Regardless of which name you use, the essentials are the same, and it's the system that's usually used in conjunction with a new subdivision, or a large piece of property that has been divided into smaller pieces usually to sell or develop separately. A *map* or *plat* or sometimes *plat map* (they are all the same — don't you wish these guys could agree on what to call things?) of the subdivision is created, showing the boundaries of each (usually numbered) lot or parcel of land. If the subdivision is large, it may be divided into blocks or sections, each of which is then divided into lots. For example, you can have Lot 2 in Block 1 or Lot 5 in Section A. In a very large subdivision you might see all three terms used, with the subdivision first divided into sections; then the sections divided into blocks and then the blocks divided into lots. Each lot has a metes and bounds description on it (see "Meeting your boundaries: The metes and bounds system," earlier in the chapter). This method is the only way a surveyor can look at the map and lay out the boundaries of the property on the actual property. So in reality, the lot and block system is a hybrid that makes use of another system.

After the surveyor draws the map, it must be filed in the local records office. The map is usually filed by the property owner, attorney, or surveyor. If the map were of a new subdivision, the subdivision would already have been approved by local zoning, planning, or other government officials. The records office goes by various names in different states and locales, but it generally is part of county or local government. The map is filed in the county (or municipality in at least one state) where the property is located and is kept on file as a public record. The filer is given a record of the filing that includes the filing date and may be marked with a specific reference number given to the map that refers to the document, what type of document it is, the book (sometimes called *liber,* which is Latin for book) in which it's kept, and the page number. This reference number helps anyone who wants to locate the map in the records office.

Now how does this work to provide a legal description, say to convey a property? Here's an example. Buyer *A* wants to buy Lot 3 in Block 2 of the subdivision I've been talking about, which by the way happens to be named Mary's Subdivision after the subdivision developer's s daughter. (Don't laugh! That sort of thing goes on more than you'd think.) So now the developer has a deed prepared that includes a property description that reads something like "Lot 3, Block 2, on the final plat of Mary's Subdivision, filed in the Office of Land Records of Washington County (State), as plat map number 12345, filed on May 15, 2004." Slight variations may occur in these descriptions, but you get the idea. All deed descriptions always refer back to that recorded plat map.

If you've been following this explanation, you may have figured something out. Because the lot and block system and the metes and bounds system are used all across the country, if the property you're describing is located in a part of the country that also uses the rectangular survey system, and the property is being subdivided into several lots, you can end up with a description that refers to the rectangular survey description and the filed map. And the filed map, which is prepared using the lot and block system, also includes metes and bounds descriptions of each lot in the subdivision written right on the map of the subdivision, even though the deed would use the lot and block number to describe the property.

### Taking it up (or down) a notch: Measuring elevations

In surveying work and in preparing property descriptions, measuring or describing space as up in the air or describing an area below the ground surface for subsurface rights sometimes is necessary. As a property owner, you can sell or lease your *air rights,* or the airspace over your land or building. (For more about air and other ownership rights, see Chapter 6.)

*Datum* is a point, line, or surface from which elevations are measured. An *elevation* is a vertical measurement either up or down. Datum for the entire United States is defined by the USGS as the mean sea level in New York harbor. Individual cities, however, may establish their own datum.

*Benchmarks* are permanent markers established by the federal government to aid surveyors in their work. They exist throughout the United States. Benchmarks are known reference points from which surveyors can work to establish property boundary lines. They are used primarily for ground level locations of distances and directions for property lines, but they're also used together with a datum to measure elevations, for example, to do a condominium description.

### Don't do that! Illegal ways to describe property

Some of the things you can't use to describe real estate from a legal point of view are:

- **The property's address:** The address is not considered an adequate description for a property from a legal perspective or for use in a deed. For one thing, it doesn't specify the boundaries of the land, and for another, in many areas, vacant parcels of land in particular, don't have addresses. Addresses are used and are acceptable for documents like leases, in which a precise description of the land is not necessary.

- **The tax assessor's parcel number:** Because many assessors use a system of identifying properties that looks similar to the recorded plat map system, tax assessor's lot, block, section, and parcel numbers can be confusing. An assessor's parcel numbers, however, can change from time to time and therefore they don't provide consistency over time. The maps sometimes contain property sizes and general boundary measurements but don't usually have detailed boundary descriptions of the likes that a metes and bounds description provides. (For more about tax assessment, see Chapter 16.)

# Getting Closure: Title Closing

*Title closing* is a point in time during a real estate transaction when all of the business of transferring ownership of a piece of property is finished and title to the property is conveyed by the grantor to the grantee. Title closing can be either a relatively simple process or extremely complicated. Complications often crop up because of problems with the title to the property. In the world of real estate brokerage, problems at closing can be the result of something so trivial as the owner of the property not mowing the lawn just before the closing. This section is not about those kinds of problems. Instead, it's about issues that can occur with the title to the property.

This section deals with activities that take place before, during, and after the closing. Closings generally are similar from one state to the next, with the exception of places that close the title in escrow. Other subtle differences may exist regarding who pays for what in terms of various fees associated with the closing, so you need to look for any major differences between the typical closing process that I describe in this section and your particular state's practices. In addition I point out specific situations that are likely to be different from state to state.

## Nearing the finish line: Before the closing

Let me give you a timeline here to put this section in perspective. Typically after all of the looking and talking and negotiation, when a buyer and seller agree on all the terms of the sale, especially price, they sign a sales contract. Essentially the seller (grantor) agrees to sell the property at a certain price to the buyer (grantee). (For more about sales contracts and other types of contracts, see Chapter 11.) A number of things happen between the time the sales contract is signed and the day of closing title when transfer of ownership of the property actually takes place. Activities after the contract is signed but before closing usually have to do with satisfying the terms and conditions of the contract and any terms and conditions the lender may set, whenever a mortgage is involved in the transaction. One main thing that occurs during the period between contract signing and closing is the *title search,* which is a look at the records of title transfers between previous grantors and grantees to determine whether any prior claims are on the title to the property.

### Proving marketable title

A typical real estate sales contract requires the seller to convey *marketable title* to the buyer, which means that the title must be free from any reasonable doubts as to who the owner is and free from any defect in title itself. The objective of establishing a marketable title is to prove that no clouds are impeding clear title to the property. A *cloud* on the title is something that casts doubts on the grantor's ownership of the property. Although strictly speaking, it doesn't constitute a cloud on the title; clear title has been expanded to mean no problems such as illegal structures or unpermitted improvements to the property. The different ways the grantor may prove marketable title vary by state and may even vary by area within a state. Check out what your state's common practice is. In general, though, proof of good title can be accomplished in several different ways. Here are descriptions of the four most common ways:

- ✔ **Abstract of title:** An *abstract of title* is a report of what was found in a title search, which is a search of essentially all public records related to the property's title, such as previous deeds and liens. (You can read about liens in Chapter 8.) These records are usually found in the county recorder's office or land records office of the county in which the property is located. Although anyone can search the public records, during a title search, an *abstractor* (someone who searches through title records) or attorney researches the chain or history of the title from one owner to the next, looking for gaps in ownership or other factors that appear to cast doubt on the validity of the current owner's claim to the property. The abstract of title then is given to the buyer's attorney to examine. When the buyer's attorney is satisfied that the seller has marketable title, and issues an *attorney's opinion of title,* the closing can proceed. Although you won't be doing a title search, these are public records and as such can be examined by anyone. Some expertise is needed to look for title issues in the deeds and related filings — like liens — but you can look through previous ownership of the property simply by working backwards from the current owner. Smith, the current owner, is the grantee from Jones the grantor. But one deed back, Jones becomes the grantee from the previous owner and backwards in time you go.

- ✔ **Certificate of title:** A certificate of title is similar to an attorney's opinion of title and may even be prepared by an attorney. It also can be prepared by a title company or an *abstractor,* the person who actually prepares the abstract. The certificate of title is an opinion about the validity of the title but not a guarantee of title. In this way, the certificate of title is similar to the abstract and attorney's opinion of title, because it doesn't protect against ownership claims that may not be in the public record. In issuing a certificate of title, an attorney examines the public records but no abstract of title is prepared.

- ✔ **Title insurance:** *Title insurance* can be purchased on its own or as a supplement to an attorney's opinion of title or a certificate of title. Normally issued after a title search, title insurance provides protection for the buyer, defending the new owner if any future claim is made against title to the property. In many cases where a mortgage loan is involved, the lender requires a title policy that at least covers the lender's portion of the purchase price. This coverage is called a *lender's* or *mortgagee's policy.* The owner may want to obtain an *owner's policy* to cover his or her interest in the property.

  Title insurance covers various defects according to the laws of the state in which the company issues the policy. The American Land Title Association sets standards for *standard* and *extended coverage.* Standard coverage policies insure against things like forged documents, improperly delivered deeds, and incompetent grantors. The standard policy is based on what is found in the public record. The extended-coverage policy, in addition to the coverage in the standard policy, insures against defects that may be found by an inspection of the property, such as someone claiming ownership or rights in the property by virtue of their use. (For more about adverse possession, see Chapter 10.)

A title company may pay the owner of the property on a claim and then pursue action for damages against some other party. Through the right of *subrogation,* the title company is entitled to the same rights as the person it insures, which means that after it pays the owner, the title company can then pursue whoever may be responsible for the title problem, say a prior owner, collect, and keep the money it gets.

✓ **Torrens system:** *The Torrens system* is based on proper registration of the title. An abstract of title and a lawsuit to quiet title, which is where you can go to court to have the court declare that you have clear title to property, are filed with the appropriate authority or office, such as the county court clerk. If approved, a certificate of clear title, called a Torrens certificate or Torrens certificate of title is issued by the court, which unlike the attorney's opinion or an abstractor's certificate of title, is considered to be proof of ownership. The Torrens system gradually is falling out of use in the United States, but some states or areas within states still use it. (Make sure to find out whether your state is one of them.)

### Removing liens

The removal of liens is another activity that takes place before closing. As part of a title search, the title company determines whether the property is subject to any liens. Liens, which are discussed in Chapter 8, are financial claims against the property. The owner/seller customarily removes all liens from the property prior to sale but under some circumstances the buyer may pay off the lien. If a lien isn't removed or satisfied through payment before the closing date, liens usually must be paid off at closing with proceeds the seller receives from the buyer.

### Examining encumbrances

Title searches also make note of any other encumbrances on the property. Encumbrances, which are discussed in Chapter 8, are limitations on the owner's use of property. They include liens but also can be an easement or a deed restriction (also covered in Chapter 8). Generally the buyer accepts ownership of the property subject to these encumbrances. They normally don't present a problem with the title to the property.

### Meeting the conditions of the sales contract

This chapter is about transferring title and all the things that affect that transaction. Although most contract conditions (such as obtaining a mortgage or having a home inspection done) don't normally affect title, note that before closing, the buyer completes all the conditions that have been put into the sales contract. So, if a sales contract has been signed and indicates that a mortgage loan has to be obtained and a home inspection by a home inspector or other professional must be completed, the buyer is responsible for completing these activities prior to closing. By the way, neither of these things is mandatory nor must they be put in the contract. You can pay cash for a house (well maybe you can but I can't) and you don't have to have it inspected. Immediately prior to closing — usually that day or the day before — the buyer personally inspects the property. The agent selling the property or the agent working with the buyer often conducts this walk-through.

## The big day: At the closing

When the big day finally arrives, the buyer, seller, attorneys, and you, the agent, meet to close on the title to the property. By the end of the day, the seller has some money and the buyer owns some property. The people who come to a closing, the roles they play, and the specific activities and papers that are signed vary greatly from state to state and even from area to area within a state. I discuss the people, roles, activities, and documentation that are most important and common, because they are what exam writers like to ask questions about.

### RESPA

*The Real Estate Settlement and Procedures Act* (*RESPA*) has to do with closing on the mortgage, which happens at the closing, and simply means signing all the paperwork necessary for the bank to give you, the borrower/buyer, the money that you don't have for very long because you give it to the seller, and for you to give them the mortgage. You can find out everything you need to know about mortgages in Chapter 15.

RESPA is a federal law designed to protect consumers who borrow money through a federally related mortgage loan (loans that are sold on the secondary mortgage market, which you can check out in Chapter 15) to buy residential properties, including condominiums and cooperative apartments. Although some of the activities required by RESPA take place before the closing, the requirements specifically impact the closing, particularly the preparation of the closing statement, so I include the discussion of RESPA here. RESPA is administered by the U.S. Department of Housing and Urban Development. RESPA's four distinct requirements are:

- ✓ **Required reading:** The HUD booklet *Buying Your Home: Settlement Costs and Helpful Information* must be given to anyone applying for a mortgage loan.

- ✓ **Estimated costs:** The lender must give the borrower a good-faith estimate of all settlement costs, or the costs associated with the closing.

- ✓ **HUD Form 1 preparation (closing/settlement statement):** When the mortgage loan closes, which is usually at the same time the title to the property is closed, a settlement statement or closing statement of costs must be prepared. The settlement statement must be prepared on a form known as HUD Form 1, which also is called the HUD Uniform Settlement Statement.

- ✓ **Prohibited kickbacks:** RESPA prohibits kickbacks. A *kickback* is an unearned fee. For example: A home inspector who pays a fee to a lender for recommending him to perform home inspections for one of the bank's customers is accepting a kickback. RESPA forbids such actions.

### Allocating expenses with proration

*Proration* is the allocation of certain expenses between the buyer and the seller. A variety of costs are associated with buying and selling a piece of property. The principal cost is, of course, the purchase price paid by the buyer to the seller for the property. Part of the settlement at closing is accounting for all the costs and fees in addition to the purchase price, making sure they are paid, and allocating them appropriately to the buyer or seller. In some states the attorneys or a representative of the title company (sometimes called a *closer*) handle this accounting; in others, it falls to the real estate agent. No matter where you are, you need to know something about this.

Two accounting words that you need to know when pondering the closing statement are credit and debit.

- ✓ A *credit* is an amount owed to the buyer or seller or something for which they've already paid. For example, the purchase price of the property always is a credit to the seller, who is owed that money (and a debit to the buyer — see the next bullet point). The down payment, on the other hand, is a credit to the buyer (here, here), who already has paid it. Remember when the buyer paid a deposit (earnest money) at the contract signing, long before the closing. A credit essentially is a financial transaction that's in someone's favor.

- ✓ A *debit,* on the other hand is a financial transaction that is not in your favor, in the case of a real estate transaction, something that the buyer or seller owes. So the purchase price of the house is a debit to the buyer, because he owes it to the seller. If encumbered by an existing mortgage loan on the property, the seller must pay off the mortgage at the closing. So it's a debit to the seller, but of course not a credit to the buyer because it's paid to a third party, that being the bank.

Various fees and charges differ from state to state in several ways. Even local differences exist as far as what fees are owed, the amounts charged, and whether the buyer or seller is responsible. Although I can't guarantee it, you probably won't see any questions on specific fees or charges. But just in case, I give you this list of the most common ones so you have some points of reference for getting the additional information you need.

- ✔ Attorney's fees
- ✔ Appraisal fee
- ✔ Broker's commission
- ✔ Loan fees
- ✔ Recording fees
- ✔ Survey fees
- ✔ Tax and insurance reserves
- ✔ Title expenses
- ✔ Transfer tax

Although this list is fairly complete, your state may have specific fees that are required or a particular transaction may involve additional fees. The fees and charges are accounted for within the closing statement as debits and credits according to who pays and who is owed.

Two types of payments and costs that are allocated between the buyer and seller at closing are either accrued items or prepaid items.

- ✔ An *accrued item* is one that is owed by the seller but is paid by the buyer. Real estate taxes that are paid in arrears (after) is an example of an accrued item. The seller lives in a house where real estate taxes are due December 31 for the entire previous year, a situation in which the taxes are being paid in arrears. The seller transfers title to the house on June 30 but has paid no taxes yet for that year, even though the seller has the benefit of living in the house for six months. The buyer has to pay the full year's taxes on December 31, but has lived in the house for only six months. Not fair you say. And you're right. The taxes are a prorated item at the closing, meaning the seller and the buyer have to share the costs and payments according to who paid and who used the property. In this case, the seller who used the house for six months owes the buyer money, because the buyer is going to pay the taxes for the entire year but only lived there six months.

- ✔ A *prepaid* item is one that the seller has paid but from which the buyer benefits. I reverse the tax example that I just gave you. Suppose that taxes are paid in advance, such that the Seller pays a full year of taxes for the coming year on January 1 but sells the property on June 30. Having paid a full year's taxes, the seller nevertheless has enjoyed the benefit of living in the house for only six months. The buyer, on the other hand, has paid no taxes for that year, yet lives in the house for six months. Not fair, again; proration to the rescue. This time the buyer owes the seller money.

In many places, real estate agents either calculate prorations or help attorneys or title companies with the calculations. In other places, attorneys or title companies handle the whole thing. Whatever the particular practice in your area, you'll probably see some questions about proration on the state exam. I take you through examples of an accrued item and a prepaid item, starting with the simple tax example that I've been using with one slight change. (For more proration math practice, check out Chapter 18.)

The way costs are divided up varies from state to state. In the following problems, I use the most common method, a 12-month year and a 30-day month. In some cases, a calendar with the actual day count is used, so the annual tax would be divided by 365 and multiplied by the exact number of days. Ownership of the property on the day of closing is assumed to belong to the seller in most places, but it may vary according to local custom. You'll want to check that out in your state. Unless your state does something different, or unless you're given specific instructions in a problem, use the 12-month year, 30-day month method and assume the seller owns the property on the day of closing.

### Accrued item example

Note that I use complete dates (year included) in these examples so that there's no doubt about what I'm talking about. It's unlikely that test writers will do the same.

The annual real estate taxes on a property are due each year on December 31 in arrears (for the year just ending). In this case, the date is December 31, 2015. The property is sold on June 1 of that year (June 1, 2015). The taxes are $1,200. Who owes what to whom?

First of all, you know that the taxes are paid for the entire year, or annually, in one payment. Then you know that they're paid in arrears, which means use it first and pay after (at the end of the year). You also know that the seller owned the property during the first five months of the year and the buyer owns the property for the last seven months of the year. Aha! I may have caught you on that one. Look again at the closing date. The math is pretty straightforward.

$1,200 ÷ 12 = $100 per month taxes

$100 × 5 months that the seller owns the property = $500

$100 × 7 months that the buyer owns the property = $700

Because the buyer owns the property on December 31, 2015, and therefore has to pay the full $1,200 in taxes for the entire year (all of 2015), the seller owes the buyer $500 for the period of time the seller lived in the house. Therefore, the $500 is a credit to the buyer and a debit to the seller. This appears in the closing statement. The $700 is not included in the closing statement, because it doesn't accrue until after the closing, when it becomes a debt of the buyer who of course has to pay it ($700) plus the $500 to the city for taxes for the whole year.

### Prepaid item example

Taxes on a property are paid in advance of the year for which they are effective, due on January 1 of that same year. In this case, the date is January 1, 2015. The property closes on August 17, 2015. Taxes are $3,600 a year. The seller will be charged for the day of closing. Who owes what to whom?

This problem tells you that the taxes are paid once a year at the beginning of the year for the whole year ahead. That year of use of the property is divided between the buyer and the seller, who share the tax payments, yet the seller (current owner — before closing) already has paid taxes for the full year.

$3,600 ÷ 12 months = $300 per month taxes

$300 ÷ 30 days = $10 per day taxes

$300 × 4 months = $1,200

$10 × 13 days = $130

$1,200 + $130 = $1,330 due to the seller by the buyer

This amount is a seller credit and a buyer debit.

Look at a couple of the steps in this problem closely. The four months that you multiply the $300 by are the four months (September, October, November, December) that the buyer will own the house. The 13 days is likewise the part of the month of August that the buyer will own the house (remember that I used the 12-month year, 30-day month method). So the buyer owns the property for four months, 13 days and needs to pay the seller the share of the taxes for that period of time.

Not all prepaid items have to be divided up. For example, a home heated with oil often has fuel left in the tank when the house is sold. For example, suppose 300 gallons of oil were purchased and paid for by the seller sometime before the closing, and the seller has used some of the oil he paid for. The remaining oil is essentially sold to the buyer, who of course will use the rest of it after she moves in. In this example, the cost of the remaining oil in the tank will be calculated and will become a debit to the buyer. There is no credit to the seller because he already used a portion of what he paid for. Similarly, in rental properties, security deposits, which in reality belong to the tenants but are held by the landlord/seller in trust, are turned over to the buyer.

### Passing title

At some point after the buyer and seller sign their names on a variety of documents, the seller (unless he's done it already) signs the deed, which is given to the buyer or more likely the buyer's attorney. Although some things have yet to happen after the closing, title, meaning ownership of the property, is conveyed when the buyer accepts the deed.

### Closing in escrow

A process that's common in some states is called *closing in escrow,* and it involves using a third party, sometimes called an escrow agent, to gather all the documents necessary for the closing and then forward them and money (as is appropriate) to all the parties involved. Sellers provide, among other things, a deed, evidence of title, information necessary for either paying off or assuming an existing mortgage, and any other documents necessary to provide a marketable title clear of all defects, encumbrances, and liens. The buyer provides funds for the purchase, mortgage loan documents if any are required, and hazard or other necessary insurance policies.

Escrow agents may be attorneys or representatives of a title or an escrow company. Real estate brokers can offer escrow services but not in transactions in which they're directly involved.

### State specific

You should find out if your state is one where closing in escrow is typical. If so, you may want to learn who can be an escrow agent, what the requirements might be, and any other information that might make for a test question or two.

## A little paperwork: After the closing

A few things take place after the closing. Although ownership of the property changed from seller to buyer at the closing, the final closing statement needs to be prepared and a variety of documents need to be recorded.

### Preparing the final closing statement

A preliminary closing statement, sometimes called a settlement statement, usually is prepared ahead of time. Until the closing is complete and final costs are allocated, the final settlement statement cannot be prepared. The most common form of closing statement for residential properties is the HUD Form 1 Uniform Settlement Statement, which is prepared at or just after closing. Copies of the statement are sent to the buyer and seller along with many other necessary documents. Closing statements can be prepared by anyone with all the appropriate information, but typically the buyer's or seller's attorneys or the title company prepares the closing statement. It's primarily a financial document stating who owes what to whom and who has already given over money that will be distributed (typically deposit money paid when the contract was signed and being held by an attorney or real estate broker).

### Recording the right documents

The act of recording the transaction documents is the final step in the closing process. The documents are recorded at the appropriate government office that is designated for this purpose. Documentation of real estate transactions usually takes place at the county level, meaning you file documents in the county where the property is located. You need to find out the name of the office or department where deeds and other such documents are filed in your location. Typically, the title company files the documents but it could also be handled by one of the attorneys or anyone else connected with the transaction, for that matter.

All documents relating to an interest in real estate need to be filed. Deeds, mortgages, liens, long-term leases (usually more than a year), and easements are typical documents that are recorded. The act of recording provides what is called constructive notice to the public. *Constructive notice* provides an opportunity for anyone who's interested to research the records. These public records provide parties who have an interest in the property in some way — brokers, attorneys, abstractors, and the public — an opportunity to investigate the ownership of the property and possible encumbrances on the title.

Recording usually involves payment of a fee, or sometimes two, usually for the act of recording itself. Perhaps a dollar a page or some other amount is charged for actually processing the document. In addition, the recording office may also be the office to which the state and sometimes local transfer taxes are paid. This state transfer tax is mentioned in the list of possible closing costs in "Allocating expenses with proration," earlier in this chapter.

You definitely want to find out whether your state charges a transfer tax on real estate transfers and/or a mortgage recording tax and how much they are (particularly the real estate transfer tax). These taxes usually are based on the sale price of the property or the amount of the mortgage loan. In some cases, states have created surcharges for high-value property sales. Local municipalities, on occasion, also have created their own transfer tax.

Be prepared for a math question or two on the subject of recording. I take you through a couple of samples.

Say, for example, the deed transfer tax in your state is $2 per $500 of the sale price, meaning that for every $500 increment of the sale price you pay a $2 tax on the transfer. So if the sale price of the property were $1,000, you'd pay $4 in transfer taxes. But if the sale price of the property were $255,000, how much is the transfer tax?

> **Answer:** $255,000 ÷ $500 = 510
>
> 510 × $2 = $1,020 transfer tax

*Note:* The number 510 is just that, a number and not a dollar amount. It's the number of times the unit of $500 is contained in $255,000.

Many deeds don't state the amount of consideration. They may state the price of the property as "$10 and other valuable consideration." No, you don't get to pay the transfer tax on the $10. You have to pay it on the total amount, and that leads to a neat trick you can use when you want to know what your brother-in-law paid for his house, but he won't tell you. Take a look at the next problem, which is the reverse of the earlier example. I'll do an obvious example first just to show you where I'm going.

If you look up the transfer tax paid on a piece of property and find out it was $2, then based on the transfer tax rate that I've been using ($2 per $500 of value), the value of the property is $500.

So you go to the county clerk's office and find the deed to your brother-in-law's property, and although it doesn't tell you how much he paid for it, you can find out that he paid $1,020 in transfer tax. The amount of transfer tax paid usually is a matter of public record and often is noted on either the deed or an attached document. Because you know the transfer tax rate is $2 per $500 of the sale price, you can calculate what he paid for the property.

$1,020 ÷ $2 = 510

510 × $500 = $255,000 sale price of the property

You see, all you did was find out how many units of $2 are contained in the $1,020 total transfer tax that was paid, and because each unit of $2 represents $500 of the sale price, the final step is to multiply.

If a mortgage is being assumed, that is, the buyer takes over the existing mortgage of the seller, the amount of the mortgage balance may be subtracted from the sale price of the property when calculating transfer taxes. So in the earlier examples, if you assumed a mortgage with a $100,000 balance, you'd only pay transfer taxes on the remaining $155,000 in some jurisdictions.

# Review Questions and Answers

Most of the questions you'll see regarding this topic on an exam are definitional or fact-based. The examiners, at the very least, want to make sure you understand what various terms mean. This is especially true for the salesperson's exam. At the broker's level, you may have to wrestle with short cases that require an understanding and application of the material. However, even handling those types of questions starts with a basic understanding of what the terms mean.

1. Typical wording in the habendum clause would be

   (A) "I hereby grant."

   (B) "In witness whereof."

   (C) "To have and to hold."

   (D) "$10.00 and other valuable consideration."

   *Correct answer:* (C). "I hereby grant," "In witness whereof," and "$10.00 and other valuable consideration" are other parts of a deed, but "to have and to hold" is typical language for the habendum clause.

2. The law that requires that a deed be in writing is called

   (A) the statute of frauds.

   (B) the tort reform act.

   (C) the acknowledgment law.

   (D) RESPA.

   *Correct answer:* (A). The tort reform act has to do with civil suits. I made up the acknowledgment law. And RESPA has to do with federal requirements for closing title.

3. Whose signature is required for a deed to be valid?

    (A) Grantor

    (B) Grantee

    (C) Both grantor and grantee

    (D) Notary public

    *Correct answer:* (A). The grantee must be named in the deed but does not have to sign. So that makes (B) and (C) wrong. A notary public witnesses the acknowledgment. The acknowledgment is not required for a valid deed, only for the deed to be recorded.

4. What is the most likely explanation when you see the words "for love and affection" as the consideration in a deed?

    (A) The grantor and grantee are related.

    (B) The grantor and grantee want to keep the actual selling price of the property a secret.

    (C) The grantor and grantee were represented by the same real estate agent.

    (D) The grantee gave the grantor the property as a gift.

    *Correct answer:* (D). The relationship of the grantor and grantee wouldn't matter because it still can be a sale. If they wanted to keep the price a secret, they probably would use "ten dollars and other valuable consideration." The nature of the representation in answer C doesn't affect the deed.

5. The guarantee of the grantor's ownership of the property is called the covenant of

    (A) quiet enjoyment.

    (B) warranty forever.

    (C) further assurance.

    (D) seisin.

    *Correct answer:* (D). You need to be able to describe each of the covenants in a sentence so that you can pick out the correct answer in a question like this. If it helps, remember that seize (the root of seisin) means to take hold of something.

6. A deed conveying title to property from a trust is called a

    (A) deed of trust.

    (B) deed in trust.

    (C) trust deed.

    (D) trustee's deed.

    *Correct answer:* (D). The first three answers have to do with using a deed to convey an interest in the property as security for a debt. Tough question.

7. The area of a section is

    (A) 43,560 square feet.

    (B) 80 acres.

    (C) 160 acres.

    (D) 640 acres.

    *Correct answer:* (D). 43,560 square feet is the area in square feet of one acre (a useful number to know). 80 acres and 160 acres are portions of a section.

8. Which section is bounded on four sides by sections 10, 14, 16, and 22?

    (A) 9

    (B) 15

    (C) 17

    (D) 13

    *Correct answer:* (B). A pretty standard exam question is locating a section within a township. If you read this question and then looked at Figure 9-1 earlier in the chapter, you cheated, because you won't have that kind of crutch on an exam. Exam writers expect you to be able to lay out a township grid with all the sections properly numbered. Remember that every section is numbered the same way.

9. A title free from any defects is a good definition of

    (A) equitable title.

    (B) marketable title.

    (C) certified title.

    (D) insured title.

    *Correct answer:* (B). You can find out about equitable title in Chapter 11. Certified title and insured title are close. A title usually is not certified or insured unless it's clear of defects. But the definition of title clear of defects is marketable title.

10. What type of notice is provided by the recording of a deed in the public records?

    (A) Actual

    (B) Inquiry

    (C) Constructive

    (D) Real

    *Correct answer:* (C). Constructive notice is provided by recording the deed. Actual and inquiry are types of notice. Real is not.

# Chapter 10

# Giving Up or Losing Property

**In This Chapter**

▶ Checking out ways of giving up your property voluntarily

▶ Discovering how others (including nature) can take away your property

▶ Understanding what happens to your property after you die

*I*n addition to simply selling it to someone who wants to buy it, property can be conveyed or transferred voluntarily through a number of means. Property can also be lost involuntarily through the forces of nature, law, or the government. And finally, in fact very finally, property is usually transferred after you die.

In this chapter, I discuss a number of the more common ways that property can be conveyed and lost involuntarily. In your real estate practice, you may never encounter or be involved with most of these issues. They do, however, involve real estate, and, as a real estate agent, you need to know something about them. Equally as important, state exam writers expect you to know something about the various ways property can be transferred or lost.

# Fine by Me: Giving Up Property Voluntarily

Most of the time, *title* to property, or the ownership of it, is conveyed or transferred voluntarily from one owner to another, which is a transaction formally known as *voluntary alienation*. Among the ways this kind of transfer can be accomplished are dedications, gifts, public grants, and sales. I explain these methods in the sections that follow. Exam questions tend to be definitional, using short cases to get the right answers out of you.

## All for the government: Dedication

*Dedication* is a term used for a specific type of voluntary transfer of property from an individual to the government. You may well ask why anyone would want to voluntarily give their property to the government. Dedication typically refers to the process by which a developer transfers ownership of the lands that are needed for roads, sewers, waterlines, and other utilities to the government as part of a land development. A person who subdivides a large piece of property into smaller residential lots for sale may build the roads as the individual lots are sold. At some point, the developer turns over title to the government, creating a public street. Dedications may also include easements that the municipality may need, such as for getting to a drainage ditch for maintenance. (Check out Chapter 8 for more about easements.) Individual property owners (as opposed to developers) can also dedicate land to a municipality, such as land for a road to allow access to a town park.

Governments vary in the way they view and treat this type of dedication. They often decide how to deal with dedications on a project-by-project basis. A local government may require a subdivision street to be dedicated, but prefer the internal roads of a condominium development to remain privately owned so it (the government) is not responsible for maintenance.

Although not technically viewed as a gift (see the next section), generally no consideration, or thing of value, is given by the government in return for the dedicated land.

## From me to you: Gifts

You know what a gift is, right? Think about Christmas and your birthday. Property can be conveyed simply by giving it to someone. A deed is executed to convey title, but the main difference in a gift situation (as opposed to a sale) is that no money or other thing of value, usually called the *consideration*, is exchanged for the property. In all other respects, the conveyance by deed is the same. I discuss deeds in Chapter 9.

## A treat from Uncle Sam: Public grants

*Public grants* — sometimes simply called *grants* — are transfers of property in which the government gives a piece of property to someone. In years past, when the federal government wanted to settle a new part of the country, it simply gave grants of land to people who agreed to settle in that location. Some of your ancestors may have received grants, or else you may be living on a piece of property that once was part of a public grant.

## The usual way: Sales

Representing someone in the sale or purchase of a property is, of course, where you make your money as a real estate agent. A sale typically involves a *grantor* (the person selling the property), a *grantee* (the person buying the property), and a *deed* (the document that transfers title). I discuss the requirements for a valid deed and different types of deeds in Chapter 9.

One important concept in a deed for a sale of property is the consideration. The exchange of money or something else of value in exchange for the property characterizes a conveyance of property as a sale rather than something else, such as a gift.

# By Force: Losing Property Involuntarily

Sometimes your property can be taken against your wishes, or for some other reason it can be lost. These types of situations generally are known as *involuntary alienation*. I go over the principal forms of involuntary alienation — adverse possession, avulsion and erosion, eminent domain, foreclosure, forfeiture, and partition — in this section. Questions on involuntary alienation will most likely be definitional, so remember the chief characteristics of each of the forms.

## It's really mine: Adverse possession

*Adverse possession* is the loss of your property or some rights to your property because of continued use by someone else. The original owner can lose complete title (ownership) to the property or only a right to use part of the property, such as an easement called a *prescriptive easement* or *easement by prescription*.

The basic premise of adverse possession is that someone other than the owner uses a piece of property openly, publicly, and without the owner's consent for a specified period of time. The conditions necessary to claim ownership under adverse possession are

- ✔ **Actual possession:** To gain possession, someone has to occupy the property.

- ✔ **Adverse possession:** Someone usurps the real owner's rights of ownership.

- ✔ **Claim of ownership:** Someone lays claim to the property.

- ✔ **Continuous use:** Someone uses the property without interruption.

- ✔ **Hostile:** Someone claims the property after using it without the owner's consent.

- ✔ **Notorious:** Someone exerts possession that isn't in secret but rather is well known to other people.

- ✔ **Open:** Someone's use of the property is visible and obvious to anyone viewing the property.

In addition, anyone who claims title by adverse possession must do everything required by law during a specified period of time, and laws governing adverse possession vary from one state to the next. When calculating the length of time someone other than the owner uses the property to claim adverse possession, a concept known as tacking comes into play. *Tacking* is the ability of a party claiming possession to count or accumulate the necessary amount of the time of possession during the ownerships of more than one owner. Say, for example, that three different people each occupy a property for six years each in an adverse possession situation. If the state in which the property is located requires a minimum of 15 years occupancy to claim title to the property, the adversary claiming ownership rights can rely on adverse use taking place during the previous occupants' ownerships to accumulate the required 15 years.

Check out the length of time of continuous use that your state requires for someone to claim title by adverse possession. Although I don't claim to know the specific law in every state, among the ones I do know, the time requirements for adverse possession can range from as little as 3 years up to 30 years. Individual states may also have variations on the requirements for adverse possession that I listed. It's unlikely that you'll be tested on anything very specific other than the number of years required. But if you're ever involved in an adverse possession situation it would be useful to research your state laws.

Being awarded title through a claim of adverse possession is not automatic. The person claiming title must file a *lawsuit* or otherwise initiate *an action to quiet title* in court. If the quiet title action is successful, the person is awarded title to the property.

An easement by prescription may also be claimed through an adverse use of a property. For example, someone driving over a part of your property every day for the statutory period of time can eventually claim the right to drive across your property forever. If successful in a legal action, that person can be awarded an easement, which is the right to use the property in a specific way as opposed to complete ownership. See Chapter 8 for details on easements.

And just in case you have your eye on a few feet of that park behind your house, most states have rules exempting government lands from adverse possession.

## *You can't fight nature: Avulsion and erosion*

Mother Nature definitely is a powerful force, even in the world of real estate. She can take away your land in a couple of different ways:

- ✔ *Avulsion,* or the sudden loss of land, can occur by natural processes. Earthquakes, landslides, and mudslides are examples of natural forces that can remove land involuntarily.

- ✔ *Erosion* is the loss of land through a gradual process. The wearing away of land by the action of a river or ocean is an example of erosion.

The opposite of losing land by natural processes is *accretion,* or gaining land by natural forces. One form of accretion describes gaining property by the natural action of water. Sand added to a beach or soil deposited by a river are examples otherwise known as *alluvium* or *alluvion* and is sometimes described as alluvial soils.

## We need that, please: Eminent domain

*Eminent domain* is the taking of land against your wishes by the government or other public agency, such as a public water district, or certain private corporations, such as utility companies, for public purposes. In addition to the requirement that the land be used for a public purpose, the owner of the property must receive fair compensation, and the authority taking possession must follow due process, or the prescribed legal requirements necessary to take the property. I discuss eminent domain as a control on land use in Chapter 8.

## Deep in debt: Foreclosures

*Foreclosure* is losing your property involuntarily to pay a debt. The most common types of foreclosure are the result of unpaid mortgage loans or unpaid property taxes. Failing to pay back borrowed money or taxes in a timely manner can result in a foreclosure. The lender or community to whom the debt is owed initiates foreclosure proceedings in court. These proceedings enable the lender or local unit of government to sell the property and collect the unpaid debt from the proceeds of the sale. In most places, homeowners' associations also have a right to foreclose on a property because of unpaid association dues or common charges. I discuss foreclosures that result from unpaid mortgage loans in Chapter 15. I cover the sale of property for unpaid taxes in Chapter 16.

## Ignoring the rules: Forfeiture

You also can lose title to your property by disobeying some condition of the deed, such as using the property for something the deed forbids or not using it for the purpose required in the deed. For example, I've seen properties that were donated to municipalities for use as parks returned to their donors for failure to abide by the deed. Conditions limiting the use of the property can also be written into the deed. If the municipality ever uses the property for any other purpose, the person who donated the property (or that person's family or estate) can demand through a court action that the property be returned.

## Making the split: Partitioning

*Partitioning* is a legal proceeding that is undertaken to divide a single piece of property that is owned in shares (in undivided ownership) by two or more people. (For more about the concept of undivided ownership, see Chapter 7.)

Two people who together own one piece of property with two vacation homes is a good example. One owner wants to rent out both units and the other wants to use the units. If the pair cannot agree on how to use the property or how to divide it, one can file a partition proceeding, asking the court to physically divide the property so that each party can own a piece of it. If for some reason the property can't be divided, the court may order the parties to sell the property and divide the proceeds from the sale proportionally according to the respective interests in the property of the two owners.

# Losing Property Very Involuntarily: Passing Title After Passing Away

You may well wonder why the subject of wills and passing title to property after death is a subject that state examiners want you to know something about. After all, wills and estates are subjects better left to attorneys and the courts, right? Although that is true, real estate agents often are called in to help sell a property that's left in someone's estate. Familiarity with some of the terminology and issues that can arise is important. Exam questions focus on very basic information about wills laws of descent or inheritance, and probate.

## Where there's a will, there are heirs and relatives

A *will* is a document that determines how a deceased person's real property (real estate and the rights that go with it) and personal property (items not permanently attached to real estate) are to be distributed after death. The person for whom the will is drafted is called a *testator*. Up to the time of death, the testator can dispose of property even if it's mentioned in the will. A will takes effect only after death. Anyone who receives title to real estate through a will is known as a *devisee;* the gift of real property is called a *devise*. An addition or change to an existing will made by the person for whom the will was written is a *codicil*.

## Where there's no will, there still may be heirs and relatives: Laws of descent

When someone dies without a will *(intestate),* he or she may still have *heirs,* or people who are entitled to inherit assets from the estate. Someone who dies with a will has died *testate*.

A good way to remember the difference between "testate" and "intestate" is that "with" is a shorter word than "without," and "testate" is a shorter word than "intestate." Someone who died with a will died testate, and someone who died without a will died intestate.

Every state has *laws of descent, a statute of descent,* or sometimes a *law of descent and distribution* covering the distribution of the assets of estates when the deceased has no will. Spouses, children, and possibly other relatives are entitled to a portion of the assets of the estate by virtue of their relationship to the deceased. If your state exam requires you to know about the subject of involuntary loss of property, check out the laws of descent in your state. If your state specifically wants you to know something about the laws of descent, make sure you at least understand the basics of who would get what from an estate if there's no will.

When people die without a will and without heirs, the state can claim the assets of the estates by something called *escheat*. For more about escheat, check out Chapter 8.

## The court has its say: Probate

*Probate* is the process of making sure that a will is legal and valid, the deceased's wishes are carried out, and the assets actually are in the estate. In the case of someone who dies intestate, the court determines who inherits the assets of the estate based on the laws of descent (see the previous section). Both processes take place in surrogate's court which is sometimes referred to as *probate court*.

An analogy that may help you remember the name of surrogate's court is that of a surrogate mother, who simply is someone standing in for the real mother. Surrogate's court means the court stands in place of the deceased.

During probate proceedings, the court appoints an *executor* of the estate to carry out the actual distribution of the assets. The executor usually is named in the will. The laws of individual states govern probate proceedings. Generally probate takes place in the county where the deceased person lived and may take place in the county where he or she owned property if different than the county of residence.

# Review Questions and Answers

The language of involuntary loss of property is pretty universal and general from one state to the next, but the specific requirements may not be. For example, all states acknowledge the concept of adverse possession, or claiming the right of title to someone else's property because of continuous use, but each state uses different time frames for it to take effect.

The review questions in this section focus on the more general knowledge that is applicable in every state. So you need to check out the details in your own state before taking the exam.

1. The law governing how heirs inherit property when the deceased has no will is called the law of

   (A) descent.

   (B) devise.

   (C) testate.

   (D) escheat.

   *Correct answer:* (A). You may have wanted to choose escheat. Remember escheat applies only when the deceased dies with no will and no heirs. Devise is real property that's inherited, and testate is when someone dies with a will.

2. By which of the following can you not lose title to your property involuntarily?

   (A) Adverse possession

   (B) Foreclosure

   (C) Dedication

   (D) Avulsion

   *Correct answer:* (C). Dedication is voluntarily giving property to the government. The other answers are ways of losing your property involuntarily; you can brush up on those methods by reviewing "By Force: Losing Property Involuntarily," earlier in this chapter. Be careful of questions like this that have a double negative. You might try restating the question to yourself, eliminating one of the negatives; in this case "By which of the following can you lose the title to your property involuntarily." Whichever answers fit that statement are all the wrong answers.

3. Mary crosses Joe's property for a number of years as she drives into her driveway. Mary sells to Alice, who continues to do the same thing. Alice sells to Barbara, who does it for a few more years and finally claims the right to do so by adverse possession. Barbara may have accumulated enough years to claim adverse possession by what concept?

    (A) Accretion

    (B) Encroachment

    (C) Notorious use

    (D) Tacking

    *Correct answer:* (D). Notorious use is one of the requirements for claiming adverse possession, but the accumulation of the required period of use by successive people is called tacking. Accretion is adding soil to your land by natural action. Encroachment is the unauthorized or illegal use of someone's property by another person (see Chapter 8).

4. Joe and Sam jointly own an apartment building. They can't agree on anything, including how to dissolve their partnership. Joe finally files a suit for

    (A) avulsion.

    (B) eviction.

    (C) escheat.

    (D) partition.

    *Correct answer:* (D). Partition is a court action to divide a single property that is owned by two or more people in shares. Avulsion is loss of land caused by a sudden act of nature like an earthquake. Eviction is the action of a landlord to remove a tenant (see Chapter 12). Escheat is when the state gets your property because you die without a will and without heirs.

5. The process by which a will is validated is called

    (A) surrogacy.

    (B) execution.

    (C) validation.

    (D) probate.

    *Correct answer:* (D). Surrogacy may confuse you because probate takes place in surrogates court. Validation is, of course a real word but has no meaning in this context. Execution in real estate terms usually refers to signing a document like a contract.

6. You subdivide some land for a residential development. You want to give the streets to the town. You do so by

    (A) descent.

    (B) dedication.

    (C) avulsion.

    (D) divestiture.

    *Correct answer:* (B). Dedication is giving land voluntarily to the government. Descent refers to a state's laws of inheritance. Avulsion is the sudden loss of land caused by natural processes. Divestiture is a general business term meaning to get rid of in some way.

7. The right of the city to take private property for a public use is called

   (A) foreclosure.

   (B) dedication.

   (C) eminent domain.

   (D) escheat.

   *Correct answer:* (C). Eminent domain is the right of a municipality to take property against the wishes of the owner. Dedication is a when a person voluntarily gives property to a municipality. Foreclosure is when a bank or a municipality takes your property for nonpayment of a mortgage or taxes respectively. Escheat is when the state gets your property because you die without a will and without heirs.

8. The person for whom a will is prepared is known as

   (A) the grantor.

   (B) the administrator.

   (C) the executor.

   (D) the testator.

   *Correct answer:* (D). The word "testator" is related to the word "testate," which means to die with a will. A grantor is a living person who conveys property to another. An administrator usually is appointed by a court to handle someone's property, as in the case of someone who may be declared mentally incompetent. An executor is appointed by the court to handle someone's estate after he dies.

9. The gradual wearing away of land by the forces of nature is called

   (A) avulsion.

   (B) accretion.

   (C) erosion.

   (D) alluvium.

   *Correct answer:* (C). Avulsion almost is the same thing as erosion, only it's a sudden loss of land, not a gradual one. Accretion and alluvium have to do with the accumulation of soil or sand by natural forces like a river.

10. Harry has a new grandson a year after he writes his will and wants to leave him a special gift. To make this change to the will, he most likely executes

   (A) a new will.

   (B) a codicil.

   (C) a devisement.

   (D) a descent.

   *Correct answer:* (B). There's a fine point here. Harry could execute a new will, but clearly the change to the existing will is a small one, which is exactly what a codicil is for. Devisement is related to devise, which is real property left to someone in a will. Laws of descent govern how property is distributed to heirs when there is no will.

# Part IV
# A House Is Made of Lots of Paper: Legal and Physical Issues

## Top Five Kinds of Real Estate Contracts

✔ Listing agreements are between an agent and a property seller.

✔ Buyer agency agreements are formed between an agent and someone who wants to purchase a property.

✔ Sales contracts indicate a buyer's and a seller's agreement to exchange property for (usually) money.

✔ Land contracts may be used to purchase property without immediately paying the full price and without obtaining a mortgage.

✔ Leases are a form of a real estate contract that gives someone exclusive use of a property for a period of time for a fee; they must contain all the elements of a valid contract.

Learn about the importance of getting everything in writing in the article "Contracts 101" at www.dummies.com/extras/realestatelicenseexams.

# In this part . . .

- ✔ With so many different legal issues connected with the sale and purchase of a property, I walk you through some basics about the types of contracts you're likely to use. I also explain how a contract is discharged and what happens when the terms of a contract aren't completed.

- ✔ Negotiating a contract is part of a realtor's job, and you examine how a contract is created and executed.

- ✔ You may never handle a lease property, but the exam requires that you have a basic understanding of leasing. I offer information about the requirements of a typical lease agreement, the different types of leases, and some ways people break leases.

- ✔ I give you an overview of some of the environmental government regulations and issues as well as the environmental effects of building property developments from waste to water.

# Chapter 11

# Contracts 101

· · · · · · · · · · · · · · · · · · · · · · · · · · · · · · · · · · · · · · · · · · · · · · · · · ·

· · · · · · · · · · · · · · · · · · · · · · · · · · · · · · · · · · · · · · · · · · · · · · · · · ·

*W*hen you agree to represent a buyer or seller as an agent, you and your client sign a contract for your services. After that, your hard work brings the buyer and seller together to sign a contract of sale. I said "signs" and "brings," not "might sign" or "could bring," because I know you're going to be a great success as a real estate agent.

A lease also is a contract, and in the real estate business you deal with a couple of other kinds of contractual agreements.

Negotiating, understanding, and in some cases, preparing contracts are important parts of your job as a real estate agent. State exam writers expect you to have some knowledge of contracts in general and specific knowledge about different types of real estate contracts.

In this chapter, I walk you through some basic information about contracts (including elements that make a contract valid). I also tell you about specific types of real estate contracts and give you some information about how a contract is discharged and what happens when the terms of a contract are not completed.

# Agreeing to Do Something: The Basics of Making a Contract

People agree to do things all the time. I agree to pay the bill in a restaurant. Someone else agrees to pay the kids to shovel the snow off the driveway. You agree to represent someone as an agent. And, of course, a buyer agrees to buy a seller's house. All of these agreements are contracts.

A *contract* is an agreement either to do or not to do something. The agreement must be made voluntarily by legally competent parties, have some form of legal payment (consideration) as part of the agreement, be about doing or not doing some legal act, and be enforceable.

In this section, I tell you about different ways that contracts can be created and give information on the elements of a valid contract. Although this section is about contracts in general, rather than real estate contracts in particular, remember that state real estate exam writers like to know that you know at least some basic information about contracts.

# Exploring how a contract is created

A contract can be created in a number of ways, which usually are defined by the actions of each party to the contract. And a contract may fit into more than one of the following categories. Pay particular attention to the contract examples in the list that follows, so that you can distinguish among the different ways a contract may be created. There are usually at least a few questions on the exam that require you to distinguish among the different types of contracts.

- An *express contract* is created when parties to the contract (the participants) clearly state in words what they agree to do or not do. The parties clearly *express* their intentions. An express contract may be either oral or in writing. Mr. Buyer agrees in writing to buy Mrs. Seller's house for $300,000. Mrs. Seller agrees to sell for that amount. This is an express written contract. Real estate sales contracts and (usually) leases for periods over a year must be in writing to be valid. On the other hand, you agree to represent a couple as the agent to sell their house, and they agree to pay you a percentage of the sale price when you sell the property. You have no written document of the arrangement, only your oral agreement. Foolish? Probably. After all, your money's on the line. And some states don't allow you to enforce an oral listing agreement when trying to collect the fee. But it's legal nonetheless — you have an express oral contract to act as the seller's agent.

- *Implied contracts* are created by the actions of the parties. A classic example of an implied contract is someone who goes into a restaurant and orders a meal. That person never says to the server, "If you bring me the steak I'll pay you what it says on the menu." The fact that the person pays the bill for the meal is implied. In real estate work, an implied contract may be created by an agent bringing a buyer to see a house that's being sold by the owner herself. No agreement exists, but Agent Ambitious nonetheless brings a buyer to the house. The seller lets the agent show the house, and the agent takes it upon herself to negotiate a deal on behalf of the seller. And the seller lets her. Eventually a deal is made. The agent expects a commission from the seller by virtue of the fact that the agent brought together the buyer and the seller and both the buyer and the seller let her. Nothing is in writing, but the actions of everyone concerned may create an implied contract.

- A *bilateral contract* is one in which two parties each agree to do something, in effect exchanging promises. For instance, I, the buyer, agree to buy your house for $300,000, and you, the seller, agree to accept my $300,000 and give me title to your house. This agreement is an express (the promises are stated) bilateral (both parties agree) contract typical of real estate sales contracts. In a bilateral contract each party can force the other to act. So I can force you to sell me your house, even if you become unwilling to do so, as long as I'm willing to pay you what I promised. A bilateral contract may be express, as in the case of a sales contract, or implied, as in the case of a tenant who has no lease and a landlord who keeps collecting the rent. Their actions imply an agreement that each can enforce.

- A *unilateral contract* is a one-sided agreement in which only one party (Party *A,* for the sake of an example) is obligated to do what is promised. The obligation exists only if the other party (Party *B*) does what is stated in the contract. Party *B,* in this case, is free not to do what is stated in the contract. An example of a unilateral agreement in real estate is an option agreement. In this example, a seller agrees to not sell his property for a year while a buyer attempts to get financing and other approvals (such as building permits). The seller further agrees to sell the property within a year's time to the buyer for $1 million if the buyer wants to buy it. The word "if" is key here. The buyer is free to buy or not to buy. But the seller must sell the property to the buyer at the stated price if the buyer wants to buy it within the years' time. The buyer is *exercising the option.*

All states have passed some version of a law called the statute of frauds. The *statute of frauds* generally requires most real estate contracts to be in writing for them to be enforceable. You need to check out your state's specific real estate exceptions to the statute of frauds requirements for written real estate contracts. For example, at least one state exempts lease contracts of less than a year from having to be in writing.

Most states also have adopted some form of the *Uniform Commercial Code* (UCC), which governs sales and contracts involving personal property like a car. For a sale of personal property to be enforceable, it must comply with the rules adopted by the state. A typical UCC rule is that all sales of personal property for more than $500 must be in writing. Although questions about the specific rules of the UCC probably won't be on the exam, you may nevertheless see a general question related to it. Cooperative apartments are considered personal property, so their sale is governed by part of the UCC. Check out those portions of the UCC in your state that deal with real estate issues.

## What makes a contract valid?

For a contract to be *valid* (binding on all parties and legally enforceable), it must contain certain elements. State exam writers expect you to have an understanding of the following five elements that must be present for a valid contract to exist.

- ✔ *Legally competent parties:* For a contract to be valid, the people making the agreement must be of legal age in the state in which the contract is executed. They must be sober, sane, and mentally competent to enter into the agreement. Parties to a contract need to be acting freely and voluntarily and be under no undue influence or duress.

- ✔ *Mutual agreement:* Sometimes referred as *mutual assent, mutual consent, meeting of the minds,* or *offer and acceptance,* mutual agreement means that all the terms of the contract must be clearly understood by all parties, who must also agree with and understand what they're agreeing to. Find out whether your state has any kind of law that requires contracts to be written in easily understandable language. These are commonly known as plain language laws. (Check out "Going back and forth with offer and acceptance" later in this chapter.)

- ✔ *Lawful object:* Sometimes referred to as *legality of object* or *lawful objective,* lawful object means that what you're agreeing to do is, in fact, legal. In the movies, the classic mob contract to kill someone is not a valid contract because the object of the contract is illegal.

- ✔ *Consideration:* Consideration is usually some clearly stated item of value that is exchanged for the promise made in the contract by the other party. The thing of value doesn't need to be money; it can be a promise to do or not to do something. In the case of a real estate transaction, it can be the exchange of one piece of property for another. You should remember that in a real estate sales contract, the consideration is the agreed-to selling price.

- ✔ *Agreement in writing:* The agreement in writing rule applies to certain kinds of contracts, including most real estate contracts, as required by your state's particular statute of frauds. (See "Exploring how a contract is created," earlier in this chapter.) Likewise, be sure to check out how the parol evidence rule relates to oral contracts. Under certain circumstances, the *parol evidence rule* enables oral agreements to complete or clarify unclear written agreements, but it also presumes that in most cases, written agreements are more valid than oral agreements and more clearly state the intentions of the parties. Here's an example: You contract to have a house built, and the contract says you're going to get Model A23 doorknobs. Later the builder agrees to install the more expensive Model B34 doorknobs at no additional cost. At the end of the project, he installs the Model A23 doorknobs. In attempting to get the better doorknobs by taking the builder to court, the court may presume that the written contract is the more valid indication of what was agreed and dismiss your case. On the other hand, if no doorknobs were specified, the court may view the oral agreement as the completion or specification for the contract, and you may get the doorknobs you want.

A *void contract* is one in which one or more of the required elements are missing. A contract to do something illegal is a void contract. A void contract, because it is missing one or more key elements, never really existed as a contract in the first place.

A couple of gray areas in the world of valid versus void contracts do exist, though:

- A *voidable contract* usually involves a situation in which one of the parties may not have the legal ability to enter into a contract but may confirm the contract at a later time. Suppose a minor who's younger than the legal age to enter into a contract signs an agreement to buy a house. The minor can either declare that agreement void within a reasonable time of reaching legal age or affirm it as a contract and move ahead with the purchase. Notice that, as is usually the case with voidable contracts, one party, in this instance the minor, can get out of the contract, but the other party is obligated to adhere to the agreement. If the contract were completely void, then neither party would have to act. The law generally views this example as a valid contract unless the minor decides to get out of it.

- An *unenforceable contract* is one that seems valid, and may, in fact, have all the elements of a valid contract, but for one reason or another can't be enforced by one party against another. Here's an example: You have a house custom-built for you. You believe that the builder didn't build the house according to the contract you signed. You sue the builder, but because the statute of limitations (the time limit set by law in which to sue somebody) has run its course for such lawsuits, you can't enforce the contract against the builder. The contract is unenforceable. However, the builder can choose to honor his obligations and make good on the contract, a situation that is described as the contract being *valid as between the parties*.

  The word "enforceable" means that the courts can, within the existing laws, make the parties to the contract do what they agreed to do. In this example, the court can't enforce the contract because the law says the time limit for enforcement has run out.

Two more words that are used to describe a contract are *executory* and *executed*. An *executory* contract is one in which one or more of the terms of the contract have not been completed. An *executed* contract is one in which everything is completed. For instance, after a real estate sales contract is signed it's considered executory. After title (ownership) passes from seller to buyer at the closing, the contract becomes executed.

# So Many Choices: Examining Types of Real Estate Contracts

A number of different types of contracts are used in the real estate business. State exam writers expect you to understand what these contracts are, how they work, and what they're used for.

# *Finding out about agency agreements*

I cover seller and buyer agency agreements in detail in Chapter 4, but you need to know a few specific details about agency agreements. Just remember that an agency agreement, signed by a real estate agent and a client, establishes the agent as the representative of the client.

### *Listing agreements*

A *listing agreement* is between an agent and a property seller. Note when I use the word *agent* here, I'm using it in the sense of the person whose listing it is, and in all cases that is the principal broker. A salesperson working for that broker may be responsible for the listing, and it may be referred to as the salesperson's listing but in fact the agent the seller is hiring is the principle broker. The following are a few common listing agreements:

- ✔ The *exclusive right to sell listing agreement* requires that compensation be paid to the broker regardless of who sells the property, the broker or the property owner. This agreement is a bilateral contract because both parties exchanged promises and can be forced to act — the agent can be forced to do his duty and the seller can be forced to pay a commission. This type of listing agreement generally requires specific promises from both parties, it is *also* considered an express contract, which means that the promises have been spoken and agreed to (or more likely have been put in writing).

- ✔ The *exclusive agency agreement* is one in which a fee is owed to the broker only if the broker sells the property. If the owner sells the property, the broker is owed nothing. This contract is unilateral because nothing is owed unless the broker produces a buyer. This type of listing agreement becomes a bilateral agreement when and if the broker produces a buyer because at that point both parties have obligations that must be fulfilled and can be enforced. This type of agreement is usually express because the listing agreement contains the details to which both parties agree.

- ✔ In an *open listing agreement,* an owner agrees to pay a fee to any broker producing a successful buyer. An open listing is a unilateral contract because only one party (the seller) is obligated to act if and when an agent produces a buyer. Open listings can be express if, for example, a seller advertises his home for sale and the advertisement states that he will work with brokers.

### *Buyer agency agreements*

*Buyer agency agreements* are formed between an agent and someone who wants to purchase a property.

- ✔ An *exclusive buyer agency agreement* requires that the buyer pay the agent whether or not the agent finds the buyer the house that the purchaser buys. So, if the buyer locates a property on his own and buys directly from a seller using no agent at all, the buyer still owes his agent a fee. This agreement is bilateral in that two parties exchange promises, and it's express because the promises are stated.

- ✔ With an *exclusive agency buyer agency agreement,* the buyer is obligated to pay the agent only if the agent produces a property that the buyer buys. It's a unilateral agreement because nothing is owed unless the buyer's agent produces a property for the buyer. It is usually express because the promises made are stated, usually in writing.

- ✔ In an *open buyer agency agreement,* a buyer essentially says he will pay any agent who finds him a property. It's a unilateral agreement because only one party is obligated to act, and it may be express if agents are notified in some way that the buyer is looking for a property and is willing to pay an agent who finds him one.

# Examining sales contracts

Real estate sales contracts indicate a buyer's and a seller's agreement to exchange property for (usually) money. I discuss the elements necessary to make a sales agreement valid and enforceable. A sales contract is a bilateral (two people exchanging promises) express (each party states what they're agreeing to) agreement.

### Making a sales contract valid (and knowing who prepares it)

For a real estate sales contract to be valid, it must comply with the laws of the state where the property is located. Although they may vary slightly by state, the following elements generally are the minimum requirements:

- Legally competent parties.
- A contract that must be in writing.
- A legal description of the property.
- Words of mutual agreement to buy and sell the property.
- Consideration, or what is being paid or exchanged and any other financial terms.
- Signatures of both (or all) parties. The signing of a contract for the sale of a property gives the buyer *equitable title,* which isn't yet ownership and which can be conveyed only by a deed. Instead, it's a contract right that essentially gives the buyer the right to demand title (ownership) to the property when the agreed-upon price is paid.
- Lawful object. This requirement's usually pretty easy to meet because the object of the real estate sales contract is to sell the real estate.

For exam purposes, you should remember what the elements for a valid contract are and what each of them means based on the list and definitions I provide above.

A direct question about who prepares the sales contract isn't necessarily one you'll find on an exam, but you nevertheless need to check out your state's approach. Typical alternatives for testing you on documentation are situations in which preparation of the sales contract is done by the real estate agent, by an attorney, or by an agent subject to review by an attorney. Agents who prepare their own sales contracts often use a preprinted, fill-in-the-blank contract form. An additional piece of information that you need to check out is what, if any, role attorneys play in selling a piece of property in your state, a factor that varies widely throughout the United States. In no case can someone who is not an attorney practice law. In most cases, brokers protect themselves against the charge of illegally practicing law in these circumstances by stating on the form that the signer needs to consult with an attorney before signing the form or that the validity of the form is contingent on an attorney's approval.

### Adding extras to sales contracts

In addition to the necessary items required for a valid contract, many sales contracts contain information about the type of deed that will be delivered to the buyer, encumbrances on the title, any money being deposited as part of the agreement, a statement of what constitutes evidence of good title, a date and place of closing, what happens in the event of destruction of the property before the closing, and other terms and conditions of the sale. (See Chapter 9 for more about deeds and title closing and Chapter 8 for the scoop on encumbrances.)

You need to check out what, if any, laws exist in your state with respect to the consequences of destruction of the property. In many states, unless the contract says differently, the buyer bears the responsibility for any loss that results from destruction of the property. States that have adopted the *Uniform Vendor and Purchaser Risk Act* require the seller to bear any loss that occurs before title is passed to the buyer.

One element that typically appears in a sales contract is a *contingency clause,* or a statement that requires that a specified condition (or conditions) must be met for the contract to be completed. Typical conditions in a real estate sales contract are a mortgage or financing contingency and an inspection contingency.

A *mortgage contingency* allows for the possibility that the buyer may not be able to afford to buy the house. Upon agreeing to purchase a house for $200,000 and coughing up $25,000 in cash for a down payment, the buyer plans to borrow the rest through a mortgage loan.

Because the sale can't go through unless the buyer can borrow the full $175,000, the buyer puts a clause in the contract that enables him or her the option of getting out of the deal if the lender refuses to approve an adequate mortgage loan amount. Without the mortgage contingency in the contract of sale, the buyer can lose the down payment, if the purchase doesn't go through as planned.

An *inspection contingency,* on the other hand, is an agreement that requires an inspection (or inspections) of the house by a home inspector. The house must pass the inspection. If this contingency clause is included in the contract, the buyer can get out of the deal if the inspector finds something wrong with the house and the seller refuses to repair it.

A third contingency that you may see is one in which the buyer must be permitted to sell his current home before being forced to buy the new home. This contingency protects the buyer from owning and having to pay mortgages on two homes at the same time.

### Going back and forth with offer and acceptance

Because real estate deals often are the result of a process of negotiation, you need to understand a few of the concepts of the offer and acceptance process. Generally this process of negotiation follows the pattern of the seller listing the house for sale, the buyer making an offer to buy the house, the seller coming back with a counteroffer for the buyer, the buyer making a counteroffer to the seller's counteroffer, and acceptance by the seller with as many counteroffers proposed between offer and acceptance as are needed for the two parties to come to a *meeting of the minds,* which is also called *mutual assent.* An exam question on the offer and acceptance process may present a case of buyer and seller going back and forth and ask you if a particular offer is binding. Remember that as soon as a seller counteroffers to a buyer's offer, the buyer's offer no longer exists.

Suppose that I list my house for sale at $250,000. You offer to buy it from me for $200,000. I counteroffer that I'll sell the property to you for $240,000. You tell me you agree to that price. That's acceptance. For this process to lead to a meeting of the minds, the two parties must agree to all terms and conditions of the contract sale. For example, because of a hot real estate market, I advertise my house for sale for $250,000 and say that I want no mortgage contingency in the contract. You agree to pay the $250,000 but want a mortgage contingency in the contract. Your offer stands until I accept or reject it. If I stick to my original conditions, I counteroffer and tell you that I'll accept your price but not the mortgage contingency. When an offer or counteroffer is rejected, it ceases to exist, and all previous offers and counteroffers cease to exist.

Here's another one for you: You list your house for sale at $250,000. I offer you $180,000. You don't think I'm really serious, but you're willing to try and negotiate. You counteroffer $230,000, but I respond with a counteroffer of only $185,000. At that point, you get annoyed and issue a counteroffer back up to $250,000. . After I counteroffered the $185,000, you effectively refused my offer and it disappeared. It was as if we were starting negotiations from scratch, so I can counteroffer anything I like.

A *binder,* or *offer to purchase,* may be the first step toward solidifying a deal in some parts of the country, in different parts of the same state, and, in recent years, among different brokers in the same market area. A binder is used for residential real estate. A similar agreement, called a *letter of intent,* is used in commercial real estate transactions. A binder is used primarily to signify that a deal has been made and an agreement has been reached to go forward with more formal contract negotiations. At the point at which there's an accepted offer, the binder is signed by both buyer and seller. A binder often is accompanied by an *earnest money deposit* or *down payment* to signal the buyer's seriousness in going forward with the purchase. In other parts of the country, binders are not used, but a sales contract is prepared immediately.

## Discovering options

An *option* in real estate terms is an agreement in which a seller agrees to sell property to a buyer at an agreed-to price within a certain time frame if the buyer wants to buy it. The seller may not sell to anyone else during the option period. Unlike a regular real estate sales contract, the buyer doesn't have to buy the property, but if the buyer wants to buy, the seller must sell. Only one party, the seller, has to act. The buyer has the option of buying or not buying. Options are express unilateral contracts.

A real estate purchase option works like this. You're selling your property for $500,000. I want to buy it, but maybe I want to find out from the local government what I can build on the property and doing so will take some time. You agree to take the property off the market and give me an option to purchase the property at $500,000 within one year. I pay you something for the option that may or may not be credited toward the purchase price, depending on the terms of the agreement. The option gives me the right (but doesn't obligate me) to buy the property for $500,000 within one year. If I choose to exercise the option, you must sell me the property. If I choose not to exercise it, you can't force me to buy the property.

In addition to the basic elements of a valid contract, which you can find earlier in this chapter, the option normally has a time limit attached to it. It's unlikely that an option would run forever.

## Looking at land contracts

A *land contract,* which may also be known as an *installment contract, conditional sales contract, contract for deed,* or *land sales contract,* may be used to purchase property without immediately paying the full price and without obtaining a mortgage. What happens is the buyer, or vendee, pays the seller, or vendor, so much money down and then pays the vendor a little at a time, usually in monthly payments over a period of years until the property is paid off. The buyer receives equitable title (the right to force the seller to give the buyer full title when the entire debt is paid off) to the property, but the seller retains full title (complete ownership of the property). The buyer can use the property and must pay all of the bills on the property, but he or she doesn't receive a deed of ownership to the property until a certain number of payments are made to the seller (see Chapter 9 for more about deeds). A land contract is generally a bilateral express contract because the two parties are required to act and the promises are expressly made to each other. For the exam, remember that if you see the words "vendor" or "vendee," the question will likely be about a land contract.

## Checking out leases

A *lease* is a form of real estate contract that gives someone exclusive use of a property for a period of time for a fee. Leases must contain all the elements of a valid contract. I talk about leases in detail in Chapter 12.

# The End of the Line: Discharging a Contract

*Discharging a contract* means ending the contract in one of several appropriate ways. Test questions on this topic tend to focus on the definitions of these different ways of ending a contract. The most common and best way for a contract to be discharged is by performance, so I list that first, but I list the others here in alphabetical order:

- ✔ *Performance:* Performance is the ideal way to end a contract, because all parties have fulfilled their obligations. "Time is of the essence" is a phrase that sometimes is used in contracts to mean that a breach of contract occurs if an obligation isn't completed within the specified time frame stated in the contract. (For more on breaches, see the next section.)

- ✔ *Assignment and delegation:* Someone else takes over or is assigned the obligations of one of the parties to the contract. The party taking over the obligations is called the *assignee*. Say, for example, that I am a builder who agrees to build you a house. For some reason, I can't do the job, but I assign the contract to another builder who builds you a house under the same terms and conditions that you and I agreed to. This example is different from *delegation,* where I'd simply hire another builder to work for me to build you a house. In an assignment, my responsibilities and obligations are transferred. In a delegation, I remain primarily responsible.

- ✔ *Death:* If you die, you definitely don't have to fulfill your obligations under a contract. However, that doesn't mean that someone else won't have to do what you agreed to do. For example, your estate may be required to go ahead and purchase a property that you contracted to buy before your death.

- ✔ *Impossibility of performance:* In a situation where the action that was contracted cannot be performed legally, the possibility of performing the task can be declared impossible. For example, suppose you hire a builder to build an addition onto your house, and after you sign the contract, you find out the town won't let you build the addition. At this point you're no longer obligated to go through with the contract because performance is legally impossible.

- ✔ *Mutual agreement:* In this situation, both parties to the contract agree to cancel it. They can agree with no penalty to either party, or they agree to some exchange of money to pay for any damage or loss to one or the other of the parties.

- ✔ *Novation:* Novation is a situation in which a new contract with different terms replaces an old one. The new contract can be between the same parties or between one of the parties to the original contract and a new party. Writing a new contract when only minor changes need to be made is not the usual course of action. Each party usually just initials and dates the minor changes to signify their acceptance. Novation is reserved for major or more severe changes.

- ✔ *Operation of law:* This type of situation can relate to some legal issue that arises that cancels the contract. For example a contract that is made on the basis of fraud is canceled when the fraud is discovered.

- ✔ *Partial performance:* Discharging a contract for partial performance refers to an acceptance by one party of incomplete work by the other party and an agreement that the incomplete work will constitute fulfillment of the terms of the contract.

✔ ***Rescission:*** A rescission of a contract sometimes is called a unilateral rescission. (Don't you wish these people could come up with normal names for this stuff?) Anyway, rescission is when one party decides not to fulfill its obligations under the contract and considers the situation to be as if the contract never existed. One party to a contract sometimes uses rescission when the other party doesn't appear to be fulfilling its obligations. For example, the painter who never shows up to paint your house may prompt you to rescind the contract.

✔ ***Substantial performance:*** With the work under contract nearly completed, a substantial performance discharge of the contract may be in order. Under these circumstances, one party may force payment from the other party. Say, for example, you contract to build an addition onto your house. The builder finishes 95 percent of the work but you still owe him a third of the agreed upon amount for the project and refuse to pay until that last 5 percent of the work is complete. The builder can sue you for payment on the basis of substantial performance. The court may let you keep a small amount of money, not the 33 percent you're holding, to finish the job. The builder receives most of his payment and his obligations to you are declared over.

# I Won't Do It! Breaching a Real Estate Contract

Sometimes people simply don't do what they promise to do, even after they sign a contract. These situations are the kind in which one of the parties but not the other refuses to do what he or she promised in the contract to do. A number of remedies and actions can be taken when a breach of contract occurs. I discuss these remedies from the buyer's side and the seller's side. (For remedies related to tenants and landlords in leases, see Chapter 12.) State exam writers expect you to know these different remedies and be able to identify them in a question.

## When the buyer refuses to go ahead with the contract

When a buyer defaults and refuses to buy the house that she signed a contract to buy, even though the seller wants to go ahead with the sale, here's what the seller can do.

✔ **Forfeit the contract:** In this case, the seller formally declares the contract forfeited. The seller typically is entitled to keep whatever money the buyer already has put into the deal. A liquidated damages provision in the contract deals with this.

✔ **Rescind the contract:** After a buyer defaults, the seller declares the contract rescinded. This statement puts everyone back in the same position as when the contract never existed. Suppose the seller receives a higher offer a few days after signing a contract of sale. The buyer's money is returned, and the seller rescinds the contract.

✔ **File suit for compensatory damages:** The seller brings a lawsuit against the buyer for monetary damages that the seller believes he has experienced because the buyer defaulted on the contract. An example is when the seller sues a buyer because he has lost a deposit on a house he was going to buy. The deposit was paid only after he had a signed contract to sell his own home.

✔ **File suit for specific performance:** The purpose of this kind of lawsuit, which the seller brings against the buyer, is to force the buyer to buy the house. In a buyer's market — one in which there are more sellers than buyers and houses are selling slowly — the seller may use this remedy whenever finding another buyer is going to be difficult.

## When the seller refuses to go ahead with the contract

When the seller defaults, even though the buyer is prepared to go ahead with the deal, the seller refuses to sell the house. Here are the remedies at the buyer's disposal:

- **Rescind the contract:** The buyer can rescind the contract and basically let the seller off the hook. The buyer's money is returned and the contract no longer exists.

- **File suit for compensatory damages:** In this case, the buyer sues the seller for monetary damages because the buyer believes she has suffered because of the seller's default. For example, a buyer sells her house and is living in a rented apartment with her furniture in storage because she'd signed a contract to buy another house, but the seller defaulted. The buyer can sue the seller for the cost of the rent and storage charges that she has to pay while looking for another house.

- **File suit for specific performance:** This type of lawsuit is designed to force the seller to go ahead with the sale. Given the fact that no two properties are exactly alike, this remedy may be pursued when monetary damages won't satisfy the buyer, and the buyer really wants a particular house.

# Review Questions and Answers

No one expects you to be an attorney, so the exam questions on contracts are going to be pretty basic. Definitions, the difference between two similar things (unilateral and bilateral, for example), and applicability (is this contract express or implied?) are the types of questions you can expect to see on the exam.

1. A real estate sales contract must be in writing because of what law?

   (A) Uniform Commercial Code

   (B) Statute of frauds

   (C) RESPA

   (D) SARA

   *Correct answer:* (B). The statute of frauds requires that real estate contracts be in writing. The Uniform Commercial Code deals with personal property.

2. A contract that depends on the actions of the parties as evidence of an agreement is referred to as

   (A) unilateral.

   (B) bilateral.

   (C) implied.

   (D) express.

   *Correct answer:* (C). A contract that depends on the actions of the parties can be unilateral or even bilateral. Express is the opposite of implied.

3. An option is an example of what kind of contract?

   (A) Implied and bilateral

   (B) Implied and unilateral

   (C) Express and bilateral

   (D) Express and unilateral

   *Correct answer:* (D). An option has to be expressed so that both parties understand their contractual obligations. Options are unilateral, because the obligation to act falls on only one party.

4. A contract to do something illegal is

   (A) voidable.

   (B) void.

   (C) valid.

   (D) executory.

   *Correct answer:* (B). A contract must have all required elements to be valid. One of those elements is that the thing you are contracting to do is legal.

5. What kind of title do buyers have when they sign an installment sales contract?

   (A) Executory

   (B) Implied

   (C) Full

   (D) Equitable

   *Correct answer:* (D). No such things as executory or implied titles exist. Full title also is not really a legal term. Equitable title is what you get in the executory stage of a contract.

6. The best word to describe a situation in which someone takes over the contractual obligations of another in a contract is

   (A) novation.

   (B) assignment.

   (C) voidable.

   (D) unenforceable.

   *Correct answer:* (B). If you missed it, the subtlety in this question is in the term "someone." A novation occurs when a new contract is written, which means both parties agree to a new contract. An assignment occurs when a third party takes over the obligations of one of the parties.

7. A buyer who will buy a house only if it passes inspection has what kind of clause placed in the contract?

   (A) An avoidance clause

   (B) An equitable title clause

   (C) A sale on demand clause

   (D) A contingency clause

   *Correct answer:* (D). Any specific action that is included in a contract and must be completed for the contract to be valid is called a contingency.

8. A minor change to a real estate contract generally is handled by

    (A) assignment.

    (B) novation.

    (C) initialing the change.

    (D) verbal agreement.

    *Correct answer:* (C). Minor changes generally can be accomplished by writing them into the contract and then having each party initial them. Novation is used when the changes are significant and require a new contract. Assignment means someone else is taking over the contract obligations. Changes must always be in writing.

9. You sign a contract to buy a house that the seller now refuses to sell to you. You still want the house. What do you do?

    (A) Sue for monetary damages.

    (B) Sue for rescission.

    (C) Sue for completion.

    (D) Sue for specific performance.

    *Correct answer:* (D). A successful suit for specific performance requires the seller to sell the house to you. Completion is not the correct term to force the sale. The other answers don't work because they don't get you the house.

10. If a buyer refuses to go ahead with a purchase of property for which he has signed a contract, what usually happens to the earnest money?

    (A) It is returned to the buyer.

    (B) It is kept by the seller.

    (C) It is kept by the seller less the broker's commission.

    (D) It is held by the title company.

    *Correct answer:* (B). The seller is usually entitled to keep the earnest money. This is considered forfeiture of the contract. No broker's commission is deducted, because the broker didn't produce a willing buyer.

# Chapter 12

# Leasing Property

. . . . . . . . . . . . . . . . . . . . . . . . . . . . . . . . . . . . . . . . . . . . . . . . . . .

*In This Chapter*

▶ Understanding some lease jargon

▶ Seeing what goes into a lease

▶ Looking at different types of leases

▶ Finding out about breaking a lease

. . . . . . . . . . . . . . . . . . . . . . . . . . . . . . . . . . . . . . . . . . . . . . . . . . .

As a real estate agent, you may represent the owners of apartment buildings, office buildings, or retail buildings like shopping centers as a leasing agent. Leasing activity is an especially important part of property management and commercial real estate work if your real estate career goes in that direction. Just as you can represent a *buyer* in a sales transaction, you can also represent a *tenant*, who is someone seeking to rent an apartment or commercial space, in a leasing transaction. State real estate exam writers expect you to know the basics of leasing. You can answer most of these questions if you simply have a clear understanding of the different related definitions.

In this chapter, I talk about various kinds of estates (interests in real estate) in connection with leases. (For a more complete discussion of estates and interests, see Chapter 6.) I also give you some information about the requirements of a typical lease agreement, the different types of leases, and some ways people break leases. I also cover some unique details of commercial space leasing.

In this chapter, I sometimes use the term *apartment,* which could mean a garden apartment, a duplex, or a single-family house as a rental. I also use *premises,* which is a common word used to describe a defined piece of land, building, apartment, or other space.

## Identifying Who's Who and What's What

When you read this section, remember that I simply cover the basic definitions and terms connected with leasing. I also give you some information about the different *interests* (estates) that exist with respect to leases. State exam writers want you to be able to identify terms and apply them to pretty simple cases.

### Owning property: Leased fee estates

A *lease* is an agreement between two parties for possession and use of a particular space, usually for a certain length of time. The person who owns the space, usually referred to as the landlord, is technically called the *lessor.* The landlord owns what's called the fee of the property. (For more in-depth information on fee simple interest and the various rights of ownership, see Chapter 6.)

A lease separates two of the rights of ownership: ownership and possession. The owner still owns the property but has given possession to the tenant. The *lessor's* (owner's) interest in a property in a lease situation is called the *leased fee estate*. The lessor has a *reversionary right* to the possession of the premises when the lease expires, which simply means she gets possession of the property back. Sometimes the owner's interest is referred to as a *leased fee estate with reversionary right*.

# Renting property: Leasehold estates

The tenant's interest in the property is called the *leasehold estate*. Another term for tenant is *lessee*. The tenant holds the lease, whereas the landlord gives the lease.

In each of the following four types of leasehold estates, I use the term *estate;* however, note that the word *tenancy* can be substituted in each case.

### Estate for years

An *estate for years* is a lease agreement with a definite starting and ending date. The tenant is required to leave when the lease expires, and the landlord isn't required to give the tenant notification to leave the premises. Neither is the tenant required to give notification to the landlord that she's leaving. Commercial property leases generally create an estate for years. No automatic renewal of an estate for years is available, but a new lease can be negotiated. Also, the agreement survives the landlord's death or the sale of the property. **Note:** In spite of the name, the lease could be for a term shorter than a year.

### Periodic estate

A *periodic estate,* also called an *estate from period to period* or *periodic tenancy,* occurs when the original agreement doesn't contain any definite period of time. A month-to-month tenancy is an example of a periodic estate, though the period can be week to week or year to year. Essentially the agreement automatically renews itself from period to period with the original terms and conditions remaining in effect unless the landlord and the tenant renegotiate the agreement. In some parts of the United States, periodic estates are commonly used in residential leases. A periodic estate can be created when an estate for years (remember, a lease with an ending date) ends, the tenant doesn't move out, and the landlord continues to accept the rent. The tenant may be referred to as a *holdover tenant.*

In the event of the death of the landlord or the sale of the property, the new landlord may be able to terminate the periodic estate by refusing to accept the rent. A typical notice for termination is usually one period, such as one month for a month-to-month lease. Periodic estates and their terminations are governed by state law, so check out how they're handled in your state.

### Estate at will

An *estate at will* is when the landlord allows the tenant to occupy the premises, but there is no definite period of time when the arrangement will expire. An owner about to sell a building may allow a tenant to occupy an apartment under this type of arrangement. The estate at will can be terminated at any time with the proper legal notice (usually defined by state law), and it ends if the landlord or the tenant dies.

### Estate at sufferance

An *estate at sufferance* occurs when a tenant who had a legal right to occupy the premises continues to occupy the space after the right of occupancy has expired, against the landlord's will. One example is a tenant who continues to stay in an apartment after the lease expires. The tenant is sometimes referred to as a *holdover.* No actual tenancy exists because the landlord is not accepting rent. In the event of the property's sale or the death of the landlord, the new owner has the same rights as the original owner to seek eviction (see "Breaking a Lease: Types of Eviction," later in this chapter).

An estate at sufferance can be converted to a periodic estate, which I describe earlier in this chapter, if the tenant pays the rent and the landlord agrees to accept it.

# The Usual Suspects: Preparing a Typical Lease

Because a lease is a legal document, I recommend that a landlord have an attorney prepare a lease. On the flip side, when signing a lease, I recommend that a tenant's attorney reviews it. Even fill-in-the-blank lease forms should be reviewed by an attorney. In this section, I focus on the requirements for a valid lease, some of a lease's typical provisions, and laws related to leases.

## Looking at laws governing leases

The *statute of frauds,* which all states have adopted in some form, usually requires that a lease for a term longer than one year be in writing (see Chapter 11 for more). Some states have also adopted another law, the *Uniform Residential Landlord and Tenant Act,* which provides additional terms and conditions that should be addressed in the lease. In the following section, I give you some of the requirements that many states use as a minimum for a valid lease.

The Uniform Residential Landlord and Tenant Act also provides protection for both landlord and tenant. Check out your state and local municipality's laws to determine if any provisions are applicable for specific tenant's rights.

Laws also govern *rent control,* which is sometimes used as a generic term for any type of government control over what a landlord may charge a tenant. These laws generally govern residential units and vary from state to state and city to city. Check out if any type of rent control exists in your state.

## Examining typical provisions of a lease

A lease is a form of a real estate contract. (For general information on contracts, see Chapter 11.) Like all contracts, a lease needs a few items to be considered valid. The main provisions of a valid lease are

- **Legally competent parties:** Also referred to as having the capacity to contract, this provision means that everyone signing the lease has met all the legal requirements of age and competence.
- **Mutual agreement:** The lease must include an offer and acceptance of the terms. All parties must clearly understand the terms of the lease.
- **Legal objective:** This provision states that what is being contracted for is lawful.
- **Consideration:** The exchange of space for money or other items of value must be enough to make the lease valid. The consideration could be in the form of services such as a janitor being given an apartment in exchange for working in the building.
- **Agreement in writing:** Depending on the provisions in your state's version of the statute of frauds, the lease may have to be in writing. Typically leases for more than a year have to be written agreements.

Your state may have additional, specific requirements for a valid lease, so be sure to check.

Although the minimum requirements technically create a valid lease, they really don't provide useful and specific details. Most leases also contain the following language to clarify certain details:

- ✔ **A description of the leased premises:** This could be an apartment number or floor number and may include an actual survey description if a piece of land is leased. I cover property descriptions in detail in Chapter 9. In a nonresidential lease the description could include a drawing that shows the dimensions and location of the space within the building.

- ✔ **The term of the lease:** The lease typically provides a beginning and ending date.

- ✔ **The amount and date of rent payments:** This statement includes how much the rent is, when the rent is due, any grace periods that may be offered, penalties for late payment, and where the rent is to be sent.

Check out when the default rent payment date is in your state. Lease provisions typically require rents to be paid in advance on the first of the month. The default position in some places is rent is due at the end of the month for the previous month (in arrears).

- ✔ **Provisions for rent increases:** Leases sometimes have provisions for automatic rent increases at certain intervals, which is sometimes called a *graduated lease*. Rent increases may be tied to the Consumer Price Index (an index that measures price increases and inflation), in which case the lease may be referred to as an *index lease*.

- ✔ **The amount of security deposit:** Lease provisions provide for the deposit amount and clarify when the landlord must return it to the tenant at the end of the lease. State laws vary as to how security deposits may be used. For example, in some places (but not all) they may be used to cover defaults on the rent. State law or local ordinances may require that the security deposit be returned to the tenant within a specified period of time or an explanation be provided as to why all or a portion isn't being returned. Find out the relevant timeframe, if any, in your state.

- ✔ **How the premises can be used:** A landlord can limit how the tenant uses the leased space. For example, commercial space couldn't be used as living quarters.

- ✔ **Whether and how improvements can be made:** Improvements to the space are often part of a commercial lease but also may be part of a residential lease. Whether the landlord or tenant does the improvements is a matter of negotiations. Typically, residential tenants are permitted to make improvements with the landlord's permission and are required to return the space to its original condition at the end of the lease.

- ✔ **Provisions outlining maintenance responsibilities:** Landlords are generally required to maintain the premises in useable and what is called *habitable condition*. Certain commercial leases may require tenants to pay for or assume certain maintenance responsibilities.

- ✔ **Details for destruction of the premises:** In cases where a tenant is leasing land or has built a building on leased land, the tenant may be responsible if the building or other structures are destroyed. Tenants aren't usually responsible for destruction of a building in which they lease only a part of the space. They would, however, always be responsible for their business equipment and personal items, just as the renter in a residential rental is responsible for their personal item insurance.

✔ **Provisions for occupancy limits:** Depending on state or local law, a landlord may or may not be able to limit occupancy of the unit to the tenant who signed the lease.

✔ **Provisions for (or against) subleasing:** The lease may provide for the renting of the space by the tenant to a subtenant through what is called a *sublease*. Provisions may also be made for someone else taking over the lease. This is called *assignment*. In a sublease, the original tenant is still liable. An assignment to a new tenant usually needs the approval of the landlord because the new tenant will usually be completely liable.

✔ **Termination on sale clause:** Under normal circumstances, if the landlord sells the building, the lease survives the sale and the new owner takes possession subject to the lease. If the lease contains a termination on sale clause, however, the new owner can evict the tenant upon proper notice or renegotiate the lease with the tenant.

✔ **The right of quiet enjoyment:** Whether stated or not, a lease generally conveys to the tenant the *right of quiet enjoyment,* a legal term that means the tenant has exclusive use of the leased premises without interference from the landlord. The landlord usually can't enter the premises without the tenant's permission except in an emergency.

✔ **Any options:** A lease also may contain a renewal clause guaranteeing the tenant the right to renew the lease or a purchase option giving the tenant the right to purchase the property at or before the end of the lease term.

# Distinguishing Among Various Types of Leases

Though different types of leases have common features and have the same minimum legal requirements, they serve different purposes. The following sections can help you distinguish among the different types. Exam questions will likely focus on the major traits of various leases and may use short case studies to ask about types of leases used under certain circumstances.

## Gross lease

A *gross lease* is where the tenant pays the same rent each month, and the landlord pays all the building's expenses, such as maintenance and taxes. The landlord may also pay some or all of the utilities, but in some gross leases, a tenant may pay his own utilities. The typical apartment lease is a gross lease.

## Ground or land lease

The *ground lease* or *land lease* is a lease where someone rents an empty (vacant) piece of land specifically to erect a building on it. These leases tend to be long term and often exceed 50 years or longer. This lease term allows the tenant time to make his investment in the building worthwhile. In a ground lease, the tenant owns the building and the landlord owns the land. Ground leases usually require the tenant to pay all property expenses, such as taxes, utilities, and maintenance. In this respect, a ground or land lease is similar to a net lease.

## Lease for oil or gas rights

Some leases give a company the right to search for and extract oil and gas from someone's property. The tenant usually pays a fee for the lease and then additional money is paid by the holder of the lease rights to the property owner according to how much gas or oil is removed. This type of lease is considered to be a limitation or cloud on the title to the property, which is anything that limits the rights you get when you buy a piece of property.

## Net lease

A *net lease* is one where the tenant pays the building expenses on top of a base rent. Whether the tenant pays all or some of the expenses is negotiable. A *triple net lease* (sometimes referred to as a *net net net lease*) generally requires the tenant to pay all expenses such as taxes, utilities, maintenance, and insurance. The net or triple net lease is commonly used in renting commercial space.

You may want to check whether a *double net lease* (or a *net net lease*) is common in your area. In some markets, the tenant pays taxes and maintenance or taxes and utilities but not all the other expenses.

## Percentage lease

A *percentage lease* usually has a minimum monthly rental charge plus a percentage of the gross earned by the business. This arrangement is sometimes used in leases with retail stores, and the percentage is based on gross sales. The percentage lease may be either a gross or net lease, meaning that the tenant pays none, some, or all of the building expenses.

## Proprietary lease

A *proprietary lease* is a lease that is given to the "owner" of a cooperative apartment. The owner doesn't actually own the apartment itself but rather shares in the corporation that owns the building. He receives a proprietary lease that allows him to occupy the apartment. (For more on cooperatives, check out Chapter 7.)

# Breaking a Lease: Types of Eviction

When a lease expires, unless the tenant and owner renegotiate it, the tenant is required to leave the premises. However, under some circumstances, the tenant may be forced to leave either by the landlord or by conditions in the building before the lease term expires. The two main types of eviction are as follows.

- ✔ **Actual eviction:** *Actual eviction* occurs when the landlord sues for possession of the premises. This usually occurs when a tenant violates the terms of the lease agreement or stays in the premises beyond the lease expiration date.

- ✔ **Constructive eviction:** *Constructive eviction* occurs when a landlord's actions are such that the premises become uninhabitable. A landlord consistently over time not providing sufficient heat during the winter months may result in constructive eviction. In such a case, as soon as the leased premises are proved to be unusable, the lease is considered ended. Don't consider this a good way to get rid of a tenant; in most places such actions by the landlord is illegal.

# Getting What You Paid For

There is a somewhat unique situation that happens when you rent nonresidential space. It's a perfectly legal and accepted practice, but the fact is you may not actually get what you paid for. Read on to learn more about this concept.

## Non-residential building layouts

Think about the last office building you visited or the one you work in. Maybe it has a nice spacious lobby, some elevators, wide hallways, men's and ladies' rooms, and finally many separate offices housing doctors and lawyers and accountants and other businesses or professionals. The same goes for the last shopping mall you went to, only this time the space is divided up into stores instead of offices. It's logical that each of the tenants in the building pay for their individual office space. But they and their clients use the lobby, the hallways, the washrooms and the elevator. Who pays for that?

Commercial property landlords and tenants understand that the so-called *common spaces* in these buildings have value and are necessary for the building to function properly. It would be relatively easy for the landlord to simply recoup the costs as part of the rent, the way apartment landlords do, if the individual rented space was more or less the same size. But a tenant renting a 1,000-square-foot office would feel that it's unfair if he has to pay the same for the use of the common space as a tenant renting 5,000 square feet. What has developed to solve this problem is the concept of rentable and useable space.

### Rentable space

Rentable space is the space that a tenant pays for when renting non-residential space, say in an office building or shopping mall. It generally contains more square feet than the tenant is entitled to use exclusively and takes into account the common spaces used by the tenant and the tenant's visitors. The rent is stated as so many dollars per square foot annually (even though it might be paid monthly) and is multiplied by the number of rentable square feet to arrive at the total annual base rent.

### Useable space

Useable space is the square footage that the tenant is allowed to use exclusively. It's the space behind the door to the hallway. It's invariably less than the total square footage the tenant pays for.

## Adding on and taking away

The difference between the rentable space and the useable space is called the *add-on factor* or the *loss factor*, depending on which way you do the calculations. It's pretty easy to remember. The add-on factor is added to the useable square footage to arrive at the rentable total square footage. The loss factor is subtracted for the rentable square footage to arrive at the useable total square footage. Both are usually stated as a percentage.

Following are a couple of simple examples that you probably won't have to do on an exam, but they help demonstrate the concept.

**Loss factor**

5,000 square feet (rentable space × 10% (loss factor) = 500 square feet lost space

5,000 square feet (rentable space − 500 square feet (lost space) = 500 square feet (useable space)

**Add on factor**

4,500 square feet (useable space) × 10% (add on factor) = 450 square feet (proportionate common space)

4,500 square feet (useable space) + 450 square feet (proportionate common space) = 4,950 square feet (rentable space)

Note that using the same numbers, the 10 percent has a different result depending on whether it's used as an add-on factor or a loss factor.

# Review Questions and Answers

Expect a few exam questions that deal with recognizing different types of leases and some of the basic terminology.

1. A retail store tenant pays $3,000 a month rent plus a portion of gross sales. This rental arrangement is most likely

   (A) a term lease.

   (B) a net lease.

   (C) an index lease.

   (D) a percentage lease.

   *Correct answer:* (D). A percentage lease requires payment of a base rent plus some portion of the income of the business occupying the space.

2. Tenant A moves out of an apartment six months before the end of the lease. Tenant B moves in and pays rent to Tenant A for the remainder of the lease. Tenant B is

   (A) an assignee.

   (B) an assignor.

   (C) a sublessee.

   (D) a sublessor.

   *Correct answer:* (C). The key to this answer is that Tenant B pays rent to Tenant A and not to the landlord. When you assign a lease, the new tenant takes over the lease and pays rent to the landlord. This isn't the case in this question.

3. A landlord refuses to repair the broken furnace in an apartment building in the middle of winter. The situation may result in

   (A) actual eviction.

   (B) constructive eviction.

   (C) abandonment.

   (D) condemnation.

   *Correct answer:* (B). Focus on the types of eviction here. When a tenant leaves as a result of the landlord creating circumstances by which the unit is uninhabitable, constructive eviction has occurred. Actual eviction is usually a result of the landlord taking action against the tenant for violating the terms of the lease.

4. Can a new owner force a tenant to renegotiate an existing lease when he takes ownership of the property?

   (A) Yes, if the lease has a purchase option in it.

   (B) Yes, if the lease has a sale clause.

   (C) Yes, under any circumstances.

   (D) No, under no circumstances.

   *Correct answer:* (B). The only circumstance under which this situation occurs is the inclusion of a sale clause in the lease. Otherwise a lease survives the sale of a property.

5. A tenant refuses to leave an apartment after the expiration of the lease. The landlord continues to accept the tenant's rent. The tenant may be said to have

   (A) a tenancy at law.

   (B) a tenancy at sufferance.

   (C) a tenancy by the entirety.

   (D) a periodic tenancy.

   *Correct answer:* (D). A tenancy at sufferance would have been created if the tenant stayed without the landlord's permission; that is, the landlord refused to accept the rent.

6. A net lease requires the tenant to pay

   (A) all or some of the building expenses.

   (B) all of the building expenses, including the mortgage payment.

   (C) none of the building expenses.

   (D) a percentage of income earned by the tenant's business.

   *Correct answer:* (A). A tenant never has to make mortgage payments. Paying none of the building expenses is the opposite of the correct answer. A percentage payment is a trait of a percentage lease.

7. The principal difference between tenancy at will and tenancy at sufferance is

   (A) the term of the lease.

   (B) the expenses paid.

   (C) whether rent is paid in arrears or in advance.

   (D) the landlord's consent.

   *Correct answer:* (D). In tenancy at will, the landlord allows the tenant to stay in the premises, but there is no definite period of time when the arrangement will expire. In tenancy at sufferance, the tenant is staying against the landlord's will.

8. A typical apartment lease with a beginning and ending date is

   (A) an estate for years.

   (B) a periodic estate.

   (C) a net lease.

   (D) a percentage lease.

   *Correct answer:* (A). This is a definitional question. A typical apartment lease has a beginning and ending date, but it isn't automatically renewed from period to period, ruling out a periodic estate. It also tends to be gross (not net or percentage).

9. The landlord's interest in a lease is called

   (A) the leasehold interest.

   (B) the leased fee interest.

   (C) the gross lease interest.

   (D) the possessory interest.

   *Correct answer:* (B). The landlord owns the fee of the property and therefore has the leased fee interest. The tenant holds the lease and therefore has the leasehold interest.

10. A tenant remains in possession of a rented house after the bank has sold the property through foreclosure for nonpayment of the mortgage, and the bank wants to evict the tenant. The tenant has

    (A) a tenancy at will.

    (B) a tenancy at sufferance.

    (C) a lawful occupancy.

    (D) a periodic tenancy.

    *Correct answer:* (B). The key here is consent. If the landlord (the bank in this case) wants you out but you stay, it's a tenancy at sufferance.

# Chapter 13

# Dealing with Environmental Government Regulations and Issues

- - - - - - - - - - - - - - - - - - - - - - - - - - - - - - - - - - - - - - - - - - - - - - - - - -

## In This Chapter

▶ Figuring out who's who in the environmental world

▶ Finding out about environmental statements and assessments

▶ Identifying some major environmental problems

▶ Looking at water supply and disposal issues

- - - - - - - - - - - - - - - - - - - - - - - - - - - - - - - - - - - - - - - - - - - - - - - - - -

*T*he public has been and continues to be concerned about the environment. This concern has gone in two directions: environmental preservation, and the study and elimination of environmental hazards. Environmental preservation has evolved into the green, sometime called eco-friendly, building concept of creating more energy-efficient homes and commercial buildings. Environmental hazards don't just come out of thin air — though of course they can affect the air. Environmental hazards also happen on the ground. And things that negatively affect the environment like air and water pollution often happen because of land development — land that is bought and sold. Enter, you, the real estate agent.

As a result of the increasing concern about the environment, many states expect real estate agents to have some knowledge of environmental issues, government regulations, and the analysis of the environmental impacts of development. Although the information in this chapter crosses state lines, for exam purposes, check out whether your state requires you to know this information for the state licensing exam.

In this chapter I give you some basic information about environmental hazards, some of their health effects, government regulations about environmental issues, and a brief analysis of the impact of development on the environment.

As you read this chapter, remember that no one is trying to turn you into an environmental scientist. In fact, most of the time in a real estate practice, you're going to recommend that buyers and sellers call in environmental scientists, engineers, planners, and attorneys who specialize in environmental issues when you or anyone involved suspects a problem. Your job is to recognize some basic laws and environmental hazards and their impacts. Liability for the real estate agent exists in these environmental issues but usually only to the extent that the agent should've known something or did know something and didn't reveal it to buyers or sellers.

# Deciphering the Federal Government Alphabet Soup

As environmental concerns have grown across the United States, the federal government has passed a series of laws, regulations, and programs to deal with environmental issues. Many of them are known by the acronyms that their letters form. In studying this information for an exam, take time to discover not only the acronyms but also the full titles. You also need to have a pretty good idea of the type of issue that the program deals with and its important points. In a few cases just knowing what the letters stand for will be enough.

In some cases, states have passed their own environmental laws to supplement or go further than federal laws. Be sure to check out these laws and find out whether you'll be tested on them. This information should be available in your prelicense course.

## CERCLA

In 1980 the federal government adopted into law the *Comprehensive Environmental Response, Compensation, and Liability Act* (CERCLA). This law's purpose is to identify sites of environmental pollution and provide funds for cleanup. The act calls for the identification of people and/or businesses responsible or *potentially responsible parties (PRP)* for the creation of uncontrolled hazardous waste sites or hazardous waste spills. The act also created a $9 billion fund called the *Superfund* to pay for the cleanup of identified hazardous waste sites.

The act considers liability for such a site and its cleanup to be strict. *Strict liability* means that the property owner has no excuse with respect to his liability. The act also considers the liability to be *joint and several,* which means that if more than one person is responsible for the hazardous waste site, the law is enforceable on the group as well as on each individual. In fact, if, for example, one of two people had no funds available for cleanup, the other party could be held responsible for the total cost. The second party would have to try and get payment from the other person through a lawsuit.

Under CERCLA, a current landowner can be held liable for the cost of cleaning up a hazardous waste site even when he or she didn't create it. The current owner can then try to obtain reimbursement from the people who originally created the site or from the Superfund itself. The term *retroactive liability* also is used in connection with CERCLA and the Superfund. It means that all previous owners also can be held accountable for the hazardous waste site.

## EPA

The Environmental Protection Agency (EPA) is the federal agency responsible for dealing with environmental issues. The agency advises Congress and the president regarding laws to protect the environment. The agency writes regulations implementing laws that have been passed, and the agency enforces all federal environmental rules and regulations. The EPA administers, among other laws, the *Clean Water Act,* the *Toxic Substance Control Act,* and the *Resource Conservation and Recovery Act.*

## HMTA

The important thing to remember for the exam here: The Hazardous Material Transportation Act (HMTA) is enforced by the United States Department of Transportation.

# HUD

The United States Department of Housing and Urban Development (HUD) isn't a major player in the federal regulation of environmental issues. However, I mention it because the agency is relevant when concerned with lead paint disclosure, which I discuss in the "Lead" section later in this chapter.

# LUST (It's not what you think)

The Leaking Underground Storage Tanks (LUST) program, sometimes referred to as the UST or Underground Storage Tank program, was created in 1984 as part of the Resource Conservation and Recovery Act administered by the EPA.

This program targets underground storage tanks used for the storage of hazardous substances such as chemicals or oil-based products like motor fuel. Such tanks must be registered with the EPA. There are a number of exceptions to the underground storage tank program, including tanks with a storage capacity of less than 110 gallons; tanks used for heating oil used on the property; and motor fuel storage tanks of less than 1,100 gallons on farms and residential properties. The program regulates such areas as tank installation and maintenance as well as spill prevention and monitoring.

Individual states may have programs that supplement the federal underground storage tank program. Check out your state law to find out whether this issue is something that you need to know for your state test. Generally the law may provide for additional registration of tanks, different minimum size tanks that have to be registered, and possibly different technical requirements.

# OSHA

The Occupational Safety and Health Administration (OSHA), which is part of the United States Department of Labor, is responsible for providing and monitoring regulations regarding worker safety particularly in factories.

# SARA

The *Superfund Amendments and Reauthorization Act of 1986 (SARA)* was passed when the original act, CERCLA, expired in 1985. (See the earlier section on CERCLA for more.) The three essential functions SARA performs are

- ✔ Providing increased funding to the Superfund for environmental cleanup.
- ✔ Creating stronger standards for cleanup of hazardous waste.
- ✔ Creating something called *innocent landowner immunity*.

   Where a property owner has been innocent of all involvement with a hazardous waste site, under certain circumstances, she may claim immunity from responsibility. In addition to having no involvement or knowledge of the situation, the property owner must have taken what is sometimes called *due care* or *due diligence* in having the property investigated for potential environmental contamination. This investigation usually takes the form of an environmental assessment. (For more on environmental assessments, see "Having suspicions: Environmental assessments" later in this chapter.) Before the innocent landowner immunity status was created, the current owner, regardless of guilt, could be held liable by the EPA to pay for cleanup of a hazardous waste site and then would have to seek reimbursement from a previous owner. SARA's immunity status can relieve a current innocent owner of this liability.

# Assessing the Environmental Effects of Building Developments

Many land development projects, which include everything from building a single house to a major shopping center or multi-lot subdivision, impact the environment. The impacts are usually proportional to the size of the project, but a small project can have a large impact if it's built on environmentally sensitive land, such as a single-family house built near a wetland. (See the sidebar "Why would you want wet land?" later in this chapter.) In this section, I discuss the primary ways that environmental engineers, scientists, and planners examine the impacts of such projects.

## Making a statement: Environmental impact statements

Laws governing the examination of the environmental impacts of a proposed project vary from state to state. If environmental issues are part of your state exam, check out the particular rules and regulations that govern the review or impact study of environmental issues with respect to a proposed development project.

An environmental impact statement or study (they may be called something else in your state) examines the environmental impact a development project may have on the environment. Depending on the state requirements, such a statement may look at everything from the number of cars that will be put on the road to the animal life that will be disturbed. The study reviews both the impact of the project when it's completed and the impact it may have while it's being built.

An environmental impact statement or study sometimes requires that alternatives be presented and examined. For example, a developer may be required to examine various access roads into a new subdivision and then explain why the one selected is best. The study also usually requires a discussion of mitigation measures. *Mitigation measures* are those things that might be done to minimize or eliminate the environmental impact of the project. For example, a developer expects the shopping center he's building to generate a great deal of car traffic (car traffic equals air pollution). He may agree to provide room at the shopping center for a bus stop to encourage people to take public transportation, thus reducing the number of cars used.

Experts in environmental matters prepare these statements or studies. The public and key agencies may be invited to comment on the study. These studies can be expensive and time-consuming depending on the project's complexity.

## Having suspicions: Environmental assessments

When someone involved in a real estate transaction suspects the presence of hazardous material on a piece of property, an environmental assessment may be performed by environmental engineers or scientists. An environmental assessment has four possible phases:

✔ **Phase 1:** A Phase 1 environmental assessment is primarily a review of the records regarding the property in question. The records that are reviewed focus on any environmental complaints, violations, special permits, or other documentation that may indicate the current or previous presence of environmentally hazardous material. This phase also includes a visual inspection of the property. Phase 1 environmental assessments are commonly done before someone purchases an industrial or commercial property and are often required by mortgage lenders before approving a loan.

✔ **Phase 2:** A Phase 2 environmental assessment involves actually testing and sampling to confirm the presence of any environmentally hazardous material or contamination.

✔ **Phase 3:** A Phase 3 environmental assessment is done after the confirmation of contamination on the property. The Phase 3 assessment examines the extent of the hazard and develops a plan to remedy the condition. Remediation is done as a result of this phase and may include removal of the contaminated material and restoration of the property.

✔ **Phase 4:** A Phase 4 environmental assessment is the development of a management plan for the contaminated site. Sometimes the contamination may be too large or extensive to be removed, and Phase 4 establishes a specific management plan to contain and manage the site so as to not affect surrounding properties.

# This Stuff Can Make You Sick: Examining Environmental Pollutants and Situations

One of the primary functions of a real estate agent is to be aware of possible environmental issues with respect to a piece of property that the agent may be involved with as a seller's or buyer's agent. State test writers therefore expect a certain basic level of knowledge about what environmentally sensitive issues might show up in a real estate transaction.

Your job certainly isn't to become an environmental expert. However, as an agent, you do have a responsibility to make yourself as aware as possible of environmentally hazardous situations that may be present. You ask how? You perform this duty by a visual inspection of the property as well as asking the property owner. It also involves being aware of commonly known hazards in the area. The agent may further recommend the services of an environmental assessor or auditor who would conduct the appropriate environmental assessment.

In this section I provide some basic information about various environmentally hazardous substances and conditions.

## Asbestos

*Asbestos* is a mineral that has been widely used in residential and commercial construction. Because of its resistance to the transfer of heat and its resistance to fire, builders have used it as insulation for pipes and heating ducts, roofing, siding, and flooring materials. The basic issue that exists with asbestos is related to its friability. *Friable* means the tendency to break down and give off dust and fibers that can be highly dangerous if inhaled. Exposure to asbestos fibers and dust can cause diseases that include lung cancer; *asbestosis*, a sometimes-fatal disease that makes breathing difficult; and mesothelioma, a cancer of the lining of the lungs.

In general, you can deal with asbestos in a building in three ways.

✔ **Leave it alone.** Leaving it alone may be appropriate if the asbestos is in good shape and doesn't appear to be disintegrating or deteriorating in such a way that fibers and dust are escaping into the air.

✔ **Remove it.** Removing it should be done only in accordance with experts who follow procedures established by the EPA and/or your state.

✔ **Deal with it.** Dealing with asbestos is called encapsulation. *Encapsulation* is sealing the asbestos in place. Doing so prevents dust and fibers from getting into the air. Make sure that appropriate professionals do all evaluations and work in dealing with asbestos or removing it.

# Brownfields

*Brownfields* are former industrial, factory, manufacturing, or storage sites that may have environmentally hazardous waste on or under them from their previous use. Federal legislation was passed in 2002 to help communities with the cost of cleaning up these areas. This legislation also protects owners of property from liability for hazardous wastes that were put there by a previous owner.

# Building-related illness

*Building-related illness,* sometimes referred to as *BRI,* is a general term to describe various health issues related to the indoor air quality of buildings. The symptoms, which may include a variety of allergic reactions and respiratory illnesses, are present both while people are in the building and continue after they leave the building. The cause of BRI is related to chemical emissions from materials like paints and glues used in the building, as well as bacteria and dust in the air.

# Electromagnetic fields

Electromagnetic fields are generated by so-called high-tension power lines and by power transfer or distribution stations and home appliances. Some research indicates that these electromagnetic fields can cause cancer as well as changes in behavior and hormone levels. This research is apparently somewhat controversial with other research indicating no health hazards. Real estate agents should familiarize themselves with the locations of the types of facilities that could generate electromagnetic fields so as to be able to advise property buyers of their presence.

# Lead

Researchers recognized lead as a health hazard a number of years ago. It's particularly dangerous to children, negatively impacting mental and physical development. Lead particles can enter a person's system if he breathes lead dust in the air, drinks from a water supply that runs through lead pipes or copper tubing joined with lead solder, or actually eats lead-based paint flakes, as may happen with small children.

In 1992 the U.S. government passed the *Lead-Based Paint Hazard Reduction Act,* which requires that homeowners in homes built before 1978 fill out a lead paint disclosure form and give it to a buyer when they sign a sales contract. This form triggers a ten-day period of time during which the buyer can have the property tested for lead. This testing isn't mandatory but at the buyer's option.

The testing, done by appropriate professionals, can be done in two ways:

- A *paint inspection* can be performed, which indicates the amount of lead present in all painted surfaces.
- A *risk assessment* also can be performed, which goes further than the paint inspection. The risk assessment actually examines sources of lead paint risk such as peeling paint and suggests how to remedy it.

If the buyer decides to have the inspection done and a lead paint hazard is found, the seller has the option of correcting it or not. If the seller refuses, the buyer has the option of getting out of the deal and getting all his *earnest* (deposit) money back.

In addition to the disclosure form that the seller must complete, she must also provide a lead paint information booklet produced by HUD and the EPA (see "Deciphering the Federal Government Alphabet Soup" earlier in this chapter for more about these government agencies), as well as the United States Consumer Product Safety Commission. The disclosure rules also apply to the landlord's obligation to reveal to the tenant any known lead paint hazard. A real estate agent's responsibility with respect to lead paint disclosure is to advise the seller about his obligations to disclose possible lead paint hazards. An agent representing a buyer advises the buyer of the fact that he should receive the lead paint disclosure.

Check whether your local state or municipality has any laws regarding lead paint hazard disclosure that supplement the federal regulations.

## Radon

*Radon* is an odorless, colorless, tasteless, radioactive gas produced by the decay of natural materials such as rocks that are radioactive. It tends to accumulate in areas with poor outside air circulation such as basements. It may spread through a building by heating and air-conditioning systems, and it's believed to cause lung cancer. Tests can be done for radon, and a real estate agent representing a buyer may recommend that the buyer have the test performed before buying the property. Professionals like private building inspectors can perform the test; do-it-yourself kits also are available for homeowners. If radon is found, the remedy generally is to introduce some kind of ventilation into the enclosed space to remove the gas.

## Sick building syndrome

Sick building syndrome, sometimes called SBS, refers to symptoms that people sometimes experience when inside a building for a period of time, but which end when the person leaves the building. (Some people may call that BBS, also known as Bad Boss Syndrome.) The symptoms may include itchiness, breathing difficulty, dizziness, and runny nose.

The cause of SBS is believed to be poor indoor air quality as a result of chemical emissions from materials such as paints and glues used in the building, as well as bacteria and dust in the air.

## Solid waste (radioactive and otherwise)

Various parts of the United States have radioactive waste sites. These sites store used fuel from nuclear power plants. The principal issue for real estate agents is to be aware of where these sites are located. People are generally aware of the potential health hazards associated with a leak of radioactive material and may choose not to live near such a site. Or if they do buy a home near a radioactive storage facility, they may expect to pay less than if the facility weren't there.

The storage of solid waste (I'm old enough to remember when it was called garbage) is more widespread. *Landfills,* which are areas that are excavated, filled with solid waste, and then covered, are located in many parts of the country. The environmental issue is primarily leakage from the landfill into nearby properties, as well as into nearby lakes, streams, and, wells. Older landfills, in particular, may cause problems because they may not have been constructed according to modern standards with appropriate liners, covering, and drainage control. Federal, state, and local governmental agencies all may be involved in monitoring landfills to prevent contamination of nearby properties and water bodies.

## Underground tanks

Underground storage tanks range in size from relatively small tanks of a few hundred gallons for home heating oil to large tanks of thousands of gallons for industrial and agricultural gasoline, oil storage, and chemical storage. The issue for real estate, of course, is leakage from the tank into the ground and then into wells or nearby water supply systems of recreational streams and lakes.

In addition to the danger posed by tanks that are in current use, the issue of tank abandonment is significant. Usually local government agencies establish proper procedures for abandoning a tank. One of the most important ones is pumping out the material in the tank so that nothing is left to leak out. The tanks are then generally filled with material like sand.

To read more about the federal Leaking Underground Storage Tank (LUST) program, check out "LUST (It's not what you think)," earlier in this chapter. Make sure you check to see whether your home state has any local programs that deal with tank registration, monitoring, or abandonment. As a real estate agent, you want to know about these specific procedures because they may affect your buyer or seller. If appropriate, you would need copies of the proper paperwork for your buyer, showing that the tanks were abandoned properly.

## A few more quick definitions to keep in mind

Exam writers may expect you to know at least a little about the following issues, such as definitions and brief explanations. So that's what I'm giving you.

- ✔ **Carbon monoxide:** This is a potentially deadly gas that occurs naturally in the burning of gas, oil, or other fuels. It can be lethal in the case of a faulty furnace or oil burner and where there is improper ventilation. Carbon monoxide detectors are mandatory in some building codes.

- ✔ **Chlorofluorocarbons:** CFCs, as they are more commonly known, are gases that were once used in aerosol cans and in the freon of older air conditioners. CFCs are thought to be responsible for the depletion of the ozone layer around the earth. Their use was banned by the *Federal Clean Air Act*. Replacing an older central air conditioning system often involves replacing equipment to handle the newer, less-environmentally hazardous gases.

- ✔ **Mold:** This is usually caused by the presence of moisture. It can be present virtually anywhere in a building and can cause allergic reactions and respiratory problems.

- ✔ **Urea formaldehyde:** This substance was used to create urea-formaldehyde foam insulation (UFFI), which the Consumer Product Safety Commission banned in 1982. Because of insufficient proof of adverse health risks associated with UFFI, the ban was changed to a warning. Gases related to UFFI are thought to cause respiratory problems and skin and eye irritations.

# Go with the Flow: Water and Waste Issues

Water supply is a major environment issue in the United States. Without a sufficient supply of clean, drinkable water, development of real estate for homes and businesses is impossible. In this section, I discuss water sources and water pollution issues, and what happens to water after you use it and it becomes sewage. I also talk about storm water, a different kind of wastewater.

## Why would you want wet land?

Somewhere in your travels you may have heard the term *wetlands*. Wetlands are properties that because of their location and soil type have the ability to act as sponges soaking up volumes of water, sometimes at a greater capacity than other types of soils.

So why is this important? For example, say you owned a 40,000-square-foot piece of commercial property. You build a small store with a parking lot and cover half of the lot with building and pavement. The next time it rains, half the water that falls on your property runs off (and it's called *runoff*) the *impervious* (water can't get through)

surface. So where does that rainwater go? Onto the part of the lot where there's still grass and the water then gets absorbed there. But suppose you paved over the whole lot to make a bigger parking area. And suppose the nearby property owners did the same thing. As more and more land is covered, the rainwater can cause street and house flooding. So wetlands in strategic places, which have the capacity to absorb more than their fair share of water, are preserved so all that rainwater running off your parking lot, driveway, or roof has someplace to go.

## *Water pollution*

The term *domestic water* is used to describe the water you drink, cook with, and take a shower in. Domestic water comes from groundwater sources, which can be either reservoirs or underground water supplies, sometimes called *aquifers*. Groundwater supplies are subject to pollution from many sources ranging from the chemicals you put on your lawn to the oil on the highways.

In some places water is supplied to homes and businesses through the local government, a public water supply agency or commission, or a privately owned water supply company. The system of supply is generally from a reservoir or series of wells through a system of pipes to your home or business. Sometimes, in between the supply and the distribution pipes, the water may be treated or filtered in some way. The *Federal Safe Drinking Water Act* requires that public water supply systems be tested regularly.

Those people who aren't served by a public or private water supply system get their water from individual on-site water supply systems called wells. Wells may (and sometimes are required to) be tested for the presence of pollutants and for adequacy of supply.

Check your local state regulations regarding mandatory testing of wells. Many places require wells to be tested for pollution and adequate pressure when a new well is drilled. Testing may be optional after that. Also find out what agency reviews the test results. Local health departments or environmental departments are typically the review agencies.

## *Sanitary waste disposal*

*Sanitary waste* is what goes out the drain pipe of your house from the sinks, showers, toilets, and washing machines. Of course, it's not sanitary but must be treated in a sanitary manner to prevent pollution and illness.

Ideally when you flush, it becomes someone else's problem. The waste from your house travels through sewer pipes and eventually is treated at a sewage treatment plant, usually operated by the city, town, or county. If you live in a large residential complex or work in an office building that has no sewers, a small, nearby treatment plant may service your building or housing complex.

In many areas, sewage disposal is handled by individual on-site disposal systems called *septic systems.* In this case when you flush, it's still your problem because septic systems have to be maintained by periodically pumping them. The septic tank is one of two parts of a septic system. The other part is the *leach fields,* which are also called *absorption fields* or *septic fields.* The size of a septic system can vary and is generally sized according to the number of bedrooms in a house. The location of the leach fields as well as even the feasibility of using a septic system is determined by the capacity of the soil to absorb what is called leachate. *Leachate* is the liquid stuff that comes out of the septic tank after all the solids have settled to the bottom of the tank. The capacity of the soil to absorb leachate is tested by doing a *percolation* or *perc test.* Where there are wells and septic systems in the same area or on the same property, local authorities establish minimum distances that have to be maintained between the septic system and the well.

## Storm water disposal

Storm water is rainwater that comes down into the streets that must be disposed of to avoid flooding of streets and houses. Generally storm drains in the streets that lead to storm sewers dispose the storm water and take it directly to lakes, rivers, or the ocean.

# Review Questions and Answers

You'll find that most answers to questions about environmental issues come down to memorizing the facts. The other important tidbit to remember is to memorize the full terms of any abbreviations or acronyms.

1. A source of money to clean up major environmentally polluted properties was originally created by

   (A) CERCLA.

   (B) EPA.

   (C) LUST.

   (D) SARA.

   *Correct answer:* (A). The trick is the word *originally.* SARA reauthorized the Superfund.

2. Immunity for a land owner innocent of creating the pollution on his property was created by

   (A) CERCLA.

   (B) OSHA.

   (C) SARA.

   (D) EPA.

   *Correct answer:* (C). Innocent landowner immunity didn't exist in the original CERCLA legislation.

3. Immunity for a landowner innocent of creating pollution on his property will most likely be dependent on

   (A) the type of pollution.

   (B) how long ago the pollution happened.

   (C) his due diligence in investigating the property.

   (D) how much money he has.

*Correct answer:* (C). Due diligence is a key requirement of innocent landowner immunity. The landowner must have done some investigation to protect himself.

4. A review of records regarding environmental problems on a property would be part of

   (A) a Phase 1 environmental assessment.

   (B) a Phase 2 environmental assessment.

   (C) a Phase 3 environmental assessment.

   (D) a Phase 4 environmental assessment.

   *Correct answer:* (A). Review "Having suspicions: Environmental assessments" earlier in this chapter and make sure that you can clearly identify what occurs in each phase.

5. A management plan for an environmentally polluted site would be developed in which phase environmental assessment?

   (A) 1

   (B) 2

   (C) 3

   (D) 4

   *Correct answer:* (D). You need to be able to identify the four phases and what occurs in each phase. (Check out "Having suspicions: Environmental assessments" earlier in this chapter for the scoop.)

6. Friability is a term associated with

   (A) BRI.

   (B) SBS.

   (C) electromagnetic fields.

   (D) asbestos.

*Correct answer:* (D). Friability is the tendency of asbestos to break down and give off dust and fibers that can be highly dangerous if inhaled. This question is a good example of how you have to remember information about various environmental hazards. For each one, you need to remember what it is, how and where it appears, associated key words (like friability and asbestos), illnesses it may cause, ways to handle it, and so on.

7. You get sick at work and the symptoms persist when you get home. You may be suffering from

   (A) BRI.

   (B) SBS.

   (C) EPA.

   (D) OSHA.

   *Correct answer:* (A). The symptoms of building-related illness are present both while people are in a building and continue after they leave the building. The symptoms of sick building syndrome end when people leave the building.

8. The size of a residential septic system is usually based on

    (A) square footage.

    (B) number of occupants.

    (C) number of bathrooms.

    (D) number of bedrooms.

    *Correct answer:* (D). This can be a tricky question because square footage or the number of occupants seems logical. But the number of bedrooms it is. Check out the section "Sanitary waste disposal" earlier in this chapter if you need to refresh your memory.

9. Odorless, colorless, radioactive gas best describes

    (A) carbon monoxide.

    (B) carbon dioxide.

    (C) radon.

    (D) methane.

    *Correct answer:* (C). All of the answers are gases, but only one is radioactive: radon.

10. The test done to locate where to place a septic system is called

    (A) a depth test.

    (B) a soils test.

    (C) a percolation test.

    (D) an absorption analysis.

    *Correct answer:* (C). This is another one of those memorization questions; the term "percolation" is unique to septic system testing (and making coffee, in the world outside of real estate).

# Part V

# You Want How Much? Valuation and Financing of Real Estate

## Conversion factors that can make your real estate life a little easier

1 foot = 12 inches

1 yard = 3 feet

1 mile = 5,280 feet

1 square yard = 9 square feet (3 feet × 3 feet)

1 acre = 43,560 square feet

A section = 1 square mile or 640 acres

A section = 5,280 feet (1 mile) on each side

1 cubic yard = 27 cubic feet (3 feet × 3 feet × 3 feet)

Learn about property values and how they're figured in the article "My Property is Worth How Much?" at www.dummies.com/extras/realestatelicenseexams.

# In this part . . .

✔ As a real estate professional, you not only need to know the value of property, but you also need to know about the appraisal process to pass the real estate exam. I show you appraisal basics so that you understand market factors that create value.

✔ For the exam, you need to know why taxes are collected, how tax rates are established, and how to calculate taxes on a specific piece of property. I define important tax terms and show you how tax deductions and credits are figured.

✔ You examine the basics of the mortgage process and the sources of mortgage funding, including several considerations that lenders take into account when making the loans.

✔ You discover different kinds of mortgages and repayment plans, do a little mortgage math, and find out about laws that require everyone be treated fairly when they try to borrow mortgage money, even if they're 70 years old and want a 30-year mortgage.

✔ I show you how to apply some simple math concepts to practical real estate problems. No one likes the math questions on the real estate license exam, but fear not — you learned most of the math on the test when you were in middle school.

# Chapter 14

# Appraising Property

- - - - - - - - - - - - - - - - - - - - - - - - - - - - - - - - - - - - - - - - - - - -

## In This Chapter

▶ Knowing what appraisals are and why you need them

▶ Recognizing the basic principles that affect real estate value

▶ Understanding different kinds of value

▶ Checking out factors that affect value

▶ Using three different methods to estimate a property's value

- - - - - - - - - - - - - - - - - - - - - - - - - - - - - - - - - - - - - - - - - - - -

An important part of every real estate sale, or for that matter almost every real estate transaction, involves the value of the property. For example, you may need to know the value of a house you inherited for estate tax purposes. Real estate agents (brokers and salespersons) are expected to know something about why one piece of property is more valuable than another. Agents also are expected to know about the methods appraisers use to estimate property values.

This chapter helps you pass the exam by giving you information about market factors that create value. It also discusses different types of value and describes the principal methodologies that appraisers use in their work.

## Figuring Out Appraisal Basics

A real estate agent is interested in a property's value for a number of reasons. An agent usually helps a seller set an asking price for a property when it's being offered for sale. An agent representing a buyer often advises his client on the values of properties that are being considered for purchase. Finally, a knowledgeable agent provides important information to the appraiser when she completes the mortgage appraisal.

### What is an appraisal?

An *appraisal* is an estimate or opinion of value. This definition often appears on state licensing exams.

The words "estimate" and "opinion" are important in this definition. Notice, for example, that I don't define an appraisal as a calculation of value. Although appraisers use a variety of mathematical techniques in their work, the act of arriving at the value of a particular piece of property can never be that precise. So appraisers never say that they calculate value.

An appraiser is a researcher, a private detective. To come up with an estimate, the appraiser investigates the following.

- ✔ **Economic factors:** Employment and interest rates.
- ✔ **Environmental factors:** The presence of pollutants in the area or on the land.
- ✔ **Physical factors:** The real estate's location, size, and condition.
- ✔ **Social factors:** Demand for a particular type of housing (such as demand by an aging population for a certain type of house).

The property being appraised is called the *subject property*. Although the definition of the term subject property isn't critical for exam purposes, you need to understand the reference whenever you're asked a question that refers to the property being appraised.

Another important item to remember is that the client hires the appraiser to provide an objective opinion of the value of the subject property. Most appraisers work independently on a fee-for-service basis; therefore, they have no interest in what the property value is. Furthermore, the code of ethics and standards that licensed and certified appraisers must follow requires them to reveal any interest in the property they're appraising to the client. Say you find a property you want to buy, and you want to find out whether the asking price is fair. You look in the yellow pages, and hire Mary Appraiser, but it turns out that Mary's mother owns the property. Mary must tell you about her interest in the property or be in violation of the code of ethics and standards.

## Seeking an appraisal: Why you need one

Hiring an appraiser for real estate transactions often is a big decision and many reasons merit such a step. Anytime value is an issue, you may want to have an appraisal done. The following list includes reasons why people most often have appraisals done.

### Assessing or appraising

Many people commonly misuse the word *assessing* when they really mean *appraising*. Assessing and appraising are two different tasks. A real estate appraisal is an estimate of value. A real estate assessment is a certain type of value estimate done for the specific purpose of collecting property taxes. Because a whole chapter on property taxes explains assessments in detail (Chapter 16 if you're really curious), I don't go any further than that here. Just remember, an appraisal isn't an assessment, and the appraiser appraises property and doesn't assess it.

# Becoming an appraiser

Although this book focuses on you becoming a real estate broker or salesperson, people often are interested in what it takes to become an appraiser. Real estate appraising also is a licensed occupation governed by individual state laws, so if you're interested in the field, I encourage you to contact your state licensing authority to obtain the specific requirements in your home state. Some states have separate volunteer boards or commissions for brokers/salespersons and appraisers. Usually, however, the same state department or agency that handles real estate broker/salesperson licenses usually also governs appraisal licensing.

Prior to 1990, no widespread licensing of appraisers existed, but the savings and loan crisis of the late 1980s changed that after authorities discovered that a lack of honest and competent appraisals was part of the reason why banks loaned so much money on properties that were overvalued.

General information about appraisal licensing can be gotten from the Appraisal Foundation in Washington DC (`http://www.appraisalfoundation.org/`). But you should check with your state to see what the local requirements are if you're interested.

I cover the details of some of the following subjects in other chapters. For exam purposes, however, what you need to remember from the following information is a general list of the reasons appraisals may be done:

- **Buying:** Buyers of real estate can hire an appraiser to determine the fairness of the asking price of the property.

- **Eminent domain:** When the government seizes privately owned real estate for public use through eminent domain, it must pay for the property. The government determines the amount of payment with the help of an appraisal (see Chapter 8).

- **Estate valuation:** When someone dies, federal or state taxes may have to be paid on the value of the estate. If the estate includes real estate, the property has to be appraised to establish the estate's value as of the date of death.

- **Exchanges of ownership:** When owners exchange real estate, rather than selling it for money, the appraiser establishes the values of the properties to determine the fairness of the exchange (find information on property exchanges in Chapter 17).

- **Mortgage approval:** Mortgage lenders, that is, banks, savings and loan associations, and other lenders order the vast majority of appraisals. When buying or refinancing a property, the borrower puts the property up as collateral. If the property owner defaults on the loan, the lender takes the property and sells it. The lender wants to be sure that if the owner defaults, the property value covers the loan. (For more information on mortgages, see Chapter 15.)

- **Property taxes:** Real estate taxes are based on assessed values, which, in turn, are based on market values. Appraisals are sometimes done for clients who want to argue with municipal (city, town, and village) tax assessors for lower assessed values to obtain a reduction in taxes (I talk about taxes in Chapter 16).

- **Selling:** People who want to sell their real estate can seek an appraisal to determine a fair and competitive asking price for their property. Most often a seller asks a real estate agent for his opinion of value when preparing to sell a house.

- **Taxes other than property taxes:** Taxes often are due when someone gives a piece of real estate to someone as a gift. Alternatively, there may be a tax benefit in the form of a deduction if someone gives real estate to a charitable organization. In both cases, an appraiser comes in to determine the property's value.

- **Various court proceedings:** Bankruptcy, divorce, and the dissolving of a partnership or corporation may all involve real estate holdings. Appraisals usually establish the value of the property in question.

# Location, Location, Location!

Many things ultimately affect the value of real estate. You've probably heard the classic real estate question: What are the three most important factors in determining real estate value? Answer: Location, location, location. Although not the only factor, location probably is the most important. I discuss this and other factors later in this chapter.

But what does location really mean? And why is it so important? And what about all the other factors affecting real estate value? This section discusses the whats and whys of the location issue and its importance to real estate values.

## You can't move it

The most important characteristic of real estate and the reason location is such an important factor in its valuation is the fact that real estate is immobile. Exam questions in this area usually focus on the issue of immobility being the reason location is such an important value characteristic.

Unlike personal property, you can't move real estate. Think about this statement: It's what makes real estate so unique and the location issue so important. Say you own a piece of real estate in a low crime neighborhood. And over time that neighborhood begins to change and becomes somewhat unsafe. You just move the real estate, right? You can sell the real estate and move, but you can't move the real estate itself. What's more, because you can't move the real estate and the environment around it has changed, the value of the real estate probably has changed, too.

Not so with your brand new car. If you think it's unsafe to park on a street, you just park on a different block or in a parking garage.

## You're not on Gilligan's Island

The fact that real estate can't be moved makes it particularly vulnerable to the effects of the surrounding area, which can be positive, such as a piece of residential real estate located in what is perceived to be a good school district. The influence on value can be negative if, for example, the real estate is located near a sewage treatment plant. My point is this: You're not on an island. Unless of course you are, in which case you have a 360-degree waterfront view — so who's better off than you?

Real estate is immobile and highly affected by its surroundings; therefore, I provide the following list of some (but not all) of the environmental factors outside of the real estate itself that may affect value. And this is what is generally meant by real estate location:

 ✔ **Access to employment:** Are there employment centers and therefore jobs available within a reasonable distance?

 ✔ **Amenities and services:** Can you find shopping centers, libraries, restaurants, and so on?

 ✔ **Hazards and nuisances:** Is the real estate too close to gas stations, waste processing plants, or other unsightly constructions?

 ✔ **Nearness to transportation:** Are you near highways or public transportation?

 ✔ **Neighborhood compatibility:** The surrounding land uses are similar to your real estate.

 ✔ **Safety:** Make sure the crime levels are as low as possible.

　　✔ **Schools:** You may want to check with neighbors about the perceived quality of the schools. (See Chapter 5 for information about possible fair housing issues when discussing the quality of schools with a client or customer.)

　　✔ **Traffic:** Are the surrounding roadways residential or commercial streets?

Going into detail on each of these points isn't important, but if you want to pass the exam, remember that many of these factors are relative to the particular piece of property in question. For example, most people don't want their homes located on a heavily traveled street, but if you own a business property, then that is exactly where you want to be located.

## You can't make any more of it

The amount of land available is limited. That may seem obvious, but think about it in the context of a car, a chair, or anything else that can be manufactured. You can make more of those products, but you can't make any more land. Only a limited amount of land is available anywhere. That of course doesn't make all land valuable, but it does say something about the value of property wherever people want to be.

If you look at the list in the previous section, I think you'll agree that most people want to live in safe neighborhoods with good schools and easy access to jobs and shopping. However, only so many of those properties are available at any point in time. Given that many people want to live in those neighborhoods, a competition ensues for those pieces of real estate and that competition raises prices.

# Arriving at Different Types of Value

Value is value, you say. How could there be different types of value? In most cases you're correct. The type of value that appraisers usually deal with is called market value. But other kinds of value may be unique to a particular situation or a particular person. In addition to discussing market value in a fair amount of detail, this section briefly covers a few of the other types of value that you or an appraiser may encounter.

Market value is the type of value most often covered in real estate exams. Being able to at least distinguish among the other types of value I cover is important for test purposes.

## Going to market . . . value, that is

*Market value* is the value that appraisers deal with most often. It's the value we're most often concerned with in the typical real estate transaction. *Typical* is a key word here. A typical buyer and a typical seller will establish market value with the price the seller is willing to sell for and the buyer is willing to pay. Keep in mind that both seller and buyer typically know as much about the property as they can, have access to needed expertise like attorneys or home inspectors, act in response to typical motives like wanting a house to live in, and have sufficient time to look at a number of properties that have been on the open market. Anything that changes these typical motivations may change the sale price of the real estate but not its value.

For example, the old family homestead where your grandfather grew up is on the market and you just have to have it for sentimental reasons. Its market value is $150,000. But because you're so anxious to get it you offer and pay $200,000 for it. Its market value is still $150,000 even though the price paid is $200,000. Why? Because your motivation was personal, not typical. Typical buyers would have paid no more than $150,000, because they'd see it only as a normal place to live.

A sale meeting the market value criteria also presumes what is known as an arm's length transaction. An *arm's length transaction* implies that no relationship exists between the parties and that the buyer and seller each act in his or her own best interest. So buying your brother's house wouldn't be considered an arm's length transaction. Most exams ask for this definition, in relation to market value.

## Value in use

*Value in use* is the value a property has to a specific person who may use it for a specific purpose that's generally unavailable to the typical buyer.

Suppose a doctor obtains special permission from the city to use two rooms in a house as a medical office. The typical buyer looks at such a house and puts a value on those rooms for family or personal use, such as a family room or den; however, another doctor looking at that property may be willing to pay a higher price because of his ability to use those rooms as a medical office. The typical buyer pays market value, while the doctor pays a higher price based on value in use.

## Investment value

*Investment value* is the value to a specific investor with a specific plan for the property. Unlike value in use, which generally presupposes a use already in place, investment value assumes a use that may be proposed. Investor A may be willing to pay $3 million for a warehouse to be used as a warehouse. Investor B wants to convert the warehouse to a multi-screen movie theater. Investor B may want to pay only $2 million for the warehouse because of the additional expenses for the movie theater conversion project. Investor B probably would look for another piece of property that meets his investment criteria.

## Assessed value

*Assessed value* is the value placed on a property for tax purposes. It is associated with the term *ad valorem,* which means according to the value. I cover assessed value in Chapter 16.

# Creating, Changing, and Affecting Values: Some Economic Factors

Value doesn't just happen; people have to create it. Most of these personal actions, usually called *economic influences,* are nothing more than normal human behavior. In fact, as I go through these influences that affect real estate values, I expect you to say, "Oh! Sure! I knew that" or "Of course people want that." What you may not have known and unfortunately what the test writers want you to know are the technical names for these normal behaviors. The definitions in the following sections are usually covered on the exam, so be sure to remember them.

The test asks two kinds of questions about these economic principles or factors. You'll see questions about the definitions and questions asking you to identify the principle involved based on an example.

## Anticipation

All property value is created by the anticipation of the future benefits the property will provide. You buy your house today (and set the price today) so you can enjoy a bigger house for years to come.

## Balance

You find a balance between land value and building value in any given area. Overall property values and builder's profits on new homes are maximized when that balance is maintained. For example, in most cases you never want to build a house that costs $100,000 on a piece of vacant land that costs $500,000 (unless of course there was gold on the property; then who cares how much the house costs). No universal magic number exists for the proper balance between land and building value. But in general the balance needs to be similar to that which exists in the surrounding neighborhood.

## Change

Change is closely related to anticipation. The idea of change is that nothing remains the same. Physical, governmental, economic, and social changes all affect property value. Physical factors can include environmental changes such as weather, pollution, and earthquakes. Governmental factors may include changes in development regulations like zoning or the construction of new roads. Economic issues may be a change in interest rates or employment levels in an area. Social factors are issues like the aging of the baby boomers. Any or all of these and others can have an impact on the values of properties.

## Competition

Competition describes the fact that in real estate, the supply side (developers and builders) tries to meet the demand side (buyers and renters) until their demand is satisfied. A developer may see a need for a new office building in a particular location. If that building is a success, other builders are likely to follow with more office buildings until the last office building a builder erects remains partially vacant because the suppliers have created a surplus of office space.

## Conformity

Value is created and sustained when real estate characteristics are similar. If you live in a neighborhood of single-family houses, you don't want an office building to be built across the street from your house. The price of your house probably will be negatively affected by that incompatible land use.

## Contribution

In real estate terms, a building or a faucet is worth the value the market places on it, not its cost. You can spend a million dollars building a house, but if it's in the wrong location or has an extremely unusual design, it may not be worth a million dollars. On the other hand, a $1,000 paint job may increase the ultimate selling price of the house by $5,000.

## Externalities

Real estate, because it stays in a fixed location, is affected by everything that happens around it. The gas station on the corner, the quality of the schools, the factory that closes in town, mortgage interest rates, and so on all have an impact on the property value.

## Highest and best use

The principle of highest and best use states that every property has a single use that results in the highest value for that property. The use must meet four criteria. It must be

- **Physically possible:** You can't build an airport on a two-acre piece of property. In fact, you can't build a regional shopping center either. But you can build a house or apartment building.

- **Legally permitted:** You may physically be able to build any of the structures I listed previously, but if the zoning or deed restriction say that all you can build is a store or an office building, then your list of possibilities has just been narrowed considerably.

- **Economically feasible:** Depending on the market conditions at the time, you may find that one or the other of the physically possible and legally permitted uses isn't economically feasible, which means that you won't make money on that use.

- **Most (maximally) productive:** If you get to this point in the analysis and you still have at least two uses that meet the first three criteria then you need to determine which use will result in the most value. That becomes your highest and best use. If you get to the economic feasibility criteria and only one use emerges from that analysis, then that's your highest and best use.

## Increasing and decreasing returns

Increasing and decreasing (sometimes called diminishing) returns relate to adding improvements to a piece of real estate. Increasing returns come in when an improvement adds more value to the real estate than its cost. A dollar spent gives you more than a dollar back. Decreasing returns occur when an improvement gives back less value than its cost. The principle of increasing and decreasing returns is based on the principle of contribution, which I discuss in the earlier "Contribution" section.

An example of this principle might be adding bathrooms in a new house (or adding them to an old house). My numbers here are for illustrative purposes only. Each bathroom may cost you $6,000, but the first one may net you back $10,000 in terms of value. The second one may net $8,000, and the third one only a break-even $6,000, the fourth one $3,000, and the fifth one nothing. The returns on each bathroom go from increasing the value to creating no additional value. It's obvious that the buyers are putting less and less value on what are essentially unneeded bathrooms.

## Opportunity cost

For every investment opportunity you choose, you lose other investment opportunities. So when Auntie dies and leaves you $100,000, you can invest it in real estate. In doing so, you miss the opportunity to invest the money in certificates of deposit at the bank. And if you can get a 4 percent return on your money at the bank, you give up that return by investing in real estate. So you better make at least 4 percent and then some in your real estate investment.

## Plottage

The plottage principle states that the whole is sometimes greater than the sum of its parts, particularly with respect to real estate. You can put together four individual 5-acre parcels of land, each worth $50,000, to create a single 20-acre piece of property. This larger piece may now enable you to do something with it that was impossible with the smaller pieces, such as building a regional-size shopping mall. It turns out the value of the whole property, or the *plottage value,* is now $300,000 rather than four times $50,000, or $200,000. The act of putting the individual properties together is called *assemblage.*

## Regression and progression

You've heard the advice that you should always buy the smallest house in the neighborhood and not the biggest one. If you ever wondered why, it's because the principle of progression says that the higher values of larger homes tend to have a positive effect on the lesser value of the smaller home. Conversely, lower-priced homes have a negative effect on the value of the higher-priced home.

## Substitution

This economic principle says that a buyer will try to pay as little as possible for the property that meets the buyer's needs. Given three houses, each of which satisfies the needs of the buyer, that buyer will buy the least expensive house.

## Supply and demand

Because only so much land can be found in any particular location, and therefore only so much of anything — houses, stores, office buildings — can be built, the balance between supply and demand affects value. If demand goes up and supply goes down or remains the same, value increases. If demand goes down and supply increases or stays the same, value decreases. Sometimes on an exam the tester mentions only one of these factors, for example what happens to prices or values when housing demand goes up? The implication is that the other factor, in this case supply, stays the same. So don't get confused.

## Surplus productivity

After the builder puts together the land, labor, materials, and coordination necessary to build a building and then sells it, the difference between the costs and the selling price is *surplus productivity*. Economists use this term to signify profit.

# Finding Value by Analyzing Comparable Sales

The principal approach that appraisers use to estimate property value involves analyzing the sales of other similar properties, called *comparables*. This approach has several names, the most common of which is the *sales comparison approach.* Some people may refer to it as *the market analysis approach* or *the market comparison approach.*

The strength of the sales comparison approach lies in its reliance on the principle of *substitution*. This principle states that no one pays more than is necessary for a piece of real estate that meets that person's needs (see the section earlier in this chapter). The principle of substitution is what most people apply as they search for a house to buy, even if they don't call it that. Because this approach is based on previous sales of similar properties, it can provide an accurate estimate of real estate value. Appraisers use the approach most often when appraising single-family and two-to-four-unit residential real estate. The weakness of the approach is when the market is slow and it becomes difficult to find comparable sales.

## Understanding the basics

The idea behind the sales comparison approach is to compare previous sales of real estate to the subject property being appraised to arrive at an estimate of the real estate's value.

For example, you ask Joan the appraiser to appraise a three-bedroom, two-bath, 2,500-square-foot house in a typical suburban subdivision. Through her research into the sales in the area, Joan finds three sales of almost identical houses in the last four months. These previously sold houses are called *comparables* or *comps*. Each of the houses sold for $250,000. Joan, by the way, is a very lucky appraiser, because even similar houses don't often sell for the same price. Joan estimates that the value of the house she is appraising is $250,000 based on the fact that three similar homes recently sold for that price. And that is the sales comparison approach at its simplest.

An appraiser normally investigates as many as ten or more comparables, finally selecting a minimum of three to five to use in the sales comparison approach. After making all the appropriate adjustments to each of the comparables (see the next section), the appraiser examines the comparables and arrives at a value estimate for the property. It seldom occurs that the three adjusted sale prices are exactly the same. In this case, the problem is easy because the prices are all the same. Where the prices are different, the appraiser never averages the three prices but rather analyzes the comparables and the various adjustments made, and through experience and trained judgment arrives at the value estimate.

## Adjusting the sales price

The situations that appraisers most often have to deal with in applying the sales comparison approach are comparables that aren't identical to the subject property. Appraisers go through an adjustment process to compensate for the differences in the properties.

The adjustment process is really quite simple and pretty intuitive. And the people who write the state tests expect you to understand it and be able to apply it.

Here's a simple example. The subject property is a three-bedroom, two-bath home. Joan the appraiser doesn't currently know the value of this house. A very similar house sold two months ago for $275,000. The comparable house, called Comparable A, is the same in all respects as the subject property except that it has four bedrooms. Comparable A is superior to the subject property. Joan's research indicates that the value of the fourth bedroom is $25,000. That means that the buyer of Comparable A paid $25,000 more for that house than he or she would have for a three-bedroom house.

Joan, when preparing her appraisal report, goes through the process of subtracting that $25,000 bedroom value from the $275,000 sales price of Comparable A. The resulting price of $250,000 is the *adjusted sales price*.

$275,000 (sale price of Comparable A) − $25,000 (value of fourth bedroom) = $250,000 (adjusted sales price)

Using the principle of substitution, the adjusted sales price for Comparable A, or $250,000, is the estimated value of the three-bedroom house.

Now look at an opposite kind of adjustment. Joan is still appraising the three-bedroom, two-bath house. She finds another comparable, which she calls Comparable B. This comparable also is the same as the subject property except that it has only one bathroom. It is inferior to the subject and sold for $240,000. Her research indicates that the value of that second bathroom is $10,000. What does she have to do to make the comparable like the subject? She has to add a bathroom, or more specifically, the value of that second bathroom.

> $240,000 (sale price of Comparable B) + $10,000 (value of second bathroom) = $250,000 (adjusted sales price)

The adjusted sales price for Comparable B, or $250,000, is the estimated value of the two-bathroom house.

The adjustment process is a matter of adding or subtracting the value of the differences between the subject property and the comparable property to or from the comparable. Take a look at that again, because this part tends to confuse people. You make the adjustments to the comparable to make the comparable property like the subject property. So keep your hands off the subject. The adjusted comparables indicate to the appraiser the estimated value of the subject property.

## It isn't old, it's mature: Making age adjustments

When I talk about age, I'm not talking about the age of the appraiser; I mean the age of a structure. The market (that is buyers and sellers) takes the age of a structure into account when deciding on what to pay.

Here's a little brain teaser: The subject property is 5 years old, and the comparable is 15 years old and sold for $190,000; otherwise, the houses are similar. The value of that ten-year difference in age is $5,000. Should you add or subtract that $5,000 from the sales price of the comparable? That's right, you need to add the $5,000 because the 15-year-old house is considered worse than or inferior to the 5-year-old house. For now, I made up the $5,000 figure but in another part of this chapter in the "How much is that hot tub worth? Finding adjustment values" section, I discuss how you can find the value of an age or any other type of adjustment.

For some reason, when age numbers are introduced into the problem of making adjustments, the direction (plus or minus) of the adjustment becomes a little muddled. But if you apply the superior/inferior test, it becomes clear immediately. Older is considered worse; therefore, you add the adjustment value to the comparable sale. Newer is considered better; therefore, you subtract the adjustment value from the comparable sale.

## Having time to adjust for time

The sales comparison approach is based on previous sales of similar houses (comparables) to indicate the current value of the property being appraised. The word "previous" can cause some difficulty, because real estate values tend to change over time. As recent history has shown real estate values can go up or down.

Take a look at an example of what is usually called a time or market adjustment. Once again, Joan the appraiser is appraising a house. She finds a comparable house that is almost identical in all respects to the subject property. The comparable house sold for $200,000 five months ago. Her research indicates that the real estate market has been quite strong in the area and property values have gone up approximately 1 percent per month during the past five months. To properly account for this rise in property values, Joan needs to ask the question, "What would the comparable have sold for if instead of selling five months ago, it sold today?" It would sell for 5 percent more. The adjustment calculation becomes

1 percent per month × 5 months = 5 percent

$200,000 (sale price of comparable) × 5 percent (increase in value for five months) = $10,000 (value of time adjustment)

$200,000 + $10,000 = $210,000 (adjusted sales price)

The adjusted sales price for Comparable B, or (again) $210,000, is the indicated value of the subject property.

You calculate a downward trend in property values over time the same way, only the value of the time adjustment is be subtracted from the sales price of the comparable to give you the value of the subject property.

And for you mathematical whizzes who are wondering about compounding the 1 percent per month, the common practice is to simply add the monthly increases in real estate value to get a total percentage increase for the period of time you're dealing with.

## How much is that hot tub worth? Figuring adjustment values

By now you're probably wondering where all these adjustment values come from. In fact many of my appraisal students think there's some kind of standardized set of numbers as to how much a bathroom or bedroom is worth. Although no such set of numbers exists, a method for getting those numbers does.

The main way appraisers find the value of an adjustment is by extensively analyzing the market and using a technique called paired sales analysis to find these adjustment values. *Paired sales analysis* is based on the idea that if two houses are similar in all respects except one, and the sales price of each home is different, the dollar amount of difference between the two houses is the likely to be value of the unique attribute or feature of one of the houses. Look at these two houses for an example. House A has four bedrooms. It sold for $400,000. House B, which sold for $375,000, has three bedrooms. In all other respects, House B is the same as House A. The only physical difference between the two houses is the fourth bedroom, along with a monetary difference of $25,000 between the two sale prices. The fourth bedroom, in this case, is worth $25,000.

The appraiser can now take that $25,000 figure and use it wherever appropriate to make adjustments to comparables when applying the sales comparison approach to estimating value.

## Finding Value by Analyzing Replacement Cost and Depreciation

Another method of estimating the value of real estate is called the cost approach. The *cost approach* is based on the idea that the components of a piece of real estate, or the land and buildings, can be added together to arrive at an estimate of value, if they're valued separately. The cost approach is particularly useful for unique properties that have few comparable sales and for new construction. If you were asked to appraise a church for example, you may use the cost approach because it would be rare to find many sales of churches.

## A journey begins with the first step . . . or a formula

The formula for the cost approach is:

Replacement or reproduction cost − depreciation + land value = value

A breakdown of the steps of this method follows:

1. **Estimate the replacement or reproduction cost of the improvement (structure).**

   Turn to the section on "How much did you say? Estimating replacement and reproduction costs" for instruction.

2. **Estimate all the depreciation of the improvement (accrued depreciation).**

   See "Estimating depreciation" section for more info.

3. **Subtract accrued depreciation from the reproduction/replacement cost.**

   Accrued depreciation is the total of all the estimated depreciation.

4. **Estimate the land value separately.**

   Flip to the section "Dirt costs money, too: Estimating land value" to discover the way.

5. **Add the depreciated cost of the structure to the land value.**

   The result is the estimate of value.

   | | |
   |---|---|
   | Reproduction/replacement cost | $200,000 |
   | − Accrued (total) depreciation | − $50,000 |
   | Depreciated value of improvements | $150,000 |
   | + Land value | + $60,000 |
   | Estimated value | $210,000 |

I devote the rest of this section to a discussion of each of these concepts.

The cost approach has a lot of terminology that may be unfamiliar. Remember, most salesperson's tests ask a lot of definition questions.

## How much did you say? Estimating replacement and reproduction costs

*Reproduction cost* is the cost to construct an exact duplicate of the subject structure at today's costs. *Replacement cost* is the cost to construct a structure with the same usefulness (utility) as a comparable structure using today's materials and standards.

For example, you may use the cost approach to appraise a house with plaster walls. A reproduction cost estimate requires estimating the cost to construct plaster walls. A replacement cost estimate, however, estimates the cost to put up sheet rock walls according to the current standard.

Replacement cost is most often used in the cost approach. Reproduction cost would be used for say historically or architecturally significant structures.

Two types of costs are included in every construction cost estimate: direct costs and indirect costs. *Direct costs,* also called *hard costs,* are those expenses directly associated with the actual construction of a building, including labor and building materials. *Indirect or soft costs* are expenses not directly related to the physical construction process, including permit fees, architectural costs, and builder's profit. Direct and indirect costs are part of the estimate of the costs.

You should know the four methods for estimating reproduction or replacement cost. For exam purposes, your ability to distinguish among the four methods by their characteristics is sufficient. Generally, no calculations are required. The four methods include

- **Square footage method:** Involves calculating the cost of construction by multiplying the square footage of the structure by the construction cost for that particular type of building. For example, you'd multiply a $100 per square foot cost to build the kind of house you're appraising by the 2,000 square foot total area of the house to arrive at a cost estimate of $200,000 to replace the structure. The square footage method is the one more commonly used by appraisers to estimate replacement or reproduction cost.

- **Unit-in-place method:** Provides the cost to construct a building by estimating the installation costs, including materials, of the individual components of the structure. So if you know you need 1,000 square feet of sheet rock to cover the walls, you need to find out the cost of buying, installing, and finishing the sheet rock on a per-square-foot basis and then multiply by 1,000 square feet. Another approach to this method is to estimate the four main steps (units) to building a house. For instance, cost of foundation, cost of roof and framing, cost of mechanicals, and cost of walls and finish work. Each step is estimated separately and then all are added together.

- **Quantity survey method:** More detailed than the previous method, it requires you to break down all the components of a building and estimate the cost of the material and installation separately. So in the sheet rock example, you estimate so many dollars each to buy the sheet rock, screws, and tape, and to pay for the installation.

- **Index method:** Requires you to know the original construction cost (without land) of the subject building. You then multiply that original cost by a number that takes into account the increase in construction costs since the building was built. National companies that do this kind of research publish these numbers. If a building cost $20,000 to build originally, and the current index in that area for this type of structure is 1.80, the calculation is $100,000 × 1.80 = $180,000, or the cost to construct the same building today.

## Estimating depreciation

Now you've arrived at the second step in applying the cost approach to estimating the value of a piece of property. *Depreciation* is the loss in value to any structure due to a variety of factors, such as wear and tear, age, and poor location, each of which I discuss in this section. I generally view depreciation as the difference in value between the perfect new structure cost that you estimate and the actual value of the structure that's being appraised.

The term *accrued depreciation* means the total depreciation of a building from all causes. You should also note that accrued depreciation isn't the kind of depreciation that concerns accountants when they depreciate a building or a piece of equipment for tax purposes. Licensing exams generally ask two types of questions about depreciation: A question asking for the definition of a particular type of depreciation and a question giving you an item of depreciation and asking you what type of depreciation that item represents. Occasionally you may get a question that asks you to calculate depreciation using a very simple technique known as the straight-line method. I review that technique in the section on "Don't be a square: The straight-line method of calculating depreciation" later in this chapter.

### *Over the hill: Physical deterioration (curable and incurable)*

*Physical deterioration* is the normal wear and tear that a building experiences as it ages and it depends on the original quality of construction and the level of ongoing maintenance. The two categories of deterioration, curable and incurable, have more to do with economics than the actual physical possibility of correcting something. As part of applying the cost approach, the appraiser analyzes these items:

- ✔ **Curable deterioration:** Refers to a form of deterioration that's economically feasible to repair. In other words, the increase in value exceeds the cost of repair. Painting is a good example of something that generally adds more value than it costs.

- ✔ **Incurable deterioration:** If the cost of repairing an item surpasses the value it adds to the structure, the item is considered incurable even if you can fix it. Usually these forms of deterioration are physical items associated with the structure of a building — significant foundation repairs probably would be classified as incurable. They're incurable because you wouldn't benefit economically by fixing them

### *Functional obsolescence*

Outmoded design in older structures or unacceptable design in newer structures usually points to a type of depreciation known as *functional obsolescence*. It too is separated into curable and incurable categories relating to economic feasibility. An older home that has four bedrooms but a single bathroom located off the kitchen suffers from functional obsolescence. This example shows incurability because the cost of constructing an entirely new bathroom probably exceeds any increase in value to the house it may generate.

A newer home built with only two bedrooms and a room for a home office would suffer from curable functional obsolescence. Most people want at least three bedrooms. Adding a closet to the home office space and converting it into a bedroom would be relatively easy. So the value of the house increases by an amount greater than what you spent to build the closet.

### *External obsolescence*

External obsolescence is a form of depreciation caused by factors external to the land itself. It's always incurable because land can't be moved. Economically, no amount of money can correct the problem. This form of depreciation can be caused by economic or physical, usually called locational, features. A gas station adjacent to a single-family house is a source of external obsolescence. Unusually bad market conditions can also be considered external obsolescence.

### *Don't be a square: The straight-line method of calculating depreciation*

The straight-line method of calculating depreciation is one of the few math questions you might be asked about the cost approach.

The *straight-line method* for estimating depreciation presumes that a structure deteriorates at the same rate each year. This method, which also is called the *economic age life method,* involves an estimate of what are called the total economic life of a building and its effective age. These numbers are somewhat subjective estimates that appraisers make when using the straight-line method. Don't worry about where the appraiser gets these numbers. For exam purposes, remember the definitions and how to do the calculations. The *economic life* of a building reflects the number of years it contributes to the value of the land. The *effective age* is an estimate of how old the building appears to be, given wear and tear, maintenance, and upgrades. For example, say you have two buildings built 40 years ago, and one has been completely upgraded and well maintained but the other has had little done to it. These two buildings will have different effective ages.

The calculation presumes that a building deteriorates at an equal rate during its economic life; therefore, if you estimate the economic life of a building to be 50 years, in one year it deteriorates 2 percent of its total value. In effect, it uses up 2 percent of its total economic life. The fraction 1/50 also is 2 percent. So the building depreciates at the rate of 2 percent per year because of physical deterioration. Just in case you get thrown a question with a different total economic life, say 40 years, the calculation would be 1/40. If you divide 1 by 40 you get 2.5 percent. Whatever the total economic life, if you divide the number one by the total economic life, you get the annual percentage that the building depreciates.

The next step is where the estimate of effective age comes in. Say the effective age of a building is ten years. That means it has used up ten years of its economic life. If the building's economic life is 50 years and from the previous calculation you know it depreciates at 2 percent per year, all you do is multiply the effective age by the annual percent of depreciation to get the total depreciation. In the example:

10 years effective age × 2 percent per year depreciation = 20 percent total depreciation

The final piece of the formula is multiplying the total percent of depreciation by the reproduction or replacement cost. To continue the example, say your reproduction cost was $100,000. The formula follows as:

$100,000 reproduction cost × 20 percent (0.20) = $20,000 total depreciation

$100,000 reproduction cost − $20,000 depreciation = $80,000 depreciated cost of improvements

For the test, you need to be able to do all these calculations when given the appropriate data.

## Dirt costs money, too: Estimating land value

The final step in the cost approach is for the appraiser to develop an estimate of the land value and add it to the depreciated value of the reproduction or replacement cost. Appraisers use a variety of methods to calculate land value. The methods vary with the type of land being appraised and the information available.

The most commonly used method for estimating the value of a single piece of property on which you'd build a house is the sales comparison approach. (For more information, see "Finding Value by Analyzing Comparable Sales" earlier in this chapter.) Features like the land's location, topography, view, and size and shape are compared to arrive at an estimate of value. The intricacies of the various methods of site appraisal are beyond the scope of sales and brokers license exams, so you need not worry about that.

# Finding Value by Analyzing a Property's Income

The third method for estimating the value of a piece of real estate involves analyzing the income that a property generates. The *income approach,* as it's called, analyzes the future financial benefits of a piece of real estate and converts it into an estimate of present value. As you may imagine, appraisers use this method to estimate value on properties that are purchased for their investment potential. Properties such as apartment houses, shopping centers, and office buildings usually are appraised using this method.

The two methods within the income approach that I review are the gross rent multiplier method and the income capitalization method. I show you some calculations, but most exam questions are about definitions and methods. Math questions in this subject area are fair game; although you don't see many, you shouldn't be surprised to see one or two.

## Grossing out the rent

*The Gross Rent Multiplier* (GRM) technique for estimating value is based on the idea that a property value can be calculated as a multiple of the gross rent. The formula states this succinctly:

Gross rent × GRM (factor) = value estimate

The gross rent is the monthly income of the building with no deductions for expenses. Another rent factor is called the *gross income multiplier* (GIM). In this case, the income used is gross annual rent rather than monthly. Other than that, all the formulas and resulting values are the same.

You're now correctly asking, "So where do I get the GRM factor?" As with all the data appraisers use, they calculate it based on the market. After getting all the information needed on the subject property, the appraiser researches the market for that type of property, which is usually the local market, to obtain a number of comparable sales. *Comparable sales* are recent sales of similar buildings. After locating a number of similar buildings, the appraiser needs to find the sales price and the gross income of each building. By dividing the sales price of the building by the gross rent, the appraiser obtains a gross rent multiplier for each of the comparables. If the buildings are similar, which they should be if they're comparable, the gross rent multipliers also will be similar numbers.

Say you're appraising a three-unit residential rental property. The gross monthly rent of this property is $600 per apartment or $1,800 per month for the whole building. You research similar buildings and find three comparable properties that are in the same location, approximately the same size, and that generate approximately the same gross monthly rent. The data is shown here:

| Sale price | Gross monthly rent |
|------------|--------------------|
| $200,000   | $2,000             |
| $180,000   | $1,800             |
| $190,000   | $1,900             |

You now apply the formula for finding the GRM to this data.

Sales price ÷ gross monthly rent = GRM

Applying the formula to the example data, you find that the GRM for each of the comparables would be 100, which means that the comparable buildings each sold for a price that was 100 times its gross monthly rent. The final step is to apply the value formula to the subject property:

Gross monthly rent × GRM = value estimate

$1,800 × 100 = $180,000

The GRM method is particularly useful for small-income-producing properties, such as one-to-four-family houses. For more math related to the GRM, see Chapter 18.

## Capitalizing the income

Another method for appraising real estate based on its income is known as the *income capitalization approach.* Like the GRM and GIM, this method converts the income of a property into an estimate of its value. Appraisers generally use this method for commercial buildings such as shopping centers, office buildings, and large apartment buildings. The basic formula for this approach, commonly referred to as IRV, is:

Net operating income (I) ÷ capitalization rate (R) = value (V)

You can break this formula down into these three steps:

1. **Estimating the net operating income.**

2. **Determining the capitalization rate.**

3. **Applying the IRV formula to arrive at a value estimate.**

Keep in mind that I cover more math related to capitalization in Chapter 18.

### Estimating net operating income

The appraiser needs to have access to income and expense statements for the subject building and for similar buildings in the area to estimate net operating income. Having that information on hand enables the appraiser to accurately estimate income and expenses for the building. Remember that all income and expenses in the income capitalization method always are annual figures. You can break down the actual process of estimating the net operating income (NOI) into four steps:

1. **Estimate the potential gross income.**

   *Potential gross income* is the income that the building generates when rented at 100 percent occupancy, at market rent or lease rent or a combination of both. *Market rent* is the rent that normally is charged for that kind of space in the market place. Lease rent is also known as *scheduled* or *contract rent.* Potential gross income includes adding in income from all sources, such as the laundry machines in an apartment house or separately rented parking spaces.

2. **Subtract a vacancy and collection loss figure from potential gross income.**

   This number, which usually is expressed as a percentage, is the appraiser's estimate from the market for these kinds of buildings in the local area, and it reflects normal loss of income caused by nonpayment of rent and periodic vacancies. Additional income, say from an antenna rental on the roof of the building is added in at this point to arrive at *effective gross income.*

3. **Estimate all building expenses and subtract them from the effective gross income.**

   Building expenses fall into three categories: fixed, variable (sometimes called operating), and reserves. *Fixed expenses* are expenses that don't change with the occupancy of the building, like property taxes and insurance. *Variable expenses* are pretty much all other expenses, some of which may vary with the occupancy of the building. These expenses include snow removal, utilities, management fees, and so on. *Reserves,* sometimes called reserves for replacements, are funds that landlords put aside for items that have to be periodically replaced but not on an annual basis. Cooking stoves in an apartment are an example of a reserve item. Note that the expenses don't include mortgage payments or building depreciation.

4. **Subtract the estimated expenses from the effective gross income.**

   The result is the net operating income.

You can put some numbers to these steps to see what the formula looks like:

| | |
|---|---|
| Potential gross income | $50,000 |
| – Vacancy and collection loss (10 percent of $50,000) | –5,000 |
| Additional income | 3,000 |
| Effective gross income | 48,000 |
| **Expenses** | |
| Fixed | $10,000 |
| Variable | $23,000 |
| Reserves | $5,000 |
| – Total expenses | – 38,000 |
| Net operating income | $10,000 |

### Determining the capitalization rate

A *capitalization rate* is similar to a rate of return; that is, the percentage that the investors hope to get out of the building in income. There are a number of ways appraisers learn to calculate capitalization rates, most of which are beyond what you're required to know. The most straightforward method and the one I teach is pretty simple. All you need are some comparable sales — buildings similar to the subject property being appraised that have sold recently.

The formula you use is

Net operating income (I) ÷sales price (V) = capitalization rate (R)

This formula is applied using the net operating income and sale price of each comparable that you're analyzing. Note in this formula, the reversal of the IRV formula for finding value (see "Capitalizing the income" earlier in this chapter).

Here's an example: A building sells for $200,000. Its net operating income is $20,000.

Applying the formula, you divide $20,000 by $200,000, which looks like $20,000 ÷ $200,000 = 0.10 or 10 percent. Capitalization rates are expressed in percentages.

Although the results may look wrong because you're always dividing a smaller number by a bigger number, remember that you're trying to get a percentage, so the answer always is less than one.

After studying the various capitalization rates that you get after applying the IRV formulas, you select the one you think is the most applicable to the building you're appraising and apply it to the final step.

### Applying the formula to estimate value

Now back to the basic income capitalization formula. You can use the numbers from the previous examples to calculate the value:

Net operating income (I) ÷ capitalization rate (R) = estimated value (V)

$10,000 ÷ 0.10 = $100,000

By dividing the net operating income of the subject property by the capitalization rate you have chosen you arrive at an estimate of $100,000 as the value of the building.

### Calculating income

Now don't panic. I didn't slip another step in here. But you may find one other part of the formula that test writers occasionally like to ask about: calculating net operating income. Notice that I said calculating and not estimating.

Suppose you have a commercial building that sells for $300,000 and its rate of return or capitalization rate is 8 percent. With that information, you can find out what the net operating income (NOI) is. In this case, you multiply the building sales price or value by the capitalization rate or rate of return.

Value (V) × capitalization rate (R) = net operating income (I)

$300,000 × 0.08 = $24,000

# I'd Like to Solve the Puzzle: Reconciling a Property's Value

The final step in the appraisal process is coming up with a final estimate of value. When the appraiser uses as many of these approaches as possible, she estimates the final value using a process called *reconciliation*.

*Reconciliation* is the process of analyzing and weighing the results of the various approaches as applied to an appraisal problem. It never involves averaging the values. The process first involves looking at each approach and relating it to the kind of property you're appraising. The appraiser relies most heavily on the approach (listed below) that's best suited to a particular kind of property.

- ✔ **The sales comparison approach:** Single-family houses
- ✔ **The cost approach:** Unique properties such as churches
- ✔ **The income approach:** Investment properties such as office buildings

The appraiser uses the other approaches to support the resulting value estimate because the differences among the three individual value estimates usually is not that great.

Finally, the appraiser prepares the report in whatever format is appropriate for the project — usually either a form report, which is how most mortgage appraisals are done, or what is referred to as a narrative report. The form, which was created by Federal agencies to provide a standardized way of preparing appraisal information, is known as the Uniform Residential Appraisal Report Form (URAR), or sometimes the Fannie Mae form, for the agency that was most responsible for its creation. A narrative report, which is used mostly for large commercial property appraisals, is like the term papers you did in school and contains more information than a form report.

# Review Questions and Answers

The exam questions you're likely to get about appraising are definitional questions and some application questions. Memorizing the terminology and knowing the math will get you through the exam.

1. What approach to value would be most suitable to appraise a shopping center?

   (A) Income approach

   (B) Cost approach

   (C) Sales comparison approach

   (D) Reconstructed value approach

   *Correct answer:* (A). Real estate that is purchased for investment, such as shopping centers generally is appraised using the income approach.

2. In the direct sales comparison approach, what type of adjustment should you make when the comparable is better than the subject?

   (A) Positive to subject

   (B) Negative to subject

   (C) Positive to comparable

   (D) Negative to comparable

   *Correct answer:* (D). Two things to remember here: First, you never adjust the subject, only the comparable. Second, when the comparable is better than the subject, the adjustment is negative.

3. A buyer who buys the least expensive house available to satisfy his needs is behaving according to what economic principle?

   (A) Supply and demand

   (B) Anticipation

   (C) Progression

   (D) Substitution

   *Correct answer:* (D). Note that this is a short case study question. The test also asks straight definition questions about these economic principles.

4. Reproductions cost is

   (A) used in the income approach to value.

   (B) the cost to construct a building using modern materials.

   (C) the cost to construct an exact duplicate of the building.

   (D) the same as market value.

   *Correct answer:* (C). Reproduction cost is the exact replacement of the structure. Replacement cost is a structure having the same utility (usefulness) but using modern materials.

5. The rent on a house is $500 per month. The gross rent multiplier is 180. What is the estimated value of the house?

   (A) $270,000

   (B) $1,080,000

   (C) $36,000

   (D) $90,000

   *Correct answer:* (D). Gross monthly rent × gross rent multiplier = value.

   $$\$500 \times 180 = \$90,000$$

   Don't multiply the rent by 12. This formula is based on monthly rent.

6. If a building's net operating income is $1,000 a month and an appraiser uses a rate of return of 10 percent, what is the estimated value of the building using the income capitalization approach?

   (A) $100,000

   (B) $1,000,000

   (C) $120,000

   (D) $1,200,000

   *Correct answer:* (C). I ÷ R = V

   $$\$12,000 \div 10 \text{ percent (expressed as } 0.10) = \$120,000$$

   Remember that with the income capitalization approach, you always use the annual income. So the first step is multiplying the monthly income by 12 months. Test writers also sometimes use the term *property* to mean any type of real estate. They also use the term *rate of return* to mean a capitalization rate. Don't be thrown by these references.

7. The reproduction cost of a house is estimated at $120,000. Its economic life is 50 years. Its effective age is 20 years. What is the depreciated value of the house?

   (A) $72,000

   (B) $48,000

   (C) $60,000

   (D) $96,000

   *Correct answer:* (A). Read the question carefully (that goes for all questions) and make sure you do every step.

   1 ÷ economic life = rate of depreciation per year

   ⅟₅₀ = 2 percent per year

   Rate of depreciation per year × effective age = total rate of depreciation

   2 percent × 20 = 40 percent

Reproduction or replacement cost × total rate of depreciation = total amount of depreciation

$120,000 × 40 percent (expressed as 0.40) = $48,000

Reproduction or replacement cost – total amount of depreciation = depreciated value

$120,000 – $48,000 = $72,000

8. A subject property has four bedrooms. A comparable has three bedrooms and sold for $160,000. In all other respects the properties are alike. The value of the fourth bedroom is estimated to be $20,000. What is the indicated value of the subject?

   (A) $180,000

   (B) $160,000

   (C) $80,000

   (D) $140,000

   *Correct answer:* (A). If the comparable is worse than the subject, you add the adjustment amount to the comparable. The comparable has one less bedroom than the subject. So you add the $20,000 value of the bedroom to the comparable.

9. A comparable sold for $110,000 five months ago. You estimate that real estate values have been rising at 1 percent per month during that period of time. How much is an identical house worth today?

   (A) $5,500

   (B) $116,600

   (C) $104,500

   (D) $115,500

   *Correct answer:* (D). 5 months × 1 percent per month = 5 percent

   $110,000 × 5 percent (expressed as 0.05) = $5,500

   $110,000 + $5,500 = $115,500

10. What appraisal approach would an appraiser most likely use to appraise a sports arena?

    (A) Cost approach

    (B) Income capitalization approach

    (C) Gross rent multiplier approach

    (D) Sales comparison approach

    *Correct answer:* (A). Sports arenas are fairly unique, and you can seldom find comparable sales. Stadiums also are built as service-type buildings rather than investment properties. The cost approach most often is used for unique real estate.

# Chapter 15

# Finding the Money: Mortgages

. . . . . . . . . . . . . . . . . . . . . . . . . . . . . . . . . . . . . . . . . . . . . . . . . . . . . . . .

## In This Chapter

▶ Understanding how real estate mortgages work

▶ Finding where to borrow money to buy real estate

▶ Checking out lenders' considerations for making loans

▶ Discovering different mortgages and how they're paid back

▶ Looking at consumer protection laws

. . . . . . . . . . . . . . . . . . . . . . . . . . . . . . . . . . . . . . . . . . . . . . . . . . . . . . . .

*I*t's no secret that most people don't buy property for cash. They borrow money from banks, savings and loan associations, and other lending institutions so they can buy a home or investment property now rather than waiting to save up the money. Part of a real estate agent's work deals with advising buyers where they may be able to borrow money to buy property. Because of all the various types of mortgages and repayment plans, real estate agents also need to be familiar with the idea that when it comes to mortgage money, one size does not fit all. Although in most cases, real estate agents ultimately refer buyers to banks and other lending institutions or mortgage brokers to get the financing they need to purchase a house, familiarity with many of the details of real estate financing is important to provide sound advice to buyers.

This chapter takes a look at the basics of the mortgage process and the sources of mortgage funding. I cover several considerations that lenders take into account when making the loans. You discover different kinds of mortgages and repayment plans, do a little mortgage math, and find out about laws that require everyone be treated fairly when they try to borrow mortgage money, even if they're 70 years old and want a 30-year mortgage.

## The Way Things Work: Mortgage Basics

The place to start a discussion about real estate financing is with some basic concepts and terminology. In this section, I cover the basic mortgage process, review some important terms, discuss several mortgage theories, and give you the scoop on conditions included in a mortgage. After you understand how real estate financing works and get used to some of the terms, specific mortgage concepts will fit in pretty nicely. All of this information probably will be covered on the exam, especially the definitions and maybe a little math.

## The nuts and bolts of the mortgage process

A buyer and a seller agree on a price and the other terms involved in the sale of a house. The buyer has some of the money in cash, say about 20 percent of the total price, for a down payment but needs to borrow the rest. The buyer goes to a bank or other lending institution to apply for a loan for the rest of the purchase price of the house. The lender considers these two things when examining the buyer's application:

- ✔ The ability of the buyer to repay the loan, which includes factors like the buyer's credit and employment history.

- ✔ The value of the real estate being purchased, which is usually determined by an appraisal, a topic that I discuss in Chapter 14. Most work in the appraisal industry involves estimating property values for mortgage purposes. Because property is considered security for the loan, lenders want to be sure that the property can be sold to pay off the loan if necessary. (See "Considerations for Lenders Accepting Mortgages," later in this chapter, for more.)

The lender issues what is known as a mortgage commitment, and on the day of closing (that's when title to the property changes hands — see Chapter 9), the buyer also closes on the mortgage loan. Closing on the mortgage simply means entering into the final and formal agreement to accept the money and pay it back. The check from the bank is given to the seller, and a short time later, the buyer begins paying off the loan under the terms of the mortgage agreement.

## Liens, notes, and a mistake most people make

Although you may sign a whole bunch of papers at the closing, the two important documents you'll sign as part of the mortgage process are the note and the mortgage. I explain these and some other terms associated with mortgage loans in this section. Definitions are important here for test purposes and basic definitions will guide you to an understanding of each term and choosing the right answers on the exam.

The process of using property as security for a loan is called *hypothecation.* In real estate circles, that process is accomplished through a *mortgage,* which is a document prepared by a lender and signed by the borrower (at the closing) that essentially serves as a *voluntary lien* on a piece of real estate. Liens are financial obligations that are attached to real estate. Remember through hypothecation the owner of the property voluntarily places a specific (meaning that property only) lien on the property in favor of the lender without giving up possession of the property. When the mortgage is signed by the borrower, the property is committed as security for the loan. A mortgage lien enables the lender to sell the property after a foreclosure process, to pay off the debt, if the borrower *defaults,* or does not pay off the debt. For more about what's included in a mortgage agreement, see "Common conditions of a mortgage loan" later in this chapter. For more about liens, see Chapter 8.

The second document that the borrower signs as part of the mortgage loan process is called a promissory note (or sometimes just *the note*). A *promissory note* is an agreement to repay a loan according to certain terms and conditions.

A *trust deed* is used in some locales to secure a mortgage loan. A trust deed also is called a deed of trust. For a deed of trust to work, a third party must be involved. The *trustor* (or borrower) gives a deed to a *trustee* (the third party). The deed gives title to the property, without the right of possession. This type of title sometimes is referred to as bare or naked title. The trustee holds the deed until the loan is paid off. The property then is reconveyed back to the trustor. If the trustor doesn't complete the terms of the loan, the trustee conveys title to the property to the *beneficiary* (the lender) for sale to satisfy the debt. (For more about trust deeds, see Chapter 9.) Now that you know about mortgages and notes allow me to clear up a common misuse of the word you just learned about — mortgage. In fact, the misuse is so common that I even hear real estate agents using it the wrong way. And in the meantime, you'll discover two other important words related to mortgages that can get you in trouble on the exam.

So, you're thinking, the buyer goes to the bank and applies for a mortgage. Wrong! Well, then, you say, "The bank gives the buyer a mortgage." Wrong! "So," you simply say, "I'm going to get a mortgage to buy my new house." Wrong, again!

Yes, wrong on all three accounts, and yet those are the things most people say, including virtually everyone in the real estate business. Why these commonly used phrases are wrong and the right way to describe the process are the focus of two words that you absolutely need to remember — mortgagor and mortgagee.

You go to the bank to borrow money. In return for that money, you agree to give the bank a mortgage on your property. Remember, the mortgage is a voluntary lien that enables the bank to take the property and sell it, if you don't pay back what you borrowed. Thus, because you're giving the mortgage to the bank, you are the *mortgagor,* and because the bank accepts the mortgage in return for lending you the money, it is considered the *mortgagee.*

Compare mortgagor and mortgagee with the words lessor and lessee in a lease situation. The lessor is the landlord. The landlord provides the lease to the tenant, or the lessee. The thing to remember about the words mortgagor and mortgagee is that *borrowers are mortgagors because they give the mortgages to the banks, which accept them and therefore are the mortgagees.* And I tell my students that if they get that one wrong on the exam, I'm coming to their houses and telling their neighbors on them.

## I have a theory . . . on mortgage loans

The differences in how mortgage loans affect property ownership are more theoretical than practical, and so they've been boiled down into the three theories in the list that follows. You need to be sure to find out which of the theories your state follows.

- ✔ **The lien theory:** Under the *lien theory,* the mortgagor (borrower) retains both the legal title and equitable title to the property. The mortgagee (lender) is granted a lien on the property. *Legal title* is the title or ownership that normally transfers in a property sale. *Equitable title,* which is fully explained in Chapter 11, gives the holder of the equitable title the right to force the transfer of title when all the conditions of a contract are met. Under the lien theory, the mortgagee must go through the legal process of foreclosure to get legal title to the property to be able to sell it for nonpayment of the debt. (For more about foreclosure, see "Shut down: Foreclosures" later in this chapter.)

- ✔ **The title theory:** In the *title theory,* the mortgagor gives legal title to the mortgagee but keeps equitable title. Because the mortgagee already has title, gaining possession of the property for sale to repay the debt is more direct than under the lien theory.

- ✔ **The intermediate theory:** Based on title theory, the borrower retains title to the property and the mortgage is a lien. If the borrower defaults on the loan, title is conveyed to the lender. *Intermediate theory* makes the mortgagee go through the foreclosure process before the property can be sold to repay the debt.

## Common conditions of a mortgage loan

Like any business arrangement, the terms and conditions of a particular mortgage loan can differ from those of any other mortgage loan. But most mortgage loan arrangements have a number of terms and conditions in common and some of them may show up on the exam, so I give you some definitions and explanations in this section that you may want to remember.

### A job (or a few) to do: Duties of the borrower

In a typical mortgage loan, the borrower commits to a number of obligations that are written into the mortgage or note documents. These include:

- Paying off the debt under the conditions as specified in the note, which includes the interest rate and payment schedule.
- Indicating the property that the mortgagor (borrower) is using as security.
- Paying all real estate taxes on the property.
- Getting permission from the lender before doing any major repairs, alterations, or demolition.
- Protecting the lender's interest by maintaining a property hazard insurance policy on the property in case unforeseen damages occur.
- Adequately maintaining the property.

### You didn't do your duty: The acceleration clause

Mortgage loan agreements frequently include stipulations that are known as *acceleration clauses,* which effectively protect the lender from a loan for which the borrower is in default. *Default* is a situation in which borrowers don't fulfill the obligations of their mortgage loan agreements (see the previous section). An acceleration clause takes effect when the buyer is declared in default. The *acceleration clause* enables the lender to require the entire debt to be repaid immediately. Yep, you read that right. So, if you defaulted on the $100,000 loan that you were going to pay off over 30 years, it may be due in full — tomorrow, that is, if your mortgage agreement includes an acceleration clause. Remember the word *acceleration* means to speed up, and that's what happens to the loan. The payments are sped up so that the entire amount is due immediately. Moral of story: Don't default. But just in case, you can read about foreclosures in "Endings You Didn't Anticipate: Foreclosures, Assumptions, and Assignments," later in this chapter.

### Point taken: Points on mortgage loans

The normal interest on most home mortgage loans is paid out over the life of the loan, but sometimes lenders charge additional interest at the beginning of the loan that is based on the amount of the loan. This additional interest is called *points* or sometimes *discount points.* A point equals 1 percent of the loan amount, and that's something you don't want to forget, because it's a common math question. And remember, a point is not 1 percent of the sale price of the house — unless, of course, the borrower is in the unusual position of being allowed to borrow the entire price of the property, but 1 percent of the loan amount.

A bank agrees to make a mortgage loan of $100,000 to a property buyer. The bank agrees to a lower-than-normal annual interest rate on the condition that the buyer pay 2 points to the bank at closing. How much does the buyer have to pay in points?

$100,000 \times 0.02 = \$2,000$

This additional prepaid interest usually results in a lower interest rate for the loan as it is paid up. For example, a lender may charge you a 7 percent interest rate with no points but give you a 6.75 percent interest rate, if you pay 1 point at the beginning of the loan. Throughout the loan's life, the lower rate means you pay about the same total amount of interest, but your monthly payments are slightly lower, and the *yield,* or overall profitability of the mortgage as an investment, stays appealing to private investors. Lenders often sell mortgages to investors to raise more money to make more mortgage loans.

The combination of the interest that is paid along the way plus the points charged in prepaid interest combine to form the *annual percentage rate* (APR), which is the real interest rate you're paying.

When points are paid to lower the interest rate, it's called a *buydown*. The buydown can be applied to lower the interest rate over the life of the loan or for a specific period of time, like the first year or two. Borrowers who use their buydowns to lower the interest rate during the short term usually are anticipating larger incomes later on during their loan repayment schedules. Builders of new homes may pay points to lower the interest rate for a few years to attract buyers to their development. When a seller pays this, it's usually referred to as a *seller incentive*.

Points sometimes are used to calculate loan *origination fees*. A borrower may pay one or two points — 1 percent or 2 percent of the loan amount — to the lender for administrative charges associated with the loan. This payment, however, won't reduce the interest rate on the loan. Origination fees sometimes are paid to mortgage brokers, who are individuals who don't lend their own money but rather arrange loans between borrowers and lenders.

Points are sometimes paid to *lock in* the interest rate for a period of time. Say interest rates look like they're going up. A borrower may want to assure himself that the interest rate in effect at the time he applies for the loan is the same rate in effect at closing. The bank usually charges a fee for this, sometimes using points to calculate how much to charge for the *rate lock*.

### A long account: Escrow

An *escrow account,* which is required by most lenders, is an account held by the bank on behalf of the borrower that is used by the lender to pay the taxes and insurance on the property. The lender normally calculates a monthly payment that includes the mortgage payment and a portion of the annual taxes and insurance costs. This is the payment the borrower makes each month to the bank. The bank pays itself with the mortgage payment and accumulates the tax and insurance portion in the escrow account, making the appropriate payments as they come due. You can check out some mortgage payment calculations in "It's Payback Time: Mortgage Repayment Plans" later in this chapter.

Tax liens are first in priority ahead of all other liens (see Chapter 8). That means if the property is sold for nonpayment of the mortgage loan, and taxes are due on the property, the taxes get paid first. If not enough money is left over from the sale to pay the mortgage loan, the lender can be stuck with the loss. To avoid this situation, the lender handles the payment of taxes, and because the lender also wants to make sure that its interests are protected in the event of damage to the property, it also collects escrow money from the property owner and sees to it that the borrower's homeowner's and mortgage insurance premiums are paid. When someone buys a piece of property with a mortgage loan, the lender may collect a substantial sum of money at closing to establish the escrow fund. You may see other terms on an exam that mean the same thing as escrow account, including *reserves, impounds,* and *trust accounts.*

# Sources of (and Insurance for) Funding

One of the important pieces of information that a real estate agent can provide a buyer is where to go for a mortgage loan, but oddly enough, it isn't something that exam writers ask questions about beyond distinguishing between the primary and secondary mortgage markets, which is what I'm going to tell you about right here. The *primary market* is composed of the lenders who lend money to people who want to buy property. The primary market is where you go to get a mortgage loan. The *secondary market* is composed of financial institutions to which the banks sell the mortgages to get more money to lend to you. You can find out more about the primary and secondary mortgage markets in the two sections that follow this one. So I'll just define some terms related to the primary and the secondary markets so you can make some sense of the topics in the rest of this chapter, which exam writers do ask questions about. On a related note, I also cover different federal loan insurance programs and private mortgage insurance in this section.

As you get into who provides the money for mortgage loans, you need to understand a few terms because they relate as much to where you get the money as they do to the terms of the loan itself. The terms I discuss relative to mortgage loans — conventional, conforming, and nonconforming — relate to the down payment, which is the cash you put into the purchase of the property, and the qualifying ratios the banks use, which are the amounts of money they think you can afford to pay for a mortgage loan. These terms further relate to whether the lender (primary market) can sell the mortgage to the secondary market. One note as you read this section: The lender and the primary mortgage market is the same thing.

- **Conventional loan:** These loans meet certain guidelines that can be set by the lender but often comply with standards set by Fannie Mae in the secondary mortgage market. You can read about Fannie Mae in "Number two: The secondary mortgage market" later in this chapter. The general terms are that the total amount of the loan won't exceed certain limits and typically that the borrower can borrow no more than 80 percent of the value of the property involved — although higher limits are possible. Conventional loans essentially are loans made within normal guidelines by lenders in the primary mortgage market. By the way, as far as I know, no such thing as an unconventional loan exists.

- **Conforming loan:** This loan meets the criteria necessary for it to be sold in the secondary mortgage market. The way conforming loans are set has to do with the amount of money the borrower can spend on monthly payments. I help you do a little math in "It's Payback Time: Mortgage Repayment Plans" later in this chapter so you can see how the numbers work with this concept.

- **Nonconforming loan:** Here's a loan that doesn't meet the criteria of the secondary mortgage market. These loans may be made by lenders under specific circumstances and may include extra requirements that the borrower must meet, but they cannot be sold on the secondary mortgage market. How this works is that Fannie Mae, for example, sets a guideline that says a borrower can spend no more than 28 percent of his or her monthly income on the mortgage payment, taxes, and insurance. If the lender (primary market) chooses to lend an amount of money that requires the borrower to use 30 percent of his or her monthly income for those payments, the lender has just made a nonconforming loan that cannot be sold to Fannie Mae (secondary market); however, it may be sold to private investors who buy mortgages for the income from the interest payments that they generate.

## Number one: The primary mortgage market

The *primary mortgage market,* which sometimes is referred to as primary lenders, is where consumers — you and I — go to borrow money to buy real estate. Although all of these institutions make loans directly to the public, some specialize in large projects, commercial properties, or residential properties. The list of typical primary lenders includes the following:

- **Commercial banks and savings and loan associations:** These lenders are sometimes collectively referred to as institutional lenders. These institutions lend money for anything from the purchase of a single-family house to a regional shopping center. These institutions are one of the principal places the average consumer goes to borrow money to buy a house.

- **Credit unions:** These institutions primarily are oriented toward lending money to the average homebuyer — consumers. Credit unions can be very popular for these types of loans, depending on the amount of assets upon which they can rely and the interest rates they charge.

- **Insurance companies:** These lenders tend to specialize in lending for large projects, such as the construction or purchase of large office buildings or shopping centers. The average homebuyer wouldn't borrow money from an insurance company to finance the purchase of the property.

✔ **Investment groups:** These groups of individuals or companies pool their money to make mortgage loans. They lend money for large real estate projects rather than to individual homebuyers.

✔ **Mortgage banking companies:** These companies are set up by investors specifically to make mortgage loans. Unlike banks or credit unions, they don't generally offer other banking services.

✔ **Pension funds:** Pension fund managers may lend money from their fund's assets for the construction of large real estate projects or purchases. Pension fund loans tend not to be made to individual home purchasers.

Mortgage brokers usually are considered to be part of the primary mortgage market, even though they don't lend money directly for mortgages. A mortgage broker is similar to a real estate broker, except that instead of bringing a buyer and seller together, a mortgage broker brings a borrower and lender together. Be sure to check out the basic requirements for becoming a mortgage broker in your state. The key elements you're looking for are whether licensing or registration is required with some state agency, the state agency involved, and whether you must meet any financial, educational, or experience requirements under state law. In the wake of the financial downturn in the housing market in 2008, states have tightened up their policies regarding mortgage brokers. Exam writers like to ask a question about the criteria to be a mortgage broker and what mortgage brokers do.

## Number two: The secondary mortgage market

The *Federal Reserve System* (the Fed) is a key player in financial markets that affect the availability of money for real estate mortgage loans. The system is regulated by two factors that have direct effects on the money that's available for mortgage loans. They are

✔ The *reserve requirement* for banks, which is the requirement that the Fed imposes on banks to maintain a specified amount of their assets as reserve funds in cash. The reserve funds may not be used for loans. By increasing or decreasing the amount of money needed for reserves, the Fed can control the levels of money that are made available for mortgage loans.

✔ The discount rate, which is how the Fed controls the flow of money. It sets and adjusts the *discount rate,* which is the rate of interest that member banks charge each other for loans between banks. Whenever the discount rate is high, interest rates on consumer loans increase and vice versa. The rate charged to the consumer impacts the way many people choose to borrow money for real estate purchases or refinancing and how much they can afford to borrow.

Banks and savings and loan associations get their money from you and me, their depositors, insurance companies get it from the premiums consumers pay, and investments groups get it from investors. Although that probably sounds pretty obvious, think about what happens when banks run out of money, or to be more precise, when their loans exceed their deposits. The *secondary mortgage market,* which buys loans from banks and other primary lending institutions, was created to prevent such a problem from happening. Although details of these transactions are fairly complicated, the essence really is pretty simple. A primary lending institution collects, packages, or pools (they all mean the same thing) its mortgage loans. These loans have value because the notes on which they're based are promises to repay specific amounts of principal and interest, plus they're backed up by a mortgage that enables the lenders to sell the properties if the debts are not repaid. The secondary market lenders pay the primary market lenders for these mortgage loans, which provide new money for the bank to lend to yet another group of home buyers. After the loans are acquired by the secondary market, the payments of the borrowers go to the secondary market institutions; however, the primary mortgage market institutions frequently retain a fee for servicing the loan, or collecting the monthly payments and sending them on to the secondary institutions.

The three major (and one minor) players in the secondary mortgage market are organizations that either are directly or indirectly associated with the federal government. The following list explains some of the major characteristics with which you need to be familiar when being tested on information about the secondary mortgage market.

- **Fannie Mae:** The Federal National Mortgage Association, or Fannie Mae, is a privately owned corporation chartered by Congress. Fannie Mae sells stocks and bonds to raise money to buy conventional bank mortgage loans. Although Veterans' Administration (VA) and Federal Housing Administration (FHA) loan programs are mortgage insurance programs (rather than direct loan programs) that insure mortgage loans made by lenders, Fannie Mae does deal in these types of mortgages in the secondary market. Fannie Mae is the leading purchaser of mortgages in the secondary market. It generally sets limits on the specific amounts of the mortgage loans that it buys. Any loan above those limits is referred to as a *jumbo loan.*

- **Ginnie Mae:** The Government National Mortgage Association, or Ginnie Mae, is a government agency administered by the U.S. Department of Housing and Urban Development. Ginnie Mae provides investors with an opportunity to invest in mortgages by selling pass-through certificates to investors. With these certificates, principal and interest payments are paid to investors as a return on their investments in the program. Ginnie Mae works primarily with Fannie Mae in secondary mortgage market activities. Don't be thrown on an exam if you see the words "tandem" or "piggyback" associated with these two agencies. It means they're working together.

- **Freddie Mac:** The Federal Home Loan Mortgage Corporation, or Freddie Mac, is a privately owned corporation that also provides a secondary market for mortgages. It sells bonds to raise funds to purchase mostly conventional mortgages.

- **Farmer Mac:** The Federal Agricultural Mortgage Corporation, or Farmer Mac, serves as a secondary mortgage market for farm loans.

You may want to remember the names of the agencies in the previous list by associating female names, Fannie and Ginnie, mostly with FHA and VA loans and male names Freddie and Mac with conventional loans.

## See your uncle . . . Sam, that is: Federal loan insurance programs

The federal government sponsors a few programs that offer insurance coverage for mortgage loans. The real estate exam may include a question or two about these programs starting with the fact that they are loan insurance programs and not direct loan programs.

A conventional loan usually must be accompanied by a down payment, frequently as much as 20 percent of the value of the property that's being purchased. The two reasons for requiring a down payment are that it provides for:

- A financial commitment on the part of the borrower. Buying property isn't all about using the bank's money; some of it has to be from you, the borrower, too.

- A cushion between the bank and possible declines in property values. When the value of a property declines, if the lender can't sell that property for its original appraised value in a foreclosure, the lender loses.

Suppose, however, that a lender is assured of getting back all of the money that it loans out for a property, even if it lends 100 percent of the value of that property. Wouldn't the lender be inclined to lend more money on the property, relative to its value? Enter the federal government with insurance programs that guarantee that the bank will get back its money from the loan. So when borrowers don't have enough money to make down payments required by their lenders, they may seek a loan insured by the FHA or VA.

Some state-run government direct-loan programs or loan guarantee programs may be operating in your state. If so, they may be fair game for questions on your state's real estate license exam. At the very least, those questions may refer to a state program as one of the potential answers to a multiple-choice question, so check out your state's programs.

## The Federal Housing Administration

The Federal Housing Administration (FHA) is an agency under the supervision of the U.S. Department of Housing and Urban Development that insures loans made by primary lenders. Even though you may hear it referred to as an FHA loan, the FHA never directly makes any loans. The most commonly used FHA program is called a 203(b) loan. The numbering refers to the section of the law that governs such loans. Here are a number of the rules for this program (some of which you may see on a real estate exam):

- FHA loans are limited to owner-occupied, one-to-four-family houses.

- A fee called a *mortgage insurance premium* (MIP) is paid at the closing by the buyer. The MIP is based on a percentage of the loan.

- An estimate of the property's value must be made by an FHA-approved appraiser. Standards govern whether the condition of the property and the neighborhood qualify for FHA assurances.

- FHA-backed loans have high loan to value (LTV) ratios. Down payments may be as low as 1.25 percent for lower-priced homes. (For more about LTV, check out the section on "Considerations for Lender Accepting Mortgages" later in this chapter.)

- Upper-end limits on property value are in effect, and they vary from one state to the next and from one area to the next within the states.

- Other borrowers may assume some FHA loans. The rules vary with the original date of the loan.

- Lenders may not charge a prepayment penalty. Prepayment penalties are explained in the "Open mortgage" section later in this chapter.

- Lenders may charge discount points, or additional fees, for the loan. The payment of these fees may be negotiated between buyer and seller.

## The Department of Veterans Affairs

The Department of Veterans Affairs (VA) provides a loan guarantee program to eligible veterans and their spouses. Eligible primary lenders make the loans, and the payment of all or part of the loan is guaranteed by the VA if the borrower defaults. Some of the important features of a VA guaranteed are

- Rules for eligibility are set by the VA. Generally those eligible are veterans of military service who served during specific periods of time and their eligible widows.

- The loans may require little or no down payment.

- The loan guarantees cover owner-occupied, one-to-four-family homes, including mobile homes.

- A Certificate of Reasonable Value (CRV) is required from an approved appraiser. The amount of the VA guarantee is based on the CRV. Although no dollar limits are set on the price of the home being purchased, the VA limits the amount of the loan that the VA will guarantee. The borrower may pay the difference in cash.

- No prepayment penalty is permitted.

- VA-backed mortgages are assumable under certain conditions.

- A funding or origination fee is charged to the borrower to be paid to the VA.

### The Farm Service Agency (FSA)

The Farm Service Agency (formerly the Farmers Home Administration) is an agency of the U.S. Department of Agriculture that sponsors programs targeted at agricultural and rural areas. It guarantees loans made by primary lenders and lends money directly to borrowers.

## A private matter: Private mortgage insurance

When making a mortgage loan that has a high LTV, the lender is lending a large percentage of the value of the property, and the borrower is making only a small down payment. In these circumstances, for its protection, the lender may require *private mortgage insurance* (PMI), which is insurance coverage that the borrower purchases that protects the lender, if the borrower defaults on paying the loan. PMI usually can be dropped when the borrower's equity in the property has increased to acceptable levels. *Equity* is the difference between the value of the property and all debt attributable to the property. Terms for PMI vary from lender to lender, and some states even established laws regarding PMI. The federal government enacted a law for loans made after July 29, 1999, that requires that lenders must drop PMI, if the borrower requests it when the borrower's equity has risen to 20 percent or more. The law further requires that PMI be automatically dropped when borrower equity reaches 22 percent. Private mortgage insurance is obtained from private mortgage insurance companies.

# Considerations for Lenders Accepting Mortgages

A primary lender has two considerations when it is making a loan for the purchase or refinancing of real estate: the value of the property and the borrower's ability to pay off the debt. In checking out the value of the property, lenders want to be assured that if their borrowers can't pay off their mortgages (default), they (the lenders) can sell the properties and get back the money they loaned to the borrowers. Assuming the property value is sufficient to guarantee the loan, a lender wants to make sure that the borrower can make the monthly payment, including taxes and insurance, for the life of the loan.

## Checking out the property value

The value of the property has a direct effect on the amount of money the lender will lend you, and you need to be prepared to do a math problem about this topic on the state exam. The percentage of value of the property that can be borrowed is called the *loan to value ratio* (LTV), an amount that is set by the bank and the secondary mortgage market. (See "Number two: The secondary mortgage market" earlier in this chapter). The value of the property is based on an appraisal (see Chapter 14). In the event that an appraised value and selling price are different, the amount of money that can be borrowed is based on the lower of the two numbers. And yes, that means that if you're paying more than the appraised value for the house, your down payment will be higher than expected. Because you may encounter a problem about LTV calculations, here are some examples.

A property sells for $200,000. Its appraised value is $200,000. The LTV ratio for the mortgage is 80 percent. How much money will the bank lend? What down payment is required?

$200,000 (appraised value) × 0.80 (80 percent) = $160,000 mortgage amount

$200,000 − 160,000 = $40,000 down payment

Notice that after the $200,000 in the calculation, I used the term appraised value and not sale price. The reason I did this becomes evident in the next problem, which shows what happens when the sale price and the appraised value are different.

The sale price of the house is $315,000. The appraised value is $300,000. If the bank offers an 80 percent LTV ratio, what down payment will be needed?

$300,000 (appraised value) × 0.80 = $240,000 mortgage amount

$315,000 − $240,000 = $75,000

A final problem shows you how to calculate the LTV, if you're given value and loan information. Say the bank will lend you $240,000 on a property valued at $300,000. What is the LTV ratio?

$240,000 ÷ $300,000 = 0.80, or 80 percent

Note that in these problems I use the appraised value to calculate the amount of the mortgage, and then I subtract the mortgage amount from the selling price to find out the down payment that's needed. In doing a problem like this, just take the numbers for what they are. Don't get hung up thinking about things like whether you'd try to renegotiate the price or maybe not buy the property at all. These types of questions are about understanding the LTV concept and the use of value rather than sale price to calculate the mortgage amount. And don't worry if the values of the properties on the state exam don't seem realistic to you. Remember these are statewide exams. I've lived in two states where the prices of real estate vary wildly from one part of the state to another.

## Examining the borrower's ability to pay

The second type of calculation involves determining how much a buyer can afford to pay for a mortgage loan. You need to understand some of the terminology and how it works.

The lender uses a qualifying ratio to determine what a borrower can afford to pay for a mortgage loan. When using a *qualifying ratio,* you work backward from the buyer's gross income, usually using monthly numbers for principal, interest, tax, and insurance expenses to arrive at what the buyer can afford to spend on housing every month. You need to note that the acronym used for the payment of *principal, interest, taxes, and insurance* is *PITI.* When lenders do affordability calculations, they use PITI as the total monthly expense for mortgage loan payment calculations.

For example, a lender may say that a buyer can afford to pay 28 percent of total gross income in monthly payments (principal, interest, taxes, and insurance expenses). This percentage is called the *front-end ratio.* The lender also establishes that the borrower's total monthly debt payments, including PITI, can't be greater than 36 percent of the borrower's total gross income. This percentage is called the *back-end ratio.*

You may or may not find a qualifying ratio calculation question on the exam, but calculating them is a service that real estate agents routinely provide for their customers and clients. And just in case you'd like to do your own calculations, here's an example.

Say you make $96,000 a year. Using the fairly standard qualifying ratios of 28 percent for principal, interest, taxes and insurance (PITI) and 36 percent for total debt, how much can you afford to pay for PITI per month?

$96,000 × 0.28 = $26,880

$26,880 ÷ 12 (months) = $2,240 maximum monthly PITI

Alternatively, you can do the calculation this way:

$96,000 ÷ 12 (months) = $8,000

$8,000 × 0.28 = $2,240

Now where, you ask, does the 36 percent back-end ratio come in?

$96,000 × 0.36 = $34,560

$34,560 ÷ 12 (months) = $2,880 maximum total monthly debt payments including PITI

Together, the front-end and back-end ratios work in such a way that the borrower's PITI and total debts have to fall below both criteria. So if in the example the borrower's total monthly long-term (usually 12 months or more like credit cards and car payments) debt payments without PITI were $2,000 a month, the lender would allow the borrower to spend $880 or less on PITI. On the other hand, if the borrower has no other debt, the lender still wouldn't allow the borrower to spend more than $2,240 on PITI.

Whatever amount of money is available for PITI, the lender uses that amount to calculate how much of a mortgage the borrower can afford to pay off.

# One Size Does Not Fit All: Types of Mortgages

Although a specific mortgage loan may not be available for every possible situation, enough variations are around to cover most people's real estate needs. And although mortgage professionals can and will help your clients and customers, real estate agents nevertheless are expected to know about the types of loans that are available for particular situations. That expectation translates into exam questions, so pay attention to the purposes and characteristics of the types of mortgage loans that I describe in the following sections so you can pick out the one that answers your exam question correctly. As a practical matter, knowing this information can help you make recommendations to a buyer who may not realize there is a mortgage product out there that can help her buy the property. And get you a commission.

## Blanket mortgage

A *blanket mortgage* is a loan that covers more than one piece of property. It sometimes is used to finance a subdivision development. (See Chapter 8 for more about subdivisions.) Say, for example, that a builder buys six lots on which he plans to build houses and sell them. The lots are in an already-approved subdivision. The builder may want to use a blanket mortgage to finance the purchase, because it usually comes with a *partial release provision*. Remember that a mortgage is a lien on the property. (I also discuss liens in Chapter 8.) A *partial release* is a provision that allows the lien to be removed separately from each parcel as it is sold to a buyer and the bank is paid a portion of the loan amount.

## Construction loan

A *construction loan* is made to finance a construction project. A typical case is when someone who owns property hires a builder to build a house. Money from the loan is released to the builder at certain points as the project progresses. At the end of the project, the loan generally is converted to a conventional mortgage.

## Home equity loan

A *home equity loan* seeks to use the equity that a mortgagor has built up in a property either for improving the property or for some other use. *Home equity* is the difference between the value of the property and the debt attributed to the property. For example, say someone paid $100,000 for a house. Ten years later, the house was appraised at $200,000, and the mortgagor has $50,000 left to pay on the mortgage.

$200,000 – $50,000 = $150,000 equity

Home equity loans are granted with various terms and conditions. The most common types either provide for a flat amount of money to be taken out or for a line of credit to be created. The borrower can withdraw money from the line of credit as needed. Sometimes the borrowed funds can be paid back and withdrawn again like a revolving fund. Home equity loans have become popular as an alternative to the second mortgages to which they are related.

## Open mortgage

An *open mortgage* is a mortgage loan that can be paid back at any time without a prepayment penalty.

A *prepayment penalty* is a fee that is charged by a lender whenever a mortgage is paid off earlier than its normal schedule. This fee can vary from one mortgage to another and from one state to the next. You need to determine what, if any, laws your state has adopted regarding prepayment penalties in conventional (non-federally guaranteed) mortgages. Some states have limited the use of prepayment penalties, so check it out.

## Open-end mortgage

An *open-end mortgage* is a loan that can be reopened and borrowed against after some of it has been paid down. For example, you can borrow $150,000 via a mortgage loan with an agreement in place that after you pay some of it down, you can borrow back up to the $150,000 limit again.

## Package mortgage

A *package mortgage* is a loan that covers real estate and personal property being sold with the real estate. The buyer of a house in which furniture is being included in the sale may want to apply for a package loan. For example, this loan can be used to purchase a furnished vacation home.

## Purchase money mortgage

The *purchase money mortgage* is the mortgage loan used to buy real estate. The term sometimes is used to mean the mortgage that a seller takes back as part of the sale price of a property. When a seller sells his property for $200,000, and the buyer has $50,000 cash, is approved for a $100,000 mortgage loan, but still falls $50,000 short, the seller can agree to take back a mortgage worth $50,000 to make the deal happen. In effect, the seller is extending $50,000 worth of credit to the buyer, which will be paid according to the terms of a promissory note the buyer signs with the seller. The mortgage is called a second mortgage and will be in second position to be paid off if the property has to be foreclosed and sold for nonpayment of the debt. Sometimes this second mortgage is referred to as a *purchase money mortgage*.

State government sets rates for interest that cannot be exceeded — called the usury rate. These seller second mortgages may not be subject to the usury limits that are set by state law, so you need to verify that information in your state. Mortgages made by lenders (not sellers) are subject to these limits. However, if the interest rate is artificially low, the Internal Revenue Service (IRS) may calculate imputed interest. The *imputed interest rate* is the interest rate that the IRS says should have been charged based on market conditions. The IRS will increase the tax owed by the seller/lender accordingly, as though the seller had been charging the higher interest.

## Reverse mortgage

*Reverse mortgages* sometimes are called *reverse annuity loans*. These loans enable a property owner to use the equity in the property (see "Home equity loan," earlier in this chapter, for more) without selling the property. Money may be paid out in periodic payments, a lump sum, or a line of credit up to a certain amount of the owner's equity in the home. No payment is due on the loan while the owner still lives in the house. These loans often are used for income by senior citizens on fixed incomes with large amounts of equity in their homes. They're usually paid off by the sale of the property after the homeowner dies or moves out.

## Sale leaseback

A *sale leaseback* isn't actually a mortgage, but can be a source of project financing and a means of obtaining the equity in a property. It traditionally is mentioned in any discussions about real estate financing. Usually used in commercial property situations, an owner-occupant uses a sale leaseback to sell the building but agrees to remain in the building under a lease. The new owner has a tenant and the old owner has gotten his money out of the building to use.

## Shared equity mortgage

The *shared equity mortgage* allows for a share of the profit on the property to be given to someone else in return for help purchasing the property. A relative, investor, or lending institution may agree to provide funds for a down payment or help with the mortgage payment. In return, when the property is sold, a predetermined share of the profit is given to the person who provided the financial help.

## Temporary loan

A *temporary loan,* also called *interim financing, bridge loan, swing loan,* or *gap loan,* is used when funds are needed for short periods of time to complete a real estate transaction. A typical situation where a temporary loan may be used is when a seller is selling one house and plans to use the proceeds from the sale to buy another house. If that individual has to complete the purchase of the new house before the sale of the old house is complete, a temporary loan can come to the rescue. Money is borrowed just long enough to buy the new house and then pay it off with the proceeds of the sale from the old house.

## Wraparound mortgage

A *wraparound mortgage* is a new mortgage that literally wraps around an old mortgage. A seller sells a property to a buyer, but the seller doesn't pay off an existing mortgage. The buyer gives a new, larger mortgage to the seller. This new mortgage includes the amount due on the original mortgage. The buyer makes payments on the new mortgage to the seller. The seller, in turn, makes payments on the old mortgage to the lender. This mortgage is used when the old mortgage won't be paid off at the time of the sale of the property.

# It's Payback Time: Mortgage Repayment Plans

One key way that loans vary is in how they are paid back. Before I explain, I need to tell you about fixed and adjustable interest rates, which will make describing several different repayment plans and doing the math the exam writers want you to know a little easier. Pay careful attention to the terminology and definitions as you go through this material, and remember that what I'm telling you about here are the terms of the note that the borrower signs, even though most people refer to it as the mortgage.

Putting the various payment plans into perspective means that I need to give you the quick version of Banking 101. A bank (any lender really) has no money of its own. People invest their money in savings accounts and other interest-bearing instruments like certificates of deposit, and they expect to receive a return on or yield from those investments. The bank, on the other hand, lends that same money out and charges interest on the loans. Part of the interest payments go to the depositors and part of them are used to operate the bank. Your former economics teacher may have made it sound more complicated because many rules, regulations, and economic conditions obviously affect banking more than I'm letting on. But the essence of the loan process is just that — the bank acting as a middleman between depositors and borrowers.

When people borrow money through mortgage loans, they must pay back the *principal,* which is the amount they borrowed, and the *interest,* which is what the bank charges you to use its depositors' money. The interest rates charged for mortgage loans vary with economic conditions, but they're often less than the interest rates on other types of loans. Mortgage loans, however, frequently are made for large sums for long periods of time. Because of the length of time the money is used, the total interest paid can be substantial. Depending on the interest rate and the length of the mortgage term, they can be even larger than the principal amount itself. As you go through the types of repayment plans, keep this in mind: The mortgage loan and the terms of the note aren't satisfied until the principal and interest are paid back to the lender.

## It's in your interest: Fixed and adjustable rates

For a long time the only type of payment plan available to a borrower was a fixed interest that never changed throughout the life of the loan. As economic times changed, it became apparent that a more flexible approach would better serve both the borrower's and the lender's needs. The particular terms and conditions of any mortgage loan are, of course, fixed by the lender within the parameters of applicable law, but some general descriptions apply to both types of payment plans. And that's what I give you here — some basics that the exam writers want you to know.

### Fixed-rate mortgages

A fixed rate of interest means that throughout the lifetime of the loan, the interest rate and the amount of the monthly mortgage payments do not change. What does change, however, in an amortized loan (see the next section) is the amount of principal and interest in each monthly payment. On a mortgage loan, interest is charged on the unpaid balance of the principal. So as you pay off the principal each month, the amount of interest being charged actually declines. And because the payments remain the same, the amount of principal you pay off each month increases.

For illustration purposes only, say you borrowed $100,000 in a 30-year mortgage loan. The amount of the interest rate is moot for purposes of this example. Your monthly payment on the loan turns out to be $665 for 360 months (that's 30 years × 12 months). The first payment may consist of $585 in interest payment and $80 in principal payment. The amount of interest is so high at this point, because you're being charged interest on the entire $100,000 loan. What that also means is that after you make that first payment, you still owe the bank $99,920 ($100,000 – $80 principal payment). Because the principal has been slightly reduced, the amount of interest owed that second month is slightly less than the first month. And because the monthly payment remains the same, the amount of principal paid off is slightly more than the first month. By the time the last payment rolls around, 30 years later, the situation essentially will be (almost) reversed, with $585 applied to payment of the principal and $80 applied toward the interest.

### Adjustable-rate mortgages

An adjustable-rate mortgage (ARM) is a mortgage for which the interest rate is subject to change during the life of the loan. An ARM can be an amortized, straight, or partially amortized loan (see the next sections for these definitions). Although the specific terms of an ARM are contained in the note, you need to be familiar with its general features.

The interest rate for the loan is tied to the *index*, a rate over which the lender has no control. A federal treasury bond rate or other federal rate of some sort frequently is used as the index. The borrower's interest rate then is calculated by adding a predetermined rate called a *margin* to the index. For example, if the index rate is 4 percent and the margin is 3 percent, the borrower's rate is 7 percent. As the index changes, so does the borrower's rate.

The borrower's rate at any point in time for an ARM loan usually is subject to two limits that are called *caps* or *ceilings,* including:

- ✔ The *annual cap,* which limits the amount that an ARM's interest rate can be adjusted upward in any given year. For example, if you start with a total rate of 7 percent (4 percent index plus 3 percent margin) with an annual cap of 2 percent and the index goes up by 3 percentage points, the resulting interest rate would total 10 percent (7 percent margin plus 3 percent index); however, because the 2 percent ceiling (the annual cap) is in place, the interest rate can increase by only 2 percent per year to a maximum total rate of 9 percent for that year. If the index increases beyond the annual cap in any given year, the additional increase usually can be carried over to the next year.

- ✔ The *lifetime cap* or *ceiling,* which limits the total upward adjustment that the lender can make to the interest rate during the life of the loan, regardless of how high the index goes. Say, for example, you start out at a total rate of 7 percent and the lifetime cap is 5 percent. That means the highest the rate can ever be is 12 percent.

Another condition of the loan to be aware of is when the loan adjusts. Some loans adjust every year, others less often. Also some adjustable loans can be or are automatically converted to fixed rate loans after a specific period of time, for example five years.

A *payment cap* also can be put in place in an ARM, meaning that even if the rate adjustments reach their maximum each year, if the resulting monthly payment increases to more than a specified amount, that payment cap keeps the payment within reasonable limits. In some cases, however, exercising the payment cap can lead to *negative amortization,* which means the loan balance increases by the amount owed but not paid. So if the adjustment in a particular year brings your payment up to $1,500 a month but you have a payment cap of $1,400, you won't have to pay the higher payment; however, that extra $100 a month you're not paying may be added on to the total balance you owe, in effect increasing your loan amount.

# Doing the math: Amortized loan

The most popular type of loan that buyers use to purchase homes is an amortized loan, or direct reduction loan. The primary feature of an amortized loan is that at the end of the *loan term* (the period during which the bank has loaned you the money), the loan is completely paid off. In other words, the borrower has completely paid the interest and principal of the loan. Each payment you make, usually monthly, is made up of principal and interest (see the earlier section on "Fixed-rate mortgages"), so that you owe the bank nothing at the end of the loan term. When you have an amortized loan, making additional principal payments or converting the loan into bi-weekly payments rather than monthly payments usually is possible. In both cases, by reducing the principal at a more rapid rate, although the future payments remain the same, the interest rate component decreases and the principal component increases, thus reducing the total amount of interest being paid over the life of the loan. Remember you're always paying interest on the unpaid principal balance. Prepaying principal also reduces the length of time you'll be paying the mortgage.

State laws may also allow the bank to impose a prepayment penalty on you for making early payments. You need to check out what your state allows in terms of prepayment penalties.

The monthly payments can be looked up in mortgage tables, which show you amortization (or payoff) rates for various percentage interest rates over a variety of loan terms in increments of $1,000 of loan amounts. (You can also do this through various online mortgage payment calculators; just do a search for *mortgage calculators* and take your pick!) But if you want to want to know the amortization rate for $1,000 at 6 percent interest for a 25-year mortgage, you can look it up in the table, and you'll discover that the factor is $6.44 per month. That factor is the amount of money it takes per month to pay off principal and interest on a $1,000 loan over a period of 25 years. So if you're borrowing $150,000, you simply drop three zeroes (the same as dividing by $1,000), and you get 150. Multiply that times the factor you looked up and see what you get.

$150 \times 6.44 = \$966$

The $966 from the equation is the monthly payment it takes to amortize a fixed-rate loan (pay off principal and interest at the same time) of $150,000 at 6 percent for 25 years.

One other thing that you definitely need to note is that mortgage loan interest rates always are quoted on an annual basis. So the interest is a certain percent a year. In the event that an exam question wants to know the monthly rate all you do is divide the annual rate by 12.

Exam writers rely on a series of math problems to test your skills calculating different aspects of an amortized mortgage. Here are examples of the more typical of these kinds of problems. (Check out Chapter 18 for more mortgage math, including ways to figure out annual and monthly interest payments.)

### Finding the monthly payment when you're given a mortgage factor

You borrow $125,000 for 20 years at an interest rate of 7 percent. The mortgage factor is $7.75. What is the monthly payment necessary to amortize this loan?

$\$125,000 \div \$1,000 = 125$

$125 \times \$7.75 = \$968.75$

Remember that the mortgage factor is the amount of money needed on a monthly basis to amortize (pay off principal and interest) on a $1,000 loan at a given interest rate over a given period of time. In this example, 7.75 (it's often written without the dollar sign) is the amount needed to pay off a $1,000 loan at 7 percent for 20 years. But because you're borrowing $125,000, you have to divide by 1,000 to find out how many units of $1,000 are in the loan amount. Multiplying this amount by the factor gives you the answer.

### Seeing how much the first month's interest is

You borrow $130,000 for 25 years at 7.5 percent interest in an amortized loan. How much interest do you pay in the first month of the loan?

1. $130,000 × 0.075 (7.5 percent) = $9,750 first year's interest

2. $9,750 ÷ 12 months = $812.50 first month's interest

Remember that you're always paying interest on the unpaid balance of the loan and interest rates always are quoted on an annual basis. So in the first month, you're paying interest on the entire unpaid balance of $130,000 at 7.75 percent interest. The first calculation gives you the total interest for the year. The second one gives you the first month's interest. Note that this calculation works only for the first month, because after that, you've already paid off a portion of the principal, so now you're paying interest on a lower principal.

### Finding the principal balance owed after the first payment

I used the same numbers as I did in the last example so you can see how that problem can have an added component, if you're given some additional information.

You borrow $130,000 for 25 years at 7.5 percent interest in an amortized loan. The monthly payment is $959.40. How much of the principal do you owe after you've made the first payment?

1. $130,000 × 0.075 (7.5 percent) = $9,750 first year's interest

2. $9,750 ÷ 12 months = $812.50 first month's interest

3. $959.40 (principal and interest payment) – $812.50 (interest) = $146.90 principal

4. $130,000 (original principal) – $146.90 (first month's principal) = $129,853.10 principal owed after the first month's payment

In Step 1, you find the total interest due for one year. Remember the mortgage interest rate is an annual rate. In Step 2, you find out the first month's interest by dividing by 12. In case you're wondering, this step works only for the first month in any 12-month period. In Step 3, you find out how much principal is contained in that first month's payment. You're given the total monthly payment, which is made up of principal and interest. If you take away the interest, you're left with the amount of principal you're paying that month. In Step 4, you subtract the first month's principal payment from the original amount of the loan, and you're left with the remaining balance of the principal.

### Finding the total interest on the loan

Another type of exam problem that sometimes gives people a hard time is the calculation of total interest paid over the life of the loan.

You borrow $100,000 for 30 years at 8 percent interest. It's an amortized loan, and your monthly payments are $734. How much interest will you pay over the life of the loan?

1. $734 × 360 (12 months × 30 years) = $264,240 total payments of principal and interest over the life of the loan.

2. $264,240 (total principal and interest) – $100,000 (loan principal) = $164,240 interest over the life of the loan.

If you took a minute and tried to do this problem before you looked at the answer, I'll bet you tried somehow to use the 8 percent interest rate. Almost everybody does, but it's useless information in this problem, because I already gave you the monthly payment amount.

In Step 1, you calculate everything you pay over the life of the loan. In Step 2, you subtract the principal from the total of what you pay. Remember that the payment you make each month, and therefore the total of the payments you make, are both principal and interest, so if you subtract the principal, what you have left is the interest.

## On the straight and narrow: Straight loan

A *straight loan* (also called a *term loan*) calls for the payment of interest only during the term of the loan. At the end of the period of the loan, a single payment of the principal is required. Straight loans sometimes are called term loans.

Say you borrow $100,000 to buy a house on a straight loan at 8 percent interest with a term of 20 years. You'd pay $8,000 ($100,000 × 0.08) in interest each year for 20 years. At the end of the 20 years, you'd have to make a single payment to the bank of $100,000, which repays the principal. These loans are used more often for commercial properties than they are for residential properties and may be fixed rate or adjustable rate. See "It's Payback Time: Mortgage Repayment Plans" earlier in this chapter for more about repayment plans. Commercial property owners who sometimes sell their property after five or ten years may want this type of mortgage, because unlike the homeowner, they're not necessarily interested in paying off the property.

## A good mix: Partially amortized loan

*Partially amortized loans* are combinations of amortized loans and straight loans (see the two previous sections). Unlike the straight loan, a portion of each monthly payment of a partially amortized loan goes toward reducing the principal and toward paying interest. However, at the end of the loan term, unlike the fully amortized loan, some unpaid principal remains. This amount is paid off in a single payment called a *balloon payment*. These loans may have interest rates that are either fixed or adjustable and are more typically used for nonresidential purchases but none the less can be used to buy a house.

## Fast times: Growing equity mortgage

A *growing equity mortgage* (GEM) uses a fixed interest rate but payment of principal increases (more than normal amortization) over time. As such, this type of repayment plan enables the borrower to pay off the loan faster. The GEM loan sometimes is called the rapid payoff mortgage, which you shouldn't confuse with a bi-weekly payment plan or making extra principal payments. I discussed both of those in the section "Doing the math: Amortized loan," earlier in this chapter. The GEM has a scheduled increase in principal payments that may, for example, be tied to the borrower's expectation of increasing income during the life of the loan.

# Endings You Didn't Anticipate: Foreclosures, Assumptions, and Assignments

There's lots of good news in owning real estate. Unfortunately there can be some bad news, too; it's usually associated with what happens when you can't pay and the lender takes your property in a foreclosure. In addition, assumption and assignment involve new parties in the mortgage. The main things to remember about these three things for the exam are the differences among them and a few of the main characteristics of each.

# Shut down: Foreclosures

When a borrower defaults on a loan, the lender may have to institute foreclosure proceedings. *Foreclosure* is the process by which the lender takes over ownership of the property and sells it for nonpayment of the debt. Mortgages may contain an *acceleration* clause that enables the lender to declare the entire balance due after the borrower is declared in default (the number of missed payments that result in default is set by the bank). Declaring the loan due in full makes the foreclosure process easier, because the entire debt is due right away and must be satisfied by sale of the property unless of course the borrower wins the lottery and pays off the loan. Any funds left after all the debts associated with the property are paid go to the borrower.

If your state has a homestead act in place, the borrower may be entitled to only a certain amount of money, the rest going to pay unsecured debts like credit card bills. See if your state has a homestead act in place and what the provisions are.

Foreclosure can occur in one of several ways:

- ✔ **Judicial foreclosure,** which is where the court orders property to be sold as a result of a foreclosure action brought by the lender. This type of foreclosure is the most common. And you can remember it by relating the word judge as in judicial.

- ✔ **Nonjudicial foreclosure,** which only some states permit, can apply to both deed of trust situations and mortgage loans. (You can read about deeds of trust earlier in this chapter in "Liens, notes, and a mistake most people make.") Nonjudicial foreclosure involves filing a notice of default in the county recorder's office and providing appropriate public notice, usually through the newspapers. After that, the property is sold to pay off the debt.

- ✔ **Strict foreclosure,** which is an action that is permitted in some states, and requires that appropriate notice be given to the borrower and a period of time established by the courts during which the borrower may pay off the debt. If the borrower fails to meet the deadline, title to the property transfers to the lender. In this case, the sale of the property isn't specifically required by the court.

Many people mistakenly believe that whenever the lender forecloses on a property for nonpayment of the loan, the borrower automatically is off the hook. If, however, the lender cannot sell the property at a price that covers the entire debt, the lender can go to court and sue the borrower for the remainder of the debt. If the lender's suit is successful, the court enters a *deficiency judgment* against the borrower, who must then cover the portion of the mortgage loan debt that the property sale didn't cover. In the case of VA and FHA insured loans this may not be true because insurance is in place to pay off the loan.

In the event of a default for nonpayment of the debt, depending on the state, the borrower may have a right of *equitable redemption,* a right that exists after foreclosure but before the sale of the property. During a specified time frame, the borrower may pay off the debt and reclaim the property. In other states, another similar time frame is effective just after the sale. During that time, the borrower can pay the debt and reclaim ownership of the property. This right to redeem the property after the sale is called a *statutory right of redemption.*

Sometimes a buyer voluntarily signs the property over to the lender by executing a deed to avoid a foreclosure action. This *deed in lieu of foreclosure,* or *a friendly foreclosure,* has a major downside from the lender's point of view. In a regular foreclosure action, all *junior* or *subordinate liens,* or liens on the property that are paid after the mortgage lien, effectively disappear. However, in a deed in lieu of foreclosure, junior liens remain in place and can become the responsibility of the next buyer. To make matters worse, the lender usually also loses any rights to FHA, VA, or private mortgage insurance. (See the section on "See your uncle . . . Sam, that is: Federal loan insurance programs" for more about VA and FHA loan guarantees and private mortgage insurance earlier in this chapter.) The deed in lieu of foreclosure is not a particular type of deed (see Chapter 9 for more about deeds) but rather is whatever type of deed to which the borrower and the lender agree.

When an existing mortgage loan on a property is not being paid off and a lender is making a new loan on the property, that lender will require the first mortgage (the first lender) to execute a *subordination agreement* to protect itself from all other mortgage lien holders. This allows the new loan to move into first position for payment if a foreclosure becomes necessary. For example, real estate agents sometimes refer to the Bank of Mom (that's your mother) lending you $100,000 to buy a house, and you give her a mortgage to secure the loan. Later on, the value of your house increases to $200,000, and you want to borrow $100,000 from the bank to do some work on the house. The bank probably will make you get your mother to sign a subordination agreement, so that if you default on your payments and the bank forecloses on the property and sells it, the bank will get paid first and then your mother. Sometimes the bank simply increases the total loan amount to cover the new loan plus pay off the old loan, so that once again the bank is in first position to be paid in the event of a foreclosure.

## Who owes whom? Assumption and assignment

A *mortgage assumption* takes place when a new party takes over the obligations of another person's mortgage debt, and it usually requires the approval of the lender. A typical situation in which someone may assume a mortgage is when a buyer buys a house from a seller who has a mortgage loan at a much lower interest rate than is currently available to the buyer. The buyer pays the seller the difference between the sale price and the outstanding balance of the seller's mortgage (which the buyer is assuming) either in cash or with a new mortgage. By assuming the old mortgage, the buyer also agrees to take over the payments on the remaining balance due.

When buying a property, you need to recognize the important distinction between taking over someone else's mortgage loan obligations by *assuming a mortgage* and not doing so by purchasing the property *subject to the mortgage*. This distinction makes a difference, if during a foreclosure, not enough money is raised from the sale of the property to cover the debt.

- ✔ If a property is purchased with the buyer *assuming the mortgage,* the buyer becomes personally liable for the portion of the debt not covered by the foreclosure sale. Say I buy a house for $200,000 paying the seller $100,000 cash and assuming a mortgage on which there is $100,000 left to pay. I lose my job, can't pay my mortgage, and to make matters worse, real estate values have plummeted. The lender forecloses and can sell the house only for $90,000. The lender holds me personally responsible for the remaining $10,000 of the mortgage debt that the sale of the house did not cover.

- ✔ If the property has been bought *subject to the mortgage,* then the buyer is not personally responsible for the remainder of the debt owed by the seller. In some cases the original owner may be liable. Say I buy a house for $200,000 with $100,000 cash to the seller subject to the seller's mortgage, which has an unpaid balance of $100,000. I lose my job and on top of that real estate values take a nosedive. The lender forecloses and because of lower real estate values can sell the property only for $90,000. The lender cannot hold me responsible for the $10,000 not paid by the foreclosure sale.

When someone is assuming a mortgage or paying off a mortgage early, the borrower (mortgagor) asks for a certificate from the mortgagee stating the amount that currently is due on the loan so they know exactly how much is due on the loan. This statement is called an *estoppel certificate* or *reduction certificate.*

An alienation clause in the mortgage loan agreement helps lenders prevent or control future assumptions of a mortgage loan by a new borrower. The *alienation clause,* which also is known as a *due on sale clause, call clause,* or *resale clause,* requires the borrower to pay off the loan in full immediately upon sale of the property. Instead of requiring immediate payment in full, the lender can permit the new buyer to assume the mortgage. If the original mortgage loan's interest rate is lower than the current market rate for the type of loan being sought, the lender may grant permission to assume the loan only at a rate closer to or at market levels.

An *assignment* of a mortgage is the change in the person or institution to whom the debt is owed on a mortgage without changing the terms of the loan. The *assignee,* the new debt holder, is entitled to payment of the debt just as the original lender was. If this is confusing remember that assignment involves a change in the mortgage, that is, the lender. Assumption involves a change in the mortgagor, the borrower.

# Being Fair: Consumer Protection Laws

As the government passed laws eliminating discrimination in housing, it also looked at discrimination in financing real estate purchases. Likewise it also passed consumer protection laws designed to inform consumers just what they're getting into when borrowing money. In this section I explain these fair lending and consumer protection laws. Get to know the names of these laws and what they cover to get you through any exam questions.

Also don't forget to check out Chapter 9 for information about the Real Estate Settlement and Procedures Act (RESPA).

## The Community Reinvestment Act

In 1977, the federal government passed the *Community Reinvestment Act* (CRA). This legislation required banks to address the financial needs of the communities where they are located, by making funds available for mortgages and other types of consumer loans to people within their service areas and to make periodic reports indicating activities that were undertaken with respect to providing loan opportunities to residents of the area.

## The Equal Credit Opportunity Act

The *Equal Credit Opportunity Act* (ECOA), enacted in 1975, prohibits discrimination in the granting or arranging (for example a mortgage broker) of credit. Lenders are prohibited from discriminating on the basis of age (must be of legal age), color, dependence on public assistance, marital status, national origin, race, religion, and sex. The act further requires that people who are not granted a loan must be given the reason why they were turned down. It also prohibits discrimination against an applicant who may have used some right under the Consumer Credit Protection Act, usually the Truth in Lending Act, which you can read about a little later in this section.

## The National Affordable Housing Act

The *National Affordable Housing Act* requires that borrowers must be notified whenever the servicing of their loans is transferred to another institution. Borrowers must be notified of the transfer at least 15 days before it becomes effective.

# The Truth in Lending Act

The *Truth in Lending Act* is the popular name for the federal *Consumer Credit Protection Act.* This act was implemented by *Regulation Z* of the Federal Reserve Board. In practice, these three names are used interchangeably when referring to this piece of consumer protection legislation. The regulation applies to all real estate credit transactions for personal (home) or agricultural purposes but not for commercial properties. The primary purpose of the act is to require that creditors provide information to consumers so they can make informed decisions about the use of credit in real estate transactions. Creditors are defined in the act as people or institutions that make more than 25 loans per year or provide credit more than five times a year, if the loans use real estate as security.

The act provides for what is referred to as a *three-day right of rescission* in most consumer credit transactions. This right enables consumers to change their minds within three days after closing on the loan. This right does not, however, apply to purchase money mortgages, first mortgages, or deed of trust loans. You can read about these types of loans in detail in the earlier section about "One Size Does Not Fit All: Types of Mortgages," but these are loans that are used to buy property. Refinancing loans, such as home equity loans, are covered by the rescission provision of Regulation Z.

Advertising of real estate financing is heavily regulated by this act. If details about financing are presented in an ad, then the annual percentage rate (APR) must be stated. You can read more about APR in the section "Point taken: Points on mortgage loans," earlier in this chapter.

In addition, if the advertisement mentions any *trigger terms,* then additional regulations kick in that require more detailed information to be included in the ad. The trigger terms are the

- Amount of any payment, such as the monthly mortgage payment.
- Dollar amount of the finance charge, that is, the interest rate.
- Down payment.
- Number of payments.
- Term of the loan, that is, how long the loan is for.

If any trigger terms are mentioned in an ad, then it must also contain the following information:

- Annual percentage rate (APR)
- Cash price (amount of the loan)
- Down payment necessary
- Number, amount, and due dates of all payments
- Total of all payments to be made

The penalties for violating Regulation Z range from penalties paid to the consumer based on the finance charge to fines of up to $10,000 per day and jail time of up to a year.

# Review Questions and Answers

Questions about mortgages include definitions and terms, distinguishing between types of mortgage and how different mortgages are used, different payment plans, and mortgage math calculations. I give you questions that use key words involving definitions as well as short case studies.

1. Borrower Sam gets a loan from a bank to buy a piece of property and offers the property as security for the loan. Which of the following is true?

   (A) Sam is the mortgagee and gives a mortgage to the bank.

   (B) Sam is the mortgagor and gives a mortgage to the bank.

   (C) Sam is the mortgagee and gets a mortgage from the bank.

   (D) Sam is the mortgagor and gets a mortgage from the bank.

   *Correct answer:* (B). Look through all these answers very carefully. The lender gives the money and receives the mortgage, so the lender is the mortgagee. The borrower who received the money gives the mortgage to the bank as security. The borrower is the mortgagor. I'm afraid you'll just have to remember this.

2. What type of lien is a mortgage?

   (A) Judgment

   (B) General

   (C) Voluntary

   (D) Involuntary

   *Correct answer:* (C). The other answers are types of liens, but voluntary is the correct answer. For definitions of the other answers, see Chapter 8.

3. Which one of the following is not a participant in the secondary mortgage market?

   (A) Freddie Mac

   (B) Fannie Mae

   (C) Ginnie Mae

   (D) Banker Mac

   *Correct answer:* (D). Just remember the three that are participants.

4. How do a mortgage broker and a mortgage banker differ?

   (A) A mortgage banker arranges loans, a mortgage broker lends money.

   (B) A mortgage banker lends money, a mortgage broker arranges loans.

   (C) A mortgage banker works for the secondary mortgage market, a mortgage broker is a primary lender.

   (D) There is no difference between them.

   *Correct answer:* (B). Other differences may be evident in how they're regulated (locally), but the essential difference is that the banker makes mortgage loans directly, and the broker arranges loans between borrowers and lenders.

5. What is the down payment on a property that's selling for $300,000, is appraised at $285,000, and the loan to value ratio is 90 percent?

   (A) $28,500

   (B) $30,000

   (C) $43,500

   (D) $256,500

*Correct answer:* (C). The down payment and mortgage amounts are calculated against the appraised value not the selling price unless by some chance the selling price is lower than the appraised value in which case the lower number is used. Remember that the selling price has to be taken into account to determine the down payment.

6. The front-end qualifying ratio is a percentage of what to what?

    (A) PITI to gross income

    (B) PITI to net income

    (C) Total debt to gross income

    (D) Total debt to net income

*Correct answer:* (A). First of all, qualifying ratios are calculated against gross income, so PITI to net income and total debt to net income are wrong. The front-end ratio is the PITI divided by gross income. The total debt divided by gross income is the back-end ratio.

7. One point is charged on a mortgage loan. It has no effect on the interest rate. It's very likely

    (A) a buydown.

    (B) a discount point.

    (C) an origination fee.

    (D) an APR.

*Correct answer:* (C). Origination fees, which have no impact on the interest rate, are sometimes calculated as points against the loan amount. A buydown is the other instance in which points are paid but it would have the effect of lowering the interest rate.

8. The amount of money a borrower can pay for a mortgage loan is determined by

    (A) the LTV.

    (B) the APR.

    (C) the points.

    (D) the qualifying ratio.

*Correct answer:* (D). The LTV is the percentage of the property's value that the lender will lend. You may argue with this question, because the APR and points definitely will determine what the buyer *has* to pay. But the qualifying ratio is what the buyer *can* pay under any given set of circumstances — and that is what the question asked for.

9. Lenders can get protection when making a low down payment mortgage loan from all of the following except

    (A) LTV.

    (B) PMI.

    (C) VA.

    (D) FHA.

*Correct answer:* (A). LTV is the calculation of the down payment. The question already presumes a low down payment. The VA and FHA provide guarantees for nonpayment of a loan so lenders are more receptive to low down payments. PMI is private mortgage insurance, which serves the same purpose.

10. A mortgage loan in which payments include principal and interest is generally referred to as

(A) an amortized loan.

(B) a term loan.

(C) a conventional loan.

(D) a conforming loan.

*Correct answer:* (A). The answer definitely isn't a term loan, because a term loan requires a payment of principal at the end of the term. The terms conventional and conforming have to do with amount of down payment made and the qualifying ratios used for the borrower.

# Chapter 16

# It's So Taxing: Real Estate Assessment and Taxes

## In This Chapter

▶ Finding out who collects real estate taxes (and why)

▶ Discovering how to calculate real estate taxes

▶ Checking out different kinds of tax exemptions

▶ Looking at ways to protest your tax assessment

▶ Getting the scoop on tax liens and sales

The only sure things in life are death and taxes. I don't know who said that, but it's true. If you own real estate, you'll pay taxes on it. You may pay more or less than someone who owns the same house in a different neighborhood, town, or city. You may have an exemption that reduces your payments or relieves you of payments for a while. Or you may not be able to pay your taxes and end up losing your property.

People who buy property are concerned about the taxes they pay and will ask you (if they ask nothing else) what the taxes are on the property. Buyers expect agents to know what amount of taxes is due each year on a piece of property. State exam writers expect you to know much more, like why taxes are collected, how tax rates are established, how to calculate the taxes on a particular piece of property, and how to protest tax assessments that may be unfair.

I cover these things and more in this chapter. I define some terms for you and show you a little math, but I hope this chapter doesn't get too taxing for you. (Sorry, I couldn't resist.)

## Who Wants Your Money, and What Do They Want with It? Collecting Taxes

This morning you probably drove your car on a street to get to work, right? Call me George Jetson, but personally I'm still waiting for those flying cars they predicted everyone would be using by now. But assuming you don't have one, you drove your car. And if you're reading this during a school year, your kids probably went to school this morning. Now think about where your water comes from and where your sewage goes. Who gave you that parking ticket last week? Who put out the fire down the street? You and I expect the government to provide these services and facilities, don't we? And it takes money to give everyone what they want, doesn't it?

The kinds of services that I'm talking about generally are referred to as municipal services, and they're provided by the town, village, or city (or *municipality*) and sometimes the county. The primary way the municipalities pay for these services is by collecting taxes on real estate.

Why tax property instead of something like income? Real estate is hard to hide. The value is somewhat predictable. It provides a relatively stable way to collect the money needed for all those services we want.

A word that you need to know in connection with taxes is the word *levy*. It just means charged against, as in, "A tax of $1,000 is levied on that property."

Taxes on real estate are called ad valorem taxes. *Ad valorem* means based on the value, and it refers to the fact that the taxes charged to a property are based on the value of the property. Ad valorem taxes sometimes are called a general tax or general real estate tax. In some communities a single, or general, tax is levied, and it pays for all municipal services. In other communities where taxing districts are set up, a property owner may also pay separate school district taxes as well as taxes for specific services like sewers.

In some communities, a property owner may have to pay four or five different taxes on the same piece of property, with each tax designated to pay for a different municipal service.

Although probably not crucial for exam purposes, you may want to see whether your state uses real estate tax revenues to pay for its operations. Most states use sales and income taxes. Some states have passed laws to limit the amount of taxes a local municipality can collect or the amount tax rates can be increased from year to year. You should check to see if your state has any laws like this.

# What's So Special About Assessments?

Another kind of tax that's levied against real estate is called a special assessment. *Special assessments* are taxes that are collected against a particular group of properties, rather than against all the properties in a municipality. They are used to pay for infrastructure improvements like sidewalks, drainage projects, and other types of improvements in a particular area of the community. The area of designated properties is called a *special assessment district.* The town, city, or county passes an ordinance or law that creates the special assessment district and designates the purpose for which the tax money will be collected.

# Go Figure! Calculating Taxes Step by Step

As a tax-assessor friend of mine observes, "If you think you're paying too much in taxes, go down the hall and complain to the mayor. But if you think the assessment on your property is too high, go see your tax assessor." The key elements in calculating the property taxes owed on an individual piece of property are its assessed value and the tax rates. In this section, I explain terms like assessed value and assessment ratio and show you how to do the calculations that you need to be able to do for the exam. (For extra practice on tax math, see Chapter 18.) I also discuss equalization rates for figuring county taxes (a good thing to know for the exam).

## Oh so valuable: Assessing property for taxes

The word *assessed* really means to assign or give a value to something. The assessed value is not necessarily the actual dollar value of the property. A municipality may, for example, assess property at 50 percent of its market value. *Market value* is the price the property would bring in a fair and open sale on the real estate market (find more about market value and appraising property in Chapter 14). The *assessed value* is the value of the property that is used for real estate tax purposes. The percentage that is used to calculate the assessed value is called an *assessment ratio.*

To find the assessed value of any given property, you simply use this formula:

Market value × assessment ratio (expressed as a decimal) = assessed value

Say that the market value of a property is $200,000. In the community that assesses at 50 percent of market value, the assessed value is $100,000.

$200,000 (market value) × 0.50 (50 percent assessment ratio) = $100,000 (assessed value)

If you take the same property in a community that assesses at 70 percent of market value, the assessed value is $140,000. And if you go to a community that assesses at 100 percent of market value, the assessed value obviously is $200,000.

To apply this fairly on a purely mechanical or mathematical basis, the key is that each municipality uses the same assessment ratio for all the properties within its jurisdiction. To fully appreciate how this works, you need to understand that the taxation of property is about equity and not objective value.

If you and I own property that has the same market value, we should be paying the same amount of taxes. And because taxes are based on assessed value, the assessed values of each of our properties should be the same. And if our properties have different market values, then the assessed values should be proportionally different, and so should our taxes. I put some numbers to this definition for you in Table 16-1, because calculating the assessed value of a property based on its market value and the assessment ratio is one of the types of calculations you may have to do on your state's real estate exam.

| Table 16-1 | Figuring Assessed Values | |
| --- | --- | --- |
| *Property* | *Market Value* | *Assessed Value* |
| A | $200,000 | $100,000 |
| B | $300,000 | $150,000 |
| C | $400,000 | ? |

In Table 16-1, properties A and B are being assessed fairly, because each of them is being assessed at the same assessment ratio of 50 percent. Remember the assessment ratio is calculated by dividing the assessed value by the market value. For Property C to be fairly assessed, you multiply the assessment ratio times the market value.

$400,000 × 0.50 (50 percent) = $200,000 assessed value

As you see, for the assessed values to be proportionally fair, it doesn't matter what the market values are for properties in a given municipality as long as the assessed value is calculated using the same percentage. Going one step further, as you look at the assessed values in the example, because taxes are based on assessed value, Property C will pay twice as much in taxes as Property A. And that's fair because Property C is worth twice as much as Property A.

## The numbers game: Understanding tax rates

Although calculating tax rates is not something you specifically need to know how to do for an exam, it is something you need to understand in general to answer non-math questions about the process. Knowing how to calculate taxes also isn't a bad thing to know, because you probably pay property taxes and may want to know how these guys at city hall come up with their numbers.

Tax rates in a municipality are based on a calculation involving the budget needs of the community and the total assessed valuation of the community. The municipality must first arrive at a dollar amount for its annual budget, and after that figure is adopted, the municipality looks at its *tax base,* which is the total assessed valuation of taxable property within the community.

So how do you figure out a basic tax rate? Easy! Just remember this formula:

Municipality budget ÷ total assessed valuation = tax rate

For example, say a city has adopted a budget of $2.5 million. Its total tax base is $50.0 million. You divide the budget number by the total assessed value to come up with the tax rate. In this case

$2,500,000 ÷ $50,000,000 = $0.05

This formula translates the fact that the municipality must collect five cents for every dollar of its total assessed value. However, tax rates never are expressed in cents.

Throughout the United States tax rates are reported in one of three different ways that vary by state and by municipality within the state. Using the basic tax rate that I calculated in the last paragraph, $0.05 of tax for every $1 of assessed valuation as an example, the three ways are

- Mills of tax per one dollar of assessed value — 50 mills/$1.

  One mill is one one-tenth of one penny, so 50 mills is $.050, which you get by dividing the number of mills, usually referred to as the mill rate or millage, by 1,000.

- Dollars of tax per hundred dollars of assessed value — $5/$100.

- Dollars of tax per thousand dollars of assessed value — $50/$1,000.

Each of these calculations is a different way of expressing the original calculation of $.05/$1.00.

## Doing the decimal diddle: Calculating the taxes due

Although you may see a few questions on the exam about how taxes work, the math question you're most likely to see on your state licensing exam is one in which you must calculate the taxes on a piece of property. The basic mathematical procedure is to multiply the assessed value by the tax rate.

Assessed value of the property × tax rate = taxes due

Because different municipalities in your state may use the three different methods, I show you three problems using mills per dollar of assessed value, dollars of tax per hundred dollars of assessed value, and dollars of tax per thousand dollars of assessed value. You need to be able to calculate taxes using all three methods.

Take note that the tax rate in the examples that follow stays the same.

### When the tax rate is expressed in mills

Tax rates frequently are expressed in mills, or as a millage (a tax rate expressed in mills per dollar of valuation). As already mentioned, a *mill* is one-tenth of one cent ($0.001). A tax rate of five cents of taxes per dollar of value is equal to a millage of 50 mills per dollar.

Conversely, and this is the more likely conversion you'll have to make, a tax rate of 65 mills is $0.065 per dollar of assessed value.

A typical question would be to calculate taxes on a property if you're given an assessed value and a tax rate expressed in mills. To convert the millage rate (sometimes called the mill rate) into something you can use in a calculation, just use the following formula:

> Millage ÷ 1,000 = Mill rate expressed in dollars or cents of tax per dollar of assessed valuation

Suppose a property has an assessed value of $60,000 and a tax rate of 40 mills. The first step is to convert the millage into dollars. There are a couple of ways you can do this.

> 40 mills ÷ 1,000 = $0.040

Or convert the mills to dollars by moving the decimal point three places to the left, remembering that a decimal is always at the right end of a whole number even if it isn't actually there.

> 40 mills = $0.040

Now that you've done the conversion, you multiply the assessed value and the millage rate (expressed in dollars).

> $60,000 (assessed value) × $0.040 = $2,400 taxes

## When the tax rate is expressed in dollars per hundred

Again, say that the assessed value of a property is $60,000, and the tax rate is $4 per $100. The tax rate, in other words is $4 for each $100 of assessed value (or $0.040). How much are the taxes?

Remember that you find the taxes due by multiplying the assessed value and the tax rate. The calculation is

> $60,000 (assessed value) × ($4 ÷ $100) (tax rate)

> $4 (tax rate) ÷ $100 (ratio of assessed valuation) = $0.04 tax rate (per $100 of assessed valuation)

> $60,000 assessed valuation × $0.04 tax rate = $2,400

The other way to do this by hand or by calculator is

> $60,000 (assessed value) ÷ $100 = 600

> 600 × $4 = $2,400

## When the tax rate is expressed in dollars per thousand

Say the assessed value of a property is $60,000 and the tax rate is $40 per $1,000 of assessed value. What are the taxes on this property?

Again, you multiply the assessed value and the tax rate, like so:

> $60,000 (assessed value) × ($40 ÷ $1,000) (tax rate)

> $40 (tax rate) ÷ $1,000 (ratio of assessed valuation) = $0.04 tax rate (per $1.00 of assessed valuation)

> $60,000 assessed valuation × $0.04 tax rate = $2,400

Doing this problem with a calculator, you'd enter the following equations:

$60,000 \div $1,000 = 60

60 \times $40 = $2,400 taxes

# A nice balance: Using equalization rates

You may have to do a problem using equalization rates, sometimes called *equalization factors*, to figure out a county property tax (as opposed to a city, town, or village property tax), so I'll explain what they are and how to use them. In a simple situation, several towns, cities, and villages within one county all levy their own taxes to pay for their own services, but the county also needs to collect taxes from all the residents in the county, and it may use the tax assessments from each town, village, and city. Equalization factors are needed in situations where county property taxes are being collected from several different towns, cities, and villages (municipalities) that are using different assessment ratios within that county. For example, House A in Town A has a market value of $200,000 and House B in Town B has a market value of $200,000, but Town A uses a 50 percent assessment ratio (for more about assessment ratios, see "Oh so valuable: Assessing property for taxes" earlier in this chapter), which results in an assessed value of $100,000, and Town B uses an assessment ratio of 40 percent, which results in an assessed value of $80,000. If you applied the same county tax rate to these two assessed values, House A would pay more county taxes than House B, even though they had the same market value. The equalization rate to the rescue.

The equalization rate is used to eliminate these differences and make sure people are paying their fair share of county taxes regardless of the assessment ratios their local municipalities use. Different counties may handle the math slightly differently, but the easiest way to look at this is that the equalization rate compensates for the individual municipal assessment ratios so that each property in the county is brought back up to its full market value. That value is then used for county tax calculation purposes. You need to note that although equalization rates are commonly used by counties — and that's the example I use — they can be used by any unit of government that collects taxes from different lower level taxing units, like a regional water authority that taxes counties or municipalities.

To figure out the county taxes on any given piece of property, you take its assessed value and multiply it by a designated equalization rate to come up with its equalized value. Don't worry — you won't be asked to calculate an equalization rate on the test.) You then multiply the property's equalized value and the tax rate (expressed in one of the three ways discussed in "Doing the decimal diddle: Calculating the taxes due" earilier in this chaper), and presto! You have the county taxes due. Here are two handy formulas:

Total assessed valuation (in the municipality) × equalization rate for the county or other taxing unit = equalized value (total assessed valuation for the county or other taxing unit)

Equalized value × tax rate for the county or other taxing unit = taxes due to the county or taxing unit

Want to see equalization rates in action? Say that Town A assesses its property at 25 percent of market value, Town B at 50 percent of market value and Town C at 80 percent of market value. (You can read about assessment ratios in "Oh so valuable: Assessing property for taxes" earlier in this chapter.) When the county applies its tax rate to all the properties in the county, properties of the same value pay different amounts of taxes, because each house is assessed at a different percentage of market value. (**Remember:** Taxes are calculated against assessed value, not market value.) A $100,000 house in each of the three example towns respectively is assessed at $25,000 (Town A), $50,000 (Town B), and $80,000 (Town C). The simplest thing to do is to raise all the properties back up to their full market value and use that to calculate the taxes.

The equalization rate is based on the different assessment ratios in each town, so that taxpayers pay their fair share relative to each other. In the example that follows, all three taxpayers pay the same amount of county taxes, because all three houses have the same market value. I've calculated equalization rates for the assessment ratios I'm using in this example to show you how and why it works out.

Assessed value × equalization rate = equalized value

$25,000 × 4 = $100,000

$50,000 × 2 = $100,000

$80,000 × 1.25 = $100,000

Notice a few factors here:

✔ I've equalized the value up to 100 percent of market value. It doesn't have to be 100 percent; it can be equalized to any level of value as long as all the individual assessments are equalized in the same manner.

✔ A different equalization rate is in effect for each property because each municipality assesses properties at a different percentage of market value.

You won't have to calculate an equalization rate, but you may have to calculate taxes using an equalization rate. Here's a sample problem. A property is assessed at $40,000. Its equalization rate for county taxes is 1.5. The county tax rate is 10 mills. What are the county taxes on the property?

$40,000 (assessed value) × 1.5 (equalization rate) = $60,000 (equalized value)

10 mills (tax rate) ÷ 1,000 = $0.01 (tax rate in dollars)

$60,000 (equalized value) ×$0.01 (county tax rate) = $600 (county taxes due)

Unfortunately, I've seen cases in which questions about equalization rates seem to indicate a lack of understanding of equalization rates on the part of the question writer. Just in case you get a question that mentions equalization rates and doesn't specify that it's for a county or school district, your best bet is to use the sample calculation that I used in this section and use the equalization rate to calculate the taxes due.

# Home Free (Sort of): Property Tax Exemptions

Some properties are exempted from paying real estate taxes, and other property owners may actually pay reduced taxes for one reason or another. In this section, I tell you about the most common situations in which tax exemptions and reduced taxes are in effect. All information in this section is subject to state and local law, so you need to check to see what kinds of properties are fully or partially tax exempt in your state and what exemptions are available for certain groups of people.

## A free ride: Fully tax-exempt properties

Government-owned properties, or properties owned by federal, state, county, town, city, village, township, borough, and any other level of government, are tax exempt to the extent that governments don't pay taxes to themselves nor do they generally pay taxes to a higher or lower level of government within which the property is located, provided that the property is also located within the borders of the government that owns it. So a town not only won't usually pay taxes to itself for a town park, but it also won't pay real estate taxes to the county for that park. The opposite also is true. The county won't pay taxes to the town for a county park within the town's borders. Federal government-owned and state-owned lands likewise are exempt from paying local real estate taxes. The one exception to this exemption is where property is owned by one government and is located in a completely different governmental jurisdiction. For example, Town A owns a reservoir in Town B. Town A may very likely pay taxes to Town B. But if Towns A and B are located in the same county, neither pays county taxes on the reservoir. Likewise, if County A owns property in County B, it probably will pay taxes to County B. This may vary by state, so check it out.

Other properties that are fully tax-exempt, in general, include the following:

- School districts, water districts, sewer districts, and similar public service organizations that own property

- Property owned by private educational institutions, religious organizations, hospitals, and charitable groups

## Just a small piece: Partial tax exemptions

Different states have different rules and programs that may exempt a portion of property taxes. You probably won't get a question on an exam about specific exemptions in your state, but you nevertheless need to check them out just in case.

A partial exemption may work in one of several ways: It can apply to the taxes directly by reducing the amount owed, it can apply to the assessment by reducing the assessment for an individual, or it can apply by reducing the assessment for a particular class or type of property. Here are a few examples:

- Partial relief of total taxes that have to be paid may be granted. This partial exemption usually is a percentage of the taxes due and may be offered to senior citizens or the disabled. Income qualifications may also be attached to the exemption. So a person may have to be 65 years old and making less than a certain amount of money to qualify for an exemption.

- Another type of partial tax exemption is a reduction in the assessment on the property. This type of exemption typically is offered to veterans. The exemption may be either a fixed dollar amount or a percentage of the assessment and may vary according to whether the veteran was in combat and/or is disabled. Special programs may also provide relief in the form of reduced assessments from various specific taxes such as for schools.

- Some states also provide different assessment ratios for different types of properties. I discuss assessment ratios in "Oh so valuable: Assessing property for taxes" earlier in this chapter. For example, commercial properties may be assessed at higher assessment ratios than residential properties. What that means is that if you have a residential and a commercial property that have the same market value, the commercial property pays a higher amount of property taxes than the residential property of equal value.

Remember, when you're an agent selling a property, you need to find out the taxes on the property as if no exemptions were applicable. Your buyer may not qualify for the same exemptions as the seller. You can find out the taxes on the property by consulting the municipal or county assessor to get the assessment information and the receiver of taxes (treasurer or department of finance) to get the tax rate. Then using the methods described earlier in "Doing the decimal diddle: Calculating the taxes due," you can figure out the taxes.

# That's Not Right: Protesting Assessments

Remember that tax assessments are about fairness, not necessarily objective reality. If your community assesses everyone at 100 percent of their property value, then you need to be on the lookout for your property being valued at a higher value than it actually is. You can argue that your property is being over assessed, because it isn't really worth what the assessor says it is. (This situation is one of the few in which you ever try to make that argument.)

The other way assessments can be unfair is when properties in the same community are assessed at different percentages of their market value (also known as the assessment ratio — see "Oh so valuable: Assessing property for taxes" earlier in this chapter). For instance, if most of the properties in town are being assessed at 50 percent of market value and yours is being assessed at 70 percent of market value, you may have a case.

All states have some method or process in place for protesting the assessment on your property. Each state may have a slightly different process. Typically, each community has some sort of review board before which you can protest your assessment, usually during a designated time of the year. If you're still unsatisfied with the review board decision, court action usually is necessary. You may be asked a question about this process on the exam, so you may want to find out just how your state handles tax assessment reviews. At the very least, you need to find out what the local tax assessment review board, if one exists, is called in your state, county, or municipality.

Before you take your first official step toward protesting your assessment, you first need to check whatever records your local tax assessor has on your property, making sure that the description of the property upon which the assessment is based is accurate. Assessors are reasonable people, and you may find that you're being assessed for the back porch that the last owner tore down but never reported.

# Pay or Lose: Tax Liens and Sales

You can read all about liens, including tax liens, in Chapter 8. But here are a couple of points you specifically must know about tax liens.

Individual state laws dictate the details of what happens when real estate taxes go unpaid. You're unlikely to get questions that deal with that level of detail. A number of practices are commonplace, however, and I discuss the ones that you need to be familiar with here. But just in case, you still should check out the details in your home state.

If you don't pay your taxes, eventually the taxing authority (call it the city) can take legal action to collect them from you. The first action taken generally is the placement of a lien against the property for the unpaid taxes. A *lien* is a financial obligation attached to a piece of property. After that, other legal action may take place that can take one of two forms.

✔ **Tax sale:** One way for the city to collect the money you owe in taxes is to conduct a *tax sale*. The city sells your tax debt to someone. That person pays the city what you owe. If you don't pay that person back, usually including some kind of interest or penalty, that person can claim ownership of the property. Before and during this action, the property owner has a right to redeem the property by paying the taxes plus any penalties or interest that apply. The right to do this before the tax sale is known as the *equitable right of redemption*. The right to do this after the tax sale is called the *statutory right of redemption*. The time frames and details of how these redemptions work are governed by individual state law. You can remember these two terms by the fact that "*e*" for equitable is near the front of the alphabet and the equitable right of redemption is before the sale, and that "*s*" for statutory is near the end of the alphabet and the statutory right of redemption is after the sale.

✔ **Foreclosure:** Another way the city can collect unpaid taxes is by *foreclosing* on the property, which means taking ownership of it and selling it to pay for the unpaid taxes. (For more about foreclosures, check out Chapter 15.) A term associated with foreclosure for unpaid taxes is in rem. *In rem* means the city takes action against the property rather than against you.

Banks that lend money for mortgages are particularly concerned about tax liens, because a tax lien takes first priority, which means it must be paid before any other liens, including the mortgage. The mortgage lender therefore is concerned that if a property must be sold for unpaid taxes, not enough money will be left from the sale to pay the balance owed on the mortgage loan. That's the reason many banks require the homeowner to pay into a tax escrow account from which the bank pays the taxes, just to be sure they get paid. You can read more about mortgages in Chapter 15.

# Review Questions and Answers

In addition to a calculation question or two, you can expect questions through which you can demonstrate your knowledge of terminology associated with taxes. Memorize all the key words and know how to calculate taxes with and without equalization rates, and you'll do great.

1. A property is assessed at 50 percent of its market value. What is the 50 percent called?

   (A) The property value ratio

   (B) The assessment ratio

   (C) The assessment

   (D) The ad valorem tax ratio

   *Correct answer:* (B). This is something you'll have to memorize. With this group of choices you can at least eliminate assessment, because you know that the word *percent* in the question is the same as *ratio* in one of the answers.

2. A foreclosure for unpaid taxes against the property is called

   (A) a judgment.

   (B) a due on sale clause.

   (C) in rem.

   (D) a general lien.

   *Correct answer:* (C). A judgment has to do with unsatisfied liens. A due on sale clause is often part of a mortgage loan agreement. A general lien is put against several properties. In rem refers to the foreclosure action against the property specifically instead of against the person.

3. While representing an owner in selling his property, you find a partial exemption of 10 percent against the assessment because the owner is a veteran. Assuming the successful buyer is not a veteran and the tax rate doesn't change, what would the new owner's taxes be relative to the previous owner's tax assessment?

   (A) Higher

   (B) Lower

   (C) The same

   (D) Not enough information given to determine

   *Correct answer:* (A). The key to answering this question is to remember that an exemption against the assessment always means a reduced assessment and therefore lower taxes. Without the exemption, the new owner's taxes would be higher.

4. The period of time after a tax sale during which a property may be redeemed is called

   (A) the statutory period of redemption.

   (B) the equitable period of redemption.

   (C) the in rem redemption period.

   (D) the lien payment period.

   *Correct answer:* (A). The equitable period of redemption is before the tax sale. Remember that "*e*" for equitable comes before "*s*" for statutory in the alphabet, just like equitable right of redemption comes before the tax sale and the statutory right of redemption period comes after the tax sale. The in rem redemption period and the lien payment period are made up.

5. Public improvements in a specific neighborhood often are paid for by

   (A) ad valorem taxes.

   (B) special assessment district taxes.

   (C) a public improvement lien.

   (D) the general tax.

   *Correct answer:* (B). Don't overthink a question like this. If you see key words like neighborhood improvements, the exam writers probably are trying to find out whether you know about special assessment districts. Although I made up the term, I imagine that some kind of lien could be placed against a specific property for an improvement benefiting only that property. The general tax essentially is the same as the ad valorem tax and wouldn't commonly be used to improve one neighborhood.

6. A property has an assessed value of $60,000 and an equalization rate of 1.25. What is the equalized value of the property?

   (A) $40,000

   (B) $48,000

   (C) $60,000

   (D) $75,000

   *Correct answer:* (D). This question really is pretty simple. Just multiply the assessed value by the equalization rate.

   $$\$60,000 \times 1.25 = \$75,000$$

7. A property is assessed at $50,000. The tax rate is 8 mills. What are the taxes due?

   (A) $40,000

   (B) $4,000

   (C) $400

   (D) $40

   *Correct answer:* (C). The thing to remember when you're working with mills is to back up the decimal by three places to the left (in other words, you divide by 1,000), and then multiply the assessed value by the millage rate.

8. A property is assessed at $76,000 and the tax rate is $5 per $100. What are the taxes?

   (A) $380

   (B) $3,800

   (C) $1,520

   (D) $152

   *Correct answer:* (B). If you had trouble with this question, check out "Go Figure! Calculating Taxes Step by Step" earlier in this chapter.

   $5 (tax rate per $100) ÷ $100 (of assessed valuation) = $0.05 (tax rate per dollar)

   $76,000 (assessed value) × $0.05 = $3,800 taxes owed

   Alternatively, you can do it this way:

   $76,000 ÷ $100 = 760

   760 × $5 = $3,800

One other thing: Don't let the size of the numbers throw you. You may think $3,800 is an outrageous amount of property taxes to pay and therefore incorrect, so you pick another answer that seems to make more sense. I think $3,800 in taxes is outrageous, too. And I think so every time I pay my property tax bill, which is more than that. So learn the math and trust your skills in doing these problems.

9. A property is assessed at $44,000. The tax rate is $11 per $1,000. What are the taxes?

   (A) $400

   (B) $4,000

   (C) $4,840

   (D) $484

   *Correct answer:* (D). This question is the same as question number eight but with a different tax rate expressed against $1,000 in assessed value.

   $11 (tax rate per $1,000) ÷ $1,000 (of assessed valuation) = $0.011 (tax rate per dollar)

   $44,000 (assessed value) × $0.011 = $484 Taxes

   Alternatively, you can do it this way:

   $44,000 ÷ $1,000 = 44

   44 × $11 = $484

10. A property's market value is $250,000. The assessment ratio is 40 percent. The tax rate is 23 mills. What are the taxes on the property?

(A) $2,300

(B) $230

(C) $5,759

(D) $575

*Correct answer:* (A). This problem ties together an assessment ratio and a tax rate calculation. If you can do this one, you can probably handle any tax math problem thrown at you.

$250,000 (market value) × 0.40 (assessment ratio) = $100,000 (assessed value)

23 mills (tax rate) ÷ 1,000 = 0.023

$100,000 (assessed value) × 0.023 = $2,300

# Chapter 17

# Investing in Real Estate

∙∙∙∙∙∙∙∙∙∙∙∙∙∙∙∙∙∙∙∙∙∙∙∙∙∙∙∙∙∙∙∙∙∙∙∙∙∙∙∙∙∙∙∙∙∙∙∙∙∙∙∙∙∙∙∙∙∙∙∙

### In This Chapter

▶ Getting in gear with investment basics

▶ Recognizing investment organizational structures

▶ Checking out ways to acquire investments

▶ Raking in cash with investments

▶ Understanding the government's relationship with investing

▶ Finding out how to analyze a real estate investment

∙∙∙∙∙∙∙∙∙∙∙∙∙∙∙∙∙∙∙∙∙∙∙∙∙∙∙∙∙∙∙∙∙∙∙∙∙∙∙∙∙∙∙∙∙∙∙∙∙∙∙∙∙∙∙∙∙∙∙∙

*R*eal estate long has been considered one of the best ways to build wealth. A real estate agent who provides services to people who are buying and selling investment properties needs to be knowledgeable about different types of investment properties, various ways you can make money by investing in real estate, and some of the tax issues that affect real estate as an investment. Although they don't expect you to become an investment analyst or financial advisor, state exam writers do expect you to know the basics of real estate investing. In this chapter, I tell you about the basics of real estate investments (including types of investment properties), how money is made in real estate investments, and how the government helps real estate investors through its tax policies. I also take you through a brief investment analysis and talk a little about how you can invest in real estate without actually owning any real estate.

 The info I'm giving you here is only what you need to help you pass the exam. If you decide that you want to find out even more about investing in real estate, check out *Real Estate Investing For Dummies* by Eric Tyson and Robert S. Griswold (John Wiley & Sons, Inc.).

## Back to Basics: Getting Started with Property Investment

Many people think that real estate investments must involve large and complicated properties, and that isn't necessarily true. Real estate investors often start small with residential properties close to home. I briefly discuss different types of properties, management issues, particular advantages and disadvantages, and getting help with your client's investments. With the exception of the list of investment properties, you can expect some state exam questions on all the material in this section.

---

### Stopping by on the way to Grandma's house

Location is an important factor in selecting any type of real estate, including investment properties. All other things being equal, location is the principal factor affecting the value of a property. But location plays another role when selecting an investment property. I once heard a piece of real estate investment advice that I'll pass on to you, and you may want to pass on to your clients: When you buy a piece of investment property (or when you help someone select a piece of property to buy), make sure it's located where the owner passes it twice a day — on the way to work and on the way home from work. This wisdom may be an idealized exaggeration, but you get the point. Even if the owner doesn't manage the property — in fact, especially if the owner doesn't manage the property — always knowing what's going on, not only on the property but also in the neighborhood, is important.

---

## *So many choices: Examining different investment properties*

An *investment property* can be almost any property for which people are willing to pay rent to use. I'm sure I may have left something out (lighthouses leased to the Coast Guard, maybe), but here's a pretty complete list of the different categories of investment properties.

- ✔ **One- to four-family houses:** These are sometimes called duplexes, triplexes, and quadriplexes in some parts of the country. Essentially, they're small houses with one to four apartments. New investors often purchase them, and sometimes the owner occupies one apartment and rents the others.

- ✔ **Apartment buildings:** These are distinguished from the one- to four-family house by the number of units, which can be anywhere from five units to hundreds of units in a single building.

- ✔ **Large residential complexes:** This term is used to describe residential developments of several buildings, each of which contains multiple apartments. These complexes can consist of several high-rise buildings or low-rise, one- to three-story buildings called garden apartments in some parts of the country.

- ✔ **Individual retail (store) buildings:** These buildings house department stores or smaller stores that usually have products and goods for sale.

- ✔ **Strip malls/shopping centers:** Open-air complexes of retail stores known by either of these two names often depending on whether they're a small (strip mall) or large (shopping center) group of stores. This type of retail complex is known for accommodating automobile traffic with sufficient parking areas.

- ✔ **Enclosed retail malls:** This term refers to large complexes of retail stores, usually all joined together in an indoor, climate-controlled configuration. They're also characterized by extensive parking.

- ✔ **Office buildings:** These buildings are used for all kinds of offices, ranging from medical to business offices.

- ✔ **Warehouses:** Refers to large buildings usually used for storage.

- ✔ **Motels and hotels:** Buildings that can be configured in low-rise, one- and two-story structures along the highway or high-rise buildings in a city center location are known as motels and hotels, respectively.

- ✔ **Industrial properties:** This term refers to factory buildings.

- ✔ **Vacant land:** This term applies to land with no buildings on it, purchased either to build something or for speculative purposes (simply waiting for the price to rise). They can also be leased to adjacent property owners for various purposes.

Land is generally not considered a good investment unless it's being purchased to build on. For more about vacant land, check out the section titled "Empty promise: Considering vacant land," later in this chapter.

Although you're not likely to get many (if any) questions about the real estate agent's role in advising clients about buying properties, it's important to know something about how investors think so you can help them achieve their investment goals. Generally, your role is to search out the type of property they want (see the previous list) and obtain relevant financial information so the client's accountants can check out the numbers to see if they'll get the return they want. You can find out more about how investors expect to make money later in this chapter in the section titled "We're in the Money: Making Money by Investing in Real Estate."

For investors who don't know that much about investing, you may have to provide some advice on financial returns and management issues. You can read more about management issues in the next section.

## *In charge: Looking at management issues*

One of the biggest decisions you first must make is whether to invest in real estate at all. Secondly, you have to select the kind of property in which you plan to invest. How you plan to manage your property is an important issue in making this decision. The two basic choices are managing a building yourself or hiring a manager. This decision usually is based on the investor's competence and experience with the kind of building, the building's location, the amount of time you have available for management duties, and whether the investment produces enough income to make hiring a manager possible.

Many investors start by investing in small residential properties (such as one- or two-family houses) close to home. They're usually familiar with residential properties, and the close proximity enables them to keep an eye on the property so self-management may be feasible. Moreover, these kinds of investments usually don't provide enough income (at least initially) to pay for outside management services.

On the other hand, someone who never has owned an office building before and has no familiarity with the needs of people who rent office space probably will hire a professional manager. Because an office building is used primarily during the day, providing on-site management or at least service people during business hours may be necessary. An office building is also more likely to generate enough income to support a property manager's salary.

---

### The rule of three

When recommending another professional's or tradesperson's services, a real estate agent should always recommend three people. Doing so minimizes the chance that you could be held liable in courts for other professionals' incompetent actions or advice. (In an era when people successfully sue for damages because they spilled hot coffee on themselves, I suggest you don't even think about this possibility too much, because it will give you a headache.) What the lawyers tell me is that by recommending at least three people, the person to whom you're making the recommendations has the chance to use his or her own judgment in the final selection and, therefore, bears at least some of the responsibility for the final choice made. So if you do recommend an attorney, accountant, or other professional or tradesperson, always recommend three. And I must add, make sure these people you recommend are professionals you'd rely on yourself. Remember, every time you recommend someone else's services to your real estate client or customer, you're putting your reputation on the line.

A real estate agent may be asked to advise a client about property management issues and possibly recommend a property management company. The agent should try to understand his client's need and experience as well as possible, make recommendations with the understanding that any decisions lie with the client, and always recommend at least three reputable companies. See "The rule of three" sidebar earlier in this chapter.

For more about property management and the duties of a property manager, see Chapter 3.

## Ask the experts: Knowing when to get help

Investing in real estate is an important decision. Locating the right property for investors and selling investment properties is something you'll be doing as a real estate agent. Knowing what you don't know is as important as knowing what you know. Good advice is crucial to making the right investment decision and maintaining that investment.

The three people who need to be consulted in making real estate investment decisions are a real estate agent (that's you), an attorney, and an accountant. These professionals need to be consulted as early in the process as possible. I cover the agent's role in finding property and handling management issues in the previous two sections, but you also need to check out the roles of an attorney and an accountant. Make sure you always refer your clients to these professionals as soon as possible.

Consulting an attorney is important any time you buy property, and doing so becomes even more important whenever you're buying property with a partner or several other people (see "Partnering Up: Real Estate Investment Organization Structures," later in this chapter). An attorney can help set up the proper organizational structure for an investment. You may also want an attorney to review any leases that exist in the building you buy.

The use of a good accountant likewise is crucial because of the tax implications of owning investment property. I talk about tax benefits in "Getting Uncle Sam's Help: The Government's Role in Investing" later in this chapter. The point to remember is that the value of the tax benefits derived from the same building sometimes varies from one owner to the next.

## Oh no: Some not-so-good news about investing in real estate

Investing in real estate is a great idea for several reasons: Over time real estate values tend to at least keep pace with inflation if not exceed it; properties often generate annual returns (income) on the investment; and investors can take advantage of tax benefits that may not be available in other investments. However, investing in real estate also has a few disadvantages. Here are three of them:

- ✔ Real estate isn't considered a *liquid* investment. Unlike stocks or bonds, it takes time to get your money out of a real estate investment.

- ✔ Real estate investments usually require substantial amounts of cash as a down payment, despite what the no-money-down gurus say. Reserve cash is also needed for unexpected repairs and vacancies.

- ✔ Real estate investments usually require some level of management and involvement in property management decisions, too.

- ✔ Real estate investments don't always turn out to be profitable. All investments carry risk; real estate is no different.

Although an agent wants to present the investment property in the best possible light, the important thing is to provide the potential buyer with factual data on current income, local vacancy rates for that type of property, and the physical condition, if known, of the property. You can guarantee very little about an investment unless you happen to have a really good crystal ball.

# Partnering Up: Real Estate Investment Organization Structures

People invest in real estate as individuals or sometimes together with another person or several other people. Different organizational structures are used to accomplish different investment goals. Does it surprise you to find out that you also can invest in real estate without actually owning property or having ownership responsibilities? You don't have to become an expert in this area, but in this section I talk about each of these types of ownership and investment situations in enough detail to enable you to distinguish one form from the other, which is what state exam writers expect of you.

## Real estate investment syndicates

A *real estate investment syndicate* is an ownership structure in which a number of people join together to invest in a single project or property. The term *syndicate* or *syndication* is more a descriptive than it is a legal term or an actual form of ownership. The actual legal structure of the syndicate also can take a number of different forms; you can find out more in Chapter 7. The key point to remember about syndicates is that they are created to invest in one piece of property.

*Private syndication* usually involves a small group of people, sometimes already known to each other. *Public syndication* involves a larger group of people, which may offer investments to the public in the form of securities or shares. Depending on factors such as the total number of investors and the value of the investment, the syndicate may be subject to federal and state securities laws designed to protect the public, which commonly are referred to as *blue sky laws*.

Two forms of syndicates used for real estate investments are general and limited partnerships. The principal difference between the two forms is the extent of management control and liability.

In the *general partnership,* all partners share management responsibility, profits and losses, and liability. If, for example, the partners are successfully sued and insurance can't cover the judgment, each partner can be held personally liable for the judgment.

In a *limited partnership,* one partner usually is known as the *general partner* and is ultimately responsible for any losses or liabilities on the project. Limited partners are entitled to certain profits (and losses, if they're beneficial to their tax situations), but the partners have no management responsibility, and their losses are limited to the amounts of their individual investments.

For more about partnerships and other forms of real estate ownership, see Chapter 7.

## Real estate investment trusts

*Real estate investment trusts* (REITs) are trusts designed to pool the money of multiple investors in real estate projects. Real estate investment trusts are like stock investments or mutual funds that usually invest in a series of projects, real estate investments, or mortgages. The REIT can continue as old investments are sold and new ones bought. REITs are available in these three different types:

- **Equity trust:** A REIT that invests in a number of different kinds of real estate and sells shares to investors.

- **Mortgage trust:** A REIT that uses shareholders' money to buy and sell real estate mortgage loans rather than properties.

- **Combination trust:** A REIT that invests shareholders' money in property equities and mortgage loans.

## Real estate mortgage investment conduits

A *real estate mortgage investment conduit* (REMIC) is a type of investment tool that uses shareholders' funds to invest in mortgage loans. A REMIC may sound like a mortgage trust, but they're two different beasts. A number of complex rules govern REMICs regarding the types of mortgages and interest payments to investors. None of these details is likely to be on an exam. In fact, REMIC may be one of the *wrong* choices in a question about real estate investments, so keep your eyes peeled.

# Spending Spree: Acquiring and Building Investments

An investor may buy one investment property and leave it at that. But great empires of wealth have been built by buying, selling, and holding multiple properties for investment. In this section, I talk about using borrowed money to increase profits in real estate investments. I also give you some information about buying one property, then another, and another. I also talk about one of the riskiest investments, land. For exam purposes, absorb the terminology, and wherever you see math, make sure you understand the basic idea.

## Getting more for less: The joys of leverage

*Leveraging* is using borrowed money to increase the return on your investment. One reason real estate is such an attractive investment is that other people's money is available for you to invest. The beauty of leveraging is that the less of your own money you use, the higher the rate of return on your investment. The fact you most likely use borrowed money to buy your home is also leveraging. But the fact is that you buy your home for one reason and an investment property for a different reason, and the advantages of leveraging a real estate investment have a direct bearing on the profit you make on the property.

The formula to calculate the percentage profit based on using borrowed money, namely using leverage to increase your profit, is a two-part equation.

Part 1: Selling price – purchase price = profit (in dollars)

The second part of the equation presumes of course that there is a profit. Leveraging doesn't really matter if there's a loss.

Part 2: Profit ÷ cash investment = percentage of profit

Here are two examples of leveraging at play. You buy an investment property for $500,000 with $100,000 of your own cash and the rest financed with a mortgage loan. After several years, you sell the property for $600,000. You made a profit of $100,000. Now here's the good part. You made that profit of $100,000 on only a $100,000 investment, because that's all the cash you put up. If you do the math:

Part 1: $600,000 (selling price) – $500,000 (purchase price) = $100,000 (profit)

Part 2: $100,000 (profit) ÷ $100,000 (cash investment) = 1 (or 100 percent of profit)

You buy the same $500,000 property, only this time you pay all cash. You again sell it after a few years for $600,000. You made the same $100,000 profit. But the math this time is:

Part 1: $600,000 (selling price) – $500,000 (purchase price) = $100,000 (profit)

Part 2: $100,000 (profit) ÷ $500,000 (cash investment) = 0.2 (or 20 percent of profit)

Comparing the first example with the second example shows how you can make the same amount of money, $100,000, with only a $100,000 investment, instead of tying up $500,000, all by using other people's money — namely the mortgage loan. (For more about mortgages, see Chapter 15.)

Now that you've seen how basic leveraging works, think about the investor who has $500,000 cash. Instead of paying cash for one $500,000 building, he puts $100,000 cash into five $500,000 buildings. Using the first example above, he would reap 100 percent profit on each of the buildings and make a total of $500,000. Investors generally want to invest as little of their own money as possible and, of course, make the most profit in the shortest time.

Make sure you can handle a math question calculating basic leverage (as shown in this section's examples) and understand that leveraging is the concept of using borrowed money to extend the impact of your own cash investment.

## Pyramiding: Not just for the pharaohs

*Pyramiding* is building multiple investments from one investment. You really need to think in terms of an upside down pyramid or triangle for this to make sense. Essentially, you start with one investment property and use the profits from it to buy two. Then, in turn, you buy four. So, the upside-down pyramid has the pointy end down — that's the one property you start with — and from there the pyramid expands up and out — that's the result of your addition of more and more investment properties. You can either sell each property and buy more properties, or refinance a property and use the resulting cash to buy another or even two more. In pyramiding, you're always aiming to increase the total number of properties you own.

The down side of pyramiding, of course, is your increasing debt load, which can be very sensitive to economic conditions. And, of course, investing in more and more buildings presumes an adequate profit greater than expenses. But pyramiding is one way that people build a real estate investment portfolio over time and end up controlling a number of properties.

## Empty promise: Considering vacant land

Traditional real estate investment advice says to avoid investing in *vacant land,* meaning land that's undeveloped. I'm talking about buying a piece of empty land and waiting for it to grow (appreciate) in value. Sometimes people wait for time to take its effect, hoping that property values will rise. Sometimes people are simply waiting for development to reach the property or a new highway to be built. In these cases, investors aren't doing anything to add value to the property. Some people have made money with this investment strategy, but in general, vacant land is not recommended as a good real estate investment.

Vacant land produces no income while you own it. The only profit to be made is when you sell it. And that profit usually depends on factors over which you have no control, such as where a new road is built. Meanwhile, you have to pay taxes on the land and possibly maintain it in some way depending on where it's located.

On the other hand, if you do something to increase the value of the property, it may become a good investment opportunity. You may be able to build on it or get the local government to permit commercial development, which usually is more highly valued than residential development. Vacant land also can be rented (leased) on a long-term basis to someone who wants to build something on it. I talk about land leases in Chapter 12. Exam questions on this subject, if any appear, are pretty simple. Just remember that vacant land is not considered a good investment because it costs you money without generating an income.

# We're in the Money: Making Money by Investing in Real Estate

You can make money in several different ways, such as capital appreciation, renting, and equity buildup, by investing in real estate. As an agent (and as a test taker), you need to be familiar with all the moneymaking methods and the appropriate terminology. In this section, I cover the basics.

The most important thing to keep in mind when it comes to making money on investments is that an investor expects these two kinds of returns:

✔ **Return of the investment:** You expect to get back your capital, the cash you invested in the first place.

✔ **Return on the investment:** You expect to receive something more than what you invested. The expected return on the investment is related to the risk of the investment. The risk in any investment is the possibility of losing all or part of your original cash investment. The higher the risk, the greater the expected return on the investment.

The several ways by which investors expect to accomplish the return *of* their investments and the return *on* their investments are covered in the following sections.

## Up and down: Buying low and selling high — capital appreciation

One of the ways investors make money in real estate is by selling property at a higher price than that which they bought it for in the first place. In this case, the value of the real estate *appreciates,* or increases, creating *capital appreciation,* or growth. The profit made from selling property for a price higher than what you paid is called *capital gain for tax purposes.* When you sell property for more than you paid for it, you get the return of your capital; that is you get your original down payment, back along with the profit or capital appreciation, which is the return on your capital. So, if I buy a property that costs $500,000 with $100,000 cash (see "Getting more for less: The joys of leverage" earlier in this chapter) and a few years later sell that property for $600,000, then I get my original cash investment of $100,000 back (return of my investment) and an additional $100,000 in capital appreciation (return on my investment). For more about capital gains, see "More than your money's worth: Capital gains" later in this chapter.

## Plenty of room: Rentals on property

Most investors get returns on their investments by means of rents paid on the property. All expenses, including the mortgage loan payment, are paid from the rent and whatever else (such as quarters from laundry machines) factors into the *building income.* Investors call the mortgage payment *debt service.* The money left over after all expenses are paid, except debt service, is called the *net operating income.* After debt service is subtracted from net operating income, what's left is called *cash flow,* or the money the investment has earned before taxes. Check out the following two-part equation:

Part 1: Building income – operating expenses = net operating income

Part 2: Net operating income – debt service = cash flow

Cash flow ideally is positive, meaning that you take money out of the investment each year. But cash flow also can be negative, meaning that the building's expenses are greater than the building's income. Three reasons why someone buys an investment with negative annual cash flow are

- The investor may believe that the shortfall is only temporary. Maybe the building isn't fully rented. Or the investor believes rents will go up faster than expenses or that expenses can be managed better and reduced.

- The investor may believe that when selling the building it will make enough profit to make up for the negative cash flow each year.

- The investor may be making a lot of money in another investment and wants to keep his income tax bracket lower by balancing a positive cash flow investment against a negative one.

## Letting someone else pay off the mortgage: Equity buildup

The mortgage payment, or debt service, always is included in the expenses of any investment property. If the borrower borrows money with an amortized mortgage, every payment made on that loan is part interest and part principal. (That's what *amortized* means.) So every time the building's income (in the form of rents and other income) is used to make a mortgage payment, usually monthly, the overall mortgage debt is reduced.

By paying off some or all of the mortgage loan, when the owner sells the property, he owes the bank less money on the balance of the mortgage loan than when he first bought the investment. The owner (investor) gets to keep more of what he sells the investment for. *Equity* is the difference between the value of the property and all debts attributable to the property. Obviously any increase in the overall value of the property also increases the equity, but investors usually use the term *equity buildup* to specifically refer to the increase in equity that comes from the mortgage loan being paid off by the rents from an investment property.

For example, suppose you borrow $200,000 to buy an investment property that costs $250,000. You keep the property for 10 years, and through the monthly loan payments, which are coming out of the rents, you pay off $50,000 of the mortgage. Assuming the property doesn't appreciate in value when you sell the property, you owe the bank only $150,000. That $50,000 you paid off of the mortgage is yours, courtesy of your tenants' rent.

I discuss mortgage loans in Chapter 15.

# Getting Uncle Sam's Help: The Government's Role in Investing

The federal tax code isn't just about the government figuring out new and exciting ways to take away your money. Much of the code is devoted to encouraging different kinds of business activities. Real estate investments benefit from several programs that help investors retain more of their profits. This section tells you about the most common programs, some of which involve a little math that exam writers want you to know how to do. I give you the basics here, but don't forget that accountant when actually owning a real estate investment.

## More than your money's worth: Capital gains

When you sell a property for more than you paid for it, you have made what, for tax purposes, is called a *capital gain*. That gain is taxable, but because the government wants to encourage people to make long-term (usually more than a year) investments over time, it treats capital gains more favorably than regular income for tax purposes.

Calculating the amount of capital gain that a property has earned starts with the *basis* of the property. The *basis* is the initial price you paid for the real estate, not just the cash you put in. The basis can change over time, because the costs of capital improvements are added to it. A *capital improvement* is a permanent improvement that adds value to the property, such as a new roof on the building or new kitchens in the rental units. This new number (original cost plus capital improvements) is still referred to as the *basis*. Depreciation, which is the government's way of enabling you to claim a loss on your property and which I discuss in the next section, is then subtracted from the total of the original cost of the property (the basis). The resulting number is called the *adjusted basis*.

Next, you subtract selling expenses, such as commission expenses and closing costs, from the selling price of the property. That total is called the *net selling price*.

Finally, the adjusted basis is subtracted from the net selling price, and the result is the capital gain. The calculations that follow show the amount of capital gain for a property initially purchased for $50,000.

$50,000 (purchase price, or basis) + $8,000 (capital improvements) – $4,000 (depreciation) = $54,000 (adjusted basis)

$90,000 (selling price to the new buyer) – $5,000 (commission expense) – $1,000 (closing costs) = $84,000 (net selling price)

$84,000 (net selling price) – $54,000 (adjusted basis) = $30,000 (capital gain)

Tax laws change from time to time, particularly with respect to the tax rate on capital gains. Expect a question or two requiring you to calculate a capital gain or to describe the basis or adjusted basis. You might even have to calculate the tax paid, but either the exam writers give you the tax rate to use or you use the one you learned in your prelicense class.

# *Feeling worn-out: Depreciation*

*Depreciation* is the recovery of the cost of an asset that wears out. Another term for depreciation is *cost recovery*. Allowing you to deduct a dollar amount of depreciation from your annual tax obligation is the government's way of acknowledging that the asset, a thing of value, wears out and that if you didn't have the asset, you couldn't earn any money on which to pay taxes. With depreciation, you wind up paying less in annual taxes on any given piece of property (and keeping more of your profits).

The government wants you to pay taxes. No surprise there. For people who need physical objects like buildings, machinery, or automobiles (as you soon see) to earn their incomes and therefore to pay taxes, the government understands that no physical object lasts forever, and without that object you have no business and pay no taxes. Depreciation is the government's way of acknowledging that these things wear out and helping investors replace these items so that they can continue earning income and — you guessed it — continue paying taxes.

Here's a non-real estate example, including the tax impact, that I use in the classroom. Suppose that you have the smallest car rental company in the world with only one car. That car cost $25,000, and you rent it out and make $8,000 in what usually is referred to as gross income (income before taxes and expenses). After gas, oil, maintenance, and insurance expenses are deducted, you end up with $6,000 left as your *net income.* You're in the 20 percent tax bracket, so your tax calculation is

$6,000 (net income) × 0.20 = $1,200 (taxes)

At least that's how much your taxes would be if the government didn't recognize the fact that cars wear out and without a car you have no business and the government gets no taxes. So, the government lets you deduct depreciation, enabling you to do so during what is called a *cost recovery period* of five years on the car.

$25,000 (cost of car) ÷ 5 (cost recovery period in years) = $5,000 (depreciation per year)

So now, instead of deducting only $2,000 in expenses from your income, you get to deduct another $5,000.

$8,000 (gross income) – $2,000 (operating expenses) – $5,000 (depreciation) = $1,000 (net income)

$1,000 (net income) × 0.20 (tax rate) = $200 (taxes)

A tax bill of $200 versus $1,200, courtesy of depreciation, sounds pretty good. And you thought those guys at the IRS were only after your money.

For more depreciation math, check out Chapter 18.

Investment properties benefit from the same depreciation calculation; however, the cost recovery period for buildings is longer than for motor vehicles, and vacant land can't be depreciated at all, because land doesn't get old and worn out like a building. And a private home can't be depreciated because it isn't considered an income-generating asset. The type of depreciation that is used for investment properties is called *straight-line depreciation,* because an equal amount of the value of the building is deducted each year. The government periodically changes the rules governing the cost recovery period, the required ownership time, and the tax rate at which capital gains generated from depreciation are taxed. I suspect because state exam writers don't want to have to change exam questions every time the federal government changes the tax law, you probably won't get any questions on the specifics. But you may get a question about deprecation in general, how it works, and how it affects the basis.

The beauty of depreciation is that it's subtracted from annual income thereby reducing your annual tax burden, as the example shows. Of course you've most likely figured out that because depreciation reduces the adjusted basis of the property, it increases the capital gains on which you'll have to pay taxes. But capital gains are traditionally given favorable treatment by the tax code, so ultimately you're paying less tax on the capital gain than you would have on the annual income.

## On the way down: Tax deductions and tax credits

A *tax deduction* is something you can deduct from an investment property's income to reduce your taxes. A *tax credit* is something you can deduct from the taxes you owe. The federal and sometimes state governments create programs that permit tax credits or deductions to encourage certain activities with respect to investment properties. Historic preservation and energy efficiency are the kinds of things the government periodically tries to encourage. Within certain limits, property owners are permitted to deduct the interest payments on their mortgage loans and local property taxes.

All things being equal, a tax credit is worth more in tax savings than a tax deduction. The credit is subtracted from taxes owed, and the deduction is subtracted from the net taxable income (your gross income after expenses). Most likely, the test will ask that question: Which is more valuable?

I doubt you'll have to do this kind of calculation, but here's an example anyway. The facts and numbers are made up.

Last year the government said you could deduct $3,000 for any work you did that increased the energy efficiency of your property. This year the government said you could take a $3,000 tax credit if you did the same kind of work. If the net income (gross income after expenses) of your building is $30,000 in each of those years, and you're in the 20 percent tax bracket, in which year are you better off?

Last year:

> $30,000 (net income) – $3,000 (energy tax deduction) = $27,000 (net taxable income)
>
> $27,000 (net taxable income) × 0.20 (tax rate) = $5,400 (taxes owed)

This year:

> $30,000 (net income) × 0.20 (tax rate) = $6,000 (taxes)
>
> $6,000 (taxes) – $3,000 (energy tax credit) = $3,000 (taxes owed)

For more about real estate taxes, check out Chapter 16.

## Let's trade: Real estate exchanges

You don't always have to pay cash for a piece of property. You can trade, just like you did with baseball cards (well, not quite). Under certain circumstances, the government allows you to exchange one piece of property for another. These exchanges are known as *1031 exchanges,* after the section of the law that governs them, or *tax deferred exchanges,* because one of the advantages is the deferral of capital gains tax. I discuss capital gains in

"More than your money's worth: Capital gains," earlier in this chapter. You don't have to get too technical in terms of what to remember about exchanges, but here are a few facts and terms you need to remember for the exam.

- ✔ **Like kind:** To qualify for an exchange, the two properties must be of *like kind* according to IRS definitions, and they must be investment properties.
- ✔ **Time limits:** Some exchanges have time limits during which they must be completed.
- ✔ **Boot:** If properties are exchanged and they don't have equal value, even if one of the properties has increased in value, capital gains tax is deferred, but it eventually must be paid when the property is sold. If the properties are not equal in value, cash or personal property sometimes is included in the deal. This cash is called *boot*. The person receiving it owes taxes on the boot.

# By the Numbers: Analyzing Investment Properties

As a real estate agent, you'll be called upon to provide information to investors about investment properties. Building condition, maintenance issues, and location issues are important in any real estate purchase, but much of the information in a real estate investment is about income and expenses for the property. Although you probably won't conduct an investment analysis yourself, you're still expected to know something about the numbers and how they're analyzed by investors. The agent's role is to provide the necessary information to the potential investor so that the investor or the investor's accountant can perform the analysis. The beginning of a real estate investment analysis is the *operating statement,* which also is called the *income and expense statement.* This statement, which usually is prepared to keep track of finances for the building and for income tax purposes, tracks the actual annual income and expenses for a building. The income tracked on the operating statement is called the *contract* or *scheduled rent,* which is the actual rent paid by the tenants. Because the operating statement is used for income tax purposes, it usually contains information about depreciation and debt service (mortgage payments). I discuss depreciation in "Feeling worn-out: Depreciation," earlier in this chapter.

The second piece of information in a real estate investment analysis is the current rent roll. The rent roll is information about the leases that exist, the rents for each lease, and the term or length of time remaining on each lease. (For more about leases, flip to Chapter 12.)

A third piece of information in the analysis is the market rents, which are what the market would pay for the kind of space or apartment in the building. Market rents may be different from contract rents for that particular building.

The final piece of information in an investment analysis is one that's created by the investor or the person doing the analysis on the investor's behalf. Called the *pro forma,* it's a financial statement of the building's potential income and expenses. By looking at the market rents for the kind of space being leased rather than the scheduled rents, a projection is made of the investment's future. The pro forma is a look at what can be. A few noteworthy characteristics of the pro forma are

- ✔ Market rents, rather than actual or contract rents, are generally used, but actual rents for existing leases may also be used under certain circumstances.
- ✔ Income figures are based on the building being 100 percent occupied, even if it currently isn't, and the figures may include other building income such as that from laundry machines.

- Other income, such as income to the building for something other than the regular rents (for example a microwave antenna rental on the roof) is usually added after the vacancy and collection loss calculation is applied.

- A vacancy and collection allowance is used, even if the space in the building is 100 percent rented.

- Expenses generally are rounded off.

- All figures are annual.

- Depreciation and debt service aren't accounted for. The value of the depreciation may vary with the owner's financial position, and the mortgage is more about the owner's financial position than the value of the building.

The basic numbers that you're looking for in a pro forma are the *net operating income* and *cash flow.* The basic formula for finding net operating income on a pro forma follows, but it will help you understand the formula if you first know the details behind some of the numbers called for in the formula.

- **Potential gross income:** Market rent at 100 percent occupancy; may also include other building income such as laundry machines or separate parking space rental

- **Vacancy and collection loss:** Used to account for periods of rent loss due to vacancies or bad debts; determined by examining other pro formas for the number they use

- **Effective gross income:** Also called effective rental income

- **Operating expenses:** Don't include depreciation or debt service

- **Debt service:** Refers to the mortgage payment

  Potential gross income – vacancy and collection loss = effective gross income

  Effective gross income – operating expenses = net operating income

  Net operating income – debt service = before-tax cash flow

If you calculate the taxes owed on this cash flow and subtract it, you get what is called after-tax cash flow.

In analyzing a building for investment, the return (the money you're going to make on your investment as well as the money you'll get back that you invested — return of investment) is calculated for a one-year period and for the project *holding period,* which is the length of time the investment will be owned.

# Review Questions and Answers

Actual math calculations on this information may or may not appear on the exam, but the exam writers expect you to be able to explain in words what each investment term means and, if relevant, how it's calculated.

1. Real estate is considered

   (A) a no-risk investment.

   (B) a liquid investment.

   (C) an investment that requires little management.

   (D) an investment that requires good professional advice.

*Correct answer:* (D). Real estate isn't considered a no-risk investment especially because of its dependence on unpredictable future market conditions. It's definitely not liquid, meaning that you can't get your money out of it quickly. It's nonliquidity is generally considered to be one of the major disadvantages of real estate investment. It does require some kind of management even if you hire a professional to handle day-to-day operations.

2. The act of using borrowed money to extend the profitability of your investment is called

   (A) a REIT.

   (B) a capital gain.

   (C) leveraging.

   (D) pyramiding.

*Correct answer:* (C). The tricky answer here is pyramiding. Pyramiding is using the appreciation from one investment to make more investments. Leveraging is what makes an investment more profitable, because you're using less of your own money. A Real Estate Investment Trust (REIT) is a type of stock investment (like a mutual fund) that invests in real estate. A capital gain is the profit made by buying a piece of real estate at one price and selling it at a higher price.

3. I put a down payment of $50,000 on a $200,000 investment property. In five years, I sell it for $225,000. The fact that my profit is 50 percent is a result of

   (A) return of investment.

   (B) leverage.

   (C) tax benefits.

   (D) depreciation.

*Correct answer:* (B). This question puts some numbers to the leverage issue without you having to do the calculation. In case you're lost here, you divide the profit of $25,000 ($225,000 – $200,000) by the $50,000 down payment to get the 50 percent profit. Return of investment is incorrect because the example talks about the money I made above and beyond my original cash investment. Nothing in the example deals with taxes or depreciation; these items are present in most real estate investments, but the example doesn't give you any information about them. So tax benefits and depreciation are also incorrect.

4. Making money by selling a property for more than you paid for it is called

   (A) capital appreciation.

   (B) return of investment.

   (C) cash flow.

   (D) tax credit.

*Correct answer:* (A). Don't get confused here with the term capital gains. Essentially, capital gains and capital appreciation refer to the same thing; however, capital appreciation describes what the question is asking and capital gains usually describes the same thing for income tax purposes. Return of investment is the return of your original investment money (capital), not any additional money you make, which would be return on the investment. Cash flow is the general term used for the annual return on the investment after all expenses, including debt service, are paid. Nothing in this question refers to taxes, so you can eliminate tax credit right away.

5. When calculating capital gains, what is subtracted from the selling price?

   (A) Depreciation

   (B) Capital investment

   (C) Operating expenses

   (D) Adjusted basis

   *Correct answer:* (D). The adjusted basis is the original purchase price of the property plus any capital improvements minus depreciation, and it's what's used to calculate capital gains.

6. The pro forma uses

   (A) scheduled rent.

   (B) depreciation.

   (C) market rents.

   (D) debt service.

   *Correct answer:* (C). You need to remember this. Debt service and depreciation are not used because they are more specific to the property owner than the property itself. Remember that scheduled rents are used as part of the overall investment analysis but are not usually used in the pro forma.

7. A few years ago you bought an investment property for $100,000. You made $10,000 worth of improvements and took $6,000 in depreciation. You sell the property for $120,000. What is the capital gain?

   (A) $20,000

   (B) $16,000

   (C) $10,000

   (D) $4,000

   *Correct answer:* (B). Here are the calculations:

   $100,000 (purchase price) + $10,000 (capital improvements) – $6,000 (depreciation) = $104,000 (adjusted basis)

   $120,000 (selling price) – $104,000 (adjusted basis) = $16,000 (capital gains)

8. You exchange properties with another person. Your property is worth $200,000. Her property is worth $250,000. You give the other party $50,000 in cash. This cash is

   (A) boot and is taxable to her.

   (B) boot and is taxable to you.

   (C) capital gains and the tax is deferred until you sell your property.

   (D) capital gains and the tax is deferred until she sells her property.

   *Correct answer:* (A). The boot is money or personal property given in an exchange when the properties are not equal in value. The person receiving the boot pays the taxes on it.

9. You own an apartment house. The potential annual gross income is $40,000. The allowance for vacancies is 5 percent. The annual operating expenses are $10,000. The debt service is $12,000 per year. What is the net operating income?

(A) $16,000

(B) $18,000

(C) $20,000

(D) $28,000

*Correct answer:* (D) You have to remember the order of how to calculate a net operating income on a pro forma. You also have to remember that you don't use debt service in the calculation. Exam writers sometimes give you information you don't need. Remember to be careful whenever you get monthly numbers because all these calculations have to be in annual figures. The calculation is as follows:

$40,000 (potential gross income) $\times$ 0.05 (vacancy allowance) = $2,000 (vacancy and collection loss)

$40,000 (potential gross income) – $2,000 (vacancy and collection loss) = $38,000 (effective gross income)

$38,000 (effective gross income) – $10,000 (operating expenses) = $28,000 NOI (net operating income)

10. An amount of money that the government allows you to deduct from taxes owed on a building's income is called

(A) depreciation.

(B) cost recovery.

(C) a tax credit.

(D) a tax deduction.

*Correct answer:* (C). You have to read this question carefully. Depreciation is deducted from income, not from taxes owed. Cost recovery is another term that sometimes is used to mean depreciation. A tax deduction is deducted from income.

# Chapter 18

# All in the Numbers: Real Estate Mathematics

**W**orking in the real estate field is more than just selling real estate. It involves many skills and a thorough knowledge of many subjects, including math. As an agent you may have to measure a room or a house, or calculate the taxes on a piece of property. And most important of all, you need to know how to calculate your commission.

A quick note to all you math phobics (you know who you are!): Those of you who suffer from math-itis, or whatever you call it, should relax. Work through the material in this chapter, and do your best. Above all, though, don't worry: The exam typically has few math problems. You'll do fine without necessarily getting the math questions right. Later on, as a friend likes to tell all her mathematically challenged students, by the time they're in the business a few months, they'll be able to calculate their commissions down to the last penny, in their heads, while waiting at a stop light.

In this chapter, I review some common math concepts and calculations. Notice I say *review*. You've already seen most of what is in this chapter in middle school and high school. You simply may not have seen it in a real estate context. I show you how to apply some fairly simple math concepts to practical real estate problems. I'm sure as you go through this chapter that it all will come back to you.

Many students ask about rounding. Test writers are interested in you knowing basic formulas and techniques. They won't give you questions where the difference between a right and wrong answer is a tenth of a number that you might get wrong due to rounding.

# Don't Lose the Faith, but You May Have to Convert

Before you start doing most of the math problems in this chapter, you need to remember that test writers often throw problems at you that contain different units of measurements in the same problem. Before you can solve the problems, you need to convert those measurements to make sure you multiply feet by feet, yards by yards, and so on. Also, you may have to calculate the area of a room in square feet but later convert it to square yards.

Memorize the following conversion factors to ease your problem solving.

1 foot = 12 inches

1 yard = 3 feet

1 mile = 5,280 feet

1 square yard = 9 square feet (3 feet × 3 feet)

1 acre = 43,560 square feet

A section = 1 square mile or 640 acres

A section = 5,280 feet (1 mile) on each side

1 cubic yard = 27 cubic feet (3 feet × 3 feet × 3 feet)

# Land and Buildings: Measuring Area and Volume

Because you'll be selling land and buildings, knowing something about figuring out what size they are is important. For exam purposes, all you really need to know is how to calculate the area and volume of land and buildings after you have the measurements.

*Area* is the amount of space on a flat surface. Calculating the *area* means figuring out how large a flat space is. It may be determining the square footage of a house, the amount of carpeting or tile needed to cover the floor of a room, or the amount of wallpaper needed to cover a wall. (Remember a wall still is a flat surface.)

*Volume* is the measurement of what it takes to fill up something. In real estate terms, calculating the volume of a warehouse, rather than just its floor area, is important when you're informing a potential buyer how much stackable space the property has.

In this section, I take you through a series of examples that cover all the standard area and volume calculations that you may encounter on a state real estate exam.

## How big is it really?

Usually, land isn't something that you as a real estate agent measure. You may occasionally walk the boundaries of a piece of property and estimate its length and width. In general, however, if someone asks you the size of a piece of land, you'll look it up in the public records like the deed, tax records, or public map filings, or you'll calculate it from information on a map drawn by a surveyor. Unless a piece of land is perfectly rectangular, square, or triangular, calculating the exact area of the property is difficult and best left to surveyors.

As an agent, you may have to measure a house or individual rooms. In general, overall house size starts with a measurement of the outside walls of the house. If you need an individual room size, measure the actual room; however, due to discrepancies in measurement over which buyers can get cranky, many agents now rely on public records when they advise the buyers of the size of the house.

## Area of a square or a rectangle

A *square* is a four-sided figure on which each side is the same length. A *rectangle* is a four-sided figure where two sides opposite each other are equal. For example, a rectangle may have two sides opposite each other that are 150 feet long, and the two other sides opposite each other are 80 feet long. See Figures 18-1 and 18-2 for examples of a square and a rectangle.

**Figure 18-1:** Square measuring 100 feet on all four sides.

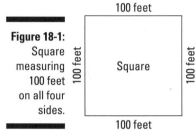

**Figure 18-2:** Rectangle measuring 150 feet by 80 feet.

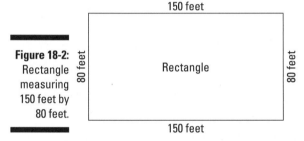

The formula for calculating the area of a square and a rectangle is the same.

Length (L) × Width (W) = Area (A)

Like most other calculations in this chapter, when calculating area, the units of measure must be the same. You have to multiply feet by feet, yards by yards, and so on. Furthermore, the answer to any area problem is always in square units. If you're multiplying feet by feet, your answer is in square feet.

You have a square piece of property that measures 100 feet by 100 feet. How big is the property?

100 feet × 100 feet = 10,000 square feet

Or, say you have a rectangular piece of property that measures 80 feet by 150 feet. What is the area?

150 feet × 80 feet = 12,000 square feet

Notice in this second question where I put the longer figure for length. It really doesn't matter in a problem like this what you call each number. On a piece of land, the distance across the front of the property generally is referred to as the width, while the distance going from the street back is the length or depth. Sometimes a problem may refer to a front foot or *front footage,* which usually is the same as the width of the property along the street.

## Area of a triangle

A triangle is a three-sided figure where all the sides join together. Look up at the end of a peaked roofed house and you'll see a triangle. That triangle is called the *gable end,* and you may have to calculate the area to determine how much paint or siding is needed to cover it.

The formula for the area of a triangle is

½ Base (B) × Height (H) = Area (A)

Figure 18-3 shows a sample triangle.

**Figure 18-3:** Triangle with a base of 30 feet and a height of 12 feet.

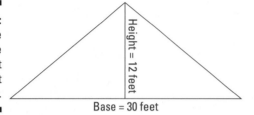

Height = 12 feet

Base = 30 feet

Similar to the way you calculate the area of a square or rectangle, when calculating a triangle's area, don't forget that all the units of measurement must be the same and the answer must be in square units. The *height* is a line that is *perpendicular,* or at a right (90-degree) angle, to the base.

Say you want to paint your roof's gable end. The width of the house at that point is 30 feet. The height of the gable is 12 feet. How many square feet are you going to have to paint?

0.5 × 30 feet × 12 feet = 180 square feet

## Area of a circle

A *circle* essentially is a single line that curves around and meets itself. Pick up that quarter in your pocket, and you've got a circle. The *diameter* is a straight line drawn through the center from one side of the circle to the other, and the *radius* is half of the diameter.

The formula to find the area of a circle is

π × radius squared (r²) (To *square* the radius, you multiply the radius by itself.)

π is the constant number 3.1416.

Check out Figure 18-4 for an example of a circle.

Maybe you're going to build a round patio. Or, if you live in farm country, you may have to rely on some of these calculations when determining the volume of a silo.

You're building a circular patio that's 16 feet in diameter. How many square feet of patio block will you use?

3.1416 × 8 (squared) = A (area)

3.1416 × (8 × 8) = 201.06 square feet

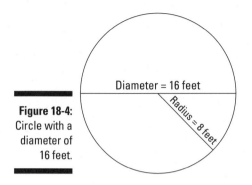

**Figure 18-4:**
Circle with a diameter of 16 feet.

## Area of an irregular shape

Unfortunately many houses aren't single squares or rectangles but rather are combinations of several squares and rectangles. A rectangular house with a small breezeway and attached garage is a good example of what I'm talking about. And the key to calculating the area of a house like this is that you have to divide the figure into squares and rectangles and occasionally even triangles, calculate the area of each individual figure, and then add them together. You can also come pretty close by using this technique to calculate the area of an irregular piece of land.

## Volume of anything

The formula for calculating the volume of any figure involves calculating the area and multiplying it by the height.

Length (L) × Width (W) × Height (H) = Volume (V)

Say you want to calculate the volume of a rectangular warehouse that measures 100 feet by 200 feet by 15 feet high. The equation would look something like:

200 feet × 100 feet × 15 feet = 300,000 cubic feet

Length × width is the formula for calculating the area, but by multiplying that answer (called the *product*) by the third dimension, the height, you get the volume. Just like when you calculate area, the measurements must always be in the same units. With volume, the answer is always in cubic units. So if all three measurements are in feet, the answer will be in cubic feet.

In the case of a triangular-shaped object like an attic, in which the triangle's height already is used to calculate the area, you multiply the area by the length of the attic. The whole formula is

½ Base (B) × Height (H) × Length (L) = Volume (V)

Finally, suppose you need to find the volume of a cylindrical object like a silo on a farm. Once again, you just have to multiply the area of the silo's base by the silo's height.

If you had a silo 20 feet in diameter and 30 feet high, what is the volume?

$\pi$ × radius squared ($r^2$) × Height (H) = Volume (V)

3.1416 × (10 feet × 10 feet) × 30 = 9,424.8 cubic feet

Remember, the area of a circle involves the radius, which is half of the diameter. (That's why this example uses 10 feet instead of 20 feet.)

# *Percentages: Pinpointing What You Really Need to Know*

Using percentages is another type of real estate math problem. Commissions usually are figured on a percentage basis. Shared ownership of a property may be on a percentage basis. Vacancy rates usually are expressed as a percent. You'll work with percents to figure out the selling price of a property. Property tax calculations may also involve percentages. So I think you can see the importance of understanding and being able to answer exam questions about percentages.

In this section, I provide the basics that you can apply to any problems asking you to use or calculate percentages. And by the way, I explain them to you as if you're doing these calculations by hand. Some calculators have percentage keys that you can use. Feel free to use them, if you know how, or ignore them.

A *percent* — which is expressed as a number like 4 percent, 8 percent, 7.5 percent, or 0.8 percent — essentially describes what part of a hundred you're talking about. The word "percent" comes from the Latin word *centum,* meaning a hundred. So 4 percent means four parts per hundred of whatever you're taking about. If 4 percent of the eggs in a truckload are bad, then four out of every hundred eggs are bad. And if you're allowed to build on 4 percent of your land area, it means you can cover 4 square feet out of every 100 square feet with a building. The calculations you do with percentages usually are most often multiplication and occasionally or division, depending on the problem.

You have two choices for turning a percentage into a number you can work with. You can either divide the percent number by 100 or move the decimal point two places to the left.

Say, for example, that you have to use 7 percent in a problem. If you divide 7 by 100, you get a number you can use in a calculator or by hand.

$$7 \div 100 = 0.07$$

That isn't 0.07 percent. It's simply 0.07, which is the same as 7 percent.

Another way to remember is that if a decimal point doesn't actually appear in the number, then it's assumed to be at the end. From there (the right side of a whole number), move the decimal to the left two spaces, even if you have to add one or more zeroes. Seven percent becomes 0.07. Check out a few more of these:

| | |
|---|---|
| 800% | 8 |
| 80% | 0.80 |
| 8% | 0.08 |
| .8% | 0.008 |
| .08% | 0.0008 |
| 8.5% | 0.085 |

*Note:* You probably won't be working too much with small percentages, such as 0.08 percent or 0.8 percent, either on an exam or in real life.

Don't forget the reverse of this concept so you can solve a problem like this.

You make a $20,000 commission on the sale of a $400,000 house. What is your commission rate? Keep in mind that the word *rate* usually means *percent.* The calculation is

$$\$20,000 \div \$400,000 = 0.05$$

Move the decimal point two places to the right to get the answer of 5 percent. Remember, to get from a decimal to a percentage, move the decimal two places to the right, or multiply by a hundred.

One other thing you need to know how to do is to convert a fraction to a decimal and, in turn, a percentage. Don't worry. If you don't remember your sixth-grade math class, this step isn't too difficult. Just divide the upper number (numerator) by the lower number (denominator). Doing so gives you a decimal. Now move the decimal point two places to the right (don't forget to add zeroes as needed) and you have a percentage. Check out the following examples:

$\frac{1}{2} = 1 \div 2 = 0.5 = 50$ percent

$\frac{3}{8} = 3 \div 8 = 0.375 = 37.5$ percent

$\frac{9}{16} = 9 \div 16 = 0.5625 = 56.25$ percent

# Commissions: Tracking Your Moolah

You probably were wondering when I'd finally get to this all-important section — the amount you get paid. Discussing percentages is foremost, because most commissions are based on a percentage of the sale price of a property. If you haven't read "Percentages: Pinpointing What You Really Need to Know" earlier in this chapter, take a few minutes to scan over it before reading this section.

In this section, I take you through a few variations on commission problems, including splitting the commission with other brokers and agents. I also have you look at how to get to a selling price working backward from a commission. Because of antitrust laws, which say that all commissions are negotiable and that brokers cannot agree among themselves (price fixing) to set certain commission rates, I make up all the figures that I use for commissions and commission splits in the examples that follow. (For more about commissions and antitrust laws, check out Chapter 3.)

## Figuring out how much you and everyone else earn

Here I start you out with a couple of basic commission problems and then move on to commission splits.

### Figuring your commission

You're a broker who sells a house. The owner has agreed to pay you a 5 percent commission. How much will you earn on the sale, if the house sells for $200,000?

Sale price × commission rate = commission earned

$200,000 × 0.05 = $10,000

Remember to turn 5 percent into a number you can use (in this case, 0.05) before you proceed with the rest of the problem.

### Figuring out your commission rate

A variation on the commission problem has you figuring out your commission rate if you know the selling price of the property and the commission earned. I use the same numbers that I did in the last problem.

You sell a listed house for $200,000. You earn a $10,000 commission on the sale. What was your commission rate?

Commission earned ÷ sale price = commission rate

$10,000 ÷ $200,000 = .05 or 5 percent

### Sharing the rewards: Commission splits

As a salesperson, your broker will pay you a share of the total commission earned for the sale. Remember that a salesperson works under the authority of a broker (see Chapter 3 for the full scoop).

All commissions and commission splits are negotiable between the salesperson and the broker. In a math problem, this split may be expressed different ways. For example, a problem may have a 60/40 split, which is 60 percent going to one party and 40 percent going to the other party. Whenever the commission shares are unequal, the problem will be clear as to what percentage each party gets. Examples of these types of problems follow.

Your firm receives a $20,000 commission that is to be split 60/40 between you and your broker. How much will you receive?

Commission amount × percentage share = commission amount share

$20,000 × 0.60 = $12,000

Why did I use the 60 percent and not 40 percent? If you read the question carefully, the 60/40 split is in the same order as the "you and your broker." If the problem doesn't give you any more information, you have to interpret what test writers mean. Scan the following problem, which contains more than one split.

Suppose a $30,000 commission is earned on the sale of a house. The listing broker and the buyer's broker agree to split the commission evenly. The listing salesperson receives 40 percent of the listing side. How much will the listing salesperson receive?

Where two brokers cooperate on a sale, they're often referred to as the listing side (the broker who originally got the listing agreement to represent the seller) and the buyer's side (the broker who finds the buyer). In this particular question, you also have to know that "split" evenly means that each of the sides gets half of the total commission.

$30,000 × 0.50 = $15,000 listing and buyer's side because the commission is split evenly

$15,000 (listing side commission) × 0.40 (listing salesperson's share) = $6,000 (listing salesperson's commission)

A variation of this question uses the same information but asks you what the listing broker's share was.

100 percent (total percentage of listing side commission) − 40 percent (listing salesperson's percentage) = 60 percent listing broker's percentage

$15,000 (total listing side commission) × .60 (listing broker's percentage share) = $9,000 (listing broker's share)

## Determining how much a house should sell for based on a commission rate

Establishing how much a house should sell for is an interesting calculation that has many uses, primarily because it enables you to work backward from a percentage to a number. But first I have a problem that I want you to try.

Your seller wants to *net* (take away from the closing table) $200,000 after paying your 6 percent commission. How much does the house have to sell for to do this?

This problem actually has two answers, $212,000 and $212,766 (rounded), but one of the answers, $212,000, happens to be wrong. Now before you start yelling or arguing or feeling bad that you got it wrong, allow me to explain. In virtually every math class that I teach, more than half the class comes up with the wrong answer. But by the time they do a few problems like the one that follows, nobody gets it wrong. Before I explain how you do this problem, I want to show you how to prove to yourself that the $212,000 is wrong. This proof may come in handy on an exam to check your answer.

Selling price × commission rate = commission paid

$212,000 × 0.06 = $12,720

Selling price − commission paid = net to seller

$212,000 − $12,720 = $199,280

The number $199,280 obviously isn't the $200,000 net the seller wants. If you got $212,000 for your answer, it's because you added the 6 percent commission to the net that the seller wanted, but that isn't how you calculate selling prices and commissions. You get a commission by taking it from the selling price, not adding onto the net to the owner figure. If you did the same proof using the $212,766 and took 6 percent from that number, the owner gets the requested $200,000.

Check out the following example if you want more clarification:

| What it is | Percentage | Dollar amount |
|---|---|---|
| Selling price | 100 percent | x (That's what you're looking for.) |
| Commission | 6 percent | You don't know this and don't need to know. |
| Net to seller | 94 percent | $200,000 |

See how the commission percentage and the seller's net percentage always equal 100 percent, which is the selling price.

If you know a dollar amount and it's part of a larger dollar amount that you want to find, and you know the percentage of the total (100 percent) that it represents, you can always find the larger dollar amount by dividing the partial dollar amount by the percentage of the total that it represents. I'll say that again with numbers:

$200,000 is the dollar amount that is part of a larger dollar amount that you want to find — that is, the selling price. $200,000 is 94 percent of the larger dollar amount, which is 100 percent. By dividing $200,000 by 94 percent, you get the larger amount, which is 100 percent of the total.

$200,000 ÷ 0.94 = $212,766

In other words, if $200,000 is 94 percent of some number that you want to find (the selling price, in this case), all you have to do is divide $200,000 by 94 percent (0.94). You get $212,766.

In this particular problem, you had to subtract 6 percent from 100 percent to get the 94 percent, which is the seller's share. But the test writers may write the problem a little differently, trying to trick you.

You earn an $18,000 commission, which is 6 percent of the selling price. How much did the house sell for?

Using the logic for this kind of problem, you can restate it like this: $18,000 is 6 percent of some number. In this case, that number is the selling price. And if you know the dollar amount and the percentage of the whole number it represents, all you have to do is divide by the matching percentage.

$18,000 (commission amount) ÷ 0.06 (commission rate) = $300,000 (selling price)

So what's the moral of the story? When figuring commissions in relation to how much a house should sell for, memorize these two formulas:

Net to seller ÷ (100 percent – commission rate) = selling price

Commission amount in dollars ÷ commission rate = selling price

# Making Mortgage Calculations without a Fancy Calculator

In this section, I do a few problems to review some of the math associated with mortgages. (Chapter 15 has the scoop on mortgages and additional math, such as problems involving loan to value ratios.) In these calculations, one important term to know is *amortized loan,* which means that each payment on the mortgage is a combination of principal and interest so that at the end of the mortgage term you have nothing left to pay.

One of the questions I'm often asked is how necessary having a financial calculator is either for real estate work or for the state exam. A financial calculator is helpful and makes life easier if you know how to use it. As for the state exams, a simple inexpensive calculator does just fine. In fact, you can probably do most of the problems on your fingers and toes (if you have enough of them).

## Calculating interest

A few standard problems that you may find on an exam deal with mortgage interest and principal payments. Here are the likely possibilities.

### Annual and monthly interest

All interest on mortgage loans is expressed as an annual interest amount, so if your mortgage interest rate is 8 percent, that's the annual rate. But most mortgages are paid on a monthly basis, so you sometimes need to calculate how much interest you actually paid in one month based on that annual rate.

First, look at an annual interest problem.

You borrow $100,000 at 8 percent for 30 years in an amortized mortgage loan. How much interest will you pay the first year?

Remember that in a mortgage loan, the interest rate is always quoted annually and is always based on the loan's unpaid balance.

Loan amount × interest rate = first year's interest

$100,000 × 0.08 = $8,000

The 30 years doesn't matter. It's extra information to confuse you.

Now here's a monthly problem with different numbers:

You borrow $150,000 at 8 percent interest for 30 years in an amortized loan. What is the first month's interest on the loan?

> Loan amount × interest rate = first year's interest
>
> $150,000 × 0.08 = $12,000 annual interest

You wind up with $12,000 for the first year's interest. To figure out the first month's interest, all you have to do is divide the first year's interest by 12.

> First year's interest ÷ 12 months = first month's interest
>
> $12,000 ÷ 12 = $1,000 first month's interest

Note that this monthly interest calculation works this way only for the first month's interest.

Test writers may go further and ask you to calculate the second month's interest. To answer the question, you need to know what the total monthly payment is, and the test writers will tell you. I'll continue using the numbers from the previous problem. In this case, the monthly payment, which includes principal and interest, is $1,101. The question is how much is the second month's interest payment.

> $1,101 (monthly payment) – $1,000 (first month's interest) = $101 (principal payment)
>
> $150,000 (loan amount) – $101 (first month's principal payment) = $149,899 (loan balance after first month's payment)
>
> $149,899 (loan balance after first payment) × 0.08 (annual interest rate) = $11,991.92 (interest owed for the next 12 months)
>
> $11,991.92 (interest owed for the next 12 months) ÷ 12 months = $999.33 (interest paid for the first month of that next 12-month period, which is, in fact, the second month of the loan term of the loan)

I continue this problem with another possible question. How much is owed on the loan after the second month's payment?

> $1,101 (monthly payment) – $999.33 (second month's interest) = $101.67 (second month's principal payment)
>
> $149,899 (owed after first month's payment) – $101.67 = $149,797.33 (remaining loan balance after second month's payment)

What you need to remember here is that in an amortized loan, you're only reducing the amount you owe by the amount of principal you pay each month and not by the amount of the total payment, because payment includes interest and principal.

### Total interest

A type of interest problem that seems to confuse people is the calculation of total interest. Total interest is the amount of interest you pay during the entire life of the loan, assuming that you pay off the loan by making the payments within the required time frame. In general, banks provide these numbers to people, but you need to be familiar with this calculation because it is fair game on an exam.

Say you borrow $200,000 at 7 percent for 30 years in an amortized mortgage loan. Your monthly payments are $1,330. What is the total interest on the loan?

Most people fool around with the 7 percent for a while, but you don't need the percentage rate of the mortgage loan to work this problem. Watch this, because you're not going to believe how easy it is.

$1,330 (monthly payment) × 12 months × 30 years = $478,800 total payments during the loan's 30-year term.

$478,800 – $200,000 (original loan amount) = $278,800 interest paid during the course of the loan.

Don't forget that every amortized loan payment contains part principal and part interest. In 30 years, you pay a total of $478,800 in principal and interest. So if you subtract the principal, or the amount you borrowed, what you have left is interest.

## Figuring out monthly payments

Unless you use a financial calculator, you're going to calculate mortgage payments using a mortgage table. These tables, which are arranged according to the percentage of interest and years of the mortgage term, provide the monthly payment to *amortize,* or pay off interest and principal, for a $1,000 mortgage loan. After you get that monthly payoff number, which sometimes is called the *payment factor,* you multiply it by the number of thousands of dollars of the mortgage loan (which you get by dividing the loan amount by $1,000).

The factor for a 20-year loan at 6 percent is $7.16. What is the monthly payment for a $150,000 loan?

$150,000 ÷ $1,000 = 150 (units of a $1,000)

150 × $7.16 (factor to pay off $1,000) = $1,074 per month

If you run into a problem like this on the exam, you'll either get a sample of a mortgage table or be given the payment factor you need to solve the problem. You'll have to remember the formula in the example.

# Oh, the Pain: Calculating Taxes

If you want the lowdown on real estate taxes, check out Chapter 16, where you also find a bit of math on equalization rates. In this section, I solve a few sample problems that you may encounter about taxes. You need to know this information not only for the test, but also because every listing of a property for sale generally requires the agent to find out what the taxes are.

## Calculating the assessed value of a property

Many municipalities use assessment ratios to assess properties. An *assessment ratio* is the percentage relationship between the market value of a property, which is the amount the property will sell for in a normal market sale, and the assessed value, which is a value tax assessors use to calculate taxes and is usually related to market value. (I discuss the details of market value in Chapter 14 and assessment ratios in Chapter 16.) The use of an assessment ratio creates the possibility of three kinds of exam problems.

A property has a market value of $200,000. The assessment ratio is 60 percent. What is the assessed value?

Market value × assessment ratio = assessed value

$200,000 × 0.60 = $120,000

What is the assessment ratio of a property whose market value is $200,000 and whose assessed value is $120,000?

Assessed value ÷ market value = assessment ratio

$120,000 ÷ $200,000 = 0.60 or 60 percent

What is the market value of a property assessed at a 60 percent assessment ratio whose assessed value is $120,000?

Assessed value ÷ assessment ratio = market value

$120,000 ÷ 0.60 = $200,000

## Calculating taxes due

You can calculate taxes due using one of the following three methods, depending on how the municipality calculates taxes or how the exam question is asked.

- ✔ **Mills:** This method bases the tax rate on so many tenths of a penny (or mills) in taxes for each dollar of assessed value.

- ✔ **Dollars per hundred:** This method bases the tax rate on so many dollars of tax for each $100 of assessed value.

- ✔ **Dollars per thousand:** This method bases the tax rate on so many dollars of tax per $1,000 of assessed value.

You need to be familiar with all three methods for exam purposes.

### Mills

The tax rate in town is 24 mills. The assessed value of the property is $30,000. What are the taxes on the property?

Assessed value × millage = taxes owed

$30,000 × $0.024 = $720

Remember, when working with a millage, move the decimal three places to the left, because millages are tax rates expressed in mills, or tenths of a cent.

### Taxes per hundred

The tax rate is $2.40 per $100 assessed value. What are the taxes on a property assessed at $30,000?

Assessed value × tax rate = taxes owed

$30,000 × ($2.40 ÷ $100) = taxes owed

$2.40 (tax rate) ÷ $100 (ratio of assessed value) = $0.024 tax rate (per dollar of assessed valuation)

$30,000 × $0.024 = $720

### Taxes per thousand

The tax rate on a property assessed at $30,000 is $24 per thousand. What are the taxes?

Assessed value × tax rate = taxes owed

$30,000 × ($24 ÷ $1,000) = taxes owed

$24 (tax rate) ÷ $1,000 (ratio of assessed value) = $0.024 tax rate (per dollar of assessed valuation)

$30,000 × $0.024 = $720

# A Good Split: Putting Proration into Perspective

*Proration* is the allocation or dividing of certain money items at the closing. (I discuss proration and closings in more detail in Chapter 9.) An attorney, a real estate salesperson, or a broker does the proration calculations at the closing. In any case, most test writers expect you to know the basics of proration math. The key to remember about prorations is that the person who uses it needs to pay for it. Here's an example that illustrates the point of proration.

The seller has paid taxes of $3,000 for the entire year ahead on January 1 and sells his property and closes title on June 1. Who owes what to whom?

The seller paid the full year's taxes, but used the property only for the five months (January through May). Read the problem carefully. The buyer needs to pay the seller for the taxes already paid for the months the seller won't own the property during the year. The rest is just the math of dividing up who paid and who pays.

$3,000 ÷ 12 months = $250 per month

$250 per month × 5 months (the time the seller owned the property) = $1,250

This is the amount of the taxes that the seller used from January through May.

$250 per month × 7 months (the new buyer's time in the house) = $1,750

This is the amount of the taxes the buyer used, because he bought the house on June 1.

Because the seller had already paid the taxes for the whole year, the buyer owes the seller $1,750 for the taxes the buyer is using but didn't pay for. In the terminology of proration, the buyer gets a debit and the seller gets a credit.

Here's another problem that has the buyer paying in *arrears* (or after the fact).

A buyer pays $2,400 in taxes in arrears for the entire year on December 31. He bought the house on September 1. Who owes what to whom?

$2,400 ÷ 12 months = $200 per month

$200 per month × 8 months (the time the seller owned the house) = $1,600

The seller used $1,600 of the paid taxes. Now to determine how much the seller didn't use:

$200 per month × 4 months (the time the buyer owned the property) = $800

Because the buyer paid the full $2,400 for the previous year, during which he owned the house for only four months, the seller owes the buyer $1,600. The buyer gets a credit and the seller gets a debit.

When you get out into the real world, find out what the local practice is for dividing up the year for prorations. Some areas and attorneys use the exact day, rather than the month. So in the previous examples, divide by 365 days to get the amount of taxes paid per day. Some people use the 12-month annual calculation and then divide by the exact number of days in a month when the closing dates occurs midmonth. As far as I know, no state law governs this practice, but rather, it's a matter of local practice. On the exam, test writers usually specify "actual days" if they want you to calculate it that way. If the time frame isn't specified or you're instructed otherwise on an exam, you need to use the third method, which is to divide a yearly cost or payment by 12 and the monthly number by 30, unless your real estate course or textbook specifies that one of the other methods is the only method used in your state. The other state-specific item that can affect proration is who owns the property on the day of closing. Unless your state says otherwise, assume that the buyer owns the house on the closing date. I'll do a problem with a mid-month closing date to illustrate the 12-month/ 30-day method.

An owner sells a house, closes on May 17, but paid a full year's taxes of $3,600 in advance on January 1. What is the proration of taxes?

$3600 ÷ 12 months = $300 per month

$300 ÷ 30 days = $10 per day

The seller/owner owned the house for four full months (January through April) and 16 days in May. (Remember, the buyer is considered to own the house on the day of closing.)

4 months × $300 per month = $1,200

16 days × $10 per day = $160

$1200 + $160 = $1,360 taxes used by the seller

$3,600 (total taxes for the year paid by the seller) – $1,360 (taxes used by the seller) = $2,240 (taxes used by the buyer)

The buyer owes the seller $2,240. The buyer gets a debit of $2,240, and the seller gets a credit of $2,240.

# Appreciating Appreciation and Depreciation

As if you weren't confused enough already, you'll find there's only one kind of appreciation but there are two kinds of depreciation. Stay with me, though, because this stuff really is pretty easy.

*Appreciation* is an increase in a property's value caused by factors like inflation, increasing demand, and improvements to the property. *Depreciation* is a decrease in the value of a property caused by lower demand, deflation in the economy, deterioration, or the influences of other undesirable factors like a new sewage treatment plant going in next door. Another type of depreciation, which I discuss in Chapter 17, is a tax benefit the government gives people on real estate investments.

Real estate salespeople and brokers, buyers, and sellers always are interested in how much a property's value has increased or decreased. Investors, real estate brokers, and salespeople may want to know what tax benefits of a property are attributed to depreciation, although more often than not, an accountant needs to be doing these calculations for an investor. Test writers expect you to know the basics of how to calculate appreciation and depreciation.

## Getting more or less: Appreciation and depreciation of a property's value

People always are interested in how much more they can sell their property for than what they paid for it. They may not want to consider a loss to their property's value, but that can happen, too. A real estate agent is expected to be able to track increases and decreases in a property's value and to apply market increases to specific properties. So if the overall real estate market values in an area have increased by 10 percent during the last year according to government or other statistics, you need to be able to apply this increase in value to a specific property. By the way, not only market values can increase. Any of the types of values that I discuss in Chapter 14 can increase or decrease. I show you some math on how to handle these problems in the real world and on the exam.

You bought a house for $200,000 and five years later sold it for $250,000. What is the rate at which the house appreciated?

The formula for this type of problem has two parts:

New value – old value = change in value

Change in value ÷ old value = percent of change in value

$250,000 – $200,000 = $50,000

$50,000 ÷ $200,000 = 0.25 or 25 percent

A different type of problem deals with a decrease in value. You bought a house for $200,000 and five years later sold it for $150,000. By what percentage did it depreciate?

The formula for this type of problem also has two parts:

Old value – new value = change in value

Change in value ÷ old value = percent of change in value

$200,000 – $150,000 = $50,000

$50,000 ÷ $200,000 = 0.25 or 25 percent

In either of these problems, you divide the change by the older value.

Keep an eye open for whether test writers ask you either of the preceding questions using the word "change" rather than "appreciate" or "depreciate." For example: "By what percentage did the value of the house change?" In that case, your answers will have either a plus or a minus sign in front of them. The appreciation answer would be +25 percent, and the depreciation answer would be –25 percent.

Now for a reverse problem:

A house sold for $260,000, which is 130 percent of what you paid for it. How much did you pay for it?

The formula for this type of problem is

Current price (or value) ÷ percent of original price = price (or value) sought

Notice in this formula that I said "percent of original price," which is always 100 percent plus the change, which is +30 percent. Now how did I know this since the numbers were not given that way? Read the wording of the question carefully. It said that the house sold for 130 percent **of** the original price, not 130 percent **more** than the original price. Another way to look at this is to say, "$260,000 is 130 percent of some number" — in this case, the original price. If you can say it that way, you know to divide the dollar amount you're given by the percentage number.

With numbers the problem looks like this:

$260,000 ÷ 1.30 = $200,000

1.30 is the decimal equivalent of 130 percent.

Another problem similar to this reverses the question:

You bought a house for $300,000, which is 75 percent of what you sell it for five years later. What price did you sell it for?

Original price (or value) ÷ the percent of selling price = price (or value) sought

$300,000 ÷ 0.75 = $400,000

Once again, you can say, "$300,000 is 75 percent of some number."

In these types of problems, you can usually get the number you're looking for by dividing the number you're given by the percent that it represents. You can find similar problems in the section on "Determining how much a house should sell for based on a commission rate" earlier in this chapter.

## Depreciation: The government kind

In Chapter 17, I explain the concept of depreciation that sometime is called cost recovery. Although in the real world, accountants working for real estate investors usually do these calculations, test writers expect you to understand and be able to apply the basics. This type of depreciation has nothing to do with a property going down in value but rather is based on government regulations that are designed to help real estate investors reduce their tax burdens.

You have a building worth $250,000. You are allowed to depreciate it over a period of 27.5 years. What is the annual amount of depreciation?

Cost of property ÷ cost recovery period = annual amount of depreciation

$250,000 ÷ 27.5 = $9,090.91

Now suppose you were asked what the annual rate of depreciation is. You don't need the dollar amounts to figure that one out. You need only the cost recovery period.

You are allowed to depreciate a building over a period of 39 years. What is the annual rate of depreciation?

$1 \div 39 = .0256$ or 2.56 percent per year

# What's It Worth? Estimating Appraised Value

If you want the lowdown on appraising property, check out Chapter 14. As a real estate agent, you won't actually be doing appraisals, but you can use these formulas to roughly estimate property values, particularly if you deal in investment properties. You can read about real estate investing in Chapter 17, but in the meantime, state test writers expect you to understand and be able to apply these formulas. In this section, the only real math-driven formulas for appraising, at least at the level that you're expected to know it, are formulas for finding value using the income approach. Two different methods are used in that approach to value. I give you formulas and examples for both.

## The capitalization method

The capitalization method uses one formula for finding a property's value, and with a couple of variations you can find the property's income and the capitalization rate. *Capitalization* is a technique for estimating a property's value based on its income. You can read all about it in Chapter 14.

The formulas use the following symbols:

- ✓ I = Income or net operating income
- ✓ R = Rate of return or capitalization rate
- ✓ V = Value or sale price

Don't be confused by the possibility that any one of these letters can mean two different things (such as income versus net operating income). Memorize these terms and the problem will be clear as to what is being asked. Also remember that in these problems, all the numbers are based on annual figures. So if, for example, you're given a monthly income number, you need to multiply by 12.

The formulas follow:

- ✓ $V = I \div R$
- ✓ $I = V \times R$
- ✓ $R = I \div V$

In the following three examples, I use the same numbers to illustrate how these formulas work.

Find the value of a building that has a net operating income of $30,000 where the capitalization rate is 10 percent.

$V = \$30,000 \div 0.10$

$V = \$300,000$

Find the income of a building that was sold $300,000 where the rate of return is 10 percent.

I = $300,000 × 0.10

I = $30,000

Find the capitalization rate of a building that sold for $300,000 and has a net operating income of $30,000.

R = $30,000 ÷ $300,000

R = 0.10 or 10 percent

## The gross rent multiplier method

The method for finding the value of a property using the gross rent is an easy matter of multiplication. The *gross rent multiplier* is used to estimate the value of small investment-type properties like small multifamily houses. You can find out more about it in Chapter 14. The formula is

Value = rent × gross rent multiplier (GRM)

The variations of this equation are

GRM = sale price (or value) ÷ rent

Rent = sales price (or value) ÷ GRM

The following examples show you how to use these formulas with numbers.

You're appraising a building that generates a gross annual rent of $36,000. You've calculated a GRM of 10. What is the value of the building?

Value = $36,000 × 10

Value = $360,000

You're trying to calculate GRM using information on a building that recently sold for $360,000 with a gross annual rent of $36,000. Find the GRM.

GRM = $360,000 ÷ $36,000

GRM = 10

You would rarely have to calculate the rent using the GRM formula, but just in case, here's one last example.

Say you were looking at a building to invest in that was selling for $360,000 with a GRM of 10. What is the annual gross rent income?

Rent = $360,000 ÷ 10

Rent = $36,000

Don't forget to note whether the numbers you're given are based on monthly rent or annual rent. You may have to convert one to the other or use the number given. Gross rent multipliers are sometimes calculated on an annual basis and are sometimes called the Gross Income Multipliers (GIM). Your course should clarify the terminology used for your exam.

# Review Questions and Answers

It would be great to get 100 percent on the state exam, but if math really sends you into a spin, don't worry. Not many math questions are on the salesperson's or broker's exam. In either case, if you really do well on the other questions, math won't make or break you.

1. Find the volume of concrete needed to pour a patio slab 30 feet by 20 feet by 6 inches thick.

    (A) 600 cubic feet

    (B) 600 square feet

    (C) 3,600 cubic feet

    (D) 11 cubic yards

    *Correct answer:* (D). Length × Width × Height = Volume

    > 30 feet × 20 feet × 6 inches

    > 30 feet × 20 feet × (6 inches ÷ 12 inches — remember you have to convert inches to feet if the other numbers are in feet)

    > 30 feet × 20 feet × 0.5 feet = 300 cubic feet

    > 300 cubic feet ÷ 27 cubic feet = 11.11 cubic yards. (Make sure that you read the problem carefully to complete all the steps. In this case, you had to convert cubic feet to cubic yards.)

2. You're selling a rectangular piece of property that measures 99 feet by 110 feet. What part of an acre is this property?

    (A) .75

    (B) .50

    (C) .25

    (D) .10

    *Correct answer:* (C). Length × Width = Area

    > 110 feet × 99 feet = 10,890 square feet

    > 10,890 square feet ÷ 43,560 square feet = 0.25 acres

The answers are all in acres so you must convert by dividing the square feet by 43,560 square feet, which is the number of square feet in an acre. Watch out when one of the answer choices is the correct number of square feet but the question asks for acres.

3. A warehouse rents for $0.60 per cubic foot per year and measures 200 feet by 300 feet by 15 feet high. What is the monthly rent?

(A) $36,000

(B) $45,000

(C) $540,000

(D) $900,000

*Correct answer:* (B). Length × Width × Height = Volume

300 feet × 200 feet × 15 feet = 900,000 cubic feet

900,000 cubic feet × $0.60 per cubic foot = $540,000 annual rent

$540,000 ÷ 12 months = $45,000 monthly rent

Note in this problem that $540,000 is a correct answer to a part of the problem. Be sure to read questions carefully or you may pick the right answer to the wrong question.

4. You sold 40 houses this year and 30 houses last year. What percent fewer houses did you sell last year?

(A) 133 percent

(B) 75 percent

(C) 66 percent

(D) 25 percent

*Correct answer:* (D). 40 (houses this year) – 30 (houses last year) = 10 fewer houses last year than this year

10 ÷ 40 = 0.25 or 25 percent

In this problem, you divide by 40 because you want to find out what percentage less than this year. If the question were how much more than last year, then you would have divided by 30.

5. How much is owed after the first month's payment on an amortized mortgage loan of $150,000 at 7 percent interest for 25 years, if the monthly payment is $1,059?

(A) 148,941

(B) 149,816

(C) 149,125

(D) 139,500

*Correct answer:* (B). See the following math.

$150,000 × 0.07 = $10,500 (first year's interest)

$10,500 ÷ 12 months = $875 (first month's interest)

$1,059 (monthly payment of principal and interest) – $875 (interest) = $184 (principal paid off in first month)

$150,000 (original loan balance) – $184 (first month's principal payment) = $149,816 (mortgage balance after first month's payment)

Take a look at "Making Mortgage Calculations without a Fancy Calculator" earlier in the chapter to find out how to go to the second month for this type of problem.

6. If a house has depreciated 30 percent since you bought it, and it's worth $200,000 now, what did you buy it for?

   (A) $285,714

   (B) $240,000

   (C) $230,000

   (D) $160,000

   *Correct answer:* (A). $200,000 is 70 percent of some number, the original purchase price of the house.

   > 100 percent – 30 percent = 70 percent
   >
   > $200,000 ÷ 0.70 = $285,714

7. The seller pays $1,200 in taxes for six months in advance on April 1. She sells her house on May 1. What is the proration on the taxes?

   (A) Seller gets a credit of $1,000; buyer gets a debit of $200.

   (B) Seller gets a credit of $200; buyer gets debit of $1,000.

   (C) Seller gets a credit of $1,000; buyer gets a debit of $1,000.

   (D) Buyer gets a credit of $1,000; seller gets a debit of $1,000.

   *Correct answer:* (C). The seller owned the property for one month of the period for which the taxes had been paid, so she used $200 worth of the taxes but had paid $1,200. She gets a credit of $1,000. The buyer will be in the house for five months of the tax period but paid none of the taxes and used $1,000 worth. He gets a debit of $1,000. The buyer owes the seller $1,000 at the closing.

   > $1,200 (taxes) ÷ 6 months = $200 per month

8. A broker receives a commission check for $13,000 based on a 4 percent commission rate. How much did the house sell for?

   (A) $52,000

   (B) $300,000

   (C) $325,000

   (D) $336,960

   *Correct answer:* (C). Commission earned ÷ commission rate = sale price

   > $13,000 ÷ 0.04 = $325,000

9. A room 14 feet by 18 feet is to be carpeted at a cost of $23 a square yard. What will be the cost to carpet the room?

    (A) $214

    (B) $579

    (C) $644

    (D) $5796

    *Correct answer:* (C). Length × Width = Area

        18 feet × 14 feet = 252 square feet

        252 square feet ÷ 9 square feet = 28 square yards

        28 square yards × $23 per square yard = $644

10. What is the area in acres of a piece of property that is one mile square?

    (A) 640

    (B) 320

    (C) 160

    (D) 80

    *Correct answer:* (A). One square mile is 640 acres. You can memorize this fact, because it's also the size of a section. Or using the Length × Width = Area formula:

        5,280 feet × 5,280 feet = 27,878,400 square feet

        27,878,400 square feet ÷ 43,560 square feet per acre = 640 acres

You may also want to remember that the phrase "one mile square" means a length of one mile on each side. Test writers also like to ask the area of a figure where the side is some portion of a mile, say ½ mile on each side. Remember that a mile is 5,280 feet.

# Part VI

# You're Ready to Pick Up Your Pencil: Taking Practice Exams

## *Top Five Reasons to Take Practice Exams*

- ✔ Become familiar with the types of questions on the license exam.

- ✔ Get an idea of where your strengths and weaknesses lie, and know what you need to study further to do well on the test.

- ✔ Know you can take the practice exams over and over until you thoroughly understand the material on the real test.

- ✔ Learn that although the practice exam test questions are grouped by similar subjects, the actual exam distributes subjects at random.

- ✔ Understand that along with the practice exam questions, there are also state-specific questions that you need to know for the actual exam.

# In this part . . .

✔ I give you a leg up on the test with four practice exams. You examine the types of questions that you'll see on the actual estate license exam.

✔ Along with the test questions, you can check out the answers to the four practice exams. You'll know what chapters you need to go back and review.

✔ I show you how to study state-specific information for the actual exam.

✔ You can retake the practice exams as many times as necessary to strengthen your core knowledge. Each time you retake the tests, your score will improve, and you'll soon feel comfortable enough to take the real exam.

# Chapter 19

# Practice Exam One

• • • • • • • • • • • • • • • • • • • • • • • • • • • • • • • • • • • • • • • • • • • • • • • • • • • • • • • • • • • • • • • • • • •

*T*his exam has 100 questions, and I've laid it out to group similar subjects together. I group them for ease of reviewing the material in any one chapter. However, different subjects probably will be randomly distributed throughout the actual exam. And don't forget that a number of state-specific questions on the actual exam will deal with particular laws and practices unique to your state. Review the items marked with the State-Specific icon throughout this book, and study both the materials that you get in your prelicensing course (such as a textbook) and your state's license law.

Mark your answers on a separate piece of paper, and try doing the entire test in less than two hours. Chapter 20 features the correct answers to this exam, plus explanations and cross-references to chapters for review. (Don't peek at the answers until you finish the test, though.) If you discover that you need to brush up on your studying and test-taking skills, be sure to head to Chapter 2 before taking the second practice exam in Chapter 21. Good luck!

1. Which type of insurance is used to insure against rent being stolen by an employee of a property management company?

    (A) Rent loss insurance

    (B) Surety bond

    (C) Business interruption insurance

    (D) Liability insurance

2. Which of the following is not a typical way that property management fees are set?

    (A) Fixed fee

    (B) Commission on new leases

    (C) Percentage of gross income

    (D) Percentage of operating costs

3. For what activity does a person generally not need a real estate license?

    (A) Collecting rents as an employee of a building owner

    (B) Representing people in the exchange of properties

    (C) Selling properties on behalf of several owners

    (D) Negotiating leases on behalf of several commercial building owners

4. Roof replacement is considered what type of expense in a building's budget?

    (A) Capital

    (B) Operating

    (C) Maintenance

    (D) Fixed

5. Which of the following is true for an independent contractor working for a broker?

    (A) The broker is required to pay the contractor's Social Security taxes.

    (B) The broker is required to withhold income taxes from the contractor's commission checks.

    (C) The broker must give workman's compensation to the contractor.

    (D) The broker is required to supervise the contractor.

6. The primary duty of a property manager is to

    (A) ensure that income is generated by the building.

    (B) maintain the building.

    (C) protect the owner's investment in the building.

    (D) maximize income while maintaining the building's value.

7. A real estate broker hired to represent someone who wants to sell his house is

    (A) a special agent.

    (B) a general agent.

    (C) a universal agent.

    (D) a representative agent.

8. Fiduciary responsibilities are always owed to

    (A) the client.

    (B) the customer.

    (C) the buyer.

    (D) the seller.

9. Fiduciary duties do not include

    (A) care.

    (B) control.

    (C) accounting.

    (D) confidentiality.

10. The client is always

    (A) the seller.

    (B) the buyer.

    (C) the principal.

    (D) the customer.

11. Which of the following would not end an agency relationship?

    (A) The property was sold.

    (B) The house was burned in a fire.

    (C) The principal got married.

    (D) The broker declared bankruptcy.

*Go on to next page*

12. When does a seller's agent earn a fee?

    (A) She accomplishes what she was hired to do.

    (B) She is the procuring cause.

    (C) She finds a ready, willing, and able buyer.

    (D) All of the above.

13. A homeowner refuses to sell his home to a family because of its race. The homeowner claims that because this is an owner-occupied home, he is exempt from all fair housing laws. The owner has violated

    (A) the 1968 Fair Housing Act.

    (B) the 1968 Fair Housing Act as amended in 1988.

    (C) the 1866 Civil Rights Act.

    (D) no law. He is correct.

14. A person who owns a 15-unit apartment building has established different security deposit amounts for different tenants based on their ethnic group and whether or not they have children. He has ten years of statistical research to back up the validity of this approach. Which of the following is true?

    (A) What he is doing is illegal.

    (B) What he is doing is legal under any circumstances.

    (C) What he is doing would be illegal if he didn't have the factual research to back it up.

    (D) What he is doing would be legal only if the owner himself lives in the building.

15. A real estate agent attempts to generate listings by contacting people in a particular neighborhood and suggesting to them that their property values might be going down soon because a particular immigrant group is coming into the neighborhood. This practice is called

    (A) soliciting.

    (B) farming.

    (C) prospecting.

    (D) blockbusting.

16. A church group decides to build housing for its members only. The church does not permit African Americans to join its congregation. Which of the following is true?

    (A) The housing can be restricted to members of the church.

    (B) The housing cannot be restricted to members of the church.

    (C) The housing can be restricted as long as they do not advertise or use a real estate agent.

    (D) The housing could be restricted if the prohibition for joining the church was not against African Americans but against some other racial or ethnic group.

17. Complaints under the Civil Rights Act of 1866 are handled by

    (A) HUD.

    (B) federal courts.

    (C) state courts.

    (D) state human rights commissions.

18. A homeowner gives a listing to the real estate broker to sell his one-family house with the warning that he does not want to sell to non-Christians. What should the broker do?

    (A) Take the listing, but ignore the homeowner's wishes.

    (B) Take the listing and follow the homeowner's wishes because of the owner occupancy exception.

    (C) Explain to the homeowner that he's violating the federal fair housing laws and refuse the listing unless he removes the request.

    (D) Take the listing, but only if the homeowner agrees to put the request in writing for the broker's protection.

*Go on to next page* ⟶

19. The First Bank of Main Street refuses to grant loans within a ten-block area of its offices because of declining property values. This practice is

    (A) redlining and illegal.

    (B) redlining and legal.

    (C) redlining and usually illegal except where values are declining.

    (D) legal in any other part of the town except in the immediate area of the bank.

20. A term used to describe land, improvements, and all the rights associated with ownership is

    (A) land.

    (B) personal property.

    (C) real estate.

    (D) real property.

21. A built-in microwave oven is an example of

    (A) personal property.

    (B) a fixture.

    (C) a trade fixture.

    (D) an attachment.

22. You want to donate a piece of land to a religious organization. The title will pass when they complete building a church on the property. The estate is

    (A) fee simple.

    (B) fee simple condition precedent.

    (C) fee simple condition subsequent.

    (D) fee simple determinable.

23. The estate that grants the most complete form of ownership is

    (A) fee simple.

    (B) fee simple condition precedent.

    (C) fee simple condition subsequent.

    (D) fee simple determinable.

24. An owner of a rental building is said to have what type of interest?

    (A) Leasehold

    (B) Leased fee

    (C) Fee simple

    (D) Fee on condition

25. Someone who has riparian rights on a navigable river owns

    (A) nothing.

    (B) to the centerline of the water.

    (C) to the high water mark on the land.

    (D) no water but to the centerline of the land under the water.

26. The term generally used to describe the rights a property owner gets when she buys a piece of property is

    (A) fee simple rights.

    (B) real estate rights.

    (C) freehold rights.

    (D) bundle of rights.

27. Unity of possession means that

    (A) each owner has an undivided interest in the property.

    (B) each owner took title at the same time.

    (C) each owner took title with the same deed.

    (D) each owner has the same interest in the property.

28. What form of ownership has no right of survivorship?

    (A) Joint tenancy

    (B) Tenancy in common

    (C) Tenancy by the entirety

    (D) All forms of ownership have a right of survivorship.

29. Joe, Sam, and Fred are joint tenants in a piece of property. Joe sells his interest to Bob. Bob now has what relationship to Sam and Fred?

    (A) Joint tenant

    (B) Tenant by the entirety

    (C) Tenant in common

    (D) Tenant in severalty

30. Condominium owners generally own their land as

    (A) tenants by the entirety.

    (B) tenants in severalty.

    (C) joint tenants.

    (D) tenants in common.

*Go on to next page*

31. Which type of co-ownership requires the signature of all owners to sell a property interest?

    (A) Tenancy in severalty

    (B) Tenancy in common

    (C) Joint tenancy

    (D) Tenancy by the entirety

32. Who owns the apartment in a cooperative building?

    (A) The individual apartment owner

    (B) The corporation that owns the building

    (C) The bank that financed the purchase

    (D) The individual owner owns the apartment, but the corporation owns the common areas.

33. Which statement is true?

    (A) All encumbrances are liens.

    (B) All liens are encumbrances.

    (C) All encumbrances are financial in nature.

    (D) All financial claims against property are voluntary liens.

34. Homeowner Bob's house has been foreclosed and sold. He has unpaid local real estate taxes from last year. He owes on the mortgage he took out five years ago. And he owes the plumber for work that was done two years ago. Who gets paid first?

    (A) They each will receive a proportionate share.

    (B) The bank

    (C) The town

    (D) The plumber

35. A judgment lien is placed against you after you lose a court case for an accident that occurred at your home. This means that the lien is placed against

    (A) all your real property.

    (B) the one piece of property where the accident happened.

    (C) all your real and personal property.

    (D) your salary only.

36. The electric company needs to put a permanent electric cable across your property to get to a nearby street. The company obtains

    (A) an easement appurtenant.

    (B) an easement in gross.

    (C) an easement by necessity.

    (D) an easement by prescription.

37. The city needs your property for a road widening, but you don't want to sell it. The city probably will take it through its power of

    (A) escheat.

    (B) encroachment.

    (C) prescriptive rights.

    (D) eminent domain.

38. The study of population characteristics is called

    (A) economic base study.

    (B) demographics.

    (C) infrastructure study.

    (D) feasibility study.

39. Which of the following is not necessary for a valid deed?

    (A) Signature of grantor

    (B) Signature of grantee

    (C) Description

    (D) Granting clause

40. On what date does a deed become valid?

    (A) Signing deed

    (B) Delivery and acceptance date

    (C) Recording date

    (D) Mortgage approval date

41. The one requirement that is not technically necessary for a deed to be valid but, in most cases, is required for recordation is

    (A) signature of grantee.

    (B) consideration.

    (C) granting clause.

    (D) acknowledgment.

*Go on to next page*

42. The type of property descriptions that use directions and distances is called

(A) metes and bounds.

(B) rectangular survey.

(C) government survey.

(D) plat map.

43. If the section you're buying is bound by section 16 on the north, section 22 on the east, section 20 on the west, and section 28 on the south, what section are you buying?

(A) 21

(B) 15

(C) 27

(D) 29

44. Elevations are measured from

(A) a benchmark.

(B) a monument.

(C) a meridian.

(D) a datum.

45. A developer wants to give the new streets in the subdivision she just built to the city. She does this by

(A) dedication.

(B) grant.

(C) avulsion.

(D) sale.

46. Which of the following is not a form of involuntary alienation?

(A) Adverse possession

(B) Avulsion

(C) Grant

(D) Eminent domain

47. You and your brother own a campground together. You and he have very different ideas about how to run it. Neither of you wants to buy the other out, but you can no longer operate the campground together. To resolve the problem, you file a suit for

(A) adverse possession.

(B) a grant.

(C) partition.

(D) prescriptive rights.

48. The process by which a will is processed is called

(A) surrogacy.

(B) a trust.

(C) execution.

(D) probate.

49. The government is giving lands away in Alaska. It does so by

(A) public sale.

(B) public grant.

(C) public possessory interest.

(D) escheat.

50. Actual title may be granted in an adverse possession situation after a successful suit

(A) for adverse possession.

(B) for partition.

(C) to quiet title.

(D) for prescriptive rights.

51. The rule that real estate contracts must be in writing is a function of

(A) contract law.

(B) the statute of contracts.

(C) RESPA.

(D) the statute of frauds.

52. As a real estate agent, you bring a buyer to a house being sold by the owner. The owner is aware that you are a real estate agent and eventually sells the house to the buyer you brought. Even though you never actually talked about it, you expect a commission because you feel you have

(A) an express contract.

(B) an implied contract.

(C) a unilateral contract.

(D) an executed contract.

*Go on to next page*

53. Joey, a 17-year-old, is big for his age. Because he wants to begin his real estate investment career, he signs a contract to buy a house a few weeks before his 18th birthday. After he turns 18, he decides he doesn't want to buy the house. He can probably get out of the contract because it is

    (A) void.

    (B) voidable.

    (C) implied.

    (D) unenforceable.

54. Which of the following is an element unique to a real estate sales contract?

    (A) Consideration

    (B) Legal description of property

    (C) Legally competent parties

    (D) Mutual agreement

55. Joe lists his house for sale at $300,000. Alice offers Joe $200,000. Joe counteroffers with $280,000. Alice offers Joe $205,000. Joe gets mad and raises his counteroffer to Alice back up to $300,000. Can he do this?

    (A) Yes.

    (B) No.

    (C) Yes, but he owes a commission on the $280,000.

    (D) Yes, but only if he counteroffers within 24 hours.

56. Jim finds a piece of property on which to build a shopping center. It's going to take about a year to get the necessary permits, and there's no guarantee that he'll get permission to build. Meanwhile, he doesn't want to lose the property to another buyer. His best bet is to sign

    (A) a contract of sale.

    (B) an option agreement.

    (C) an easement.

    (D) an executory contract.

57. Harry's House of Hats can no longer pay its landlord, Jim. Nancy's House of Shoes agrees to take over the space and executes a new lease with Jim. This situation is

    (A) a sublease.

    (B) an assignment.

    (C) a novation.

    (D) a graduated lease.

58. A landlord does not keep a building in good repair, including not fixing a broken boiler in the middle of winter. The tenants want to move out and go to court to prove

    (A) constructive eviction.

    (B) actual eviction.

    (C) invalid possession.

    (D) lease violation.

59. Georgia's House of Mirrors agrees to pay its landlord a flat rental fee plus a portion of its gross sales each month. This situation is best described as

    (A) a gross lease.

    (B) a net lease.

    (C) a percentage lease.

    (D) a proprietary lease.

60. A person in a cooperative apartment gets what kind of lease?

    (A) Gross lease

    (B) Net lease

    (C) Ground lease

    (D) Proprietary lease

61. Alice refuses to move out of her apartment after her lease expires. The landlord refuses to accept the rent she offers to pay. This is

    (A) an estate at will.

    (B) an estate at sufferance.

    (C) an estate for years.

    (D) a periodic estate.

*Go on to next page* ⟹

62. A typical commercial lease is

    (A) a tenancy for years.

    (B) a tenancy at will.

    (C) a tenancy at sufferance.

    (D) a periodic tenancy.

63. The agency primarily responsible for dealing with environmental issues is

    (A) CERCLA.

    (B) HUD.

    (C) LUST.

    (D) EPA.

64. Under CERCLA, liability is considered to be

    (A) joint and several.

    (B) joint and strict.

    (C) strict and several.

    (D) joint, strict, and several.

65. The possibility of claiming innocence of responsibility for prior hazardous waste dumping on land you bought was made available by

    (A) SARA.

    (B) CERCLA.

    (C) OSHA.

    (D) HMTA.

66. Which phase of environmental assessment would confirm the presence of hazardous material?

    (A) 1

    (B) 2

    (C) 3

    (D) 4

67. You get sick every day at work but the symptoms disappear on your drive home. You may have

    (A) building related illness.

    (B) sick building syndrome.

    (C) asbestosis.

    (D) building radon illness.

68. Which program requires registering various types of underground storage tanks?

    (A) LUST

    (B) OSHA

    (C) SARA

    (D) CERCLA

69. An appraisal is

    (A) an estimate of value.

    (B) a calculation of value.

    (C) an educated guess of value.

    (D) an analysis of value.

70. The most important reason that location is such an important factor in the value of real estate is its

    (A) neighborhood compatibility.

    (B) amenities and services.

    (C) safety.

    (D) immobility.

71. In the sales comparison approach, if a comparable is better than the subject, what do you do?

    (A) Make a positive adjustment to the subject.

    (B) Make a negative adjustment to the subject.

    (C) Make a negative adjustment to the comparable.

    (D) Make a positive adjustment to the comparable.

72. Which of the following is not a type of depreciation used in the cost approach?

    (A) Functional obsolescence

    (B) Physical deterioration

    (C) Straight line deterioration

    (D) External obsolescence

*Go on to next page*

73. You buy the smallest house in a neighborhood of larger, more expensive homes. What economic principle will most likely affect the value of your house?

    (A) Regression

    (B) Progression

    (C) Increasing returns

    (D) Opportunity costs

74. The gross rent multiplier is a factor that relates

    (A) expenses to net income.

    (B) net income to value.

    (C) rent to value.

    (D) expenses to value.

75. Effective gross income is potential gross income minus

    (A) operating expenses.

    (B) debt service.

    (C) vacancy and collection loss.

    (D) vacancy and collection loss and operating expenses.

76. Al borrows money from the First Bank of Main Street. He is

    (A) the mortgagor.

    (B) the mortgagee.

    (C) the lien holder.

    (D) the note holder.

77. The Annual Percentage Rate could not be described as

    (A) points plus interest rate.

    (B) the actual interest rate.

    (C) the discount rate.

    (D) the yield.

78. Equity is best defined as

    (A) the down payment.

    (B) the amount owed on the mortgage.

    (C) the difference between the value and the debt attributable to the property.

    (D) the amount of cash taken out after the house is sold.

79. The VA requires what in order to secure a loan?

    (A) LTV

    (B) CRV

    (C) PMI

    (D) FSA

80. Which of the following is not a part of the secondary mortgage market?

    (A) Fannie Mae

    (B) Ginnie Mae

    (C) Freddie Mae

    (D) Farmer Mac

81. A single word to describe a loan where nothing is left to pay at the end of the term is

    (A) a term loan.

    (B) a balloon loan.

    (C) a variable loan.

    (D) an amortized loan.

82. Mom and Dad help you buy a house by lending you some money. They don't want any payments right away but tell you that when you sell, if you make a profit, they'll take a portion of the profit as payment of the loan. You have

    (A) a growing equity mortgage.

    (B) an open-end mortgage.

    (C) a shared equity mortgage.

    (D) a reverse annuity mortgage.

83. The rate that is used to adjust taxes among several towns in the same county is called

    (A) the equalization rate.

    (B) the capitalization rate.

    (C) the mill rate.

    (D) the assessment rate.

*Go on to next page*

84. A town's property tax rate is typically determined by
    - (A) dividing the total assessed value of taxable property by the town budget.
    - (B) dividing the town budget by the total assessed value of taxable property.
    - (C) multiplying the total assessed value of taxable property by the town's budget.
    - (D) dividing the total assessed value of taxable property by the assessment ratio.

85. The right to redeem foreclosed property by paying the taxes after a tax sale is called
    - (A) equitable right of redemption.
    - (B) statutory right of redemption.
    - (C) in rem right of redemption.
    - (D) post foreclosure right of redemption.

86. A combination REIT can invest in
    - (A) mortgages and bonds.
    - (B) equity real estate investments and bonds.
    - (C) mortgages and stocks.
    - (D) equity real estate investments and mortgages.

87. The tax deferred in a real estate exchange is tax on
    - (A) income.
    - (B) capital gains.
    - (C) corporate profits.
    - (D) net operating income.

88. Another term for depreciation is
    - (A) recapture.
    - (B) capital loss.
    - (C) adjusted basis.
    - (D) cost recovery.

89. All other things being equal, which of the following is worth more in tax savings?
    - (A) Deduction
    - (B) Credit
    - (C) Adjusted basis
    - (D) Capital gains

90. A building whose expenses are higher than its income is described as having
    - (A) positive cash flow.
    - (B) negative cash flow.
    - (C) negative amortization.
    - (D) excessive depreciation.

91. In general, in a real estate investment, the higher the risk,
    - (A) the higher the expected return.
    - (B) the lower the expected return.
    - (C) the greater likelihood that the return remains unchanged.
    - (D) the harder a property is to manage.

92. A seller wants to net $200,000 after she pays the real estate agent a 6 percent commission. What must the house sell for?
    - (A) $200,000
    - (B) $206,000
    - (C) $212,000
    - (D) $212,765

93. A buyer wants to know the size of a square piece of property that measures 264 feet by 264 feet. What do you tell him?
    - (A) 1 acre
    - (B) 1.3 acres
    - (C) 1.6 acres
    - (D) 2 acres

94. A peaked roof barn is used to store hay. The width of the barn is 40 feet. The height of the ridge beam above the second floor is 15 feet, and the barn is 60 feet long. If hay is stored only in the upper peaked roof portion of the barn, how much hay can be stored?
    - (A) 36,000 cubic feet
    - (B) 24,000 cubic feet
    - (C) 18,000 cubic feet
    - (D) 6,000 cubic feet

*Go on to next page*

95. Five hundred houses were sold in your county this year. Four hundred were sold last year. What percentage more of houses were sold this year than last year?

    (A) 100 percent

    (B) 50 percent

    (C) 25 percent

    (D) 20 percent

96. If the cost recovery period on a property is 25 years, at what percentage does the property depreciate each year?

    (A) 25 percent

    (B) 10 percent

    (C) 5 percent

    (D) 4 percent

97. If the annual gross rent on a building is $20,000 and the gross rent multiplier for this type of building is 16, what is the estimated value of the building?

    (A) $320,000

    (B) $150,375

    (C) $125,000

    (D) $118,750

98. How much interest do you owe for the first year on an amortized mortgage loan of $250,000 at a 7 percent interest rate?

    (A) $1,458

    (B) $1,750

    (C) $14,580

    (D) $17,500

99. A property is assessed at $42,000. The mill rate is 22. What are the taxes on the property?

    (A) $9,240

    (B) $924

    (C) $1,900

    (D) $190

100. You bought a house for $200,000, which is 80 percent of what you sell it for six years later. At what price did you sell the house?

    (A) $160,000

    (B) $240,000

    (C) $250,000

    (D) $260,000

# Chapter 20

# Answers and Explanations to Practice Exam One

. . . . . . . . . . . . . . . . . . . . . . . . . . . . . . . . . . . . . . . . . . . . . . . . . .

*A*ll right! You're just minutes away from finding out how well you did on the practice exam in Chapter 19. Give yourself one point for each correct answer, and add up your total score.

Find the range that corresponds to your score in the following list:

- ✔ **Between 90 and 100:** Congratulations! You're on your way to your first million as a real estate agent.

- ✔ **Between 80 and 90:** Take a breath, pat yourself on the back, and keep reviewing the material so you don't forget what you've already picked up.

- ✔ **Between 75 and 80:** Too close for comfort. Check out your weakest areas, section by section, and review the corresponding chapters again, using the review questions at the end of each chapter for practice. If you got more than half of the questions wrong in any one section, that's a good indication you need more work with that chapter.

- ✔ **Below 75:** Don't be discouraged. The difference between this score and a higher one is time, and that time needs to be spent with this book. Check out your weakest areas in the exam, review the corresponding chapters, do the review questions at the end of each chapter, and try this exam again and the next three. By the way, I've chosen 75 percent as the passing grade, though your state may use a different one.

Don't forget that no matter how well you did on this exam, the information here is general to most states. You still need to study the information unique to your state. Review the material noted with the State-Specific icon throughout this book as well as the list of subjects in Chapter 23. You can get state-specific information from your prelicensing course's materials, textbook, and instructor, too.

1. **(B) Chapter 3**

   A surety bond insures against employee misdeeds like theft. Rent loss insurance (also known as business interruption insurance) insures against the landlord losing rent because of a disaster like a fire, and liability insurance covers losses caused by injuries that are the result of negligence on the part of the landlord.

2. **(D) Chapter 3**

   Did the "not" in the question throw you off? A good way to handle this question is to repeat each answer in a positive way and ask yourself whether it's true or false. For instance, you say, "Fixed fees are a way to set a property management fee." True or false? Well, that's true, so it can't be the right answer. Percentage of operating costs is the only answer that doesn't fit.

3. **(A) Chapter 3**

   Real estate license laws generally require a person to hold a real estate license when performing any number of particular duties for another person for a fee. You don't have to have a real estate license to do any of these things for your own property. An employee of a person who owns and rents out buildings is effectively acting directly on behalf of the owner, as if, in a sense, the employee were the owner. This could vary slightly by state, so check yours out just in case.

4. (A) Chapter 3

A capital expense is usually a major expense to improve or repair something that does not last as long as the life of a building, like a roof. An operating expense is an annual expense to keep the building running, like the gas or oil bill. A maintenance item is usually a repair that may happen occasionally and sometimes unpredictably like a furnace repair. A fixed expense is a term used to describe insurance and tax payments.

5. (D) Chapter 3

The first three answers are characteristics of being an employee, not an independent contractor. However, even when you're an independent contractor, the broker is responsible for your work and must supervise you.

6. (D) Chapter 3

The keys to this question are the word "primary" and avoiding confusion when partially correct answers are among the choices. Maximizing income while maintaining the building's value encompasses the first three answers and is considered the primary duty of a property manager. Looked at another way, the first three answers are each a part of the more correct total answer (D).

7. (A) Chapter 4

A special agent represents a client for one real estate transaction. A general agent represents a client in a range of activities, and a universal agent represents a client in all or almost all activities. I made up "representative agent."

8. (A) Chapter 4

Fiduciary responsibilities are defined as being owed to the client. A seller or a buyer can be your client. A customer is the third party in a transaction. The only thing that is always true in this question is (A), the client.

9. (B) Chapter 4

The duties are accounting, care, confidentiality, disclosure, loyalty, and obedience. A question about these duties is so fundamental to being a real estate agent that I can almost guarantee you will see a question about this on the exam.

10. (C) Chapter 4

Watch out for the word "always." The buyer or seller *could* be the client but not *always*. The principal is always the client; the two terms are interchangeable.

11. (C) Chapter 4

If an individual property owner contracts with a real estate agent to sell his property, that arrangement isn't affected by his getting married because the property ownership hasn't changed.

12. (D) Chapter 4

The first three choices all are essentially the same thing.

13. (C) Chapter 5

There are no exemptions for race to the 1866 law, plain and simple.

14. (A) Chapter 5

Changing the terms of rentals for any group in a protected class is illegal, no matter how many supporting facts one may have.

15. (D) Chapter 5

Blockbusting is the deliberate attempt to generate profits by scaring people into selling their houses under the circumstances stated in the question. The other answers are all legitimate ways to get listings of houses to sell, provided blockbusting isn't used.

16. (B) Chapter 5

The church housing exception applies only if membership in the church or religion itself is not restricted. Because the church in question discriminates in its membership policies against African Americans, the housing exception does not apply; therefore, the housing can't be restricted to only church members.

17. (B) Chapter 5

HUD enforces the 1968 Fair Housing Act, but the federal courts enforce the 1866 law.

18. (C) Chapter 5

Even if a homeowner has the exemption (in this case, the owner of a single-family home who doesn't own more than three units), a real estate agent may not be used. Real estate agents are always held to higher standards when it comes to fair housing issues.

19. (A) Chapter 5

Redlining, which is discrimination in the lending of mortgage money based on location, is always illegal.

20. (D) Chapter 6

Land is the physical "dirt." Real estate is the dirt and the structures attached to it. Real property is the land, everything attached to it, and the rights associated with owning it. Personal property is tangible, movable, portable things that are not real estate.

21. (B) Chapter 6

A fixture is personal property that becomes permanently attached to the real estate and is expected to stay with it when it is sold. Personal property is something tangible, moveable, and not attached to the real estate. A trade fixture is used to conduct a business and usually expected to be removed at the end of a lease period or when the property is sold. An attachment can mean anything attached to real estate.

22. (B) Chapter 6

Fee simple condition precedent is ownership subject to a condition that must be satisfied before title is actually conveyed. Fee simple is ownership without condition. Fee simple subsequent is ownership in which the grantor has the right to reclaim the property through court action if a condition isn't met after title is conveyed. In fee simple determinable, if a condition isn't met, the property automatically reverts to the grantor without the necessity of court action.

23. (A) Chapter 6

Fee simple is ownership without condition and is the most complete form of ownership. The other choices all have limitations.

24. (B) Chapter 6

Leased fee is the most correct answer. The owner may have a fee simple interest or a fee on condition interest, but when a question involves leases, the most correct answer involves either leasehold or leased fee interests. (The tenant has the leasehold interest.)

25. (C) Chapter 6

If the river is navigable, the property owner owns to the edge of the river or to the mean high water mark. If the river isn't navigable, the property owner owns to the centerline of the water. You just have to remember this difference.

26. (D) Chapter 6

The bundle of rights refers to *all* the rights a property owner generally gets when she receives ownership of a piece of property and is the most complete answer. The terms "fee simple" and "freehold" refer to estates or interests that a person may have in a piece of property. There really is no such thing as real estate rights in the context of this question.

27. (A) Chapter 7

Each owner taking title at the same time refers to unity of time, each owner taking title with the same deed refers to unity of title, and each owner having the same interest in the property refers to unity of interest.

28. (B) Chapter 7

This question can have a state-specific variation if your state does not recognize the right of survivorship in joint tenancy. But tenancy in common never has a right of survivorship.

29. (C) Chapter 7

A joint tenant can sell his share to another person. That new owner becomes a tenant in common to the other joint tenants, unless everyone executes new documents to create a new joint tenancy.

30. (D) Chapter 7

Condominium owners generally own the airspace encompassing their units in fee simple ownership. The land under and around the units is owned by all of the owners as tenants in common. A good way to jog your memory is to remember that condominium owners would want to leave their condo to their heirs, which is a feature of tenancy in common rather than joint tenancy.

31. (D) Chapter 7

Of course, tenancy in severalty needs "all" the signatures because there's only one owner, but it is not a form of co-ownership. Tenants in common and joint tenants can sell their individual interests with only their signatures. This action does not convey ownership to the whole property, so the word "interest" is crucial in this question. Tenancy by the entirety views the interest of the husband and wife as a single interest that can't be sold separately, so both spouses have to sign the deed to sell their interest.

32. (B) Chapter 7

The corporation owns the entire building. The individual tenant owns shares in the corporation and has a proprietary lease that enables him to occupy his apartment.

33. (B) Chapter 8

The statement that all liens are encumbrances is true. Liens (which can be voluntary or involuntary) are just one type of encumbrance, and encumbrances in general can be financial in nature or can limit the use of property.

34. (C) Chapter 8

Real estate taxes take first priority in all liens. After taxes are paid, liens generally are settled in the order in which they were recorded in the public record.

35. (C) Chapter 8

A judgment lien is involuntary and general. That means that it's placed without your consent and against all your real and personal property. There may be state-specific laws that limit the judgment being placed to property in the county where the lawsuit took place. Check this out in your state, but in the way this question was asked this answer is generally correct.

36. (B) Chapter 8

An easement in gross benefits a person, and an easement appurtenant attaches itself to the land. An easement by necessity is one that must be given to another person by a court order. An easement by prescription occurs against your will by someone continuously using your property. In this case the "person" that benefits is the electric company.

37. (D) Chapter 8

The right of a municipality to take your property against your will for a public purpose is called eminent domain. In escheat, the state gets your land if you die without a will and without heirs. The other answers don't involve the state taking your land.

38. (B) Chapter 8

Studies of demographics are used for planning purposes in a municipality.

39. (B) Chapter 9

The person getting the property (the grantee) doesn't have to sign (though he or she does have to be clearly named), but the person selling the property (the grantor) does.

40. (B) Chapter 9

Delivery and acceptance is the handing of the deed by the grantor to the grantee, though it is not generally done in any formal manner.

41. (D) Chapter 9

An *acknowledgment* proves that the person who signs a deed (the grantor) signed it voluntarily and is, in fact, who he says he is (or who she says she is). This question may be state-specific in a few places. Consideration and a granting clause are always required, and the signature of the grantee is never required.

42. (A) Chapter 9

The metes and bounds method of description uses locations, distances, and compass directions to define property boundaries. The rectangular and government survey systems, which are two names for the same thing, describe property boundaries using squares and rectangles determined by longitude and latitude. The plat map system uses a map of a property, usually a subdivision, which is filed in the local recording office. The map divides properties into blocks and lots for description purposes.

43. (A) Chapter 9

If you check Figure 9-1 of a township divided into sections (part of the rectangular survey system) and are able to duplicate it, you can answer any question like this.

44. (D) Chapter 9

Benchmarks and monuments are markers used by surveyors, but a datum is specific to measuring elevation. A meridian is a feature of the government survey system and has nothing to do with elevations.

45. (A) Chapter 10

Dedication it is! The government gives land to people with grants. Avulsion is the sudden loss of land by natural forces. A sale is, well, selling property to someone else.

46. (C) Chapter 10

The government voluntarily gives land to people with grants. The other choices are involuntary ways of losing property.

47. (C) Chapter 10

Partition is a legal proceeding that divides property when the owners can't agree on how to do it themselves.

48. (D) Chapter 10

Probate is the way that a will is legally processed. It's done in surrogate's court, so surrogacy may have confused you.

49. (B) Chapter 10

The key word in this question is "give." The government gives property to a person in a public grant, but a sale involves the exchange of money or something of value for a piece of property.

50. (C) Chapter 10

A suit to quiet title is what you sue for when you claim ownership through adverse possession. A suit for partition involves co-owners who can't agree on how to divide the property they own. The other two answers sound good but are made up.

51. (D) Chapter 11

The statute of frauds governs certain kinds of contracts, including real estate contracts, and says that contracts must be in writing to be enforceable. Contract law itself has no such requirement; other kinds of contracts can be oral. RESPA deals with closing title, and as far as I know, no statute of contracts exists.

52. (B) Chapter 11

An implied contract occurs because of the parties' actions. An express contract clearly states what the parties agree to do or not to do, and in a unilateral contract, one party has to act only if the other party acts. An executed contract has all of its terms fulfilled. In some states the absence of a written contract may affect your ability to collect a commission.

53. (B) Chapter 11

The contract is voidable, because Joey can go ahead with it if he wants to, and it is enforceable on the other person. A void contract never actually existed because it didn't meet some requirement to be valid. An implied contract exists because of the actions of the parties rather than any express agreement. An unenforceable contract is one that may appear valid but cannot be legally enforced by either party.

54. (B) Chapter 11

Remember that a contract in general requires consideration. It logically requires legally competent parties and mutual agreement about what is being promised. A real estate sales contract has all this and more. A real estate sales contract would have to have the legal description of the property being sold to be valid.

55. (A) Chapter 11

As long as neither person accepts the other's offer, no valid deal exists. A person absolutely can raise his offer as long as no other offer has been accepted.

56. (B) Chapter 11

An option will enable Jim to get his approvals while the property cannot be sold. With an option, in the event that Jim can't get the approvals, he would not have to buy the land, whereas with a standard sales contract he would.

57. (C) Chapter 11

A novation is a new lease agreement to replace the old one. The other answers, which don't involve completely new leases, are explained in Chapter 12.

58. (A) Chapter 12

The key in this question is that the tenants want to move out rather than get the items repaired, so lease violation — on the part of the landlord, in this case — is not a good answer. In actual eviction, the landlord seeks to evict the tenant for some reason and goes to court to do it. I made up invalid possession.

59. (C) Chapter 12

The best answer is percentage lease because it involves some payment based on a percentage of something, usually sales in a store. This lease may be a net lease, but you would need to know if the tenant is paying building expenses as well as rent.

60. (D) Chapter 12

The proprietary lease entitles the cooperative owner to use the apartment for which he has purchased shares in the corporation that owns the building. A gross lease is a typical apartment lease. A net lease is often used in commercial buildings. A ground lease is one where only vacant land is leased.

61. (B) Chapter 12

In an estate at sufferance, the tenant remains in possession of the apartment after the lease expires without the landlord's permission. An estate at will is when the tenant can stay in the apartment with the landlord's permission for an indefinite period of time. An estate for years is one that has a definite period of time associated with it. A periodic estate keeps automatically renewing itself from period to period.

62. (A) Chapter 12

I use the word "tenancy" here. Remember that when talking about leases, it means the same as "estate." In a tenancy for years, the lease is for a definite period of time, providing a beginning and ending date for the commercial tenant.

63. (D) Chapter 13

EPA is the Environmental Protection Agency. HUD is the Department of Housing and Urban Development. The other two are environmental laws, not enforcement agencies.

64. (D) Chapter 13

Joint and several liability means that if there is more than one owner of a contaminated property, each one is personally liable, and if only one is able to pay, he must bear the total cost and attempt to collect from the other owners. Strict liability means that the contaminated property's owner has no excuse for any injury done by the contamination.

65. (A) Chapter 13

The Superfund Amendments and Reauthorization Act increased funding of the Superfund, which was created by CERCLA. It also created innocent landowner status for current owners not responsible for contaminating property.

66. (B) Chapter 13

The phases of environmental assessment are 1) a review of records and a physical inspection of the property; 2) testing; 3) cleaning up the contamination; and 4) managing the contamination.

67. (B) Chapter 13

The main difference between the first two answers is that with sick building syndrome, the symptoms disappear on the way home, and with building-related illness, they remain even after you leave the building. Asbestosis is a disease specifically caused by exposure to asbestos. And there is no such thing as building radon illness.

68. (A) Chapter 13

The goal of the Leaking Underground Storage Tanks program is to identify and prevent the failure of underground storage tanks. The main provision is tank registration.

69. (A) Chapter 14

Analysis of value may sound right, but the market gets analyzed to estimate the value. A calculation of value is wrong because while calculations may be used, the result is still an estimate of value. A guess, educated or not, is still a guess. An estimate of value is the definition as used in the appraisal industry. Sometimes the word *opinion* is also used to mean the same thing.

70. (D) Chapter 14

The first three answers are some of the things that real estate agents use to measure a location's value. However, it is the fact that property cannot be moved that makes location so important as a determining factor in the property's value.

71. (C) Chapter 14

If the comparable is better than the subject, what must you do to make it like the subject? You take something away. So, it is a negative adjustment to the comparable. You never adjust the subject.

72. (C) Chapter 14

There's no such thing as straight-line deterioration. However, there is a straight-line method of estimating depreciation. Beware answers that have one or two words that sound right (like straight-line).

73. (B) Chapter 14

Progression is the positive effect on value that larger houses have on a smaller house. Regression is the opposite or negative effect on value that smaller houses have on a larger house.

74. (C) Chapter 14

Don't get put off in a question like this because it doesn't have the exact wording like "gross rent." Rent to value is the best answer because the gross rent multiplier technique uses rents and converts them to value using the GRM. Net income to value may look right, but that's the technique used with the income capitalization approach to value. As for the other two answers: You never convert expenses to value.

75. (C) Chapter 14

Gross income minus vacancy and collection loss is effective gross income. When you subtract operating expenses from the effective gross income, you get net operating income. The other two answers don't give you any meaningful numbers.

76. (A) Chapter 15

With mortgage loans, the borrower gives the mortgage to the bank. The borrower is the mortgagor; the bank is the mortgagee. The bank is the lien holder and the note holder. The mortgage lien entitles the bank to foreclosure for nonpayment, and the note signifies that the borrower owes money to the bank.

77. (C) Chapter 15

The discount rate has to do with loan rates established by the federal government (and has nothing to do with the APR). The other three answers are all related to the APR. Take special care not to confuse discount points and the discount rate.

78. (C) Chapter 15

The difference between the value and the debt attributable to the property and the amount of cash taken out after the house is sold are pretty close. The difference is that you don't have to actually sell the house to calculate equity. Note the use of the phrase "best defined" in the question; the difference between the value and the debt attributable to the property is the best answer.

79. (B) Chapter 15

The Certificate of Reasonable Value is required for a Veterans Administration guarantee.

80. (C) Chapter 15

Freddie Mac (not Freddie Mae) is part of the secondary market for mortgages. Always read the questions carefully.

81. (D) Chapter 15

A variable loan refers to how the interest rates are set. A term loan and a balloon loan require a payment at the end of the term.

82. (C) Chapter 15

A shared-equity mortgage allows for a share of the profit on the property to be given to someone else in return for help purchasing the property. You must be able to distinguish among types of mortgages by a few of their principal characteristics.

83. (A) Chapter 16

Remember the term "Equalization rate" simply with the word "equalize," which is what it does. The capitalization rate is used to estimate value in the income capitalization approach. The mill rate is an actual tax rate in any community. The assessment ratio is the percent of market value used to calculate the assessed value.

84. (B) Chapter 16

Divide the town budget by the total assessed value of the town, which is also called the tax base, and you get your answer.

85. (B) Chapter 16

Here's a trick to remember: *E,* for equitable right of redemption, comes early in the alphabet, so it's what you can do before the tax sale. The statutory right of redemption (*S* for statutory) comes late in the alphabet; it's what you can do after the tax sale. In rem right of redemption and post foreclosure right of redemption are made up, but the phrase "in rem" relates to taxes and means "against the thing," meaning the property.

86. (D) Chapter 17

A combination Real Estate Investment Trust (REIT) invests in equities, which are real estate investments, and mortgages. The others are partially correct, but REITs don't invest in stocks and bonds. An equity REIT invests only in properties; a mortgage REIT invests only in mortgages.

87. (B) Chapter 17

A real estate exchange is designed to defer payment on taxes of capital gains. The exchange takes the place of a regular sale.

88. (D) Chapter 17

Remember that depreciation is the government's way of helping you recover the cost of the building, which is wearing out, so to speak.

89. (B) Chapter 17

A credit comes off taxes owed, whereas a deduction is subtracted from income. The other two answers don't really apply here.

90. (B) Chapter 17

Negative cash flow is when you have to put money into a building every month because its income cannot cover its expenses. Positive cash flow is the opposite: You have money left over each month after expenses are paid out of the building's income.

91. (A) Chapter 17

The answer that the harder the property is to manage may be true, but don't overthink the question. The expected answer is "the higher the expected return."

92. (D) Chapter 18

What you know here is that after you deduct your commission, the owner is getting 94 percent of some dollar amount (the sales price). Just divide the dollar amount to the owner by the percentage to the owner, and presto! You have the selling price.

100 percent – 6 percent = 94 percent

$200,000 ÷ 0.94 = $212,765

93. (C) Chapter 18

Multiply the length times width, and you get the area in square units (in this case, feet). To find the area in acres, you divide the number of square feet by 43,560 square feet, which is how many square feet are in an acre.

264 feet × 264 feet = 69,696 square feet

69,696 square feet ÷ 43,560 square feet (one acre) = 1.6 acres

94. (C) Chapter 18

You're looking for the volume of the peaked roof part of the barn. For you city folks, that's like the attic. The formula for the volume of a triangular-shaped structure is

½ Base × Height × Length

0.5 × 40 feet × 15 feet × 60 feet = 18,000 cubic feet

95. (C) Chapter 18

First you find the difference between the number of houses sold this year and the number sold last year. Because you want to find the percentage of more houses sold this year than last year, you need to divide by last year's amount.

500 – 400 = 100

100 ÷ 400 = 0.25 = 25 percent

96. (D) Chapter 18

Calculate any cost recovery problem by dividing the number of years of cost recovery into the number 1.

1 ÷ 25 = 0.04 or 4 percent

97. (A) Chapter 18

Multiply the rent by the gross rent multiplier to find the value. Easy!

$20,000 × 16 = $320,000

98. (D) Chapter 18

You always pay interest on the unpaid balance of the mortgage, which is the whole thing in the first year.

Mortgage amount × interest rate = total first year's interest

$250,000 × 0.07 (7 percent) = $17,500

99. (B) Chapter 18

Always divide the mill rate by 1,000 to get the number you have to multiply by. Then multiply that number by the assessed value.

22 ÷ 1,000 = 0.022

$42,000 × 0.022 = $924

100. (C) Chapter 18

If you have a dollar figure and the portion of 100 percent that the figure represents, you can get the total number (100 percent) by dividing the dollar figure you have by the percent it represents. In this problem, $200,000 is 80 percent of some number.

$200,000 ÷ 0.80 (80 percent) = $250,000

# Chapter 21

# Practice Exam Two

. . . . . . . . . . . . . . . . . . . . . . . . . . . . . . . . . . . . . . . . . . . . . . . . . . . . . . . . . . . . . . . . . .

*A*re you ready for another round of test-taking fun? Like the first practice exam in Chapter 19, this practice exam has 100 questions and is laid out with similar subjects grouped together, even though on the actual exam, subjects will be distributed randomly. I've grouped the questions so you can have an easy time determining what your strong and weak areas are. Also remember that a number of state-specific questions on the actual exam will deal with particular laws and practices unique to your state. Review the items marked with the State-Specific icon throughout this book, and study both the materials that you get in your prelicensing course (such as a textbook) and your state's license law.

Mark your answers on a separate piece of paper, and try to complete the entire test in less than two hours. Chapter 22 contains the correct answers to this exam, plus explanations and cross-references to chapters for review. (Be strong: Don't check out the answers until you finish the exam.)

You should take this exam only after you've completed the first practice exam in Chapter 19 and reviewed the chapters featuring your weaker areas. You also may want to take this exam a second time right before you take your state exam as a refresher. Good luck!

1.  A rental building has several different types of insurance. A property manager may want to have which of the following?

    (A) Fire and hazard insurance

    (B) Errors and omissions insurance

    (C) Casualty insurance

    (D) Rent loss insurance

2.  Rents are typically set

    (A) after an analysis of the building by a certified appraiser.

    (B) somewhat arbitrarily.

    (C) based on the expenses of the building.

    (D) based on market rents and vacancy rates.

3.  Salesperson Sally works for Broker Bob. Unknown to Bob, Sally has been particularly rude to Vietnamese customers. If she is charged with a fair housing violation, will Broker Bob also be held responsible?

    (A) Yes

    (B) No

    (C) Only if she is an employee

    (D) Only if Bob had known

4.  A property manager analyzing a building's risk may recommend all except which of the following?

    (A) Retain risk

    (B) Transfer risk

    (C) Avoid risk

    (D) Contain risk

5.  Broker A and Broker B meet to discuss a listing that both of them are working on. They discuss the commission they will share. Which of the following is true?

    (A) They have violated antitrust laws on price fixing.

    (B) They have violated local real estate board practice if the fee they are discussing is beyond the standard fee schedule.

    (C) They really can't discuss anything because the state real estate commission sets fees.

    (D) No violation of the law has occurred.

6.  Broker A and Broker B, who have real estate agencies on opposite sides of town, meet at the beginning of the year and agree that each one will handle sales only in his part of town and not interfere with sales in the other broker's area.

    (A) They have violated the antitrust law prohibiting price fixing.

    (B) They have violated the antitrust law prohibiting market allocation.

    (C) They have violated the antitrust law on group boycotting.

    (D) They have violated no antitrust law.

7.  Seller Sam hires Broker Bob to sell his house. Bob brings Buyer Betty to see the house. Assuming there is no dual agency, which of the following is correct?

    (A) Sam is the customer; Bob is the agent.

    (B) Sam is the customer; Betty is the client.

    (C) Sam is the client; Betty is the customer.

    (D) Betty is the client; Bob is the agent.

8.  An agency established with a written document is always

    (A) an express agency.

    (B) an implied agency.

    (C) an agency by estoppel.

    (D) an agency by ratification.

9.  Fran notifies all the brokers in her area that her house is for sale and says she will work with any broker who brings a buyer. She is creating

    (A) a seller's listing.

    (B) a free-for-all listing.

    (C) an open listing.

    (D) an exclusive right to sell listing.

10. Seller Sara agrees to let Broker Ben keep any amount over the $200,000 that she needs if he sells her house. This is called

    (A) an open listing.

    (B) a gross listing.

    (C) a net listing.

    (D) a buyer's listing.

*Go on to next page*

11. You are representing Seller Sharon and bring Buyer Barbara, your customer, to see the house. Barbara makes an offer. Barbara has confidentially told you about the bankruptcy she went through two years ago, but she thinks she will be financially approved to buy the house. What, if anything, should you do with the information about the bankruptcy?

    (A) Tell Sharon.

    (B) Keep the information confidential as Barbara asked you to.

    (C) Keep the information confidential unless the deal doesn't go through.

    (D) Contact the bank to verify Barbara's financial status.

12. Several people are involved in most real estate transactions. The duty of loyalty requires you to put their interest in what order of priority?

    (A) Yourself, customer, client

    (B) Yourself, client, customer

    (C) Customer, client, yourself

    (D) Client, yourself, customer

13. A homeowner refuses to rent an apartment in his two-family house to an African American family. Which of the following is true regarding this action with respect to fair housing laws?

    (A) This is legal because there is an exception to the law for one- to four-family houses.

    (B) This is legal only if the owner lives in the house himself.

    (C) This is legal as long as the homeowner does not use discriminatory advertising.

    (D) This is illegal.

14. "Christians only" is the advertisement for a house that's for sale. This is

    (A) legal if the house is owner-occupied.

    (B) illegal unless a real estate agent is used.

    (C) legal because it's a one-family house.

    (D) illegal.

15. A young married woman's income is discounted by 50 percent by a bank when she applies for a mortgage loan because she is of childbearing age. This is

    (A) illegal discrimination.

    (B) legal discrimination because of the business aspects of banking.

    (C) called redlining.

    (D) legal because protection of a depositor's money supersedes other laws.

16. A Portuguese couple looking for a house asks a real estate agent to show them houses in Portuguese neighborhoods. Which of the following is correct?

    (A) The agent can accommodate this request because the buyers are asking for it.

    (B) The agent should tell the buyers that she will show them houses in a number of different neighborhoods that meet their needs.

    (C) The agent should refuse to work with the buyers.

    (D) The agent should agree, then show the buyers houses in other neighborhoods.

17. Advising people on which neighborhoods they would be happy in may be construed as

    (A) redlining.

    (B) blockbusting.

    (C) steering.

    (D) canvassing.

18. The *Jones versus Mayer* decision basically confirmed

    (A) the constitutionality of fair housing laws.

    (B) the legality of the various exceptions to fair housing laws.

    (C) no exception for race in fair housing laws.

    (D) the owner-occupied exemption for fair housing laws.

*Go on to next page*

19. A young woman is refused the right to buy a condominium in a complex that restricts purchases to people 50 years of age or older. This is

    (A) illegal.

    (B) legal.

    (C) legal if there is a restrictive covenant in the condominium deed.

    (D) legal if the complex is specifically designated as senior citizen housing for people over the age of 50.

20. The lumber for a deck that has not yet been built is

    (A) personal property.

    (B) a fixture.

    (C) a trade fixture.

    (D) real estate.

21. The interest of a tenant in a rented building is most properly known as

    (A) leasehold.

    (B) leased fee.

    (C) tenant's rights.

    (D) tenancy in fee.

22. Reversion of title is a feature of what type of interest?

    (A) Fee simple

    (B) Fee simple condition precedent

    (C) Fee simple condition subsequent

    (D) Fee simple determinable

23. I give my sister permission to live in a house I own until the death of her son. I have created

    (A) an ordinary life estate.

    (B) a life estate pur autre vie.

    (C) a leased hold interest.

    (D) a tenancy for life.

24. Littoral rights for properties abutting the ocean give ownership

    (A) to the mean high water mark.

    (B) to a point 200 feet out from the shore.

    (C) to the state ownership line.

    (D) to nothing because littoral rights have to do with non-navigable rivers.

25. Jewelry cases in a jewelry store are an example of

    (A) fixtures.

    (B) personal property.

    (C) trade fixtures.

    (D) real estate.

26. A fixture

    (A) is always assumed to accompany a property that is sold.

    (B) is always assumed to belong to the seller and may be removed.

    (C) is usually sold separately with a bill of sale.

    (D) is not considered real estate.

27. In what way does a PUD generally differ from a condominium?

    (A) Condominiums have homeowners associations; PUDs do not.

    (B) Condominiums have monthly common charges; PUDs do not.

    (C) Condominium owners individually own the airspace occupied by their unit and the land under and around their units as tenants in common; PUD owners own the land under and around their units individually.

    (D) Condominium owners own shares in a corporation; PUD owners own the real estate.

28. Three people each buy pieces of property next to each other for farm use. As a matter of efficiency, they hire one person to manage the farm as a single unit even though the properties are owned separately. How is the property owned?

    (A) Joint tenancy

    (B) Tenancy in common

    (C) Tenancy by the entirety

    (D) Tenancy in severalty

29. A proprietary lease is a unique characteristic of what form of ownership?

    (A) Condominium

    (B) Cooperative

    (C) Time share

    (D) PUD

*Go on to next page*

30. A corporation usually owns property in

    (A) joint tenancy.

    (B) tenancy in common.

    (C) tenancy by the entirety.

    (D) tenancy in severalty.

31. Liability that is limited to the investment does not apply to

    (A) partners in a general partnership.

    (B) a corporation's shareholders.

    (C) limited partners in a limited partnership.

    (D) limited liability corporations.

32. The type of co-ownership that allows an owner's property to be left to her heirs is

    (A) tenancy by the entirety.

    (B) tenancy in severalty.

    (C) tenancy in common.

    (D) joint tenancy.

33. You want to build your house ten feet closer to the road than the zoning ordinance permits. You will likely try to get

    (A) a zoning ordinance change.

    (B) a variance.

    (C) a deed restriction amendment.

    (D) an infrastructure change.

34. You own a factory that has been in your family for 100 years. Houses have sprung up all around it, and the zoning is now residential. How would your factory most likely be classified?

    (A) Temporary use

    (B) Transitional use

    (C) Interim use

    (D) Nonconforming use

35. The drawing showing an entire subdivision and the lots it is being divided into is most properly called

    (A) a survey map.

    (B) a plat map.

    (C) a filed map.

    (D) a metes and bounds map.

36. A mortgage is most accurately described as what type of lien?

    (A) Involuntary and general

    (B) Voluntary and general

    (C) Voluntary and specific

    (D) Involuntary and specific

37. A restriction in the deed says you cannot run a business out of your home. The zoning ordinance says you can. Which of the following is true?

    (A) You cannot run a business out of your home.

    (B) You can run a business out of your home.

    (C) You can run a business out of your home if you get the town to give you a special permit.

    (D) The deed restriction is invalid because it is against the public interest.

38. The loss of a right to enforce a deed restriction is called

    (A) prescriptive rights.

    (B) adverse possession.

    (C) escheat.

    (D) laches.

39. The assignment of costs between the buyer and the seller at the closing is called

    (A) finishing fees.

    (B) proration.

    (C) closing accounting.

    (D) real estate settlement and procedures.

40. How many acres does a section contain?

    (A) 640

    (B) 320

    (C) 160

    (D) 40

*Go on to next page*

41. The deed that provides warranties only for the duration of the grantor's ownership is called a

    (A) general warranty deed.

    (B) special warranty deed.

    (C) quitclaim deed.

    (D) grantor's deed.

42. If the seller paid taxes in advance for the whole year and he sells the house on July 1, which of the following is true?

    (A) The grantor gets a credit, and the grantee gets a debit.

    (B) The grantor gets a debit, and the grantee gets a credit.

    (C) The grantor and grantee both get credits.

    (D) The grantor and grantee both get debits.

43. A deed often used to clear up a cloud on a title is

    (A) a trust deed.

    (B) a referee's deed.

    (C) a special warranty deed.

    (D) a quitclaim deed.

44. The act of recording a deed provides or accomplishes

    (A) actual notice of ownership.

    (B) constructive notice of ownership.

    (C) proof of ownership.

    (D) transfer of ownership.

45. Which of the following is not a form of voluntary alienation?

    (A) Gift

    (B) Sale

    (C) Dedication

    (D) Forfeiture

46. You have just lost a large portion of the hill you live on due to a sudden mudslide. You are the victim of

    (A) erosion.

    (B) avulsion.

    (C) escheat.

    (D) forfeiture.

47. A religious group was given property for use in building a church. Instead, they lease the property out to raise money for their missionary work. The group loses the property for violation of the deed condition through a process called

    (A) avulsion.

    (B) escheat.

    (C) foreclosure.

    (D) forfeiture.

48. The process by which multiple owners can accumulate the statutory time necessary to claim adverse possession or a prescriptive easement is called

    (A) accumulation.

    (B) accretion.

    (C) tacking.

    (D) notorious possession.

49. If you die intestate, the law distributes your assets according to the laws of

    (A) descent.

    (B) inheritance.

    (C) probate.

    (D) surrogacy.

50. The court that handles wills is called

    (A) inheritance court.

    (B) civil court.

    (C) surrogate's court.

    (D) devisee's court.

51. You sign an option agreement to purchase some land while a zoning change is being sought. Which of the following is true?

    (A) You must purchase the land.

    (B) You must purchase the land if the zoning change is granted.

    (C) The seller must sell you the land.

    (D) The seller must renegotiate with you if you want.

*Go on to next page*

52. A buyer wants to make sure everything is okay with the house he's buying. He most likely would

    (A) have every house he looks at inspected by a qualified home inspector.

    (B) sign an option on a house he likes so that he doesn't lose it while it is inspected.

    (C) put an inspection contingency clause in the sales contract.

    (D) rely on the homeowner's disclosure of the property's physical condition.

53. The parol evidence rule generally says that

    (A) written contracts take precedence over oral contracts.

    (B) oral contracts take precedence over written contracts.

    (C) written contracts can be modified by oral contracts.

    (D) real estate sales contracts may be oral or in writing.

54. Forcing a buyer to go through with a property purchase that he does not want to do is

    (A) a novation.

    (B) an assignment.

    (C) a suit for compensatory damages.

    (D) a suit for specific performance.

55. A contract for the sale of property is said to be

    (A) executed.

    (B) executory until the closing.

    (C) executory until the closing whereupon it is executed.

    (D) executed until closing whereupon it is executory.

56. Joe agrees to buy Sally's house. When Joe can't come up with the money, Tim agrees to take over the contract and buy Sally's house under the same terms. This is called

    (A) a mutual agreement.

    (B) a novation.

    (C) an assignment.

    (D) a delegation.

57. A landlord who is selling a building allows a tenant to stay until the building is sold. This is

    (A) an estate at sufferance.

    (B) an estate at will.

    (C) an estate for years.

    (D) a periodic estate.

58. A tenant's lease expires, and the landlord does not give the tenant a new lease but instead allows her to stay and collects rent from her every month. Which of the following is true?

    (A) An estate for years has become a periodic estate.

    (B) A periodic estate has become an estate for years.

    (C) A periodic estate has become an estate at will.

    (D) An estate for years has become an estate at sufferance.

59. The fact that a lease of longer than a year must be in writing is a typical provision of

    (A) RESPA.

    (B) UCC.

    (C) the statute of frauds.

    (D) the parol evidence rule.

60. Landlord *A* rents space to Tenant *B*. Tenant *B* agrees to rent the same space to Tenant *C*. This is most likely

    (A) an assignment.

    (B) a novation.

    (C) a sublease.

    (D) a net lease.

61. A tenant rents an apartment from a landlord. The tenant pays rent and the landlord pays all the expenses. This is

    (A) a net lease.

    (B) a proprietary lease.

    (C) a triple net lease.

    (D) a gross lease.

*Go on to next page*

62. A feature unique to a ground lease is that

    (A) the tenant pays all expenses.

    (B) the tenant pays no expenses.

    (C) the term may be unusually long.

    (D) the tenant pays rent based on the revenues the property generates.

63. What phase of environmental assessment creates a management plan for the hazardous waste area?

    (A) 1

    (B) 2

    (C) 3

    (D) 4

64. Various allergic and respiratory symptoms that develop in an office building and then persist even after leaving the building may be

    (A) BRI.

    (B) SBS.

    (C) OSHA.

    (D) CERCLA.

65. Homes built before what year require lead paint disclosures?

    (A) 1978

    (B) 1979

    (C) 1980

    (D) 1981

66. A colorless, odorless gas that may cause cancer is

    (A) asbestos.

    (B) electromagnetic fields.

    (C) radon.

    (D) BRI.

67. Typically, individual on-site sanitary waste disposal systems are sized by the number of

    (A) square feet.

    (B) bedrooms.

    (C) bathrooms.

    (D) people.

68. The test done to determine the soil's capability to absorb leachate from a septic system is called

    (A) a site test.

    (B) an absorption analysis.

    (C) a percolation test.

    (D) a leach field analysis.

69. Investment value is

    (A) the same as market value.

    (B) the same as value in use.

    (C) the value to a typical investor.

    (D) the value to an individual investor.

70. The value usually associated with real estate taxes is

    (A) market value.

    (B) appraised value.

    (C) assessed value.

    (D) tax value.

71. A transaction in which a father sells property to his son would not be used in an appraisal because

    (A) it is not an arm's length transaction.

    (B) it is an invalid transaction.

    (C) it is a value in use transaction.

    (D) such a sale can use only the cost approach.

72. A comparable sale has four bedrooms compared to the subject's three bedrooms. The fourth bedroom is worth $30,000. What do you do with that number?

    (A) Add it to the subject's value.

    (B) Subtract it from the subject's value.

    (C) Add it to the comparable's sale price.

    (D) Subtract it from the comparable's sale price.

*Go on to next page*

73. The method of estimating replacement or reproduction cost that requires you to know the original cost of construction of the building is

    (A) the square foot method.

    (B) the quantity survey method.

    (C) the unit in place method.

    (D) the index method.

74. The total number of years a building is considered to contribute to the value of the property is a good definition of

    (A) chronological age.

    (B) effective age.

    (C) economic life.

    (D) remaining economic life.

75. A number that relates net operating income to value is

    (A) the gross rent multiplier.

    (B) the capitalization rate.

    (C) the depreciated cost factor.

    (D) the effective gross income factor.

76. Which of the following does not fit in a group?

    (A) Consumer Credit Protection Act

    (B) Truth in Lending Act

    (C) Regulation Z

    (D) Equal Credit Opportunity Act

77. A person buys a furnished house and wants to finance the purchase of both the house and the furniture through a mortgage loan. She tries to get

    (A) a blanket mortgage.

    (B) a purchase money mortgage.

    (C) a temporary loan.

    (D) a package mortgage.

78. Which of the following is not a typical obligation of the mortgagor?

    (A) Maintain the property.

    (B) Keep a hazard insurance policy in force.

    (C) Get permission for alterations.

    (D) Advise the mortgagee of a change in the escrow account balance.

79. Which one of the following does not affect the interest rate adjustment in an adjustable-rate mortgage loan?

    (A) Index

    (B) Equity

    (C) Margin

    (D) Cap

80. In a fixed-rate amortized loan, which one of the following does not vary from month to month?

    (A) Monthly payment

    (B) Interest paid

    (C) Principal paid

    (D) Remaining principal owed

81. The discount rate is

    (A) the amount of points you pay to reduce your interest rate.

    (B) the amount of interest federal reserve banks charge each other for loans.

    (C) the amount of interest paid on treasury bonds.

    (D) the amount of money as a percent of total deposits that banks must keep in cash.

82. A property is foreclosed and sold for non-payment of the mortgage loan. The sale does not cover the remaining balance of the mortgage loan. The bank goes to court to seek

    (A) judicial foreclosure.

    (B) statutory redemption.

    (C) equitable redemption.

    (D) deficiency judgment.

83. The term most closely associated with real estate taxes is

    (A) ad valorem.

    (B) appraised value.

    (C) market value.

    (D) cost approach.

*Go on to next page*

84. The assessment ratio is used to

    (A) determine the tax rate.

    (B) convert market value to value in use.

    (C) convert market value to assessed value.

    (D) determine property tax exemptions.

85. Someone protesting his assessment has to prove that

    (A) his taxes are too high.

    (B) his taxes are higher than those of similar properties.

    (C) his assessment is too high.

    (D) his assessment is unequal to those of similar properties.

86. Capital gains is calculated using

    (A) the depreciated basis.

    (B) the original price of the property.

    (C) the adjusted basis.

    (D) the capital gains basis.

87. A reason people invest in real estate is because real estate is

    (A) low risk.

    (B) highly liquid.

    (C) easy to manage.

    (D) highly leveraged.

88. Real estate investors expect to make money all the following ways except through

    (A) tax benefits.

    (B) staying liquid.

    (C) capital appreciation.

    (D) positive cash flow.

89. When calculating the adjusted basis for capital gains purposes, depreciation is

    (A) subtracted from the total cost of the property.

    (B) subtracted from the value of the building only.

    (C) added to the adjusted basis.

    (D) subtracted from taxes due.

90. In analyzing a possible real estate investment, potential gross income minus vacancy and collection loss minus operating expenses equals

    (A) effective gross income.

    (B) net operating income.

    (C) debt service.

    (D) cash flow.

91. If properties are not equal in value in an exchange, one person will have to pay the other

    (A) capital gains.

    (B) loot.

    (C) boot.

    (D) adjusted basis value.

92. A property was sold for $260,000, which was 130 percent of what the owner paid for it. What had the owner paid for the property?

    (A) $100,000

    (B) $160,000

    (C) $200,000

    (D) $230,000

93. A building generates gross rent of $30,000 and just sold for $360,000. What is the gross rent multiplier?

    (A) 12 percent

    (B) 8 percent

    (C) 10

    (D) 12

94. A building has a net operating income of $45,000. Buildings like this are appraised using a capitalization rate of 11 percent. What is the estimated value of the building?

    (A) $409,000

    (B) $450,000

    (C) $495,000

    (D) $540,000

*Go on to next page*

95. How many cubic feet are in a warehouse that measures 80 feet by 50 feet by 18 feet high?

   (A) 72,000

   (B) 4,000

   (C) 2,340

   (D) 145

96. Seller Sally pays $1,200 in taxes in advance for the year on January 1. She sells her house to Buyer Brian and closes on June 1. Who owes what to whom?

   (A) Seller owes the buyer $700.

   (B) Buyer owes the seller $700.

   (C) Seller owes the buyer $500.

   (D) Buyer owes the seller $500.

97. If the tax rate is $30 per $1,000, what are the taxes on property assessed at $80,000?

   (A) $240

   (B) $2,400

   (C) $800

   (D) $300

98. The factor for a 25-year loan at 6 percent interest is $6.85. What is the monthly payment on a mortgage loan of $175,000?

   (A) $1,199

   (B) $875

   (C) $583

   (D) $618

99. What is the commission if a property sold for $250,000 and the commission rate is 5 percent?

   (A) $15,500

   (B) $12,500

   (C) $10,500

   (D) $7,500

100. What is the total interest you will pay on an 8 percent amortized 25-year mortgage loan of $200,000 if the monthly payments are $1,400?

   (A) $420,000

   (B) $300,000

   (C) $220,000

   (D) $200,000

# Chapter 22

# Answers and Explanations to Practice Exam Two

Y our performance on the second exam in Chapter 21 should tell the story of how well you've mastered the material and how ready you are for the state exam. Give yourself one point for each correct answer and note the blocks of questions by subject. You'll have two scores: an overall exam score and a score for each of the sections by subject. At this point, I'm assuming you took the practice exam in Chapter 19, reviewed the answers in Chapter 20, and studied your weakest areas. If you've done that and your score for this exam is below 80, take a close look at your weakest areas on this exam. If you got more than two or three questions wrong in any subject, go back and review the corresponding chapter. Spend some time reviewing the material in your weakest areas, but unless you got everything right in a particular subject, don't neglect the areas that you did well in. Remember: Every point counts. After you've finished reviewing all the material you need to continue on to the next two exams in Chapters 23 and 25. Take all the practice exams more than once. I bet you'll be amazed at how much your score improves.

Don't forget that no matter how well you did on this exam, the information here is general to most states. You still need to study the information specific to your state. Review the material marked with the State-Specific icon throughout this book as well as the list of state-specific subjects in Chapter 27. You also can get state-specific information from your prelicensing course's materials, textbook, and instructor.

1. (B) Chapter 3

   A property manager gets errors and omissions insurance for his own protection and the other three for a building. Reread the question in light of this explanation, and you'll see how the correct answer makes sense.

2. (D) Chapter 3

   The word "typically" is important. An owner usually looks at market rents of similar buildings and the vacancy rate of other buildings and his own to determine a proper rental rate.

3. (A) Chapter 3

   Broker Bob is responsible for everything that Salesperson Sally does. Her status as an employee or an independent contractor doesn't matter. And if (D) confused you, the point is that Bob should have known.

4. (D) Chapter 3

   Retaining, transferring, and avoiding risk are three ways to deal with risk. The fourth way to deal with risk (which isn't listed) is to control it.

5. (D) Chapter 3

   The antitrust law doesn't apply to cooperating brokers for a particular transaction. All real estate commissions are individually negotiated, so B and C don't exist.

6. (B) Chapter 3

   The question describes market allocation, or dividing up the market, and it's illegal.

7. (C) Chapter 4

The agent represents the client, who may be a buyer or a seller. The person not represented by the agent is the customer.

8. (A) Chapter 4

If the agreement is in writing, it's expressed. All of the other choices are agencies established by the actions of the parties rather than any specific agreement.

9. (C) Chapter 4

An open listing gives several brokers a chance to sell the property. Seller's and free-for-all listings are not types of listings. An exclusive right to sell a listing is an agreement with one broker who is paid whether the broker or the owner sells the property.

10. (C) Chapter 4

Be sure to check out whether net listings are illegal in your state. An open listing gives several brokers a chance to sell a property. Gross and buyer's listings are made up.

11. (A) Chapter 4

Your fiduciary duties include disclosure to your client of all important information, even if it's personal to the customer and you've been asked to keep it confidential. You don't owe your customer the duty of confidentiality.

12. (D) Chapter 4

The fiduciary principal of loyalty requires you to put the client's interest above all other, even your own. You don't owe loyalty to the customer; you owe only honest and fair dealing, reasonable care, and disclosure of material facts and latent defects.

13. (D) Chapter 5

There's no exception for race as per the Civil Rights Act of 1866.

14. (D) Chapter 5

Even if there's an exception to one of the antidiscrimination acts, discriminatory advertising, which includes any mention of religion, isn't permitted.

15. (A) Chapter 5

Gender is a protected class in housing discrimination.

16. (B) Chapter 5

Real estate agents may not participate in steering, even if the customer directs it. Steering is directing people to various neighborhoods on the basis of any protected class. Keep in mind that you can accommodate someone's request to see properties in a particular neighborhood or subdivision if he specifies it by geographic location.

17. (C) Chapter 5

Advising people on where they would be happy may not appear to be steering because you may not be doing it to discriminate, but the word "construed" indicates that it can appear to be steering.

18. (C) Chapter 5

The 1866 Civil Rights Act, which prohibited discrimination on the basis of race, allowed no exceptions. It was largely forgotten. The 1968 Federal Fair Housing Act, which also prohibited discrimination on the basis of race, among other things, permitted some exceptions. The *Jones vs. Mayer* decision confirmed that the 1866 law was still in effect and superseded the 1968 law, permitting NO exceptions for race.

19. (A) Chapter 5

Housing may be restricted to people 62 years of age and older or 55 years of age or older in cases where at least one occupant per unit is 55 and at least 80 percent of the units are occupied by people 55 or older.

20. (A) Chapter 6

Personal property is tangible, moveable, and not permanently attached to real estate. The lumber can become a fixture (and therefore, real estate) if the deck is built. A trade fixture is something used in conjunction with a business.

21. (A) Chapter 6

The words "most properly" signal that the exam writers are looking for a precise legal answer (if possible), so the best answer is leasehold.

22. (D) Chapter 6

You may have been tempted to answer fee simple condition subsequent, which allows the right of reentry (the grantor's right to go to court to reclaim the property). In fee simple determinable, the title reverts back to the grantor if a certain condition isn't met.

23. (B) Chapter 6

In an ordinary life estate, the length of time of the estate interest is the lifetime of the person receiving the life estate. The length of a life estate pur autre vie is for the lifetime of a third party rather than the person actually receiving the life estate.

24. (A) Chapter 6

Littoral rights give owners of property next to large bodies of water ownership of land up to the average or mean high water mark. Riparian rights involve rivers and streams.

25. (C) Chapter 6

Jewelry cases may be considered personal property because they're usually removable by the owner, but the best answer is trade fixtures, which are used in association with a business use of property.

26. (A) Chapter 6

A fixture becomes real estate when it is attached and is always assumed to go with the property when sold. Personal property is normally sold with a bill of sale.

27. (C) Chapter 7

Both PUDs and condominiums generally have homeowners associations and monthly common charges. Cooperative owners own shares in a corporation.

28. (D) Chapter 7

Look for key words in a question, and above all, read the question carefully and completely. Don't confuse how a property is owned with how it is managed. The key words are "each buy pieces of property" and "owned separately." This is a case of three individual owners. Sole ownership is tenancy in severalty. Joint tenancy, tenancy in common, and tenancy by the entirety all apply to ownership of one property by more than one person.

29. (B) Chapter 7

Cooperative ownership provides for ownership of shares in a corporation that owns the building. The proprietary lease allows occupancy of the unit.

30. (D) Chapter 7

Corporations are considered a single person, and ownership by a single person is tenancy in severalty. The other choices are all forms of ownership with other people.

31. (A) Chapter 7

Watch the negative in this question; three of the choices feature limited liability, and only one (a general partnership) doesn't.

This question is a good example of what to do if you have no clue. Two answers have the word "limited" in them, as does the question. I know you think the exam writers want to trick you, but your best bet is to eliminate those two answers. If you think about how most corporations work (many stockholders and a few people running the company), it may seem logical that liability would also be limited in that case as well. That leaves you with the correct answer of general partnership.

32. (C) Chapter 7

Tenancy in common has no right of survivorship, which means that a person's shares of property go to heirs upon the person's death, not to the other owners of the property. And watch out for especially tricky wrong answers. In this case, tenancy in severalty is not a form of co-ownership; it's ownership by one person.

33. (B) Chapter 8

You can try to get a change in the actual zoning ordinance itself, which you're unlikely to get because it involves only one property. You'll apply for a variance, which is a change in the zoning ordinance for one lot.

34. (D) Chapter 8

A nonconforming use is one that existed before the current zoning.

35. (B) Chapter 8

A plat map is the technical term for a map of lands that have been approved for subdivision. A discussion of a survey map, the filed map system (another name for the lot and block system), and the metes and bounds system can be found in Chapter 9.

36. (C) Chapter 8

No one can force you into a mortgage agreement, so it's voluntary. And a mortgage applies to only one property, so it's specific.

37. (A) Chapter 8

If a conflict arises between a deed restriction and public law, the stricter rule applies.

38. (D) Chapter 8

Laches is correct. Two wrong answers may have thrown you off. Someone may gain prescriptive rights over the property of another by continuous use. Adverse possession is similar to prescriptive rights, only it may involve actually obtaining ownership.

39. (B) Chapter 9

In the proration process, costs and payments are debited and credited between the buyer and the seller. If real estate settlement and procedures looks familiar, that's because the Real Estate Settlement and Procedures Act governs most closings.

40. (A) Chapter 9

Remember that a section is one mile long (5,280 feet) on each side. If you do the area math (5,280 feet × 5,280 feet), and then convert square feet into acres (by dividing by 43,560), you'll come out with 640 acres.

41. (B) Chapter 9

The general warranty deed provides warranties back to the beginning of time (basically). "General" is broader than "special," so you may remember that a special warranty deed provides warranties only for the ownership period of the grantor.

42. (A) Chapter 9

The grantor is the seller, and the grantee is the buyer. A credit means an amount is owed to you. A debit means that you owe an amount. The grantor paid for the whole year, and the grantee will live in the house for part of the year. Therefore, the grantee owes the grantor money for that part of the year.

43. (D) Chapter 9

A quitclaim deed provides no warranties and often is used to clear up title problems. Make sure you have a basic knowledge of the different types of deeds.

44. (B) Chapter 9

Constructive notice is essentially setting up a situation in which someone who's interested can get information. Recording the deed in the public records does that.

45. (D) Chapter 10

Voluntary alienation is giving up title to property of your own free will. Gifts, sales, and dedication are voluntary. Forfeiture is an involuntary loss of the title to a property because of a violation of condition in the deed.

46. (B) Chapter 10

Avulsion is the sudden loss of land through natural processes such as earthquakes. It's often grouped with erosion, which is the loss of land through a gradual natural process, so you may have answered (A).

47. (D) Chapter 10

The two you may confuse are forfeiture and foreclosure. Forfeiture is the loss of ownership of a property because of a violation of a deed condition. Foreclosure is the seizing of your property for nonpayment of a debt such as taxes or the mortgage loan.

 48. (C) Chapter 10

"Tacking time" may be a good way to remember this answer. None of the other answers have a *T*.

49. (A) Chapter 10

Exam writers expect you to know that "intestate" means without a will. The laws of descent govern the distribution of your assets after death. Some of the other answers may ring true; probate, which is the processing of a will, occurs in surrogate's court.

 50. (C) Chapter 10

Surrogate's court handles an estate on behalf of someone else, namely the deceased. (Think of surrogate mothers to help you remember this.)

51. (C) Chapter 11

A simple option agreement is a unilateral agreement, in which only one person is obligated to do what is promised. In this case, the seller has to sell the land to the buyer (option holder) if the buyer wants to purchase the land. The simple option agreement doesn't require the buyer to act. If the buyer refuses to buy at the terms originally stated in the option agreement, the seller is under no obligation to renegotiate the deal. Answer B would apply if this were a conditional contract instead of an option.

52. (C) Chapter 11

The buyer can choose to do any of the options listed, but he probably will add an inspection contingency clause to the sales contract. A contingency clause in a contract requires that something be completed before the closing can take place.

53. (A) Chapter 11

The parol evidence rule says that written contracts take precedence over oral contracts and that oral modification of written contracts may not be enforceable. All real estate sales contracts must be in writing.

54. (D) Chapter 11

You want the buyer to perform, that is, to do or act in the manner he agreed to and buy your house. Novation involves a whole new contract, assignment is the same contract with a different buyer, and a suit for compensatory damages is a suit for money.

55. (C) Chapter 11

I wanted to give you a taste of a bad question. Executory until the closing is technically correct, but executory until the closing whereupon it is executed is the better, more complete answer. A real estate sales contract is said to be executory until closing because all the terms have not yet been fulfilled. It is executed at closing because at that point, all the terms have been fulfilled. Look out for answers that are partially correct; the test writers want you to give the best, most complete answer possible.

56. (C) Chapter 11

There is mutual agreement for Tim to take over the contract, but it's an assignment of the existing contract. The tricky part is telling the difference between assignment and delegation. Assignment is when Party *B* takes over the obligations of Party *A* and Party *A* no longer has any liability. Delegation is when Party *A* asks Party *B* to fulfill the terms of Party *A*'s contract. Party *A* is still responsible.

57. (B) Chapter 12

In an estate at will, the tenant will stay as long as the landlord lets him. In an estate at sufferance, the landlord 'suffers' when the tenant stays, because the landlord wants him to leave. A year is a period of time, and an estate for years lasts for some definite period. And a periodic estate renews itself as each period expires.

58. (A) Chapter 12

An estate for years is the regular lease tenancy with a beginning and ending date. A periodic estate is (in this case) a month-to-month lease that automatically renews itself from period to period and in which the landlord accepts the rent.

59. (C) Chapter 12

The statute of frauds (adopted in some form in every state) usually requires that all real estate contracts, including leases of more than a year, be in writing.

60. (C) Chapter 12

In a sublease, the original tenant remains responsible for the lease provisions but executes a lease between herself and the new tenant. An assignment is similar, but it's in fact taking over the original tenant's lease as is, with the new tenant liable.

61. (D) Chapter 12

A gross lease is the one described in the question. In a net lease, the tenant pays some part of the building's expenses. In a triple net lease, the tenant pays all of the building's expenses. A cooperative apartment owner has a proprietary lease.

62. (C) Chapter 12

Because ground leases often involve someone leasing vacant land to build a building, they tend to be for unusually long terms, 50 to 100 years not being unusual.

63. (D) Chapter 13

The phases of environmental assessment are 1) a review of records and a physical inspection of the property; 2) testing; 3) cleaning up the contamination; and 4) managing the contamination.

64. (A) Chapter 13

The symptoms of building related illness persist even after you leave a building, and the symptoms of sick building syndrome are present only when you're in a building. The Occupational Safety and Health Administration can make employers sick when it finds safety violations in the workplace, and the Comprehensive Environmental Response, Compensation, and Liability Act is designed to prevent everyone from getting sick by cleaning up contaminated sites.

65. (A) Chapter 13

Sorry, gang; this is something you're just going to have to memorize. The federal government requires lead paint disclosure for houses built before 1978.

66. (C) Chapter 13

Radon is gas formed from radioactive rocks usually beneath a house. It comes up through basements and can be alleviated by ventilation.

67. (B) Chapter 13

The problem with this question is that answers like bathrooms and square footage make sense. Just remember that you can have many bathrooms in a very large house and still have only a few people. The number of bedrooms, however, often determines a choice in buying a house for a family. By the way, the specific onsite sanitary waste disposal system in the question is usually called a septic system.

68. (C) Chapter 13

An absorption analysis may sound right, but an absorption analysis actually looks at how fast space, houses, or apartments will be absorbed by the market. "Site test" is too vague. A leach field analysis may look right, but remember that you're testing the soil. The leach field, which is part of the septic system, isn't there yet.

69. (D) Chapter 14

Investment value can be the same as market value by coincidence. A typical investor will pay market value for a building. A specific investor will look at investment value for a particular use.

70. (C) Chapter 14

There's technically no such thing as tax value. Market value may be used in tax work, but real estate taxes are based on assessed value; it's the best answer. Appraised value is an estimate of value and is usually but not exclusively associated with market value.

71. (A) Chapter 14

If this question was tricky for you, remember that all appraisals depend on the use of market value transactions, which presume an arm's length transaction. An arm's length transaction technically is one in which no relationship exists between the parties. (The transaction is valid because no law forbids a father from selling his property to his son, or anyone else for that matter; the transfer of ownership took place.)

72. (D) Chapter 14

Remember, you never touch the subject in the sales comparison approach. Instead you make adjustments to the comparable. If the comparable is better than the subject, you subtract; if it's worse than the subject, you add.

73. (D) Chapter 14

The three incorrect answers all are methods for estimating reproduction or replacement cost that involve either calculating building costs per square foot or pricing out the various construction components.

74. (C) Chapter 14

The economic life of a building reflects the number of years it contributes to the value of the land. Chronological age is the actual age of the building. The effective age is the current apparent age of the building taking into account the level of maintenance and upgrades the building has had. Remaining economic life is the number of years left in which the building will contribute to the value of the land.

75. (B) Chapter 14

You divide the net operating income by the capitalization rate to get value.

76. (D) Chapter 15

The first three answers are essentially interchangeable names for the same act, which controls advertising and the provision of information with respect to loans. The Equal Credit Opportunity Act prohibits discrimination in granting credit.

77. (D) Chapter 15

A package mortgage loan covers real and personal property. You need to be able to identify all the types of mortgage loans covered in Chapter 15.

78. (D) Chapter 15

This question requires you to know who the mortgagor (borrower) and mortgagee (lender) are. The first three answers relate to the borrower's duties. The mortgagee does the advising about the escrow account balance; the borrower contributes money to the escrow account only according to the lender's accounting of what it needs.

79. (B) Chapter 15

Equity is the difference between the value of the property and all the debts owed on the property. It bears no relationship to adjustable-rate mortgages.

80. (A) Chapter 15

In an amortized loan, the monthly payment remains the same while the portion of the principal you pay goes up, the amount of interest goes down, and you pay off more and more of the overall principal.

81. (B) Chapter 15

The two answers to watch out for are discount points (A) and the discount rate (B). Discount points are prepaid interest that you pay at the beginning of a loan to reduce the interest rate that you pay.

82. (D) Chapter 15

A deficiency judgment makes a borrower personally obligated to pay the balance of a debt. Judicial foreclosure is wrong here because foreclosure has already happened. Statutory and equitable redemption are rights of the person whose property was foreclosed to pay off the debt and get the property back.

83. (A) Chapter 16

Appraised value and market value can be used to figure out assessed value for tax purposes. However, the term "ad valorem," which means "based on the value," relates directly to real estate taxes because taxes are based on the value of the property. The cost approach is an appraisal technique for estimating value.

84. (C) Chapter 16

Multiply a property's market value by the assessment ratio to get the assessed value.

85. (D) Chapter 16

Note the word "assessment" in the question. This should help you eliminate (A) and (B), which are about taxes, not assessments. Although you may think your assessment is too high, remember that assessments are about being equal among similar properties.

86. (C) Chapter 17

Some of these answers *almost* make sense. For example, the adjusted basis is calculated using depreciation and the original value of the property, so you may have thought (A) or (B) was correct. But the adjusted basis is the best answer because it's the last number you use in figuring capital gains. (I can't stress it enough — watch out for wrong answers that may be partially correct.) I made up the capital gains basis.

87. (D) Chapter 17

Believe it or not, real estate isn't considered a low-risk investment unless it can be held for an unknown length of time. It also isn't considered liquid, which means you can't get your money out of it quickly. Those midnight phone calls about the broken furnace don't make real estate easy to manage. Generally you can borrow money easily to buy property. And that's what leverage is.

88. (B) Chapter 17

Real estate isn't considered a liquid investment; you can't get your money out of it quickly.

89. (A) Chapter 17

Depreciation is subtracted from the total cost of the property (for instance, the purchase price plus capital improvements) to get the adjusted basis. Remember that depreciation is calculated only against the value of the building; buildings depreciate, but land doesn't.

90. (B) Chapter 17

Here's the whole breakdown of the pro forma (analysis of an investment):

Potential gross income – vacancy and collection loss = effective gross income. (Some analysts add what's called other income right after vacancy and collection loss is subtracted to arrive at effective gross income. Other income is, for example, leased space on the roof for a radio antenna.)

Effective gross income – operating expenses = net operating income

Net operating income – debt service = before-tax cash flow

91. (C) Chapter 17

I know, it may be loot, but that's still not the right answer — boot is. And watch out: Don't be thrown off by capital gains. A capital gains tax is deferred in a real estate exchange, but one person doesn't pay that tax to the other.

92. (C) Chapter 18

The question says 130 percent of what he paid for the property, not 130 percent *more than* what he paid for it. State the problem this way: $260,000 is 130 percent of some number. When you can state a problem like that, you can divide the number you have by the percentage you're given and get the number you're looking for. And don't forget: You can convert any percentage into a decimal number you can work with by dividing the percentage by 100 or moving the decimal point two places to the left.

130 percent ÷ 100 = 1.30

$260,000 ÷ 1.30 = $200,000

93. (D) Chapter 18

A multiplier always is just a number. A rate is a percentage, so you know 12 percent and 8 percent are wrong. The formula for finding the gross rent multiplier follows:

Price ÷ gross rent = gross rent multiplier

$360,000 ÷ $30,000 = 12

94. (A) Chapter 18

Net operating income ÷ capitalization rate = value

$45,000 ÷ 0.11 = $409,090 (Answers like this are usually rounded, hence the given answer of $409,000.)

95. (A) Chapter 18

    Length × width × height = volume

    80 feet × 50 feet × 18 feet = 72,000 cubic feet

96. (B) Chapter 18

    A credit is an amount owed to you, and a debit is an amount you owe. Seller Sally paid taxes for the whole year, but she lives in the house for only five months. Buyer Brian lives in the house seven months and paid nothing. Brian owes something to Sally.

    $1,200 of taxes ÷ 12 months = $100 per month

    The seller is in the house 5 months, and the buyer is in the house for 7 months. So, 7 × $100 = $700.

97. (B) Chapter 18

    Assessed value × tax rate = taxes owed

    $80,000 × ($30 ÷ $1,000) = taxes owed

    $30 ÷ $1,000 = 0.03 tax rate

    $80,000 (assessed value) × 0.03 (tax rate) = $2,400 taxes owed

    You also can do the following:

    $80,000 ÷ $1,000 = $80

    $80 × $30 = $2,400

98. (A) Chapter 18

    Amount of mortgage ÷ $1,000 = units of $1,000

    Units of $1,000 × payment factor = monthly payment

    $175,000 ÷ 1,000 = 175

    175 × $6.85 = $1,198.75 (rounded off to $1,199)

    The payment factor includes the interest rate (6 percent) and the loan term (25 years), so this information actually isn't needed for your calculation. And no, the exam writers don't expect you to be able to calculate the factor.

99. (B) Chapter 18

    The formula for calculating a commission, which I'm sure you'll grow to love, follows:

    Sales price × commission rate = commission earned

    $250,000 × 0.05 (5 percent) = $12,500

100. (C) Chapter 18

    Each payment in an amortized mortgage loan contains principal and interest, and at the end of the loan, you've paid a lot of interest and the original amount of the mortgage loan (principal). The following formula will handle a typical problem like this.

    Monthly payment (principal and interest) × 12 months × term of loan in years = total payments of principal and interest

    Total payments of principal and interest − original loan amount (principal) = interest

    $1,400 × 12 months × 25 years = $420,000 in total payments

    $420,000 − $200,000 (original loan amount) = $220,000 interest

# Chapter 23

# Practice Exam Three

⋅ ⋅ ⋅ ⋅ ⋅ ⋅ ⋅ ⋅ ⋅ ⋅ ⋅ ⋅ ⋅ ⋅ ⋅ ⋅ ⋅ ⋅ ⋅ ⋅ ⋅ ⋅ ⋅ ⋅ ⋅ ⋅ ⋅ ⋅ ⋅ ⋅ ⋅ ⋅ ⋅ ⋅ ⋅ ⋅ ⋅ ⋅ ⋅ ⋅ ⋅ ⋅ ⋅ ⋅ ⋅ ⋅ ⋅ ⋅ ⋅ ⋅ ⋅ ⋅ ⋅ ⋅ ⋅ ⋅ ⋅ ⋅ ⋅ ⋅ ⋅ ⋅ ⋅

*Y*ou've completed two exams, but you can't get too much practice. So here is another exam with the answers in the following chapter. This exam offers you some new questions as well as some old questions asked in a different way. Don't forget to use a separate sheet of paper for your answers so you can do the exams again. As before the questions are grouped by chapter so you can easily analyze your weak areas which by now I'm sure are getting fewer.

Don't get over confident. Read the questions and answers carefully. By the time you're done with all four practice exams, know you are ready for the state test.

1. Maximizing income and maintaining property value are the general goals of what aspect of the real estate business?

   (A) Appraising

   (B) Brokerage and sales

   (C) Property management

   (D) Property inspection

2. When managing risk, transferring it usually means

   (A) making the property manager responsible.

   (B) making the owner responsible.

   (C) complying with all local laws so that the municipality is responsible.

   (D) purchasing insurance.

3. What type of insurance would usually pay a financial claim for injury by a person who falls on the icy sidewalk in front of a building?

   (A) Liability

   (B) Errors and omissions

   (C) Casualty

   (D) Fire and hazard

4. Although a property management agreement can be for any length of time, the generally recommended minimum is

   (A) six months.

   (B) one year.

   (C) two years.

   (D) no minimum.

5. An agent who represents someone in a group of activities such as a property manager is considered what type of agent?

   (A) Special

   (B) General

   (C) Universal

   (D) Individual

6. In general, which of the following is not an agent's duty to a customer?

   (A) Confidentiality

   (B) Honest and fair dealing

   (C) Disclosure of material facts

   (D) Reasonable care

7. Which of the following is true?

   (A) A latent defect is always a material defect.

   (B) A latent defect is never a material defect.

   (C) A latent defect always affects a buyer's decision.

   (D) A material defect may affect the buyer's decision.

8. Seller Sam agrees to allow Broker Betty to keep anything she makes above the $250,000 Sam wants for his house. This is an example of

   (A) an open price listing.

   (B) a violation of accounting.

   (C) a net listing.

   (D) an auction listing.

9. A seller can be

   (A) a principal only.

   (B) a principal but not a client.

   (C) a principal, a client, but not a customer.

   (D) a principal, a client, and a customer.

10. A buyer wants to be represented by only one broker and understands that the broker will spend time and money working for him. He agrees that it is only fair that the broker be compensated even if he, the buyer, finds a house on his own. The buyer signs

    (A) an open buyer agency agreement.

    (B) a buyer agent guaranteed compensation agreement.

    (C) exclusive agency buyer agency agreement.

    (D) exclusive buyer agency agreement.

11. Disclosure as part of an agent's fiduciary duties mean

    (A) full disclosure of all facts to buyer and seller equally.

    (B) disclosure of latent defects to the seller only.

    (C) disclosure of all material facts to the client.

    (D) disclosure of all pertinent information to the client.

*Go on to next page*

12. A seller's agent earns her commission when

    (A) she is the procuring cause of the transaction.

    (B) produces a ready, willing, and able buyer.

    (C) there is a meeting of the minds.

    (D) all of the above.

13. There are no exceptions to the

    (A) 1866 Civil Rights Act.

    (B) 1968 Fair Housing Act.

    (C) Community Development Act of 1974.

    (D) Fair Housing Amendments Act of 1988.

14. A landlord requires a higher security deposit from families with children than those without children. According to Federal Law this is

    (A) not discriminatory.

    (B) not discriminatory if there are more than two children.

    (C) discriminatory in all cases.

    (D) not discriminatory if the owner only rents one single-family house.

15. "There are a lot of children in this neighborhood" said by a real estate agent to a buyer

    (A) is acceptable if there are a lot of children in the neighborhood.

    (B) is acceptable steering since people want to know about the demographics in a neighborhood.

    (C) is considered steering and is therefore illegal.

    (D) is not steering because it's stating a fact.

16. A real estate agent

    (A) is subject to all fair housing laws with no exceptions.

    (B) can assist clients with legal exceptions to fair housing laws.

    (C) cannot use federal acceptations but can use local state exceptions.

    (D) can only use the exception to the 1866 Civil Rights Act.

17. "This apartment/house is not available"

    (A) is permitted as a polite way to avoid renting to an African American couple.

    (B) is a good way to avoid discriminatory advertising as an exception to fair housing law to the owner of four or more single-family houses.

    (C) is permitted if the apartment has already been rented.

    (D) is never permitted because a reason for not renting always has to be provided.

18. The fact that you could own an office building but rent it to someone else is explained

    (A) by the theory of prior possession.

    (B) by the bundle of rights theory.

    (C) by the theory of eminent domain.

    (D) by the unlimited estates theory.

19. When using the term *estate* with respect to property rights, it

    (A) refers only to ownership of a large piece of property.

    (B) refers only to ownership only through inheritance.

    (C) refers only to purchased property.

    (D) does not necessarily refer to ownership.

20. Which of the following is not considered an estate with limitations?

    (A) Fee simple absolute

    (B) Fee simple defeasible

    (C) Fee simple qualified

    (D) Fee simple determinable

21. The right of a husband to a portion of his wife's property is called

    (A) community property or curtesy.

    (B) community property or dower.

    (C) dower or curtesy.

    (D) community property and homestead.

22. The best definition of tenancy is

    (A) being a residential apartment renter.

    (B) being a property owner.

    (C) being a commercial property renter.

    (D) having an interest in real estate.

23. Property inherited by one spouse under community property law

    (A) is considered community property.

    (B) is considered separate property.

    (C) may only be sold by joint action of both spouses.

    (D) becomes community property after five years.

24. Which of the following is not a unity required in joint tenancy?

    (A) Unity of trust

    (B) Unity of time

    (C) Unity of title

    (D) Unity of possession

25. In a condominium you generally own your unit

    (A) as a tenant in common.

    (B) as a tenant in severalty.

    (C) as a joint tenant.

    (D) under a proprietary lease.

26. A subdivision is zoned for one acre lots. The town agrees to allow the developer to build all the houses on quarter-acre lots and leave the remaining land in open space. The developer is likely being subject to

    (A) density zoning.

    (B) limited zoning.

    (C) a special permit.

    (D) cluster zoning.

27. When a property owner sues the government because an action it's taken reduced the owner's property value, she will claim what as a basis for her lawsuit?

    (A) Escheat

    (B) Eminent domain

    (C) Due process

    (D) Inverse condemnation

28. An owner fails to exercise his right of legal actions against his neighbor for violating a deed restriction and then loses that right because he failed to exercise it in a timely fashion has fallen victim to the doctrine of

    (A) prior authority.

    (B) laches.

    (C) escheat.

    (D) adverse possession.

29. Property owner A has a driveway easement across property owner B's property. Property owner A eventually buys property owner B's property. The easement

    (A) continues despite the joining of the two properties.

    (B) is considered abandoned.

    (C) continues by prescription.

    (D) disappears by merger.

30. A shared driveway is usually a case of

    (A) easement in gross.

    (B) easement appurtenant.

    (C) easement by prescription.

    (D) easement by necessity.

31. A judgment lien is

    (A) specific and voluntary.

    (B) specific and involuntary.

    (C) general and voluntary.

    (D) general and involuntary.

32. The dominant tenement in an easement situation

    (A) is the one who benefits from the easement.

    (B) is the one who gives the easement.

    (C) can be either part.

    (D) does not exist in an easement in gross.

33. Demographics is the study of

    (A) job growth.

    (B) topography.

    (C) earthquake activity.

    (D) population characteristics.

*Go on to next page*

34. Title to property is actually conveyed by
    (A) deed.
    (B) contract.
    (C) ttle insurance.
    (D) acknowledgement.

35. The words "to have and to hold" are typical of
    (A) the words in the sales contract.
    (B) the words in the habendum clause of the deed.
    (C) the words in the acknowledgement.
    (D) the consideration clause.

36. The words "for love and affection" in the deed usually mean
    (A) the property is part of an estate.
    (B) the property is jointly owned by a husband and wife.
    (C) the property is a gift.
    (D) the property is to be retained in a life estate.

37. Person A conveys his property to Person B to hold as security for a loan made by Person C to Person A most likely executed what kind of deed?
    (A) Quitclaim
    (B) Bargain and sale with no covenants
    (C) General warranty
    (D) Deed in trust

38. A legal description of property is any description
    (A) that can locate the property for the U.S. postal service.
    (B) that can locate the property for tax purposes.
    (C) that can be used in a deed.
    (D) that can clearly identify the location of property in the community.

39. In the government survey system
    (A) a township has 36 sections.
    (B) a section has 36 townships.
    (C) a quadrangle has 36 sections.
    (D) a township has 36 quadrangles.

40. What do surveyors use to measure elevations?
    (A) Datums
    (B) Benchmarks
    (C) A and B
    (D) Neither A nor B

41. In the proration process a credit for an item can be owed
    (A) to the buyer only.
    (B) to the seller only.
    (C) to the buyer and seller.
    (D) to the buyer or seller.

42. RESPA is monitored by
    (A) the Department of Commerce.
    (B) the Department of Justice.
    (C) the local Department of State.
    (D) the Department of Housing and Urban Development.

43. The estate of a person who dies without a will is usually divided according state laws of
    (A) intestation.
    (B) testation.
    (C) probate.
    (D) descent.

44. An owner of property in common with others who wants to divide the property against the will of the other owners would file a suit to
    (A) divide the property.
    (B) partition the property.
    (C) dissolve the tenancy in common.
    (D) create a joint tenancy.

45. The sudden loss of land through natural forces is called
    (A) erosion.
    (B) declination.
    (C) accretion.
    (D) avulsion.

46. A contract formed by the actions of two parties is

    (A) express unilateral.

    (B) express bilateral.

    (C) implied unilateral.

    (D) implied bilateral.

47. An unenforceable contract where the parties choose to honor the agreement is said to be

    (A) valid in law.

    (B) unvoided.

    (C) enduring between the parties.

    (D) valid as between the parties.

48. A person two weeks under the legal age of consent signing a contract is likely to create a situation known as a

    (A) void contract.

    (B) unenforceable contract.

    (C) fraudulent contract.

    (D) voidable contract.

49. A real estate sales contract is usually

    (A) an express bilateral contract.

    (B) an express unilateral contract.

    (C) an implied bilateral contract.

    (D) an implied unilateral contract.

50. Person A makes an agreement to let his neighbor (Person B) buy Person A's house at a certain price if he wants to within the next six months. What kind of agreement have they reached?

    (A) Express bilateral

    (B) Express unilateral

    (C) Implied bilateral

    (D) Implied unilateral

51. What does the landlord own in a lease situation?

    (A) A leasehold interest

    (B) A leased fee interest

    (C) A reversionary interest

    (D) B and C

52. A month to month tenancy is an example of

    (A) a tenancy at will.

    (B) a periodic tenancy.

    (C) a tenancy at sufferance.

    (D) an estate for years.

53. Generally a lease longer than a year has to be in writing according to

    (A) the Statute of Frauds.

    (B) the Uniform Residential Landlord and Tenant Act.

    (C) the Uniform Commercial Code.

    (D) the State Real Estate Commission.

54. In which of the following might it be said that no actual tenancy exists?

    (A) Tenancy at will

    (B) Periodic estate

    (C) Estate for years

    (D) Tenancy at sufferance

55. The federal agency responsible for most environment rules and regulations is

    (A) HUD.

    (B) CERCLA.

    (C) HTMA.

    (D) EPA.

56. Innocent land owner status was established by

    (A) the Comprehensive Environmental Response, Compensation, and Liability Act.

    (B) the Superfund Amendment and Reauthorization Act.

    (C) the Environmental Assessment Act.

    (D) the Landowner Liability Release Act.

57. Development of a management plan for a contaminated site too large to remove would fall under which phase of environmental assessment?

    (A) 1

    (B) 2

    (C) 3

    (D) 4

*Go on to next page*

58. A colorless, odorless, hazardous gas originating from rocks under the earth would most likely describe

(A) carbon monoxide.

(B) radon.

(C) chlorofluorocarbons.

(D) electromagnetic fields.

59. The number of bedrooms most likely determines

(A) whether or not you can connect to the public sewer system.

(B) whether or not you can use well water.

(C) the size of your septic system.

(D) the amount of sanitary waste the house produces.

60. In an estate appraisal for tax purposes, what date is used as the appraisal or valuation date?

(A) Date the appraisal is ordered

(B) Date the person died

(C) Date set by probate court

(D) Any time within the calendar year of the death

61. All other things being equal, what characteristic of real estate makes location the most important value factor?

(A) The federal government's policy of encouraging home ownership

(B) Ready access to mortgage money in certain communities

(C) The dependence on the automobile

(D) The immobility (can't be moved) of real estate

62. A real estate broker who obtains special permission from the town to use part of his house as a real estate office may have his house appraised for

(A) value in use.

(B) market value.

(C) assessed value.

(D) all of the above.

63. A surplus of condominiums in a town may be the result of the principle of

(A) balance.

(B) conformity.

(C) competition.

(D) substitution.

64. A man wants to buy a warehouse and convert it into a movie theatre. What types of value is he most likely to want?

(A) Assessed and market

(B) Investment and assessed

(C) Market and value in use

(D) Investment and market

65. House A is worth $300,000 and is surrounded by $500,000 homes. In a neighborhood of homes similar to House A, it would be worth $250,000. This is an example of

(A) conformity.

(B) competition.

(C) progression.

(D) regression.

66. Curable deterioration

(A) can be fixed.

(B) is just a paper loss.

(C) costs more to fix than it's worth.

(D) costs less to fix than the value it adds to the property.

67. Which one of the following is not a method by which to estimate a property's value?

(A) Capitalize the net income

(B) Multiply the gross rent by a multiplier

(C) Compare the values of several similar properties

(D) Estimate the cost to replace the building

68. The formula for estimating a property's value by comparing similar properties and making adjustments is

    (A) comparable better add the adjustment to the comparable.

    (B) comparable worse subtract the adjustment from the comparable.

    (C) comparable better subtract the adjustment from the comparable.

    (D) comparable worse add the adjustment to the subject.

69. Who does what with respect to mortgages?

    (A) Mortgage broker lends money.

    (B) Mortgage banker arranges loans.

    (C) Real estate broker and mortgage broker arrange loans.

    (D) Mortgage banker lends money, mortgage broker arranges loans.

70. Why is the person lending the money called the mortgagee and not the mortgagor?

    (A) Because they receive the mortgage payments.

    (B) Because the mortgage industry language evolved that way.

    (C) Because the borrower gives the mortgage to the lender.

    (D) Not correct. The lender is called the mortgagor because he gives the mortgage to the borrower.

71. The clause that enables the lender to declare that the entire balance of the loan is due is called the

    (A) acceleration clause.

    (B) maintenance clause.

    (C) forfeiture clause.

    (D) lien clause.

72. Which of these does not insure mortgage loan?

    (A) The Veterans Administration

    (B) The Federal Housing Administration

    (C) Private insurers

    (D) The Government National Mortgage Association

73. The Certificate of Reasonable Value is a requirement of what type of loan?

    (A) VA

    (B) FHA

    (C) Credit union

    (D) Jumbo

74. The difference between a property's value and the debt on the property is a good definition of

    (A) the loan to value ratio.

    (B) equity.

    (C) investment value.

    (D) A and B, but not C.

75. What type of loan is expected to convert to a conventional mortgage in a relatively short time?

    (A) Construction loan

    (B) Home equity loan

    (C) Package loan

    (D) Reverse mortgage

76. An index is a feature of what type of mortgage loan?

    (A) Adjustable rate mortgage loan

    (B) Reverse mortgage loan

    (C) Package loan

    (D) Jumbo loan

77. In a 30-year amortized mortgage loan, the interest for the third year is calculated by multiplying the interest rate by

    (A) the original amount of the loan.

    (B) the original amount of the loan and dividing by 30.

    (C) the original amount of the loan and dividing by 27.

    (D) the unpaid balance of the loan.

*Go on to next page*

78. A feature of the growing equity mortgage is

    (A) that the interest rate starts low and steadily increases.

    (B) that the principal payments increase over time.

    (C) that the principal payments decrease over time.

    (D) that the interest rate decreases over time allowing more rapid payoff.

79. An interest-only loan is called

    (A) an adjustable rate loan.

    (B) a blanket loan.

    (C) a straight loan.

    (D) a reverse loan.

80. The formula for calculating a tax rate is

    (A) municipality budget / (divided by) total assessed valuation.

    (B) total assessed valuation / (divided by) municipality budget.

    (C) total assessed valuation × assessment ratio.

    (D) total assessed valuation × equalization rate x municipality budget.

81. If there are three towns in a county, each using different assessment ratios, what does the county need to do to make the assessments and the taxes fair to each taxpayer?

    (A) Reassess all the properties in the county.

    (B) Make the towns reassess all the properties in each town.

    (C) Equalize the assessed values using an equalization rate.

    (D) Nothing because assessments are up to each town.

82. If you multiply the market value by the assessment ratio you get

    (A) the tax rate.

    (B) the assessed value.

    (C) the equalization rate.

    (D) the total municipal budget.

83. Market value × tax rate = taxes due under what circumstances?

    (A) Always

    (B) Never

    (C) When the assessment ratio is 50 percent

    (D) When the assessment ratio is 100 percent

84. The assessment ratio can be calculated by

    (A) dividing the assessed value by the market value.

    (B) dividing the market value by the assessed value.

    (C) by multiplying the equalization rate by the market value.

    (D) by dividing the assessed value by the equalization rate.

85. Which of the following would not be considered a liquid investment?

    (A) Bank certificate of deposit

    (B) Stocks

    (C) Real estate

    (D) Savings accounts

86. A group of investors wanting to invest in real estate could legally form

    (A) a syndicate and a corporation.

    (B) a partnership and a corporation.

    (C) a syndicate but not a corporation.

    (D) a corporation but not a syndicate.

87. The use of borrowed money to invest in real estate is called

    (A) leverage.

    (B) syndication.

    (C) selling shares.

    (D) investment trust.

88. Joe buys an investment property and three years later sells it for enough profit to buy two buildings. Five years later he refinances one building and buys two more. His actions may be described as

    (A) leveraging.

    (B) pyramiding.

    (C) capitalizing.

    (D) depreciating.

89. A real estate investment that works like a stock market investment is probably

    (A) an equity trust.

    (B) a mortgage trust.

    (C) a combination trust.

    (D) all of the above.

90. Which is not one of the benefits of investing in real estate?

    (A) Tends to keep pace with inflation

    (B) Favorable tax treatment

    (C) Non-liquid, making it a stable investment

    (D) Annual returns on one's investment

91. A property is assessed at $225,000. What is the equalized value if the equalization rate is 2.35?

    (A) $528,750

    (B) $95,745

    (C) $957,447

    (D) $52,875

92. What is the principal balance of a $100,000, 30-year amortized mortgage loan at 6 percent interest after the first monthly payment of $600?

    (A) $99,400

    (B) $99,500

    (C) $99,700

    (D) $99,900

93. The taxes on a property are $3,575. The tax rate is $30 per $1,000. The assessment ratio is 70 percent. What is the market value of the property?

    (A) $107,250

    (B) $153,214

    (C) $162,765

    (D) $170, 238

94. If the net operating income of a commercial building is $156,000, and the capitalization rate is 12 percent, what is the value of the building?

    (A) $1,872,000

    (B) $1,300,000

    (C) $1,560,000

    (D) $15,600,000

95. A building has a potential gross income of $350,000, a vacancy and collection loss of 5 percent, and total expenses of $140,000. What is the effective gross income?

    (A) $192,500

    (B) $210,000

    (C) $217,000

    (D) $332,500

96. A comparable that sold for $280,000 has a fourth bedroom valued at $20,000 that is not present in the subject. You think the subject might be worth about $290,000. What is the indicated value of the subject?

    (A) $260,000

    (B) $270,000

    (C) $290,000

    (D) $300,000

*Go on to next page*

97. A house sells for $480,000 with a commission rate of 4 percent. The listing salesperson receives 40 percent of the listing side commission, which is 50 percent of the total commission. How much does the listing broker receive after paying the salesperson?

    (A) $3,840

    (B) $4,800

    (C) $5,760

    (D) $9,600

98. Taxes for the year of $3,600 are paid in arrears on January 1 for the previous year. The sale of the property closed on September 23. Use 12 months, 30 days per month, and the buyer owns the property on the day of closing — now prorate the taxes.

    (A) $2,620 debit to buyer and $2,620 credit to seller

    (B) $2,620 debit to seller and $2,620 credit to buyer

    (C) $3,600 credit to buyer and $3,600 debit to seller

    (D) $3,600 credit to buyer and $2,620 debit to seller

99. If effective gross income is $180,000, the vacancy and collection loss is 7 percent, and expenses are $73,000, what is the net operating income?

    (A) $167,400

    (B) $107,000

    (C) $99,510

    (B) $94,400

100. If a building sells for $1,200,000 and has a net operating income of $130,000, what is the capitalization rate?

    (A) 9.23 percent

    (B) 11 percent

    (C) 12 percent

    (D) 12.34 percent

# Chapter 24

# Answers and Explanations to Practice Exam Three

* * * * * * * * * * * * * * * * * * * * * * * * * * * * * * * * * * * * * * * * *

*1* assume you've already taken the first two practice exams, so by the time you're done reviewing your answers for this exam there should be a big smile on your face. Once again, review the answers carefully. I wrote the explanations of the correct answers in such a way as to give you a little more than the basic information, so study these answers as another way to learn and remember the material.

As you did with the last two exams, go through all the answers and give yourself one point for each one correct. After you've noted all your correct and incorrect answers go through the exam answers one more time and note how many wrong answers you got by chapter. Both your overall score and your chapter-by-chapter score should be getting higher at this point. But keep studying. You've put a lot of effort in so far, and the finish line is almost in sight.

1. (C) Chapter 3

   The key to this answer is that only the correct answer has any actual control over what happens to a piece of real estate. The three incorrect answers are all specific functions that an agent or other real estate professional may perform to provide a limited service that would have no ongoing impact to the property.

2. (D) Chapter 3

   There's a tendency when answering questions to look for the most complicated answer as the correct one. This question is an example of the simplest answer being correct. The idea of dealing with risk by transferring it is that no individual involved in the property has to assume the risk. One must always comply with municipal laws.

3. (A) Chapter 3

   This can be a tricky question because of the titles of some of the other insurances. You might think that words like *hazard* or *errors* would relate to the fact that you didn't clean the sidewalk, and that casualty might be correct because the person who fell was a casualty of your negligence. Just remember that liability insurance covers the owner for injury that someone sustains due to negligence.

4. (B) Chapter 3

   The generally recommended minimum is one year. This gives the manager time to recoup his initial investment in setting up systems to manage the building and provides sufficient time for the owner to adequately judge the performance of the manager.

5. (B) Chapter 4

   Review the other types of agents. There is no such thing as an individual agent unless you consider the fact that every agent is an individual.

6. (A) Chapter 4

   Not only do you not owe confidentiality to the customer, but your duty to your client requires that you reveal all information to your client that you may learn from your customer.

7. (D) Chapter 4

A latent defect is something not readily visible and may or may not affect a buyer's decision. A material defect is one that may affect a buyer's decision and, therefore, a reasonable buyer would want to know about and will most likely affect a buyer's decision. Latent defects may be material or not.

8. (C) Chapter 4

Answers A and D are made up. B does not apply as long as the client is kept fully informed of all financial dealing. Remember net listing may or may not be illegal in your state or if legal may be subject to specific requirements which you should learn about for the exam.

9. (D) Chapter 4

The terms *principal* and *client* mean the same thing. A seller can be the client of the broker he hires to represent him and the customer of the buyer's broker.

10. (D) Chapter 4

Answer B is made up, though descriptive of what happens in the case described. The open buyer agency agreement allows the buyer to work with multiple brokers and pay only the one, if any, who find him a house. The exclusive agency agreement, Answer C, is with one broker but compensation is earned only if the broker finds the buyer a house.

11. (D) Chapter 4

An admittedly tricky question that should be read through carefully and all answers considered. When you see *client* instead of *buyer* or *seller* in this kind of question, it's a good bet that *client* is the answer. Remember you owe fiduciary duty to the client and this question did not provide enough information to determine if the buyer or seller was the client. Answers C and D are both correct, but D is more correct because you should disclose any and all information to your client that might affect the transaction and allow the client to decide what is material or not.

12. (D) Chapter 4

Procuring cause and producing the buyer (answers B and C) describe the agent's role. The meeting of the minds describes the point at which all the sale conditions are agreed to and met.

13. (A) Chapter 5

The 1974 and 1988 Acts in effect amended the 1968 Act by expanding the protected classes but the 1968 exceptions remained in place. The 1866 Act is the only one with no exceptions.

14. (D) Chapter 5

This is generally always discriminatory. The exception is when an owner of three or fewer single-family houses offers them for rent.

15. (C ) Chapter 5

Any language directing people to or from a neighborhood based on a protected class is steering and it is illegal whether based on facts or not.

16. (A) Chapter 5

A real estate agent may not participate in any exceptions even if they are legal to an individual. There are no exceptions to the 1866 Act.

17. (C) Chapter 5

Answer A is incorrect in that there are never any exceptions with respect to race. The exception in Answer B applies to three or four single-family houses owned by one owner. Answer D is incorrect. Provided one is not discriminating or is partaking of an acceptable exception to the law, one need not provide a reason for not renting to someone.

18. (B) Chapter 6

    Answer A is made up but I made it sound like the prior appropriations theory related to water rights. Eminent domain has to do with government rights of taking. Answer D is also made up. Remember that the bundle of rights theory explains the ability of someone to separate rights like ownership and occupancy or possession.

19. (D) Chapter 6

    The term *estate* refers to the extent or type of interest someone has in a piece of land. It includes any interest including non-ownership interests like a lease or an easement.

20. (A) Chapter 6

    Answers B and C are the same thing. Answer D is a form of conditional estate.

21. (A) Chapter 6

    This is a tricky question because at least two of the answers — C and D — are partially correct. Community property deals with the rights of either spouse. Curtesy deals with the husband's rights specifically, so Answer A is the most correct answer.

22. (D) Chapter 7

    Technically all of the answers are correct but the first three answers are limited because they each deal with only one aspect of tenancy. The most inclusive and therefore best answer is D.

23. (B) Chapter 7

    Only property purchased during the marriage is considered community property and would require joint action to sell it.

24. (A) Chapter 7

    The missing one is unity of interest. I have no idea what unity of trust is but it sounded like a good false answer.

25. (B) Chapter 7

    Don't get confused here by answer A. Condo owners usually own the common areas as tenants in common but they own their individual units — or more accurately the air space their unit occupies — as sole tenants or tenants in coin severalty. The proprietary lease is associated with cooperative ownership.

26. (D) Chapter 8

    This is a classic description of the cluster zoning subdivision. The density zoning subdivision would have lots of varying sizes. Some town may have something called *limited zoning*, but it's generally not a common term associated with zoning.

27. (D) Chapter 8

    Inverse condemnation is essentially the owner claiming that the government has taken away her land value without due process or proper use of eminent domain.

28. (B) Chapter 8

    There is no such thing as prior authority. Escheat has to do with the government claim of ownership. Adverse possession actually conveys ownership of property that has been used against the owner's will.

29. (D) Chapter 8

    A and C are incorrect; the easement disappears because it's no longer needed. It could be considered abandoned, though that's not precisely what's happened because an easement could be abandoned if the properties were not joined.

30. (B) Chapter 8

A shared driveway could be created in a number of ways, but generally speaking (and the best answer because you don't have any other facts) the answer is B. Remember an easement appurtenant or appurtenant easement is one where the adjacent property benefits form the easement. In this case the property on the right half side of the property has an easement for use of the left side. The left side owner has an easement for the right side.

31. (D) Chapter 8

Keep in mind what a judgment line is. A judgment line is usually the result of a lawsuit someone has filed (and won) against you for money. This is certainly involuntary. And because it's about money, it's not about a specific piece of property like a mortgage.

32. (A) Chapter 8

There is always a dominant and servient party in any easement. The servient tenement (remember to serve) is the one giving the easement even if it was not given voluntarily.

33. (D) Chapter 8

Demographic studies are associated with creating master plans for the community. Things like age, salary, gender, and marital status are typically studied.

34. (A) Chapter 9

A contract is an agreement to transfer title to the property at some future date. Title insurance insures against any problems with the title after it's conveyed. The acknowledgement is witnessing the grantor's signature for filing purposes.

35 (B) Chapter 9

The sales contract would not contain these words. The consideration deals with what things of value are being exchanged for the property. The acknowledgment is a witnessing of the signature of the grantor.

36. (C) Chapter 9

These words are peculiar to the consideration clause in deed when a property is a gift since there has to be something of value mentioned even if it's not monetary. The words would not normally be found in property conveyed in an estate or owned by a married couple. It's possible that the property could be conveyed as a gift AND be required held in a life estate, but C is the best answer with the information given.

37. (D) Chapter 9

All of the incorrect answers are types of deeds which are distinguished by the warrantees they provide. The situation described would have the grantor use a deed in trust to accomplish creating security for the loan.

38. (C) Chapter 9

The term legal description has a specific meaning, which none of the other answers fit.

39. (A) Chapter 9

The correct order of division is quadrangle to townships to sections. A quadrangle has 16 townships; a township has 36 sections.

40. (C) Chapter 9

Datums are the primary points used for measuring elevations, but benchmarks — which are used primarily for ground surveys — are also used to help surveyors measure elevations.

41. (D) Chapter 9

   This is a tricky question, mostly because of the last two choices. You need to read this question and the answer choices carefully. It would be impossible for the buyer and the seller to receive credit for the same item, though a buyer and seller could receive a credit for different items for the same property.

42. (D) Chapter 10

   Just remember that RESPA — the Real Estate Settlement and Procedures Act — has to do with closing for homebuyers as in housing.

43. (D) Chapter 10

   The first two answers are made up and are derived from the words *testate* (with a will) and *intestate* (without a will). Probate occurs when there is a will. Your state may call these statutes of descent and distribution.

44. (B) Chapter 10

   This is a tough question unless you memorize the answer because all the answers seem logical except D which would not solve the problem. But you are going to be real estate agents and need to know proper terminology so a suit to partition the property is it.

45. (D) Chapter 10

   Erosion is gradual loss of land. I made up declination. Accretion is actually adding land through natural processes.

46. (D) Chapter 11

   A contract formed by the actions of the parties instead of a written or oral agreement (express) is considered implied. A contract formed by two parties implying promises made to each other is bi-lateral. Unilateral would be if only one party promised anything.

47. (D) Chapter 11

   I got very creative here with three answers that sound good but are made up.

48. (D) Chapter 11

   The most correct answer is voidable because in a very short time the person could choose to void the contract or go ahead with it. You could argue that the contract is void but because it can be validated in a few weeks, D is the better answer. The contract itself isn't fraudulent because there's nothing in the question that implies that the underage party was agreeing to something they had no intention of doing.

49. (A) Chapter 11

   Two parties agreeing in writing to do something is the definition of an express bilateral contact. Remember unilateral means only one party promises, and implied usually means that no agreement has ever been discussed or signed.

50. (B) Chapter 11

   The contract is express because they have both reached the agreement. The contract is unilateral since only one has to act (A) only if B wants buy the house, B is not required to act. This kind of agreement would go by the more common name — option.

51. (D) Chapter 12

   The leasehold is the interest the tenant has. Note that in the questions on leases I use both the terms tenancy and estate because I don't know which terms your particular exam will use. As noted in Chapter 12 the terms are interchangeable.

52. (B) Chapter 12

A tenancy or estate at will is where the landlord allows the tenancy to occupy the premises but there is no definite point at which the arrangement will expire. A tenancy or estate at sufferance is where a tenant remains in the premises after the lease has expired against the landlord's will. An estate for years has a definite beginning and ending date.

53. (A) Chapter 12

All states have adopted some form of the statute of frauds. The Uniform Residential Landlord and Tenant Act provides provisions for minimum requirements for a lease to be valid. The Uniform Commercial Code which all states have in some form governs personal property transactions. The real estate commission — your state may have a different name for it — generally handles license law issues rather than real estate transactions themselves.

54. (D) Chapter 12

In the case of tenancy at sufferance, in which the tenant remains against the landlord's will, the landlord doesn't collect the rent. In effect no tenancy, therefore, exists.

55. (D) Chapter 13

This is an easy question if you remember the meaning of all the acronyms, which you should. The Department of Housing and Urban Development; The Comprehensive Environmental Response, Compensation, and Liability Act; and the Hazardous Material Transportation Act are all important but not the correct answer.

56. (B) Chapter 13

Answers C and D are made up, but they sound good, don't they. Answer A was the original Superfund funding act, but innocent landowner immunity was not conveyed until SARA.

57. (D) Chapter 13

Phase 1 is examination of the site records; phase 2 is testing; phase 3 is remediation.

58. (B) Chapter 13

Carbon monoxide and chlorofluorocarbons don't come from rocks, and are by-products of other materials or processes. Electromagnetic fields are just that, not gasses.

59. (C) Chapter 13

Connecting to a sewer system is usually a matter of location. The use of well water is governed by quality and quantity of water available through a well. The amount of sanitary waste produced is generally a function of the number of people in the house.

60. (B) Chapter 14

None of the other answers have any bearing. For tax purposes the value of the estate on the date of death must be established.

61. (D) Chapter 14

If Answer A were correct it would affect all locations Mortgage money is now available from regional banks that may not even be in the same community as the property. Dependence on the automobile is certainly one factor that contributes to the idea that location is very important, but it's not the only factor.

62. (D) Chapter 14

You probably were tempted to go for answer A because this is a case where value in use would apply. But there may be an occasion to want market value to see how it compares to value in use or assessed value to fight a high assessment.

63. (C) Chapter 14

These questions about the economic factors at work in real estate value can be tough because the various factors can be hard to distinguish. In all cases, try to go for the best answer that most closely fits the definition and examples given in the book. In this case builders, the supply side, usually go in when they see a demand until that demand is satisfied. The building cycle is slow, however, so by the time the last project is built there is a surplus.

64. (D) Chapter 14

The investor may eventually want assessed value so it is unlikely that he would want a value in use appraisal. He wants to know what the property should cost him in order to make his project successful — investment value. He also should want to find out whether the market value is higher or lower than the investment value because he might be getting a bargain if it's lower, or the property may not be a good investment if the market value is higher than the investment value.

65. (C) Chapter 14

Conformity creates value by houses being similar. Competition often results in a surplus, driving values down. Regression is the opposite of progression. Remember in progression a smaller house benefits from being near larger, more expensive homes.

66. (D) Chapter 14

Curability when speaking of deterioration is an economic concept not necessarily a physical one. Answer C could be applied to incurable deterioration; it can be fixed but costs more than the value it would add to the property.

67. (D) Chapter 14

OK. Stop yelling. If you answered this question correctly I won't worry about you passing the state exam. This is probably not the normal way a question like this would be asked, but just in case some state examiners decide to get cute you're ready. You may wonder why answer D was not correct because the cost approach calls for determining the replacement or reproduction cost of the building. You're half right, and that's why this answer is wrong. Without subtracting depreciation and adding land value, you won't even come close to the appraised value of the property.

68. (C) Chapter 14

Answer D is wrong because you never add or subtract the adjustment form the subject. In answer A the market has already increased the value of the comparable (added) due to its superior features. The same is true in reverse for answer B. The adjustment process is designed to compensate for what the market has already done.

69. (D) Chapter 15

This is a basic question of definitions. Real estate brokers may recommend sources for mortgage loans but generally don't actually arrange loans unless they are also certified in some way by their state to be mortgage brokers.

70. (C) Chapter 15

The lender gives the money to the borrower, but the borrower gives the mortgage to the lender. Remember — the mortgage is the document that the borrower signs to allow the lender to take the property in the event of a foreclosure.

71. (A) Chapter 15

Answers C and D are made up. The due on sale clause which is typical in most mortgages is that the loan must be paid off if the property is sold.

72. (D) Chapter 15

Ginnie Mae is a secondary market organization that buys mortgage loans.

73. (A) Chapter 15

All lenders require an appraisal to determine the value of the property. The CRV, which is based on an appraisal, is unique to the VA

74. (A) Chapter 15

This is a tricky question because answer B is pretty close to being correct. Equity, however, is expressed in dollars. The loan to value ratio would be a percentage calculation. Investment value is an appraisal concept.

75. (A) Chapter 15

A construction loan is used to build a house and is expected to convert to a conventional mortgage at the end of construction. A home equity loan can be refinanced into a new mortgage, but that's not the general expectation. A package loan covers the real estate and personal property and continues without the necessity of conversion to anything else. The expectation with a reverse mortgage is that it will be paid off (not converted) upon the death of the property owner.

76. (A) Chapter 15

Given the information in the question, answer A is the best answer because it's always a feature of these loans and is part of the way the interest rate is calculated. Any of the other types of loans could have adjustable rates, but an index would not be considered a standard feature of these loans because they could just as well be fixed interest rate loans.

77. (D) Chapter 15

First of all I'm finding more of these no-number math questions in exams. So you need to know how the math works without having to actually do any calculations. Don't worry — I've got plenty of math questions with numbers coming in a little while. Meanwhile, the amount of interest due on this type of mortgage is always calculated on the unpaid balance of the principal at any point in time. No need to divide by the number of years because the mortgage rate is an annual rate.

78. (B) Chapter 15

I tried to make all the wrong answers seem plausible, especially answer D. The fact of the matter is the interest payments (not the interest rate) would likely decrease over time because you pay off a reducing balance. See the answer to question 77.

79. (C) Chapter 15

An adjustable rate loan deals with how the interest rate is calculated. The other two incorrect answers are types of loans for special purposes. The straight loan, also called a term loan, calls for payment of interest only until the end of the loan when the whole principal is due.

80. (A) Chapter 16

I'm afraid you're going to have to remember this. One hint might be that taxes are expressed as dollars of taxes per thousand (or hundred) of assessed value, which means that assessed value is always the bottom number in a fraction, or the number you're dividing by.

81. (C) Chapter 16

Answers A and B could be possibilities under certain circumstances, none of which are mentioned in this question. So the best answer given the information is C. In fact, this is the purpose of the equalization rate.

82. (B) Chapter 16

    Market value × assessment ratio = assessed value

83. (D) Chapter 16

    There are so few circumstances in which something is always or never, it's a good bet these answers are incorrect. You need to think through this question, or just remember it. When municipalities assess properties at full market value, they're essentially using a 100 percent assessment ratio. In that case, the assessed value used to calculate taxes is the same as the market value, making D the answer.

84. (A) Chapter 16

    Assessed value ÷) market value = the assessment ratio. This is a reverse of the formula to find assessed value market value × assessment ratio = assessed value. Answers C and D must be incorrect because the answers to these equations are in dollars. Remember a number representing a rate or ratio is always a percentage.

85. (C) Chapter 17

    *Liquid* means that you can get your cash relatively quickly. If you're wondering about certificates of deposit, you can usually cash them in any time; you most likely have to pay a penalty to access it, but the money is readily available.

86. (B) Chapter 17

    A syndicate is a descriptive term rather than a legal entity. Corporations and partnerships are two forms a syndicate may take.

87. (A) Chapter 17

    You may have been fooled by some of the other answers that implied use of other people's money like selling shares. The difference is shares are not borrowed money. Investors in syndicates and corporations expect a direct return on their money. In a sense they are actual owners of the real estate investment.

88. (A) Chapter 17

    You might argue that leveraging applies because he's using refinanced (borrowed) money to build his empire. But of the four choices answer B is the most correct.

89. (D) Chapter 17

    You might have gotten fooled into thinking that A was the answer because equities are the properties themselves, but all of these are ways to invest in the real estate market.

90. (C) Real estate isn't liquid, but that doesn't make it stable or unstable; that's the work of the economy having nothing to do with liquidity.

91. (A) Chapter 18

    Assessed value × equalization factor (rate) = equalized value

    $225,000 × 2.35 = $528,750

92. (D) Chapter 18

    Remember that the monthly payment in an amortized mortgage consists of principal and interest, so each month a portion of the payment goes to reducing the principal balance.

    Mortgage amount × Interest rate = Annual interest owed

    $100,000 × .06 (6 percent) = $6,000

    Annual interest ÷ 12 months = first month's interest because the whole balance is due at this point

    $6,000 ÷ 12 = $500

Monthly payment – monthly interest = principal portion of the payment

$600 – $500 = $100

Total principal due – monthly principal payment = balance due

$100,000 – $100 = $99,900

The fact that the loan is for 30 years is irrelevant.

93. (D) Chapter 18

You're being asked to work backwards to arrive at the market value of the property. Generally these kinds of problems involve division rather than multiplication.

Taxes ÷ the tax rate = assessed value

$3,575 ÷ $30/$1,000 ($30 of taxes per $1000 of assessed value) = 119,166.67

The logic of this equation is that each $30 in taxes represents $1,000 in assessed value. So divide by $30 and multiply by $1,000.

Assessed value ÷ assessment ratio = market value

$119,166.67 ÷ .70 (70 percent) = $170, 238.10

If you know the number and the percentage it represents, divide to find the whole.

94. (B) Chapter 18

Net operating income ÷ capitalization rate = value

$156,000 ÷ .12 (12 percent) = $1,300,000

95. (D) Chapter 18

This is a trick question. I know how much you love them. You don't need to know the expenses to calculate effective gross income.

Potential gross income – vacancy and collection loss = effective gross income

$350,000 – 5 percent = $332,500

96. (A) Chapter 18

The rule for this is comparable better subtract. And you never, ever touch the subject regardless of what you think it's worth.

Sales price of comparable – adjustment amount = indicated value of subject

$280,000 – $20,000 = $260,000

97. (C) Chapter 18

After you've calculated the commission, the easiest way to do this unless you're very comfortable with math is to break down the entire commission into everyone's shares. Also you need to read this question carefully because the information leads you to believe that they want to know the listing salesperson's share when in fact they want to know the listing broker's share.

Sale price × commission rate = commission

$480,000 × .04 (4 percent) = $19,200

The first split is between the buyer's broker and the seller's broker. Because they each get 50 percent you can just divide by 2.

$19,200 ÷) 2 = $9,600

Commission × percentage shares = dollar amounts

$9,600 × .40 (40 percent salesperson's share) = $3,840

Total listing side commission – salesperson's share = broker's share

$9,600 – $3,840 = $5,760

Saving one step, you could also conclude that if the salesperson gets 40 percent, the broker gets 60 percent, and multiply the $9,600 by that.

98. **(B) Chapter 18**

Proration questions always seem more complicated than they really are. It comes down to finding out the monthly and daily amounts of money involved and apportioning it out taking into account whether the buyer or the seller has paid. I kept the numbers themselves easy because I want you to see the methodology clearly. Expect more difficult numbers on the exam.

Because taxes are paid in arrears and the house has closed prior to the tax due date you know that the buyer (the new owner) has to pay the entire year's taxes a few months after he's moved in even though he's only lived in the house for less than the full year. So the seller is going to owe the buyer money at closing — a debit to the seller and a credit to the buyer.

Annual taxes ÷ 12 months = monthly taxes

$3,600 ÷) 12 = $300

Monthly taxes /(÷ 30) = Daily taxes

$300 ÷) 30 = $10

The buyer owns the property on the day of closing so the seller owns the property for 8 months (January through August) and 22 days of September.

8 months × $300 (monthly taxes) = $2,400

22 days × $10 (daily taxes) = $220

$2,400 + $220 = $2,620 that the seller owes the buyer for the time he owned the house without paying the taxes which the buyer had to pay later.

99. **(B) Chapter 18**

This question requires you to remember the format for arriving at the net operating income.

Potential gross income – vacancy and collection loss = effective gross income

Effective gross income – expenses = net operating income

Note that the question already provides the effective gross income. The vacancy and collection rate is an unnecessary number to solve the problem.

$180,000 – $73,000 = $107,000

100. **(B) Chapter 18**

Income ÷ value = rate

This formula assumes the value and sales price are the same. In questions like this, you can assume that value and sales price are the same.

$130,000 ÷ $1,200,000 = .11 or 11 percent

# Chapter 25

# Practice Exam Four

........................................................

*O*K. This is it, your fourth practice exam. If you've completed the first three practice exams regardless of how well you did you should be very comfortable answering the type of questions you'll see on the state exam. You've gotten comfortable with the material and the vocabulary. You're reviewed your strong areas and studied your weak ones. In short, you are ready!

You're familiar with the routine by now. Take a separate piece of paper, check the clock to time yourself, and get to it. Go through the exam as quickly as you can, answering the questions to which you immediately know the answers. There are a lot of them. Then go back through to take your time with the others. Make sure you do each math question twice. Not that I think you will, but don't start to slow down your studying as you get close to the finish line. You may have done well on the first three practice exams. In fact I'm sure your scores are improving. I've tried to ask different questions and tackle the same subject matter in different ways in these exams, so use this exam as one more opportunity to be as absolutely prepared as you can be for the state exam. I'd wish you good luck, but you won't need it. So I say congratulations in advance of you passing your state exam and becoming a licensed real estate agent.

1. Property management remuneration should not be based on

   (A) a fixed fee.

   (B) a percentage of gross income.

   (C) a lease fee.

   (D) amount of remuneration from contractors.

2. One of the primary differences between independent contractors and employees is that independent contractors

   (A) pay their own social security.

   (B) don't have to obey office policy.

   (C) can't deduct work related expenses.

   (D) work a different set of standard hours than an employee.

3. Broker A and Broker B met on January first and agreed that during the year A will service only sellers on the north side of town and B will service only sellers on the south side of town.

   (A) This is legal market division because everyone is guaranteed to get serviced

   (B) This is illegal price fixing.

   (C) This is boycotting because they left Broker C out of the arrangement.

   (D) This is illegal market allocation.

4. The case that dealt with real estate broker price fixing was

   (A) Brown vs. the Board of Education.

   (B) United States vs. Foley.

   (C) Dred Scott.

   (D) Jones vs. Mayer.

5. A special agent is one who

   (A) handles a single transaction.

   (B) is appointed by the broker only in dual agency situations.

   (C) is the typical agency for a property manager.

   (D) always represents the seller.

6. "The landscaping on this house is beautiful," which in reality consists of two scraggly bushes in the yard is an example of

   (A) puffing.

   (B) fraud

   (C) negligent misrepresentation.

   (D) intentional misrepresentation.

7. Which of the following need not be disclosed to a seller client?

   (A) Recent customer bankruptcy

   (B) Self dealing

   (C) Current customer divorce

   (D) All of the above must be disclosed

8. Joe is Mary's seller client. Fred is Sally's buyer client who is interested in Joe's house. Based on this information, which of the following relationships is accurate?

   (A) Mary and Sally are designated agents.

   (B) Mary and Sally are dual agents.

   (C) Joe is Sally's sub agent whereas Fred is Mary's sub agent.

   (D) Fred is Mary's customer and Joe is Sally's customer.

9. Using your best efforts on behalf of your client even if they conflict with your own self-interest is

   (A) loyalty.

   (B) care.

   (C) obedience.

   (D) accountability.

10. Broker Allen has a listing and is the agent for the seller Sam. Buyer Ben hires Broker Allen as his buyer's agent and wants to see Sam's house. Broker Allen

    (A) must refuse to work with buyer Ben as his agent.

    (B) must disclose his relationship to Sam and Ben.

    (C) must engage another broker to represent Ben.

    (D) must obtain informed consent to continue with this arrangement.

*Go on to next page*

11. Seller Cindy asks Broker Bob to help her sell her house. Broker Bob agrees, and they settle on a fee but nothing is put in writing. This appears to be

    (A) an express agency.

    (B) an implied agency.

    (C) a designated agency.

    (D) an agency by ratification.

12. Seller Slim agrees to let Broker Barbara list his house for sale and agrees to pay her a 4 percent commission if the sale goes through. But Slim continues to advertise the house himself, and Barbara agrees that there will be no commission owed if he sells his own house. What type of listing agreement did Slim sign?

    (A) Open listing

    (B) Owner acting as seller listing

    (C) Exclusive right to sell

    (D) Exclusive agency

13. A buyer asks you to show them homes in a Christian neighborhood

    (A) You can comply with their request because they initiated the request.

    (B) You must immediately stop working with the buyer.

    (C) You can tell them where the Christian neighborhoods are, but you can't show them houses there because real estate agents are held to a higher standard

    (D) You may show them houses in a variety of neighborhoods that meet their financial and other housing needs.

14. Which of the following is not a protected class under federal fair housing law?

    (A) Gender

    (B) Race

    (C) Marital status

    (D) National origin

15. The unique enforcement provision of the 1866 Civil Rights Act is that

    (A) all complaints are brought to the department of Housing and Urban Development.

    (B) suits are always brought in state court.

    (C) suits are brought directly in federal court.

    (D) the FBI is charged with investigating the complaint.

16. What is the rule regarding a housing exemption for religious organizations?

    (A) No limits on the exception due to freedom of religion

    (B) Limited to three or fewer units

    (C) No limits as long as no real estate agent is used

    (D) The religion itself must not discriminate in its membership rules

17. Because there's a significant Jewish population in a particular community, two multiple listing organizations have been established — one Jewish and one non-Jewish. Real estate agents may belong to one but not both.

    (A) This is legal market allocation.

    (B) This is no problem.

    (C) This is discriminatory but not a fair housing violation.

    (D) This is a fair housing violation.

18. The rights of an owner to the waters of an abutting river or stream are called

    (A) littoral rights.

    (B) riparian rights.

    (C) prior appropriation rights.

    (D) homestead rights.

*Go on to next page*

19. Title to property donated to the county park system has automatically reverted back to the original owner because the parks department is no longer using it for the purpose for which it was donated. The donation was probably made as

    (A) fee simple absolute.

    (B) fee simple condition precedent.

    (C) fee simple condition subsequent.

    (D) fee simple determinable.

20. You give your aunt the right to live in your second home until your cousin dies. You've likely given her

    (A) curtesy rights.

    (B) homestead rights.

    (C) a life estate pur autre vie.

    (D) an ordinary life estate.

21. Personal property attached to a building

    (A) remains personal property.

    (B) becomes a fixture.

    (C) becomes personalty.

    (D) is assumed to not remain with the property upon sale.

22. Another term for tenancy in severalty is

    (A) sole ownership.

    (B) common ownership.

    (C) joint ownership.

    (D) community property.

23. Tenancy by the entirety

    (A) means one owns the entire property rather than shares.

    (B) is the way several people can own equal shares of the property.

    (C) is characterized by the four unities.

    (D) is specific to property ownership by a married couple.

24. A person who buys the interest of someone who owns property in joint tenancy becomes

    (A) a new joint property owner.

    (B) a tenant in common.

    (C) a tenant by the entirety.

    (D) a tenant in trust.

25. Tenancy in common owners always have

    (A) equal shares.

    (B) the right of survivorship.

    (C) divided ownership.

    (D) ability to sell without permission of the other owners.

26. Which of the following statements is correct?

    (A) All encumbrances are financial limitations on property ownership.

    (B) Encumbrances are only physical limitations on properties.

    (C) Easements are not considered encumbrances.

    (D) Encumbrances may be physical or financial.

27. A mortgage lien is

    (A) voluntary and specific

    (B) involuntary and specific

    (C) voluntary and general.

    (D) involuntary and specific

28. An easement by prescription is created by

    (A) the actions of a person.

    (B) utility companies only.

    (C) agreement.

    (D) eminent domain.

29. An easement that benefits a person rather than a property is called an easement

    (A) by necessity.

    (B) by prescription.

    (C) in gross.

    (D) appurtenant.

*Go on to next page*

30. The cat that I must paint my house white is probably because of

    (A) an easement.

    (B) a deed restriction.

    (C) a lien.

    (D) an infrastructure clause.

31. Which of the following is not considered a public land use restriction?

    (A) Deed restriction

    (B) Zoning

    (C) Building code

    (D) Special permit use

32. If a density zoning ordinance is applied to a subdivision all the lots must

    (A) be grouped in a small area

    (B) allow for at least 30 percent of the land to be left open.

    (C) total the lot count in a normal subdivision.

    (D) be below the normal size called for by the zoning.

33. If a person dies without a will and without heirs, the state government obtains the property by

    (A) eminent domain.

    (B) claim of prior appropriation.

    (C) escheat.

    (D) lien rights.

34. Title to property is actually conveyed

    (A) when the contract is signed

    (B) when all the conditions in the contract are met.

    (C) when title insurance is issued

    (D) when the deed is delivered to the buyer and accepted by him.

35. The allocation of certain expenses between a buyer and a seller is called

    (A) proration.

    (B) settlement and procedures.

    (C) kickbacks.

    (D) payoffs.

36. The section due east of section 36 in the rectangular (government) survey system is section

    (A) 36.

    (B) 31.

    (C) 25.

    (D) 1.

37. In the rectangular (government) survey system a principal meridian and a baseline cross to form a

    (A) township.

    (B) section.

    (C) quadrangle.

    (D) nothing; they never cross because they are parallel.

38. A deed commonly used in family property transfers that gives no warrantees is

    (A) bargain and sale deed

    (B) deed in trust.

    (C) grant deed

    (D) quitclaim deed

39. Whose signature is required to make a deed valid?

    (A) Grantor only

    (B) Grantee only

    (C) Grantor and grantee

    (D) Grantor, grantee, and the title company representative

40. In a warranty deed the covenant of quiet enjoyment means

    (A) that no one will come along to claim ownership of the property.

    (B) that the grantor must compensate the grantee if any later claims of ownership turn out to valid

    (C) both A and B

    (D) neither A nor B

41. In the proration, an accrued item

    (A) is paid by the seller.

    (B) is paid by the buyer.

    (C) could be paid by either.

    (D) has been paid by the mortgage lender.

*Go on to next page*

Part VI: You're Ready to Pick Up Your Pencil: Taking Practice Exams

42. Constructive notice of a real estate transaction is generally provided by

(A) registered mail.

(B) the title company notifying the town tax assessor.

(C) the buyer to the seller.

(D) registering the deed in the public records.

43. The continuous use of property by someone other than the owner could result in a claim of

(A) eminent domain.

(B) avulsion of title.

(C) adverse possession.

(D) grant of title.

44. Title to park created as part of a new development might be given to the local town by

(A) grant.

(B) dedication.

(C) possessory interest.

(D) partition.

45. When the town takes property for unpaid taxes the process is called

(A) foreclosure.

(B) eminent domain.

(C) public grant.

(D) forfeiture.

46. Person B wants $300,000 for her house. Person A offers $250,000. Person B counteroffers $280,000. Person A counteroffers $252,000. Person B gets disgusted and counteroffers $310,000 back to Person (A) Can Person B do this?

(A) Yes

(B) No

(C) Only if the negotiations are conducted verbally

(D) Only as long as both real estate brokers agree

47. A contingency in a real estate sales contract

(A) must be satisfied for the contract to be enforceable.

(B) can be dropped from the contract by mutual agreement.

(C) can be dropped by the party who placed the contingency in the contract.

(D) all of the above.

48. The words vendor and vendee are often associated with what type of contract?

(A) Lease

(B) Real estate sales contract

(C) Option agreement

(D) Installment or conditional sales contract

49. Forcing someone to sell you their house in accordance with the contract you both signed is called

(A) specific performance.

(B) forfeiture.

(C) compensatory damages.

(D) rescission.

50. A building contractor taking over the contract of another builder is called

(A) the assignee.

(B) the vendor.

(C) the sub-contractor.

(D) the contractor of record

51. The owner of a two-family (duplex) house with two tenants might want to put what clause in the lease that would allow the new owner to evict either or both of the tenants.

(A) Sale clause

(B) Use clause

(C) Occupancy clause

(D) Subleasing clause

52. What kind of lease is typically used in an office building?

(A) Gross lease

(B) Percentage lease

(C) Proprietary lease

(D) Net lease

*Go on to next page*

53. If the date/day is not stated in the lease legally when is the rent due on a rental apartment?

    (A) The monthly anniversary of when the lease was signed

    (B) The last day of the month

    (C) The first of the month

    (D) Whenever the state stipulates as the default payment date

54. The principle difference between a net lease and a triple net lease is

    (A) there is no difference other than terminology.

    (B) the type of building.

    (C) the number of different expenses paid by the tenant.

    (D) the term of the lease.

55. Friable is a term generally associated with

    (A) lead paint.

    (B) asbestos.

    (C) sewage disposal.

    (D) brownfields.

56. Which phase of environmental assessment deals with remediation of the polluted area?

    (A) Phase 1

    (B) Phase 2

    (C) Phase 3

    (D) Phase 4

57. The cutoff below which tanks are generally exempted by the LUST program is

    (A) 2600 gallons.

    (B) 2100 gallons.

    (C) 1600 gallons.

    (D) 1100 gallons.

58. Brownfields refer to

    (A) former military bases.

    (B) Former industrial sites.

    (C) Farms where the soils are depleted

    (D) Sanitary landfills.

59. Chlorofluorocarbons are associated with

    (A) lead in water.

    (B) mold

    (C) sewer gases.

    (D) air-conditioning equipment.

60. At what vacancy rate is potential gross income calculated?

    (A) 100 percent

    (B) The actual rate

    (C) 0 percent

    (D) 80 percent

61. Reconciliation in appraising involves

    (A) averaging the value estimates from each approach.

    (B) weighing the value estimates from each approach and relying most on the appropriate approach for that type of property.

    (C) adjusting the three values so they're no more than five percent apart.

    (D) eliminating any value that doesn't meet the expectation of the client.

62. Which of the following is not a formula in the income capitalization approach?

    (A) Value ÷ income = rate

    (B) Value × rate = income

    (C) Income ÷ rate = value

    (D) Income ÷ value = rate

63. Vacancy and collection loss is subtracted from

    (A) potential gross income.

    (B) net operating income.

    (C) effective gross income.

    (D) gross rental income.

64. The formula for determining the gross rent multiplier is

    (A) gross rent × gross rent multiplier.

    (B) potential gross income ÷ capitalization rate.

    (C) sales price ÷ gross rent.

    (D) value × rate.

*Go on to next page*

65. Of the various approaches to appraising property what approach would be most suitable to appraising a unique nonresidential property with few comparables?

(A) Sales comparison approach

(B) Gross rent multiplier approach

(C) Income capitalization approach

(D) Cost approach

66. In the cost approach, a severely broken foundation that could be repaired would be classified as what kind of depreciation?

(A) Functional obsolescence curable

(B) Functional obsolescence incurable

(C) Physical deterioration curable

(D) Physical deterioration incurable

67. A gas station near a house is a form of

(A) functional obsolescence.

(B) external obsolescence.

(C) physical deterioration.

(D) straight-line depreciation.

68. If the subject has a newly remodeled kitchen and the comparable does not, you

(A) add the adjustment value to the comparable.

(B) add the adjustment value to the subject.

(C) subtract the adjustment value from the comparable.

(D) subtract the adjustment value from the subject.

69. Other than the borrower's ability to repay the loan what is the most important thing in consideration of how much the lender will lend?

(A) LTV

(B) NOI

(C) Property value

(D) Property cost

70. Which piece of federal legislation dealt with banks making loans within their community?

(A) The Community Reinvestment Act

(B) The Equal credit Opportunity Act

(C) The Truth in Lending Act

(D) The Neighborhood Affordable Housing Act

71. In which case does the buyer become personally liable for the balance of the mortgage loan?

(A) Estoppel

(B) Presumption

(C) Subject to

(D) Assumption

72. You can calculate the first month's interest on an amortized 30 year mortgage by multiplying

(A) the loan amount by the interest rate and dividing by 30.

(B) the loan amount by the interest rate and dividing by 12.

(C) the loan amount by the interest rate and dividing by 30 then dividing by 12.

(D) the monthly loan payment by the interest rate.

73. The interest rate on an adjustable rate mortgage is calculated as follows:

(A) Index plus margin

(B) Annual cap plus margin

(C) Lifetime cap minus margin

(D) Index minus margin

74. What is negative amortization?

(A) Additional money borrowed on a home equity loan

(B) An increase in the principal balance of a loan due to money owed but not paid

(C) The total payment due at the end of a term loan

(D) The result of a drop in the index from one year to the next in an adjustable rate loan

*Go on to next page*

75. I'm in contract to sell my house. I've bought another house and the seller wants to close before I can close on my own house. What kind of financing might help me?

    (A) Temporary loan

    (B) Swing loan

    (C) Bridge loan

    (D) All of the above

76. The total monthly payment on an amortized loan is composed of

    (A) principal and interest.

    (B) principal only.

    (C) interest only.

    (D) principal, interest, taxes, and insurance.

77. Mom and dad lent you money to buy a house with the stipulation that you not only pay them back what you borrowed but also a portion of the profit you make on the house when you sell it. This is probably a

    (A) blanket mortgage.

    (B) package mortgage.

    (C) purchase money mortgage.

    (D) shared equity mortgage.

78. A partial release provision is characteristic of what kind of mortgage?

    (A) Blanket mortgage

    (B) Construction loan

    (C) Package mortgage

    (D) Open end mortgage

79. Another name for the estoppel certificate is

    (A) reduction certificate.

    (B) certificate of reasonable value.

    (C) assumption certificate.

    (D) payoff certificate.

80. Which of the following is not the same tax rate as the others?

    (A) $8 per $100

    (B) $80/$1000

    (C) 8 mills

    (D) 80 mills

81. Assuming no special exemptions, properties with the same market value should

    (A) pay the same taxes but not necessarily have the same assessments.

    (B) pay the same taxes and have the same assessments.

    (C) have the same assessments but may pay different taxes.

    (D) not be concerned if their taxes differ periodically.

82. An equitable right of redemption with respect to a tax sale comes

    (A) after the tax sale.

    (B) before the tax sale.

    (C) either before or after the tax sale.

    (D) after the in rem proceeding.

83. What property does a tax lien have over other liens?

    (A) All liens are prioritized by date

    (B) Tax liens come last

    (C) Tax liens takes priority over all other liens

    (D) Tax liens take the second position right after the mortgage regardless of when other liens were filed

84. A protest against high taxes should be brought to

    (A) the tax grievance board.

    (B) the tax assessor.

    (C) small claims court.

    (D) elected officials.

*Go on to next page*

85. When rent from an investment is used to pay off an amortized mortgage it's called

    (A) capital appreciation.

    (B) cash flow.

    (C) depreciation.

    (D) equity buildup.

86. An owner of an investment building gets to deduct from the taxes he owes a certain amount of money he spent making his building environmentally more efficient. Most likely the government has given him

    (A) a grant.

    (B) a tax credit.

    (C) an exemption.

    (D) a tax deduction.

87. The cash owed to someone in an uneven property exchange is called

    (A) boot.

    (B) like kind

    (C) capital gains.

    (D) deferred depreciation.

88. In a real estate investment, which of the following is correct with respect to risk and expected return?

    (A) Risk up, return up

    (B) Risk up, return down

    (C) Risk down, return the same

    (D) Risk up, return the same

89. Another term for cost recovery is

    (A) capital gains.

    (B) profit.

    (C) return on investment.

    (D) depreciation.

90. The fact that equal amounts of deprecation are taken every year is referred to as

    (A) accelerated

    (B) cost recovery

    (C) straight line

    (D) limited

91. You're selling the NW 1/4SW1/4 S 1/2 W1/2 section 31. How many square feet of land are you selling?

    (A) 435,600

    (B) 43,560

    (C) 21,780

    (D) 4,356

92. An owner wants to net $300,000 from selling his house after she pays you a 5 percent commission. What price must she sell her house for?

    (A) $315,000

    (B) $315,789

    (C) $300,000

    (D) 320,000

93. You sold 20 houses last year and 25 houses this year. What percent fewer houses did you sell last year than this year?

    (A) 25 percent

    (B) 20 percent

    (C) 10 percent

    (D) 5 percent

94. A couple gets a 30-year amortized mortgage loan for $200,000 at 5 percent interest. The monthly payment for principal and interest is $1,074. They make 15 years of payments when they come into some money and are able to pay off the remaining $120,000 balance of the loan. Approximately how much total interest did they pay on the mortgage loan?

    (A) $113,000

    (B) $105,000

    (C) $93,000

    (D) $78,000

95. What is the first month's interest on a 20-year mortgage loan for $90,000 at 4 percent interest?

    (A) $3,600

    (B) 300

    (C) $200

    (D) 180

*Go on to next page*

96. A couple has $24,000 a year available to buy a house. Annual taxes are $4,000; one year's insurance is $1,000. The mortgage rate they've secured calls for a payment of $4.50 per month per $1,000 of mortgage. The couple has $30,000 to put down on the house. What is the highest price house they can afford?

    (A) $474,444

    (B) $444,444

    (C) $381,851

    (D) $138,000

97. The market value of a property is $400,000. The town's assessment ratio is 80 percent. The tax rate is 15 mills. What are the annual taxes for this property?

    (A) $480

    (B) $600

    (C) $4,800

    (D) $6,000

98. Six months taxes of $3,600 are paid in advance on February 1. Sale of the house closes on August 1. Who owes how much to whom?

    (A) Buyer owes the seller $3,600

    (B) Seller owes the buyer $3,600

    (C) Seller and buyer owe each other $1,800

    (D) Buyer owes seller nothing

99. The subject property has a third bathroom that is not present in the comparable; however, the comparable has a renovated kitchen that the subject property does not have. If the bathroom is valued at $5,000, the renovated kitchen has a value of $10,000, and the comparable recently sold for $330,000, what is the indicated value of the subject?

    (A) $315,000

    (B) $325,000

    (C) $335,000

    (D) $345,000

100. Three multifamily properties sold as follows:

| Sales Price | Gross Annual Rent |
| --- | --- |
| $700,000 | 70,000 |
| $650,000 | $65,000 |
| $720,000 | $72,000 |

The property you are interested in purchasing has a gross annual rent of $68,000. Using the gross rent multiplier method, what's the value of the property you want to buy?

    (A) $680,000

    (B) $710,000

    (C) $780,000

    (D) $6,800,000

# Chapter 26

# Answers and Explanations to Practice Exam Four

*1* assume that you took these practice exams in order, at least the first time through. If so, your score on this should be great. If not, don't worry. After you've checked through all your answers, go back as you did in the earlier exams and see in which areas you need more study. You'll see that once again I've grouped the questions by chapter to make it easier for you to identify the subjects that you may need to go over.

Your goal on all of these exams is to get at least 85 correct answers out of a 100. This should give you a safe margin for the actual state exam. If you've used a separate piece of paper for your answers, re-do any and all of these exams until you get an 85 or better. And you'll soon be on your way to your first million dollars in real estate.

1. **(D) Chapter 3**

   Remuneration is one of those four dollar words exam writers occasionally like to use. It simply means *pay* and in this case means kickback, which is a payment the owner doesn't know about from a contractor hired by the property manager. It's illegal.

2. **(A) Chapter 3**

   Everyone must obey office policy. In fact it's the independent contractor rather than the employee who usually can deduct work expenses. The word standard in Answer D should tip you off that this is wrong because independent contractors can't be made to work certain hours.

3. **(D) Chapter 3**

   There is no such thing as market division. The arrangement is illegal so although leaving Broker C out of it could be considered a boycott, leaving someone out of an illegal scheme is not what boycotting refers to. Price fixing has to do with illegally setting commission rates.

4. **(B) Chapter 3**

   The three wrong answers may look familiar because they're all cases that dealt with fair housing or other discrimination issues.

5. **(A) Chapter 4**

   A special agent is typically the type of agency created for a single real estate transaction. Property managers are usually general agents. As you already know, agents can represent either the seller or buyer. An agent might be appointed in a dual agency situation but it's not the "only" case in which this might happen.

6. **(A) Chapter 5**

   You might argue that the statement intentionally misrepresents the quality of the landscaping but the term is generally used for cases of misrepresenting items that can't be readily checked and is usually another term for fraud. Negligent misrepresentation is not revealing something you should have known but didn't.

7. (D) Chapter 4

Both A and C are situations that could affect the buyer's ability to buy the property. Self-dealing is where an agent wants to buy his own listing.

8. (D) Chapter 4

This is an easy question to get lost in because of the poor wording. Yes, I did this on purpose. First thing to do is to organize the players on scrap paper if you can.

Mary = Agent representing

Joe = Client/seller

Sally = Agent representing

Fred = Client/buyer

The third party in a transaction is the customer. So in this case from Mary's perspective Fred is the customer. From Sally's perspective Joe is the customer. Give yourself a pat on the back if you got this one right.

9. (A) Chapter 4

No fair, you say! Using your best efforts is care but putting your client's interests above your own is loyalty. Don't be too literal here. Loyalty is the best answer because care doesn't address the self-interest issue.

10. (D) Chapter 4

This is often the way dual agency occurs. Informed consent means giving full disclosure to both parties and obtaining both their consents to represent both of them.

11. (A) Chapter 4

A designated agency occurs when there is a possibility of a dual agency. Agency by ratification occurs after the fact when an implied agency is accepted. The tough choices here are A and B because nothing in writing would imply an implied agency. (Sorry I couldn't resist). But the fact that an agreement was made orally makes this an express agency though in some states the agent would have a hard time collecting her commission.

12. (D) Chapter 4

I made up C. Exclusive right to sell guarantees Barbara a commission regardless of who sells the property. Open listing allows multiple brokers to sell the property.

13. (D) Chapter 5

As a real estate agent you may never initiate or participate in steering, which this is.

14. (C) Chapter 5

Marital status may be a protected class in some states but is not one of the protected classes under federal law.

15. (C) Chapter 5

All civil rights complaints are brought to HUD for enforcement except the 1866 Civil Rights Act.

16. (D) Chapter 5

The limitation is that the religion may not discriminate as to who may become a member. Even though a real estate agent and no advertising should be used the limits still exist so answer C is wrong.

17. (D) Chapter 5

This question can be tricky since it included a reference to an antitrust issue: market allocation, which is never legal. If you're wondering how something can be discriminatory but not illegal, think about some of the exceptions to the fair housing law that in effect permit legal discrimination.

18. (A) Chapter 6

Riparian rights involve large bodies of water like lakes. Prior appropriation rights are the state's rights to water in certain states. Homestead rights have nothing to do with water rights.

19. (D) Chapter 6

You're really going to have to memorize the fine points of these definitions, especially C and D. The big difference is that C requires action on the part of the owner. D is an automatic reversion of the title.

20. (C) Chapter 6

Answers A and B have nothing to do with the question. An ordinary life estate gives the right for the life of the person receiving the life estate. Pur autre vie means for the life of another person, in this case your cousin.

21. (B) Chapter 6

Answers A and C are both incorrect. Personalty is another word for personal property. A fixture is assumed to remain with the property upon sale.

22. (A) Chapter 7

The three wrong answers describe some form of ownership by more than one person. You have to memorize this one.

23. (D) Chapter 7

This is another one of those definitional questions. Tenancy by the entirety is only for use by married couples. Answer A most likely is tenancy in severalty. B and C refer to joint tenancy.

24. (B) Chapter 7

Answer A seems to be the logical answer, but in fact because of the unity of time a new owner buying into an existing joint tenancy becomes a tenant in common.

25. (D) Chapter 7

Tenants in common can have equal or unequal shares. The right of survivorship is a feature of joint tenancy. Both tenancy in common and joint tenancy have undivided ownership.

26. (D) Chapter 8

An encumbrance is a limitation on property ownership. As such it can be either physical like an easement or financial like a lien.

27. (A) Chapter 8

A is a voluntary action for one piece of property.

28. (A) Chapter 8

An easement by prescription may result when an individual continually uses the property of another person without an agreement. Such a situation may arise with a utility company, but it's also possible for this to occur by the actions of a private individual.

29. (C) Chapter 8

This is a tricky question because two of the answers A and B are strictly speaking not types of easement but rather two ways an easement can be created. An easement appurtenant benefits an adjacent property.

30. (B) Chapter 8

An easement allows someone else to use a portion of your property. A lien is a financial encumbrance on the property. Infrastructure clause sounds like it should mean something, but I made it up.

31. (A) Chapter 8

   These negative questions — pick the wrong answer (really it's the answer that doesn't fit the group) — are not the easiest because you'll be generally doing most questions looking for the right answer. It's a good reminder to always read the question carefully. The three incorrect answers are all types of public land use controls.

32. (C) Chapter 8

   You're going to have to re-read this section to fully understand the concept. Density zoning allows lots to be various sizes, bigger or smaller than what zoning requires, but the total lot count must be the same as if it were a regular subdivision. Grouping the lots close to each other is a characteristic of cluster zoning.

33. (C) Chapter 8

   Eminent domain is the government's right to take one's property against the owner's will. The claim of prior appropriation has to do with water rights. A lien usually means that taxes haven't been paid and the property is seized by the town or city, not the state.

34. (D) Chapter 9

   Delivery and acceptance of the deed, usually at closing (which is why I didn't include that as a choice) is when title to a property transfers. The other three conditions are typical as preliminaries leading up to the transfer of title.

35. (A) Chapter 9

   Settlement and procedures might remind you of the RESPA act that applies to closings. Kickbacks are illegal payments. If you've watched too many gangster movies you know what a payoff could be, but remember one of your goals as a homebuyer is to pay off your mortgage loan.

36. (B) Chapter 9

   Check out Figure 9-1 and remember that every township is divided into 36 sections in the same manner. So if you lay one township grid next to the other you'll always know what sections are next to each other.

37. (C) Chapter 9

   Quadrangles are the principal divisions in this system and are further divided into townships and sections. Principal meridians run north and south whereas baselines run east and west, so they aren't parallel.

38. (D) Chapter 9

   Bargain and sale deeds are used in many typical real estate transactions and may or may not have certain warrantees. Deeds in trust are used for loan guarantee purposes. Grant deeds have limited warrantees.

39. (A) Chapter 9

   You have to remember this because it is a little tricky. Most people think that the buyer (grantee) should have to sign the deed to accept the property but the only required signature is the grantor. The title company representative is not involved in signing the deed because he or she has no ownership interest in the property.

40. (C) Chapter 9

   You might want to remember the differences of each of the warrantees in the general warrantee deed. Because these are generally legal terms there is no easy way to remember them easily other than to memorize them.

41. (B) Chapter 9

I suggest you read through this section and the math examples carefully since this can be complicated. An accrued item is one that's owed by the seller and paid by the buyer, usually a later date. A seller who lives in a house for the first six months of the year then sells it where the taxes for the year are paid on December 31 for the previous year owes the buyer the six months taxes that he used for the first half of the year. So the taxes are owed by the seller to the buyer, but the buyer pays all the taxes for the year to the town.

42. (D) Chapter 9

Constructive notice is accomplished by making the transaction records available to the public. This is done by recordation. The other activities may occur incidentally but have nothing to do with constructive notice.

43. (C) Chapter 10

Eminent domain is taking property by the government. There is no such thing as avulsion of title. A land grant is usually given to someone by the government.

44. (B) Chapter 10

Grant is the government giving you land. Possessory interest may be an interest in property but it's not a way to transfer title. Partition involves a lawsuit to divide property between owners.

45. (A) Chapter 10

Eminent domain is used by the government to take property against the owner's will and has nothing to do with unpaid taxes. A public grant is where the government gives property to private individuals. Forfeiture is where property may be lost due to the owner disobeying some condition in the deed.

46. (A) Chapter 11

Either you know the answer to this question right away, or you're going to have to think it through. Because real estate contracts including offers and acceptances have to be in writing to be valid, if negotiations are conducted verbally anything goes until a contract is signed. Agents works for clients, not the other way around. An agent must obey all lawful orders of a client. In these circumstances every time a counteroffer was made, it negated the previous offer so B is free to raise the price as she did.

47. (D) Chapter 11

Many places are dropping all of the above questions but I wanted to include one, and I thought this would be a good place to give you all the information about contingencies you need to know after you read the section in the chapter. The contingency is usually placed by one party and agreed to by the other so if both agree to drop the contingency or the party that the contingency protects wants to drop it the contract can proceed. If neither of those things happens, the contingency must be satisfied. You sharp readers may also note that if A is correct, because I use the word *must*, B and C can't be correct.

48. (D) Chapter 11

The installment contract that usually conveys title after a number of payments have been made often uses the terms in the question. A typical real estate sales contract uses the words *grantor* and *grantee*. A lease uses the words *lessor* and *lessee*. An option agreement may use the words *optionor* and *optionee* but can also use the terms *grantor* and *grantee*.

49. (A) Chapter 11

Compensatory damages might be storage costs for the buyer's furniture. Forfeiture might be when the buyer refuses to buy and forfeits his deposit. Rescission is when both parties agree to rescind, that is dissolve the contract.

50. (A) Chapter 11

This could be a little tricky because in fact the new contractor might now be considered the contractor of record by the town. Also in some cases anyone selling a service or product could be called the vendor. So I admit this is probably not a great question, but you may get some not so great questions which is why I include one or two. The best answer is assignee because it appears from the information in the question that the existing contract was assigned to the new contractor.

51. (A) Chapter 12

The sale clause (sometimes called the termination on sale clause) allows the new owner after proper notice to evict the tenant. The use clause controls the uses to which the rental unit can be put. The occupancy clause limits the number of people who can live in the unit. The subleasing clause governs subleasing activity.

52. (D) Chapter 12

Net lease is the best answer of these choices but see question 54. Meanwhile the gross lease is usually used in residential rental situations. A percentage lease is generally used with retail stores. The proprietary lease is given to cooperative owners.

53. (D) Chapter 12

This is a state specific question but I wanted to use it to remind you to check what your state's default date is. In some places the usual practice of payment on the first of the month is nothing more than the standard language in a lease, without which the rent would be due on the last day of the month.

54. (C) Chapter 12

All the wrong answers essentially have no bearing on anything to do with this question. In a net lease the tenant will pay some of the expenses like taxes or insurance of the building. In a triple net lease the tenant will pay all of the expenses. Note that even in a triple net lease the tenant never pays the mortgage.

55. (B) Chapter 13

*Friable* refers to how easily asbestos can crumble or give off particles and dust.

56. (C) Chapter 13

Memorize the various phases.

57. (D) Chapter 13

All the other answers are irrelevant. Another one you have to memorize.

58. (B) Chapter 13

Brownfields are former industrial sites that may have pollution issues. Although the other answers may or may not have environmental issues, brownfields generally focus on industrial, manufacturing, and storage facilities that may have hazardous waste from a previous use. This could be a tricky question, but the best answer is B.

59. (D) Chapter 13

Chlorofluorocarbons (CFCs) are elements in the gases in older air conditioning equipment and aerosol cans.

60. (C) Chapter 14

OK. This is my read the question. Potential gross income in the income capitalization approach to value is calculated at 100 percent occupancy, which is zero percent vacancy.

61. (B) Chapter 14

I thought I'd go easy on you and give you one obviously false answer, D. An appraiser never averages the values nor does he manipulate the values in any way.

62. (A) Chapter 14

Value is generally larger than income. If you divided value by income you'd come up with a multiplier (whole number) not a rate (percentage).

63. (A) Chapter 14

You have to memorize the sequence to arrive at net operating income and it starts with vacancy and collection loss being subtracted from potential gross income.

64 (C) Chapter 14

The other three answers were a variety of terms thrown together none of which result in anything useful. There are several formulas in this chapter that should be memorized. Make every effort not to mix up terms from one appraisal approach to another, as I did in this question.

65 (D) Chapter 14

Technically you could use the cost approach on residential property also but I didn't want you to get confused and pick A as the answer because you know that's the approach most suitable to appraising homes. B and C are both ways to appraise income producing properties that are usually bought for investments.

66. (D) Chapter 14

Functional obsolescence usually are design flaws in the building not deteriorating physical condition. Curable and incurable are economic not construction concepts. Curability means that the cost to fix the item will add at least the same or more value to the property. Incurability means that the cost to fix the item will not result in a commensurate increase in value even though the item is fixable.

67. (B) Chapter 14

Physical deterioration is wear and tear on the building itself. Functional obsolescence is design flaws in the building. Straight line depreciation is a method for estimating depreciation. External obsolescence are things negative to value that occur off the property. It's always incurable, by the way.

68. (A) Chapter 14

You never touch the subject in the sales comparison approach, so B and D are incorrect. If the subject has something that the comparable does not have it makes the comparable inferior to the subject. If the comparable is inferior you have to compensate for that lack by adding the adjustment. Remember, what do you have to do to the comparable to make it like the subject?

69. (C) Chapter 15

This is a pretty sophisticated question that I think at this point you're ready for. The loan to value ratio is important, but the ultimate amount of the loan is based on the value. The lender considers the cost in determining the loan amount, but only if it's lower than the value. The net operating income contributes to the determination of the value of a commercial property, but is not the basis for the loan.

70. (A) Chapter 15

Answers B and C do provide for non-discrimination and greater information respectively in the mortgage lending process. I made up answer D by changing one word National to Neighborhood in the title of the actual act. I didn't want to make the question too easy.

71. (D) Chapter 15

Estoppel is the certificate signed to verify the loan balance. Presumption is made up. In a subject to the mortgage purchase the new buyer is not personally responsible for the balance, though he would make the payments on the loan.

72. (B) Chapter 15

In an amortized loan, the interest rate is stated an annual rate so multiplying the total amount of the loan — because that's the unpaid balance in the first year — by the rate gives you that year's total interest. Divide by 12 months and you have the first month's interest.

73. (A) Chapter 15

The three wrong answers are completely made up.

74. (B) Chapter 15

In an adjustable rate loan if the annual interest rate exceeds the annual or lifetime cap there is money owed to the lender but not paid. It is sometimes added to the outstanding loan balance creating negative amortization.

75. (A) Chapter 15

You already know that an amortized loan is paid off over time rather than in a lump sum at the end so each payment has a portion of the principal as well as the interest. The confusing answer might be answer D because many of us pay our property taxes and insurance through an escrow account with the bank. The fact is, however, that total we send to the bank each month is not the mortgage payment but is the payment plus these other items.

76. (D) Chapter 15

This is a pretty simple question if you did your reading (which I know you did). I wanted to give you chance to review all the names that this type of gap or interim (two more names) financing goes by.

77. (D) Chapter 15

This is a difficult question because answer C may technically be correct also because the mortgage loan is used to purchase the property. But the better and more correct answer is D. You will probably get some questions on your exam that require you to pick the best answer out of two or more that are very close.

78. (A) Chapter 15

A blanket mortgage covers more than one piece of property. The partial release provision is used to release the lien on each individual piece of property as it's sold.

79. (A) Chapter 15

The CV is part of the VA loan process. There I no such thing as an assumption certificate, and although payoff certificate sounds right, it too is made up.

80. (C) Chapter 16

Answers A and B are pretty obviously the same; B being A with both numbers multiplied by 10. Remember when using a mill rate you move the decimal which is at the end of the number, three paces to the left. 8 mills is 8 dollars per thousand of value so it's the one unlike the other three.

81. (B) Chapter 16

People should always be concerned about paying unequal taxes for the same market value property. If market value is the same a consistent application of the assessment ratio will result in the same assessed value and the same taxes due, which is the desired result.

82. (B) Chapter 16

Remember E comes before S as in statutory right of redemption, which comes after the tax sale. In rem refers to foreclosure, which is a different procedure.

83. (C) Chapter 16

Memorize this and remember that this is why banks want escrow accounts for taxes so mortgages won't go into second place behind an unpaid tax lien.

84. (D) Chapter 16

Read this question carefully and remember what my tax assessor friend said. Complaints or grievances about unfair tax *assessments* can be brought to any of the agencies named in the first three answers depending on your state. But if taxes are too high, that's the responsibility of the elected officials no matter where you live.

85. (D) Chapter 17

Remember equity is the difference between what the property is worth and the debts attributed to the property. If the mortgage is getting paid off there is less of a balance to pay at the end; therefore, equity has been — you guessed — building up.

86. (B) Chapter 17

A tax deduction is deducted from income before taxes are calculated. A grant is actual money given. An exemption is usually something we don't have to pay taxes on that we own or certain types of income that might not be subject to taxes.

87. (A) Chapter 17

Tax on the boot is payable by the person receiving it. The boot can be due to capital gains but not necessarily.

88. (A) Chapter 17

Yes, there are questions this easy on the exam, though not many. As the risk goes up, so does the expectation of a higher return.

89. (D) Chapter 17

Profit can be anything you make beyond your investment. Return on investment is much the same as profit. Capital gains is the positive difference (if there is one) between what you paid and what you sold a property for.

90. (C) Chapter 17

Accelerated depreciation allows more depreciation to be taken in the early years of an investment.

91. (A) Chapter 18

Remember to drop the directions and replace them with multiplication signs. Also remember two important facts needed to answer this question: A section is always 640 acres and an acre is 43, 560 square feet.

$\frac{1}{4} \times \frac{1}{4} \times \frac{1}{2} \times \frac{1}{2} \times 640 = 10$ acres

10 acres $\times$ 43560 sq. feet = 435600 sq. ft.

92. (B) Chapter 18

You and the owner are partners in this deal whether the owner knows it or not. Because the commission comes off the sale price, she gets what's left after you get your 5 percent commission, which means she gets 95 percent of the sale price. If you know the dollar amount and the percent of the whole it represents, you can calculate the whole by dividing the percent into the dollar amount.

$300,000 \div .95$ (95 percent) = \$315,789

93. (B) Chapter 18

    You know the numerical difference is five houses. The trick is knowing which number to divide by. Because you're "going backward," you use this year's number.

    $5 \div 25 = 20$ percent

94. (A) Chapter 18

    This question looks far more complicated than it is. The total loan was for $200,000 and the couple paid off in a lump sum $120,000 right after the 15th year, so in the first 15 years of the loan they must have paid off $80,000 in principal.

    $200,000 - $120,000 = $80,000$

    But they made 180 monthly payments of $1,074, which included principal and interest.

    15 years $\times$ 12 months = 180 months

    $180 \times $1,074 = $193,320$ in total payments

    If they paid $80,000 in principal during this time the rest must be interest.

    $193,320 - $80,000 = $113,320$ interest

95. (B) Chapter 18

    Interest is always calculated for the year on the unpaid balance.

    $90,000 \times .04$ (4 percent) = $3,600 interest

    $3,600 \div 12$ months = $300 for the first month

96. (C) Chapter 18

    This is a typical problem in real world real estate as you help someone determine the price house they can afford to buy. The idea is to work backward from their income.

    Note the couple doesn't have $24,000 available to pay the mortgage. They actually have:

    $24,000 - $4,000 - $1,000 = $19,000$ because the lender includes taxes and insurance in their affordability calculation.

    If every $4.50 buys $1,000 worth of mortgage on a monthly basis, then

    $19,000 \div 12$ months = $1,583.33 per month available

    $1,583.33 \div $4.50 = $351.85 units of $1,000 worth of mortgage

    $351.85 \times $1,000 = $351,851.85 mortgage amount

    $30,000 down payment + $351,851.85 mortgage amount = $381,851 rounded total maximum house price

97. (C) Chapter 18

    You may be doing this calculation a lot and not just on the exam.

    Market value $\times$ assessment ratio = assessed value

    $400,000 \times .80$ (80 percent) = $320,000

    Assessed value $\times$ tax rate = taxes due

    $320,000 \times .015 = $4,800

    Don't forget when dealing with mills to move the decimal point three places to the left before multiplying.

98. (D) Chapter 18

    The taxes are paid in advance to cover the period February 1 to July 31. The new owner takes title the day the new tax period begins.

99. (B) Chapter 18

    Don't get overwhelmed by the fact that this question has two adjustments. Just take one at a time.

    Remember if the comparable is better than the subject subtract the adjustment from the comparable. If the comparable is inferior to the subject, you add the adjustment amount to the comparable.

    Subject has a third bathroom. The comparable does not have a third bathroom, which makes it inferior to the subject, so you add the adjustment value of $5,000 to the comparable's selling price of $330,000.

    The comparable has a renovated kitchen that the subject does not have, which makes the comparable superior to the subject so you subtract the $10,000 kitchen value.

    $330,000 – $10,000 + $5,000 = $325,000

100. (A) Chapter 18

    Two formulas to memorize for this problem:

    Sales price ÷ gross annual rent = gross rent multiplier

    Gross annual rent × gross rent multiplier = value

    $700,000 ÷ $70,000 = 10

    $650,000 ÷ $65,000 = 10

    $720,000 ÷ $72,000 = 10

    The gross rent multiplier derived from comparable properties – 10

    $68,000 × 10 = $680,000 value of subject property

# Part VII
# The Part of Tens

Enjoy an additional Real Estate License Exams Part of Tens chapter online at www.dummies.com/extras/realestatelicenseexams.

## In this part . . .

✔ Real estate laws can be extremely specific from one state to another and are ever changing either by legislative action or court decree. I offer my own personal list of the ten most important state-specific subjects that you need to research.

✔ I give you more test-prep techniques to help you sail through the exam with less stress and worry.

✔ When you get stuck on a question, you learn to always go with your gut instincts and don't overthink the answers.

# Chapter 27

# Ten Things to Find Out From Your State's Real Estate Law

*In This Chapter*

▶ Finding out about agency, fair housing, and license laws

▶ Checking out rules regarding land use, money, property, and rentals

▶ Getting the scoop on various ownership issues

*L*icenses for real estate brokers and salespersons are granted by each state. The problem that creates in writing a book about taking the real estate license exam is that every state has its own laws governing real estate procedures, practices, and license law. Enough factors don't vary from state to state to fill an exam review book, which, of course, is what you're reading right now. On the other hand, some space inevitably must be devoted to information that may be specific to each state.

This chapter gives you a list of issues (in alphabetical order) that you need to find out about in your own state before you take the real estate exam. I touch on ten categories of subjects that you need to research. For more information on the general subject matter you can consult the chapter on that particular issue. (Fear not — I provide handy cross-references for you. Now that's service!)

The two things I need to warn you about are the following:

✔ This is my list of the most important state-specific items. Some instructors and exam writers may disagree with what's on the list. The research I did in writing this book led me to create this list, and I constantly was on the lookout for items that may be state-specific rather than general topics across state lines.

✔ Real estate laws can be extremely specific from one state to another and are ever changing either by legislative action or court decree, even as you're reading this book. So as you're researching these topics in your home state, try to get the most current and complete information you can find. Often you can go online to get your state's latest version of its real estate license law. You can be assured that there will be questions on the exam based on what's in that law. You also need to consult your prelicensing course textbook, handouts, and the instructor.

# Agency Law

*Agency law,* simply stated, is the law that governs the relationship between a client and an agent, in this case a buyer or seller and you their real estate agent. Every state has its own version of how it defines the relationship between a broker/salesperson and a client (the person represented by a broker/salesperson). Of all the state-specific exam information, agency law is perhaps the most complicated and the most important. See Chapter 4 for more info. Look for what your state has to say about the following topics:

✔ Agency disclosure

✔ Buyer agency

✔ Buyer agency agreements

✔ Dual agency

✔ Listing agreements (including net listings)

✔ Transactional or facilitating brokerage

✔ Any other type of permitted or prohibited agencies in your state

# Fair Housing

In essence, the goal of fair housing laws is to prevent discrimination in housing sales and rentals. Most fair housing laws come from the federal government. Many states, however, and some large cities, have supplemented the federal regulations with their own. The local rules and regulations usually are stricter than the federal rules. In the case of two different laws covering the same thing, the stricter law applies. (See Chapter 5 for more.) Check out

✔ **Protected classes:** Fair housing laws regarding race and religion are among the protections offered these groups. You need to check out additional groups that are protected by fair housing standards in your state, for example sexual orientation may be a protected class in your state even though it's not a protected class in the federal law.

✔ **Exceptions to the exceptions:** Some municipalities may not permit the same exceptions to the rules that the federal government does.

✔ **Additional prohibited activities:** Federal law is pretty complete in addressing prohibited activities, but check out any supplemental state or local laws.

# License Law

Every state has its own procedures for obtaining and maintaining a real estate license. Find out everything you can about your state's licensing law. Something as minute (and silly, in my opinion) as knowing the fee for filing a change of address has been asked on exams. So study your state's law carefully. You probably can check out your state license law online, and you may get a copy of it when you take your prelicensing course. For more, flip to Chapter 3.

# Limitations on Land Use

A variety of local governmental controls govern how you use your property; see Chapter 8 for the scoop. Questions you may want to ask about local regulations include the following:

✔ What board or agency adopts and amends the zoning ordinance?

✔ What board or agency grants variations (variances, special permits) from the zoning ordinance?

✔ What local procedures are required for approval of a subdivision and who or what board or agency gives the approval?

✔ What are the statutory time limits for protesting deed restriction violations?

✔ Are any statewide historic preservation programs or environmental review laws in effect?

✔ Does your state require you to know something about construction?

# Money Stuff

Money makes the world go round, including the world of real estate. A few things that you may want to check out in your state with respect to money issues include:

✔ State-sponsored mortgage loan or guarantee programs that may make money available to homebuyers under favorable conditions like lower-than-normal interest rates.

✔ Special incentive, rebate, or exemption programs for property taxes, such as a senior citizen tax exemption.

✔ How you protest your property tax assessment.

For the scoop on mortgages, see Chapter 15. I cover taxes (including property tax assessments) in Chapter 16.

# Ownership Rights, Forms, and Theories

You may want to check out the following ownership issues in your home state:

✔ The applicability of the following terms in your state: community property, curtesy, dower, and homestead.

✔ Whether your state recognizes the right of survivorship in joint tenancy.

✔ Whether the terms town house and condominium mean the same thing.

✔ If your state is a title theory or lien theory state.

✔ Whether your state uses tenancy by the entirety or some other form of ownership specific to married couples.

Chapter 6 provides details about the rights involved with owning real estate; Chapter 7 covers the different forms of real estate ownership. For specifics on theories, see Chapter 15. And check out the two sections about transferring ownership later in this chapter.

# Property Disclosure

The general fiduciary duties (the overall responsibilities of an agent to a client) regarding disclosure of information to your principal or client (the person an agent represents) are pretty standard from state to state. The issue of what must be disclosed to the customer, which in most cases is the buyer, can vary. As an agent, you may want to check out the following responsibilities of an agent as well as an owner with respect to disclosure:

✔ Latent defects

✔ Material defects

✔ Stigmatized property

✔ Megan's Law

✔ Disclosure procedures

✔ Penalties

✔ Special environmental hazards such as earthquake prone areas

See Chapter 4 for more, and check out your state licensing law for fraud and negligent misrepresentation penalties.

# Tenants' Rights and Rent Control

Check out any laws in your state that specifically guarantee certain protections to tenants in rental buildings. If any are in effect, they may be on a state level or an individual city level. These types of laws can cover anything from placement of window guards and other security features to notification about rent increases. Pay particular attention to the number of units a building must have for the laws to apply.

The other thing to check out is whether your state or any municipalities in your state have laws that control rental rates and rent increases. I'm not talking about public housing here but rather control over rents in privately owned rental buildings. Check out what the rules are and to what buildings or tenants they may apply. And be aware that even within the same state, two ways for controlling rents may be in effect — one in the cities and one in the suburbs. Head over to Chapter 12 for more about renting and leases in general.

# Transferring Ownership Involuntarily

To find out more about involuntarily giving up property, check out Chapter 10. Two state-specific factors to check out regarding the loss of property against your will are

✔ The statutory time period needed to claim adverse possession or prescriptive rights against someone else's property.

✔ The laws of descent, which govern the distribution of your estate if you die intestate (without a will). Because as an agent you may help heirs dispose of real estate that they've inherited, many states want you to know something about these laws.

# Transferring Ownership Voluntarily

Voluntary transfer of property ownership is the area where you'll be spending most of your time after you get your real estate license. Perhaps the most important item you need to check out for exam and for practical purposes is to what extent you'll be involved in the legal side of things. In some places, real estate agents handle most, if not all, of the work in actually transferring ownership of the property from one person to another. In other parts of the country, attorneys pick up the ball right after an offer is accepted on a piece of property.

Regardless of your role in the actual ownership transfer process some of the specific things that you need to check out for your state's exam include:

✔ The type of deed most commonly used.

✔ Requirements for a valid deed. These can vary a little from one state to another.

✔ The type of property description most commonly used in a deed.

✔ The use of title insurance, abstract of title, or other systems for certifying marketable title to the property.

✔ Who pays what closing costs.

✔ Who owns the property on the day of closing.

✔ Who's responsible if the property is destroyed while under contract for sale.

✔ Whether property transfers commonly close in escrow.

With respect to property descriptions, you folks who live in states that came along after the original 13 colonies should know something about how to calculate area and locate property in the rectangular survey system.

# Chapter 28

# Ten Tips to Help You Succeed on the Exam

*In This Chapter*
▶ Understanding some basic exam preparation techniques
▶ Finding techniques to use during the exam

*I* once had to go to the doctor, and I knew he would test my blood pressure. I stayed up all night studying so I could pass the test. (Groan!) But seriously folks, everyone's taken tests, and yes, even the calmest, most well prepared of all of us get nervous about being tested. As you know, there are tests and then there are tests. You probably don't want to fail your blood pressure test. And you sure didn't want to fail your driving test back when you first took it. That, after all, is serious stuff. So I won't minimize the anxiety you're probably already feeling about taking the state real estate exam. Yet I do want to put this into perspective for you. The worst that can happen is that you have to take the exam again. And, of course, the best thing that can and will happen to you is you'll pass the first time around. I had a student take the test twice in the same day, figuring that would double her chances of passing at least one of them. Yes, she did pass both. So don't let exam anxiety get in your way. If you've done your homework in your prelicense class and used this book to help you prepare, boys and girls, you're there. Trust me. You'll be selling real estate before you know it.

But just to give you one last bit of help, I wrote this chapter to provide you with a few more strategies to use while you're taking the exam and a few ideas for preparing for the exam. Don't think of these ten topics as guarantees for success; just know that if you follow the advice in this chapter, you can maximize your chances of passing the state license exam the first time you take it. For more exam preparation tips, check out Chapter 2.

## Taking the Exam as Soon as You Can

Given the fact that the vast majority of states require some kind of coursework before you can get your real estate license, most of you probably will have completed a number of hours of real estate classes before taking the exam. You never will know the material better than you do right when you finish the course. And you're likely to forget the specifics that you need from the material soon after your coursework is completed, especially if you must take an exam to complete the course. One of the most creative exercises you'll ever do in your life is come up with a laundry list of excuses for putting off taking the state exam. Don't!

I hope you use this book along with the course material as you complete the prelicensing course. If you haven't taken the practice exams in Chapters 19, 21, 23, and 25, do so. Take a quick review of your weakest points, and then go take the state exam. If you need to make an appointment to take the exam, make the appointment before you finish your course so there is little delay after you finish real estate school.

# Knowing the Rules (and Following Them)

You must adhere to a number of rules for any state exam. Find out what they are and obey them. Although you may encounter others, here are a few rules that you may want to check out. (For more on figuring out the rules of your state's exam, see Chapter 1.)

- ✔ **Calculators:** What kind can you bring and what kind are forbidden? Some states forbid any calculator (or electronic device with a calculator) that can store text, so no cell phones.

- ✔ **Entry permit:** If your state requires an entry permit, don't forget to bring it. States that require them typically have some sort of application procedure for you to go through just to take the exam. Follow all the instructions to apply for your entry permit, put it in a safe place when it comes in the mail, and then (did I say this already?) don't forget it when you go to take the exam.

- ✔ **Exam fee:** If you must pay the fee at the time you take the exam, make sure you have it and can pay it the way the test makers want it, by check, credit card, in cash, or with a money order; but you need to know which so you are prepared. Most of the time, though, you pay the exam fee when you apply to take the test.

- ✔ **Food:** You may be prohibited from bringing food to the test. If you have a medical condition that requires you to eat at certain times, get permission ahead of time by contacting the state licensing agency or the people administering the test since some states use contracted services.

- ✔ **Handicapped accessibility:** If this is an issue for you — say, for example, you use a wheelchair — find out ahead of time how your state licensing agency is making accommodations.

- ✔ **Identification:** Find out the specific types of identification you need and whether more than one is necessary. Photo IDs are common requirements, but check it out first and make sure you bring what you need.

- ✔ **Location:** Some states have more than one exam location. Pick the one most convenient and least stressful to you. Note I didn't say the one closest. You may be more relaxed driving a longer distance to a suburban location, knowing you won't have to struggle for parking downtown.

- ✔ **Time:** Find out what time you need to arrive at the exam and be there at least 15 minutes early. At the very least, doing so can help relax you by avoiding the last-minute rush and possibly being late.

- ✔ **Writing implements:** If the test materials say to bring two No. 2 pencils, then bring at least two or more. And you may want to bring a pen with you, just in case you have to sign something.

- ✔ **What you can and cannot bring in:** Some states have strict rules about what can and cannot be brought into the actual exam room. Follow those instructions carefully, or you may find yourself having to leave your laptop computer in the hallway outside of the exam room — never to be heard from again.

# Studying Your State License Law

Make sure that you read your state's real estate license laws (see Chapter 3) before you take your state exam. These laws can cover everything from agency relationships, which you can read about in Chapter 4, to how much continuing education you have to have to keep your license. Even if you've covered some of the material in your real estate course, you're expected to be familiar with the law itself. You may be given a copy of the law when you take a prelicensing course. If not, you usually can obtain a copy directly from your state licensing agency, and often can do so online with your computer. Try using a search engine like Google and type in your state's name followed by the words real estate license law. Because states vary in who issues real estate licenses, you can also type in your state's name followed by the words real estate license commission or real estate license board.

Don't neglect knowing about the silly little stuff like license fees. Every real estate exam I've ever taken asked some question or another about how much it costs to get a license or change an address or something like that.

# Remembering Important Vocabulary

Not having taken the real estate exams in all 50 states, I can't say the following with absolute certainty, but I believe you can pass most state license exams for real estate salesperson by simply mastering the vocabulary (no small task). At the initial stage of licensing, state officials want to make sure that you at least understand the basics. If you can master all the terms that are in italics in this book, and any other words that are new to you, I think you'll pass the state exam. By master them, however, I mean committing to memory a one- or two-sentence definition for each term. As for the more complicated concepts, memorizing the major differences between two similar terms probably will get you through.

Exams beyond the salesperson exam, such as the broker's exam, require you to memorize more terminology and be able to apply it in various situational questions, almost like mini-case studies. A mastery of the vocabulary, however, shouldn't be overlooked, even for the broker's exam. That mastery can help you answer case studies and other questions on the broker's exam.

# Focusing on Key Concepts

Real estate studies include many key concepts that go beyond simple vocabulary (see the previous section). For example, the fact that a salesperson must work under a broker is a key concept (see Chapter 3). The idea of fiduciary responsibility is a key concept (see Chapter 4). Math formulas are key concepts (see Chapter 18). Most key concepts can be reduced to a few sentences. The way this book is organized, every key concept has its own heading. Look for the words in italics and a few key sentences that describe what I'm talking about. If it helps, reduce it all to a sentence or two or a list of important characteristics. In addition, when a key concept doesn't warrant its own section, I highlight it with the (you guessed it) Remember icon. Make sure you learn, understand, and remember them for the exam.

# Eating Something

I'm a big believer in the food, energy, blood sugar, and alertness relationship. Eat your normal meals for the day. If eating and the exam schedule are a problem, make other arrangements. For example, if you're traveling to an exam site or actually taking the exam when you normally would be eating, get some energy or meal replacement bars and eat them as close to your regular meal time as possible. If you're allowed to bring food into the exam, by all means, bring something if you want — just don't go overboard.

# Staying Cool, Calm, and Collected

Okay! I grant you staying calm before a test always is easier said than done. But let your nerves work for you rather than against you. Get just anxious enough to motivate you to study, do the practice exams in this book, and review the material you didn't do well on in class and practice questions. At some point, you'll begin to feel comfortable enough with the information that you'll begin to relax. Keep in mind that you probably have accomplished much harder things in your life, that you're being tested on real estate issues and not rocket science, and that you can always take the test over if you don't pass.

I think activities like relaxation exercises, meditation, and deep breathing all can help. Before any exam that I take, I close my eyes for just a few seconds and take a couple of deep breaths. If you're so inclined, say a short prayer. What you're looking for is to become calm and focused.

# Paying Attention (without Overthinking)

Take what is presented in each question at face value. Avoid "what-iffing" as you read the question. Don't be afraid to select the obviously correct answer. Examiners don't write questions that are intentionally designed to trick you. They do write questions that sometimes require knowledge of the fine differences between two points. Pay attention to unnecessary material that is designed to give the question a sense of reality or throw you off. Here's an example with a topic from Chapter 7.

> **Question:** Tenancy in common is a common form of ownership for
>
> **Answers:** married couples, cooperative apartment owners, time share owners, condominium owners.

The answer is condominium owners, and you can read why in Chapter 7. If you started to overthink this question, you may want to pick cooperative apartments, because that's a form of group ownership, and married couples can own property as tenants in common, but it isn't typical. Time share ownership generally is individual ownership. So if you overthink this question, you may find justification for at least one if not two of the incorrect answers. This question, again, points out the benefits of mastering terms and key concepts that I discuss in "Focusing on Key Concepts" earlier in this chapter. I've tried to give you examples of various types of test questions in the four practice exams in this book.

# Going with Your Initial Instinct

The advice you've been given since the time you started taking tests needs to be engraved on Mount Rushmore: Go with your first answer on a multiple-choice question. I have corrected enough of these types of exams and have seen enough right answers changed to wrong answers to tell you that for the most part, it's true. I don't know enough about how the brain works to explain it, but on recognition-type exams, or exams where the answers are right in front of you, the first answer that comes to mind usually is the best one.

The two exceptions to this rule are:

✔ If a later question gives you information that makes a better choice likely in an earlier question.

✔ When checking your answers to the math questions. Do the math questions at least twice or until you get the same answer twice. Once upon a time, I decided that 100 minus 4 equaled 94. That cost me a perfect score on a math test in seventh grade. Although not that important in the grander scheme of things, I never forgot after that to do math questions twice over just in case.

# Finishing the Job

Above all, don't leave any answers blank. Go through the test quickly the first time to answer as many of the easy questions that you know the answers to right away. Then go back and take your time with the harder ones. Guess if you have to. There will inevitably be a few answers you know right off the bat in the last 10 or 15 questions. It would be a shame to miss those answers because you spent too much time on a few questions earlier in the exam. The last thing you need to do is actually count the number of marks on the answer sheet to make sure the number corresponds with the number of questions on the exam. While you're at it, make sure you didn't fill in two answers for the same question. Many states are using computerized testing. Make sure you understand how the system works, how to finalize your answers or leave them open to change, and to make sure you've answered all the questions. And if you're not sure, ask the exam proctor and don't be embarrassed to ask in front of the kids in the room who probably grew up with computers in their cribs.

# Index

government agencies and regulations, 174–175
pollutants and situations, 177–180
review questions and answers, 182–184
water and waste, 180–182
Environmental Protection Agency (EPA), 174, 179
Equal Credit Opportunity Act (ECOA), 232
equalization rate
assessment ratios and, 243
defined, 242
in tax determination, 242
in tax determination example, 243
use of, 242
equitable redemption, 230
equitable right of redemption, 245
equitable title, 213
equity buildup. *See also* real estate investments
defined, 259
example of, 260
equity trusts, 256
erosion, 141–142
errors and omissions insurance, 35
escheat, 114
escrow account, 215
estate at sufferance, 164–165
estate at will, 164
estate for years, 164
estate valuation, as reason for appraisal, 189
estates
bundle of rights, 81–82
defined, 81
dominant, 102
fee, 82
fee simple, 82
fee simple qualified, 82
freehold, 82–83
leased fee, 163–164
leasehold, 83, 164–165
legal life, 83
life, 82–83
life, pur autre vie, 83
ordinary life, 82–83
servient, 102
estoppel (reduction) certificates, 231
estoppel, agency by, 48
evaluation, in exam preparation, 18
eviction, 168
exam four. *See also* practice exams
answers and explanations, 375–385
instructions, 363
questions, 364–373

exam one. *See also* practice exams
answers and explanations, 307–316
instructions, 295
questions, 296–305
exam three. *See also* practice exams
answers and explanations, 351–361
instructions, 339
questions, 340–349
exam two. *See also* practice exams
answers and explanations, 329–338
instructions, 317
questions, 318–327
exams
analyzing, too much, 21
application for, 11–12
calculators at, 11, 396
details, checking on, 10
eating before, 398
entry permit, 11, 396
finishing, 399
focus during, 398
food at, 396
format, 10
getting information about, 16
guessing on, 21
handicapped accessibility, 396
identification at, 396
initial instinct during, 399
key concepts, focusing on, 397
location of, 396
math questions on, 22
needed, identifying, 9
reading carefully, 20
registering for, 10–11
relaxation during, 398
retaking, 13
rules, following, 396
salesperson versus broker, 8–10
score determination, 12–13
second-guessing on, 22
single, 10
state license law on, 397
success tips, 395–399
taking as soon as you can, 395–396
time of, 396
two-part, 10
vocabulary, 397
walk-in, 11
what to take to, 11–12, 396
writing implements, 12, 396
exclusive agency buyer agency agreement
defined, 50, 153
in payment, 57
exclusive agency listing, 49, 153
exclusive buyer agency agreement, 50, 153

exclusive right to sell listing, 49, 153
executors, 144
executor's deeds, 121
existence of agreement, as legal test, 81
express agency, 47
express contracts, 150
external obsolescence, 201
externalities, 194

## • F •

Fair Housing Act of 1968
age exception, 71
defined, 64
enforcement of, 65
exceptions to, 70–71
owner-occupied exception, 71
private clubs exception, 71
public-law occupancy standard exception, 71
religious organizations exception, 71
single-family housing exception, 71
violations, complaints regarding, 72
Fair Housing Amendments Act of 1988, 70
fair housing laws
basics of, 63–66
concept and goal of, 63
disabilities and, 72
discriminatory actions, 66–69
enforcing, 72
exceptions to, 70–71
federal, 64–65
FRESH CORN acronym, 65
protected classes, 70, 390
review questions and answers, 72–75
state and local, 65–66, 390
fair housing poster, 66
faithful performance, 53
Fannie Mae, 218
Farm Service Agency (FSA), 220
Farmer Mac, 218
federal antitrust laws
group boycotts, 39
market allocation, 39
price fixing, 38–39
tie-in arrangements, 39
federal fair housing laws, 64–65, 70
Federal Housing Administration (FHA), 219
federal loan insurance programs, 218–220
Federal Safe Drinking Water Act, 181
fee simple, 82
fee simple qualified estate, 82

National Affordable Housing
    Act, 232
National Apartment
    Association, 35
National Association of Home
    Inspectors, 33
National Association of Realtors
    (NAR), 28
national franchises, 31
national origin, as prohibitive
    advertising language, 67
negative amortization, 226
negligent misrepresentation,
    55–56
net leases, 168
net listing, 49
net operating income. *See also*
    income capitalization
    approach
  calculating, 206
  defined, 259
  estimating, 204–205
  finding on a pro forma, 264
  in real estate investment
    analysis, 264
net operating income,
    estimating, 204–205
net selling price, 260
nonconforming loans, 216
nonconforming uses, 109
nonjudicial foreclosures, 230
non-residential building
    layouts, 169
notes, 212
notorious, 104, 141
novation, contract, 157

### • O •

obedience, as fiduciary duty, 53
obligations
  agent to customer, 54
  meeting, 53–56
  seller disclosure, 52
Occupational Safety and Health
    Administration (OSHA), 175
offer to purchase, 156
office buildings, 252
office management, 37
office policy, 37
one- to four-family houses, 252
open, in claiming ownership
    under adverse
    possession, 141
open buyer agency agreement,
    50, 153
open listing agreement, 49, 153
open mortgages, 223
open-end mortgages, 223
operating expenses, 264
operating statement, 263
operation of law, 157
opportunity cost, 194
option listing, 50

options, 156
ornamental trees and bushes, 80
OSHA (Occupational Safety and
    Health Administration), 175
overhead (aerial) easements, 103
ownership
  by business, 93–94
  concurrent (co-ownership),
    90–91
  condominium, 95
  cooperative, 94–95
  estates, 81–83
  exchanges, as reason for
    appraisal, 189
  forms of, 89–98
  in marriage, 91–92
  planned unit developments
    (PUDs), 95–96
  review questions and
    answers, 85–88
  sole, 90
  state law, 391
  terms, understanding, 79–81
  time shares, 96
  transferring, 117
  in trust, 92
  undivided, 90
ownership limitations
  deed restrictions, 105–106
  easements, 102–104
  eminent domain, 113
  encroachments, 106–107
  encumbrances, 99–107
  escheat, 114
  foreclosure, 114
  government, 112–114
  land-use regulation, 107–112
  liens, 100–102
  review questions and
    answers, 114–116
  taxation, 114
ownership rights
  air, 84–85, 127
  development, 85
  littoral, 85
  mineral, 85
  riparian, 85
  subsurface, 85
  surface, 85
  types of, 83
  water, 84
  watering, 85

### • P •

pacing during exam, 19–20
package mortgages, 223
paired sales analysis, 198
partial performance, 157
partial release, 222
partial release provision, 222
partial tax exemptions, 244
partially amortized loans, 229
partitioning, 142

partnerships
  defined, 93
  general, 255
  limited, 255
  ownership by, 93
party walls, 104
passing title, 119, 134
payment, agent. *See also*
    commissions
  process, 30–31
  when, 57
  who, 56–57
payment cap, 226
payment factor, 280
pencils, No. 2, 12, 396
pens, at licensing exam, 12, 396
pension funds, 217
perc tests, 182
percentage leases, 168
percentages
  calculating, 274–275
  commissions and, 274
  decimal points, 274–275
  fraction conversion to, 275
  percent, 274
performance
  in discharging contract, 157–158
  faithful, 53
  impossibility of, 157
  partial, 157
  substantial, 157
periodic estate, 164
perpendicular, in triangle, 272
personal property
  defined, 80
  as fixtures, 80
  questions, 81
personalty, 80–81
photo ID, at licensing exam,
    12, 396
physical deterioration, 201
physical responsibilities,
    property managers, 34
PITI (principal, interest, taxes,
    and insurance), 221–222
planned unit developments
    (PUDs), 95–96
plat maps, 124
plottage, 195
PMI (private mortgage
    insurance), 220
points, mortgage loan, 214–215
police power, 107
potential gross income, 204, 264
practice, in exam preparation, 18
practice exams
  exam four, 363–373
  exam one, 295–305
  exam three, 339–349
  exam two, 317–327
  scoring, 307
prelicensing course certificate, at
    licensing exam, 12
prepaid items, 132–134

# Notes

# About the Author

On the first night of class, **John Yoegel** always quotes one of his former real estate teachers to his students: "Most of us don't start out in real estate, but an awful lot of us end up there."

After serving in the United States Air Force and with a master's degree from New York University in hand, John pursued a career in his chosen field — urban planning. Working in local government, specifically Westchester County, New York, he earned a PhD in public administration and urban planning, also from New York University. During this time, John found himself getting more involved in county real estate matters, first as property supervisor for the county parks department and eventually as director of real estate for Westchester County. Along the way, John picked up his New York State broker's license and studied appraising with the Appraisal Institute.

After teaching courses in urban planning and public administration at the college and graduate-school levels, John began teaching real estate courses in 1987. As president of John Yoegel Seminars, he currently teaches prelicensing and continuing education courses for salespeople, brokers, and appraisers. John has served on a number of professional committees, including test-preparation review committees for the New York State Department of State and an ad hoc curriculum study committee of real estate educators. The recommendations of this committee resulted in a complete overhaul of real estate licensing requirements in New York State.

John is a member of the Real Estate Educators Association (REEA) and holds the DREI (Distinguished Real Estate Instructor) designation. He also holds the C-CREC (Consumer-Certified Real Estate Consultant) designation from the National Association of Real Estate Consultants and completed training with the Instructor Training Institute. In addition to this book, John also has written four other real estate books and articles that were published in the *REEA Journal* and *The Real Estate Professional* magazine.

When John isn't teaching or writing about real estate matters, he's performing weddings as an ordained Interfaith Minister and priest with the Orthodox Catholic Church of America and teaching at his old Seminary, The New Seminary for Interfaith Studies. And when time permits, he's an avid amateur home winemaker.

He lives with his wife, the lovely Marina, in Connecticut.

# Dedication

This book is dedicated to my beautiful and loving wife, Marina. Throughout this book she was there every day, scheduling things around my writing schedule and taking care of what needed to be taken care of as I wrote. I owe her at least one vacation that she canceled and much more. Thanks, honey, for being my biggest fan. I love you.

# *Author's Acknowledgments*

No book ever is written alone. Even if it's a work of pure fiction that comes straight from an author's imagination, other people still must inspire that imagination, teach the author the discipline to write it all down, support and encourage the author's writing, and generally take care of business while the author writes. It's those people, past and present, whom I want to acknowledge.

On the production side of the first edition of this book , I want to thank Natasha Graf, the acquisitions editor who was my first contact with Wiley Publishing. Whatever ability she recognized in me is the reason you're holding this book in your hands. My project editor, Georgette Beatty, has been a true joy to work with. Without a doubt, this book, in its final version, is due in large part to her abilities. And I want to acknowledge all the copy editors who worked on this book, including Josh Dials, Chad Sievers, and especially Neil Johnson, who kept me on my toes and gave me a few laughs along the way. Their work made me a better writer than I am and ultimately gave you a better book to read. I'd also like to thank Mikal Belicove, who graciously and patiently listened to my marketing suggestions. Finally I want to thank the technical reviewer, Donna Pfafman. Her experiences and knowledge as a real estate broker and an educator ensure that you, the reader, will reap the benefits of this test-preparation tool.

For this revised edition I'd like to thank Michael Lewis for initiating the project and Susan Hobbs the editor. I'd also like to thank my two technical editors, real estate professionals Cheryl Crawford and Libby Cyman.

Many people are connected to the chain between the idea for a book and its production. Without my agent, Grace Freedson, this project never would've happened for me. Thanks, Grace, for that first phone call three years ago, for keeping me in your address book, and for getting me this project — not to mention listening to my occasional rants about contracts and the publishing industry.

Who I am today is in no small measure the result of the influence of a few very important people in my life. First of all I want to thank my parents, John and Angela, for giving me the education to get where I've gotten. I regret that my father, for whom education was an unfulfilled dream during his lifetime, is not here to see his son's name on the cover of a book. As an educator, I value the role teachers play in their students' lives, so it's with great humility that I attest to the inspirations that Remo Ianucci and Perry Norton were in my life.

On the professional side, I want to thank my fellow members of the Real Estate Educators Association for all their knowledge and willingness to share it. In particular, I want to express my appreciation to Eileen Taus, director of education with the Westchester County, New York, Board of Realtors. She gave a fledgling instructor his first real estate teaching job and since then has served as mentor and cheerleader. I also want to thank my friend Richard O'Donnell for being there (as always) with his expertise when I needed answers to questions for the chapter about taxes. I also want to thank all the students I've taught over the years. It was a rare class that I did not learn something from them.

While writing the first edition of this book, my friends and extended family were support-ive, encouraging, and wonderfully patient I want to thank them all: Al and Lee Tramelli, Marco Tramelli, Dr. John Paulmann, Dr. Ray and Susan Griffin, Victor and Gloria Consiglio, Greg and Janice Arcaro, Dale and Bob Terwilliger, and Anna and Danny Guadagnoli. They never failed to ask how the book was going and were enthusiastic in the most supportive of ways — as if the project were their own, listening patiently as I ruminated about the joys and pressures of writing a book. Thanks, pals. You're the best.

The most important thanks go to my family: my children Alex and his wife Porscha, my daughter Angelique and her fiancé Joseph Capozzi, both talented writers in their own right, for their enthusiasm and love; Christine, who someday may read this and know that her father is thinking about her; and Jennifer, who is always with me. I also want to acknowl-edge my grandson Alexander and my grandson Aydin who will be born by the time this book is on the shelves. Someday they will be old enough to know that they were never far from their grandfather's thoughts while he worked on this book.

Finally, I want to thank my wife, Marina. Her support and enthusiasm for this project never wavered, even as she was rearranging our lives around my writing. You wouldn't be reading this book if it weren't for her.

*Publisher's Acknowledgments*

**Acquisitions Editor:** Mike Lewis

**Project Editor:** Susan Hobbs
  *(Previous edition: Georgette Beatty)*

**Copy Editor:** Susan Hobbs
  *(Previous edition: E. Neil Johnson)*

**Technical Editors:** Cheryl Crawford, Libby Cyman

**Art Coordinator:** Alicia B. South

**Senior Project Coordinator:** Kristie Rees

**Cover Image:** ©iStockphoto.com/Victor Correia